Mapping the American Revolutionary War

Published for the Hermon Dunlap Smith Center
for the History of Cartography
The Newberry Library

Series Editor/David Woodward

Previously published
Maps: A Historical Survey of Their Study and Collecting
by R. A. Skelton (1972)

British Maps of Colonial America
by William P. Cumming (1974)

Five Centuries of Map Printing
edited by David Woodward (1975)

Mapping the American Revolutionary War

J. B. Harley, Barbara Bartz Petchenik, and
Lawrence W. Towner

The Kenneth Nebenzahl, Jr., Lectures in the History of Cartography at The Newberry Library

The University of Chicago Press · Chicago and London

J. B. Harley is Montefiore Reader in Geography, University of Exeter. Barbara Bartz Petchenik is on the staff of Cartographic Services, R. R. Donnelley & Sons, Chicago. Lawrence W. Towner is President and Librarian, The Newberry Library.

The University of Chicago Press, Chicago 60637
The University of Chicago Press, Ltd., London
© 1978 by The University of Chicago
All rights reserved. Published 1978
Printed in the United States of America
82 81 80 79 78   5 4 3 2 1

Library of Congress Cataloging in Publication Data

Harley, John Brian.
    Mapping the American Revolutionary War.

    (The Kenneth Nebenzahl, Jr., lectures in the history
of cartography at the Newberry Library)
    "Lectures were given 11–14 November 1974."
    Bibliography: p.
    Includes index.
    1.   United States—History—Revolution, 1775–1783—
Cartography—Addresses, essays, lectures. I. Petchenik,
Barbara Bartz, joint author.   II.   Towner, Lawrence W.,
joint author.   III. Title.   IV.   Series.
GA405.5.H37   911'.73   77–8023
ISBN 0–226–31631–9

Contents

Editor's Note | vii

1 The Contemporary Mapping of the
American Revolutionary War | 1

   J. B. Harley

2 The Spread of Cartographical Ideas between the
Revolutionary Armies | 45

   J. B. Harley

3 The Map User in the Revolution | 79

   J. B. Harley

4 The Mapping of the American Revolutionary War
in the Nineteenth Century | 111

   Lawrence W. Towner

5 The Mapping of the American Revolutionary War
in the Twentieth Century | 125

   Barbara Bartz Petchenik

Notes | 149

Selected Bibliography | 173

Index | 183

Editor's Note

The Kenneth Nebenzahl, Jr., Lectures in the History of Cartography are now sufficiently well established that some explanation of our approach to their subject matter and format is in order. With the first and second series of lectures, given by R. A. Skelton and William P. Cumming respectively, the authors were chosen for their widely known competence in the field, and were invited to speak on a topic of their choice. With the 1972 lectures on the history of map printing, we experimented with a different concept: that of starting with the subject matter that needed to be covered in the young and growing field of the history of cartography, and then selecting scholars who could provide a sound treatment of the needs and opportunities for study in that chosen area. A symposium format for the lectures resulted, and the division of subject matter among the participants was carefully planned in advance.

The concept of a symposium was preserved for the series of lectures from which this book results. The lectures were given 11–14 November 1974 at The Newberry Library. We felt that a treatment of the military cartography of the Revolutionary War was an underdeveloped yet potentially important topic, and proposed a structure for the symposium based on a distinction between the study of the contemporary mapping of events and the historiographic treatment of later centuries.

The book is thus divided into two parts: the contemporary mapping of the war, which accounts for three of the five chapters, and the retrospective mapping of the war, which is treated in the remaining two. The distinction is not hard and fast; some eighteenth-century mapping could certainly be termed historiographic in nature, but the basic division in the book remains.

We were fortunate to enlist the services of J. B. Harley, Montefiore Reader in Geography, University of Exeter, who was already engaged in similar studies, to cover the contemporary mapping of the Revolution. His two lectures given in the Fall of 1974 were expanded into three chapters of this book. Lawrence W. Towner, President and Librarian, The Newberry Library, with his wide ranging background in American history, tackled the lecture treating the nineteenth century historiographic mapping of the war in his inimitable style. For the twentieth century, we knew that Barbara Bartz Petchenik, then Cartographic Editor of the *Atlas of Early American History,* had conceived a simple and effective method of mapping the theatres of activity of the Revolutionary War for the *Atlas,* and we invited her to provide a critical appraisal of the cartography of the war in recent times.

It is a pleasure to acknowledge the help and patience of the contributors to this book. In addition, I should like to acknowledge the help of Joseph Narun, staff editor at The Newberry Library, who spent many long hours checking references, smoothing out inconsistencies, and attending to many of the small details that surround the production of a book before final submission to the press.

David Woodward

1 | The Contemporary Mapping of the American Revolutionary War

One historian of the American Revolution, reflecting on the almost overwhelming number of surviving eyewitness accounts—diaries, journals, letters, and narratives—has written that it "ranks as one of history's most literate wars."[1] It might also be called one of the most "carto-literate," in view of the considerable number and diversity of surviving military maps from the period, both manuscript and printed.

Historians and cartographers are confronted by maps, charts, and plans varying from small crudely executed sketches of local areas and temporary fortifications to large-scale beautifully colored surveys. The maps, a form of instant shorthand and a *lingua franca* to the military officers of the period, were surveyed and drawn by American, British, French, and German cartographers. Printed maps were published in large numbers not only in London and Philadelphia but also in the main European capitals, with editions in several languages. Randolph G. Adams, a pioneer student of Revolutionary War maps, wrote nearly fifty years ago, "A complete list of the maps of the American Revolution, in print and in manuscript, would be a pretty piece of work."[2] True then, his observation is even more true now, as hardly a year passes without the discovery of some new cache of maps to augment the mass already available for study.

A few researchers have started to feel their way toward a classification of the varied and sometimes bewildering cartographic output of the Revolutionary War. William P. Cumming described "The Cartography of Conflict" as including "charts of harbors and rivers, . . . maps of terrain in which campaigns must be waged, . . . quickly made maps of campaigns and of battles to be fought at some small outpost, careful maps to keep account of what has happened and where troops are, maps that are reports of officers to their superiors, diagrams of enemy forts to be taken or of new forts to be built. And, finally, there are commercial maps to keep the public informed."[3] Similarly, if more crisply, Peter J. Guthorn wrote in his study of the British maps of the American Revolution: "The maps . . . fall into six broad categories: military geographical surveys, surveys of encampments and fortifications, casual offhand sketch

For author's acknowledgments, see page 149.

maps, public information news maps, formal documentary battle or campaign maps, and finely finished artistic renderings to serve as personal souvenirs for public or private exhibition.''[4] That two authors, writing within a couple of years of each other, should adopt different categories and terminology to describe a group of maps with at least a classic unity of purpose, time, and place suggests that a necessary first step in the historical study of the military maps of the Revolution is to establish an objective classification.

At one time or another, most of the major subtypes of maps that can be classified as "military" have been described in the literature, and many of them have been illustrated. The point at issue, therefore, is not whether a classification can be devised to accommodate all the known variants of military maps—aiming solely at some crude measure of comprehensiveness—but whether its rationale is suitable for its stated historical purposes. This is not the place to digress into philosophical discussion of the principles and procedures of cartographic taxonomy, but it is nonetheless clear that classifiers of cartography have sometimes failed to define their objectives.[5] In some cases, these aims will be obvious. The distinction between manuscript and printed maps, for example, is useful for a cartobibliographer concentrating on published maps. In the use of maps by military commanders, as during the Revolutionary War, however, the distinction is irrelevant. Failure to delineate the objectives, rationale, and limitations of classification can engender confusion. Similarly, unless the classifications are preliminary to a further study of the relationships or origins of the maps involved, it may be worth questioning the diagnostic value of other familiar distinctions—such as those between sketch maps and finished maps, accurate and inaccurate maps, maps of terrain and exploration drawings, maps made by geographical engineers and those made by other military specialists or civilians employed by the army, and maps distinguished by the different types of geographical areas to which they relate. In other words, a classification has to serve as a means to an end; it should throw new light on some aspects of the maps under discussion.

The classification eventually adopted in this chapter looks forward to the two main arguments presented in chapters 2 and 3. They are:

(a) that most of the military maps of the Revolutionary period are most easily understood in the light of a European military culture that, in both educational theory and operational practice, was prevalent in most European states throughout the eighteenth century and from them was transmitted to (and modified in) North America; and

(b) that to assess the part maps played in the military and political decisions of the Revolution, it is necessary to pay greater attention to the map user and his operational environment than to any actual or arbitrarily perceived characteristics of maps, which are too often assessed only by the technical criteria of the individual map historian.

There are undoubtedly several classifications that would assist in a study of these aspects of the cartographic history of the Revolution. For example, given the initial assumption that most maps produced (or used) in the campaigns of the Revolution do reflect European experience, an attractive yet simple classification might involve the subdivision of a general European map culture into national groups, then into other progressively smaller ones, finishing up with single maps. The approach is illustrated in figure 1:1, representing what archaeologists have called a hierarchical system arranged in ascending order of system complexity:[6]

(a) at the lowest level is the single map or atlas;

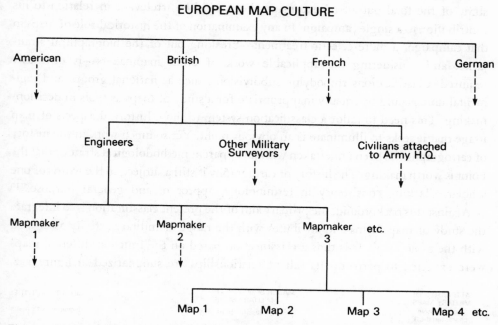

Fig. 1:1 Stages in the logical division of a European map culture as represented in the American Revolutionary War. Stages similar to the British one (illustrated above) would apply to the American, French, and German cartography.

(*b*) above this is the total cartographic output of one mapmaker;

(*c*) next would come a group of all maps produced by a specialized technical unit such as the British corps of engineers, the geographers attached to George Washington's Continental Army, or the *ingénieurs géographes* (topographical engineers) associated with Rochambeau's expeditionary force in North America;

(*d*) the penultimate level is a national one, bringing together the associated sets of contemporary maps originating from cartographers attached to the American, British, French, and Hessian forces;

(*e*) the apex of the hierarchy is a European military map culture.

This arrangement, although it has not been explicitly formulated by the researchers concerned, has doubtless been implicit in their selection of topics for investigation; thus, as well as being a potential organizing concept for the study of Revolutionary mapmaking, it is also a partial guide to the existing literature on this subject. All stages except the most complex—the European military map culture—are represented in recent writings. At a national level there are studies of American,[7] British,[8] French,[9] and Hessian[10] mapmaking. At the regimental level there are studies of the British engineers,[11] the French *ingénieurs géographes*,[12] and the American geographers.[13] There are also numerous studies focused on individual mapmakers and, equally, on the characteristics of single maps and atlases.[14]

The only disadvantage is that much of this work has been undertaken in relative isolation with different objectives and specifications; it does not necessarily provide data suitable for a general examination of Revolutionary mapmaking. Furthermore, a hierarchical approach has built-in disadvantages for the questions to be examined in chapters 2 and 3. In particular, although it allows stress to be laid on the development of physical and stylistic differences between maps, relating to their role in military decisions, it tends to divorce the maps from their original historical context, that is, from the specific events that gave rise to their production. As a simple example, a study of the total output of one mapmaker would be irrelevant in relation to his contribution to a single campaign. In any examination of the historical role of maps in that campaign, a more eclectic treatment—breaking out of the biographical strait-jacket and considering the applicable work of other mapmakers—is obviously required. Classifications embodying subdivisions, such as national groups and regimental units, could be equally inappropriate for a study of maps as tools in decision-making. This need to tailor a classification system to those historical aspects of map usage that it seeks to illuminate is an obvious point. Yet so much work in the history of cartography has been undertaken without apparent methodological strategy that the point is worth making. The history of cartography is still a subject, in the words of one scholar, "lacking consistency in terminology, approach, and general purpose."[15]

Against this background, the primary aim of the present classification is to integrate the study of map forms and attributes with the range of military activity associated with the same maps. It is thus a classification based on the function different maps were expected to perform. Its salient relationships are summarized in figure 1:2,

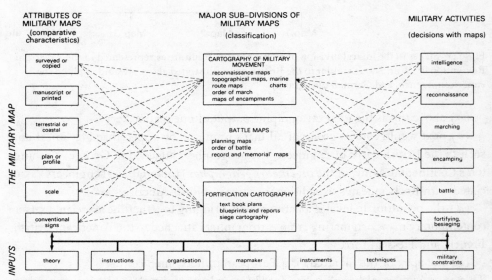

Fig. 1:2 The connections between the attributes and uses of three major classes of military maps.

which is designed to set out the more important features in a systematic study of military maps—features which, despite their complexity, can be arranged and linked in a meaningful way. Four facets of the design can be amplified:

(a) Its main role is to provide a basic threefold classification of military maps, together with subdivisions, which occupies the central column. The three groups of maps are those associated with fortification, with military movement, and with battle.

(b) These maps are a result of the military activities displayed in the right-hand column (the maps in turn influenced these activities as they were used in making decisions). This column does not contain a definitive list but summarizes those military activities that consistently demanded (and used) maps.

(c) Although the main raison d'être of the classification is to link function with map type, it can be demonstrated that all the cartographic attributes set out in the left-hand column (for example, conventional signs or scales) are consistently associated with particular types of map in the central column. This is again an illustrative rather than a definitive listing, but consistency of association—often transcending the maps of different national groups—is a valuable criterion in the analysis of a European military map culture.

(*d*) The boxes in the lower part of the diagram (inputs) represent recurrent factors that impinged on the making of the military maps of the Revolution, and these again interact with other aspects of the classification. Many of these topics, ranging from the education of military surveyors to their field techniques and from the organization of mapmaking at different army headquarters to the available surveying instruments, are proper subjects for thematic research in their own right. Here, they are usually subordinated to the general objective of this study. The diagram is one way of organizing the characteristics of the corpus of surviving maps for a particular purpose. All that can be said is that it may be of sufficient general validity to accommodate most Revolutionary maps; any that fall outside its divisions are likely to be of unusual historical significance.

The extent to which the classification matches reality can, moreover, be partly tested by the application of three criteria: first, that the military functions with their associated maps can be identified in contemporary military textbooks (that is, they have a basis in the military theory of the period); second, that these functions and the maps are also described in documents relating to the military activities of the Revolution (that is, practice at least partly reflects theory); and third, that the maps were broadly capable of serving these functions. The evidence for such criteria will be discussed below. In summary, the advantages of the approach are:

(*a*) It enables maps to be studied in the historical situations that created them rather than in the circumstances of their survival, which may or may not be relevant to an interpretation of military events in the period 1775–83. By grouping together maps designed to fulfill similarly perceived functions (even if they vary technically and stylistically), it can be shown how they were often interrelated rather than discrete objects. The historian, if he is to be assisted by historical studies of maps, may find the identification of central cartographic purposes more useful than an exposition of minor stylistic quirks. Revolutionary maps, in particular, often had single and ephemeral purposes, and these are relatively unintelligible unless restored to their military context.

(*b*) Since military maps are so diverse in both physical format and technique, discussion of their attributes is possible only in relation to subtypes. It would not be very meaningful to talk about the surveying methods, cartographic style, or conventional signs of military maps as a whole, even though better defined cartographic genres can be dissected in that way. Because of the variety of his roles, the military mapmaker relied on much of the cartographic experience of the eighteenth century.

(*c*) The approach overcomes one limitation of the evidence for a study of maps in military decisions. As R. A. Skelton often reminded us, all maps have high mortality rates.[16] With the maps of the American Revolution, this was doubly so since two of the armies had lines of supply across a perilous ocean. It is therefore necessary to reconcile a situation in which there are plenty of maps without documents. Conversely, many documentary sources refer to maps that have not survived. Through classification by function, these two imperfect strands of evidence may be more easily woven together.

Fortification cartography is one of the best defined groups within eighteenth-century military cartography. The object of much of the warfare in eighteenth-century Europe was to control, attack, or defend fortified places, whether they were single fortresses or whole towns. Not surprisingly, fortification plans were especially familiar to both amateur and professional students of the military sciences.[17] Indeed,

THE CARTOGRAPHY OF
FORTIFIED PLACES

the extent to which they had permeated a wider culture is reflected by their appearance in both the art and the literature of the seventeenth and eighteenth centuries. A knowledge of fortification enhanced the education of a gentleman as well as that of a professional soldier. English travelers on the Grand Tour, for example, viewed the fortifications to the north of Venice as part of the "standard package."[18] Atlases of fortification plans were published in several European countries in the seventeenth and eighteenth centuries and were sold to the libraries of laymen as well as military experts.[19] At the more purely military level, too, fortification plans were often cast as central objects in great military events. In paintings of some of the more famous sieges of the eighteenth century (in effect they were pictorial variants of perspective plans), an attacking general was sometimes shown with a plan of the enemy works in his hand. This was true in the paintings of the siege of Yorktown undertaken by Louis-Nicholas Van Blarenberghe, one of several battle painters (*peintres de batailles*) attached to the Dépôt de la Guerre in Paris, in whose landscape a group of officers, including engineers, are studying a plan.[20] In the illustrations of many military textbooks on fortifications, engineers were similarly shown constructing forts with the help of plans, and elsewhere they were depicted as directing sieges with plans in hand.[21] The view that a thorough knowledge of such plans was fundamental to the education of a staff officer is given emphasis by a nineteenth-century edition of the collected works of Frederick the Great; an illustration shows two young officers slumped in exhaustion after studying Frederick's military instructions and plans.[22]

Such random examples serve to indicate the wide currency that plans of fortification enjoyed in the eighteenth century. As everyday tools in the hands of military engineers and commanders, these plans had become fairly well standardized by the second half of the eighteenth century. There can be little doubt that the engineer officers attached to the headquarters staffs of the different Revolutionary armies frequently acted, whatever their educational or national background, with similar basic principles and models in mind. Jeduthan Baldwin, for example, had no formal training, but when he entered the Continental Army in March 1776 as captain assistant engineer, his work showed the same approach to the planning and cartographic recording of fortifications as did that of technical officers trained in European military academies.[23] A trend towards relative standardization in both the objectives and results of plan making was also aided by the fact that most fortifications, even by an eighteenth-century yardstick, were relatively small features in the landscape. Subject to variety in local topography, they tended to require only the application of one of several standard designs (such as the star, triangular, or square forts) by the engineer (see plate 1). Plans of these fortifications, either projected or existing, were usually executed at one of the relatively large fortification scales discussed below. Except in the heat of battle, they were usually surveyed with the help of the standard instruments available to the eighteenth-century military engineer—including the small theodolite or compass, the plane table, and the chain—and this also contributed to the broad cartographic formality that characterizes many of the surviving examples.

In a systematic study of fortification plans, further subdivision is necessary beyond the general scheme outlined above. That adopted in figure 1:2 conforms to the approach in this chapter and is intended to mirror the functions, both in theory and practice, that plans served when they were first made and used. Subtypes therefore range, in an idealized sequence, from those plans illustrating (and explained in) the textbooks of military writers, through the numerous blueprints of intended fortifications or reports on existing fortifications, to the use of fortification plans in the conduct and recording of sieges.

Textbooks and instructional manuals illustrate and describe survey and drawing methods and demonstrate the practical uses of military maps. As will be emphasized throughout this study, the textbooks often provide an invaluable guide to the contemporary use of all types of military maps, including the plans associated with fortification. Not all eighteenth-century texts were printed; they include manuscript treatises as well as other instructions and specifications which codify contemporary practice.[24] In four respects they shed important light on both the making and use of fortification plans.

Textbooks As a Guide to Surveying Methods. Many military textbooks, either directly or by implication, describe the instruments and techniques to be adopted by an engineer engaged in fortification. In the treatises on fortification (1774) by John Muller,[25] professor of artillery and fortification at the Royal Military Academy in Woolwich, which ran through several editions and were widely used in Britain and North America at the time of the Revolution, there is, for example, a detailed account of both the theory and practice of surveying and drawing fortification plans. In Muller's words, "The elementary part consists in teaching the plans and profiles of a fortification on paper, with scales and compasses."[26] A series of exercises in large-scale plan drawing were in effect prescribed for the engineering cadets in training. In the practical portion, instruction was offered to prepare a military engineer more directly for service in the field and to give guidance on matters like "How to make the Plan of a Fortress" and how "To trace the plan of a Fortress on the ground" using either plane table or theodolite. In both cases the instructions concerning surveying methods were explicit:

When a plain table is used, the plan must be drawn on a large scale, at least of 30 fathoms to an inch, which is fastened with sealing wax to the table, so as to lay quite smooth and even; then, by means of a ruler with sights, the angles are laid down on the ground, and the lengths of the lines measured by a chain and rod: but when the theodolite is used, the lines and angles must be found by trigonometry, in the manner given in our *Elements of mathematics.*[27]

These particular instructions continue for a further six pages in the text. They are not untypical of detail in similar works, not only containing the basic arithmetic, geometry, and trigonometry required by the engineer but also providing practical and illustrated examples, in some cases from actual fortifications.

Textbooks do not invariably provide a specification for a particular plan. Other things being equal, they allow the possibilities to be narrowed and the correct technique to be inferred from the plan itself or from additional written evidence. Since the same instruments are sometimes referred to in documents associated with the work of military engineers and in the textbooks, this lends support to the view that the majority of fortification plans made during the Revolutionary War were surveyed by variations of a few very basic techniques that, despite their elusiveness in the sources, were widely understood and practiced. Thus, Louis Lebègue Duportail, commandant of engineers in the Continental Army from 1777 to 1783, was careful to equip himself with three surveying compasses (*boussoles*), and three alidades to be attached to plane tables (*alidades de planchettes*), to be used, respectively, for the

Fortification Plans in the Textbooks

measurement of horizontal and vertical angles. These he described as the indispensable instruments of his profession.[28] Similarly, the journal of John Montresor, chief engineer of the British forces in North America, contains references to the surveying compass, the plane table, and the theodolite in various professional assignments (although not all were connected with fortification).[29] Even Jeduthan Baldwin, working for the relatively poorly equipped Continental Army, refers to his use of a "Surveyors compass or theodiler" in taking plans of the "Fortification at leachmor point."[30] Even where documents are silent, it may be safe to extrapolate from a limited number of examples. The sparseness of references to surveying techniques during the Revolutionary War does not mean that the methods employed were especially esoteric: it could equally mean that they were sufficiently commonplace to make their repetition in standard accounts, or on the face of every plan, largely superfluous. That a plan was drawn to scale in some multiple of a hundred feet to an inch in itself suggests the use of the standard chain supplied to the British engineers.

Textbooks As a Key to the Standard Scales Employed in Fortification Plans. Among the attributes of military maps itemized in figure 1:2, the scale is crucial for the overall definition and subdivision of fortification cartography. Concerning the definition, it is possible, although with some overlap, to isolate relatively large-scale fortification plans from topographical maps at smaller scales.

The textbooks imply that there were three main types of fortification plan. First, engineers were usually expected to make detailed topographical plans of a fort's surroundings. These might include the roads and tracks leading to the fort, settlements and military installations outside the main fortress area, and the distribution of woodland and scrub—trees could be cut down to form an abatis and were often so depicted in the environs of a fort. Second, even more detailed large-scale plans, at "particular scales," were made of the actual fort. Although these sometimes appear as an inset, they were often separate drawings with their own insets of features such as magazines and redoubts. Third, adding a vertical dimension to the horizontal, cross sections or longitudinal profiles through fortifications gave a distinctive subtype. They were almost invariably incorporated in large-scale plans (even where they were crudely sketched) and, by the early eighteenth-century, the drawing of profiles was a recognized subbranch of fortification cartography. A profile was distinguished as the "orthography of a work" (that is, of a fortification) as opposed to its "ichnography" or drawing in plan.[31] Since these profiles showed positions in which guns were to be mounted (or the potential lines of fire for other troops), they gave particular attention to the measurement of elevation. It is accordingly on such cross sections that some of the earliest values for height occur in military cartography, especially the relative heights between places (required for fortification purposes) rather than absolute heights.[32] On "A Map of the Pass, at Jamaica Long Island Surveyed by Order of His Excellency General Sir Henry Clinton, K.B. Commander in Chief . . . By George Taylor Captn. of Guides," for example, the cross sections, but not the map itself, record relative heights (see plate 2).[33] Such measurements, coupled with data on distances between points designed for gun emplacements, gave the artillery officer precise information about the way a site commanded the surrounding terrain.

These three categories constantly recur in the textbooks and in the surviving plans, but when numerical values for their associated scales are sought, the evidence of the textbooks is more ragged. For a plane table survey of a fort, Muller recommended a minimum scale of 30 fathoms (approx. 180 feet) to an inch.[34] He was explicit in his opinion that profiles could not be drawn on a scale of less than 30 feet to an inch.[35] For British fortification plans, however, the fullest statement of eighteenth-century practice, still current at the time of the Revolution, was included in unpublished instructions to British engineers issued about 1740. These were to fulfill a cartographic role similar to that of the textbooks in the process of technical standardization:

The following Measures for Geometrical Scales are certainly the most useful, being applicable to all sorts of Practice and being aliquot parts each of the other, the Plans Surveyed to any one of them may be readily enlarged or contracted as occasion shall require:—

1st. A Scale of 1600 Feet to an Inch for the General Map of a Coast or small Island &c.

2nd. A Scale of 800 Feet to an Inch for the Plan of a Town and parts adjacent.

3rd. A Scale of 400 Feet to an Inch for a particular Plan of Town or Settlement.

4th. A Scale of 200 Feet to an inch to Survey the same by.

5th. A Scale of 100 Feet to an Inch for a particular Plan of a Fort Battery or the Like.

6th. A Scale of 10 feet to an Inch for a Magazine or particular Building, Sections, or Profils of the same.

7th. A Scale of 5 Feet to an Inch for a Draw-Bridge, Gun Carriage, or any other Carpenter's Work.[36]

This data can assist the study of fortification cartography in the Revolutionary period. It allows the relationship to be established between the scales of the plans and the surveying instruments used. This is made clear by the instructions which, as well as noting that these scales could be easily enlarged or reduced, stress the advantage of their natural relationship with the 100-foot chain. "A Chain of One Hundred Links, each Link one Foot in Length," it was stipulated, "is the most proper to be used with the above Scales."[37] Moreover, a definition of "fortification scales" appears to be incorporated in the instructions, with a break at 800 feet to an inch. Scales above that (such as 1,600 feet to an inch) were regarded as more appropriate for a "General Map of a Coast or small Island". At 800 feet to an inch and larger, however, the scales were designed for "plans" rather than maps; these were suitable for plans of towns and (at the largest scales) for drawings of single buildings. Finally, the listing of a series of basic scales offers a standard against which surviving fortification plans can be compared.

As these particular instructions were issued to British engineers, they have been compared with the scales either given or calculated for British fortification plans. Similar analyses need to be made where comparable evidence exists for French and German plans. For the British plans, there is a discernible relationship between theory and practice. Certainly, in the crop of cartographic schemes relating to North America in the years immediately preceding the Revolution, the results of a standard training for British military engineers were in evidence from Quebec to Florida. The use of scales at 800 feet to an inch and below, apparently based on the 100- or 50-foot chain, is amply illustrated in those major collections—such as the King George III Topographical Collection in the Map Library of the British Library[38] or the Gage and Clinton papers in the William L. Clements Library at the University of Michigan[39]—where engineers' work is amply represented. To give one example, the detailed plans of Quebec in the James Murray survey of the Saint Lawrence valley (1761–63) were drawn at 800 feet to an inch; the seven plans that illustrated the defense of its fortifications were at 400, 100, and 50 feet to an inch; and longitudinal profiles were at 25 feet to an inch.[40] The small group of trained engineers at work in North America on the eve of the Revolution obviously tended to think along similar lines in carrying out their fortification assignments. Hugh Debbeig, who had served his apprenticeship with William Roy on the military survey of the Scottish highlands (1747–55), after being posted to Newfoundland, submitted a proposal to the British colonial administration in 1764 for a "General Military Survey of the Great Ports and Harbours on the . . . Coast of America."[41] Although Debbeig's ideas were not taken up in the face of competition from somewhat similar schemes, he clearly recognized the standard engineer scales. Three points in his specification for his proposed survey illustrate this. First, the surveys of all the great harbours were to be executed on a uniform scale of 400 feet to an inch.[42] Second, cross sections at 100 feet to an inch were to be taken of "Commanding Grounds, of all spots that appear fit to receive any kind of Works of Fortification Batteries &ca."[43] Third, "Particular plans" were also required of these fortifiable sites at a scale of 100 feet to an inch. The cumulative impression is of a standard approach to fortification cartography. If this is accepted, then interest focuses on a historical explanation of the exceptions to this pattern.

To assess the range of conformity and exception, a wider sample is required. For British fortification plans of the Revolution, this is conveniently provided by the headquarters maps and sketches used by Sir Henry Clinton as commander-in-chief of the British forces in North America.[44] These can, moreover, be supplemented by similar collections made by other general officers.[45] Figure 1:3 is a simple histogram,

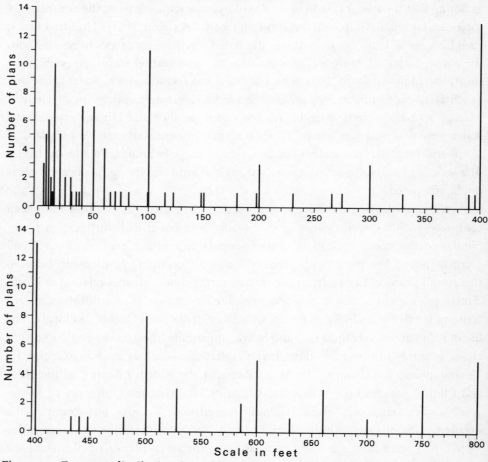

Figure 1:3 Frequency distribution chart of fortification scales of British plans in the Revolution.

based on data in the Clinton and Percy collections and on plans in the Public Record Office, showing the incidence of the scales of plans in the fortification range, at 800 feet to an inch or larger.[46] Analysis reveals a much wider scatter of scales than the six values given in the 1740 instructions. There was in practice, therefore, much greater flexibility than in theory. This was especially true under campaign conditions, and several explanations of this variation may be noted. First, cartographers with backgrounds other than that of trained engineers were employed at British army headquarters in North America from 1775 to 1783. Second, an assumption that standard instruments—the 100- and 50-foot chain—were always available is likely to be wrong: where a scale of multiples of 66 feet to an inch is recorded, this presumably denotes use of the Gunter's chain.[47] Third, where no chain was available, fortification scales had to be calculated in paces.[48] Even here, orthodox practice was not entirely excluded, and the engineer had been prepared for an absence of proper surveying instruments. The 1740 instructions noted that 100 feet was equivalent to "20 Geometrical Paces or 40 Common Paces."[49] The underlying trend, even during the disturbed conditions of Revolutionary campaigns, was toward standardization in the use of military fortification scales.

Textbooks as an Explanation of Color Conventions. The same tendency towards standardization can also be adduced in the use of color in the production of fortification plans. In this, as in the matter of scale, trainees in the drafting, engineering, and geographical branches of most European armies were often drilled in standard plan styles rather than encouraged to engage in artistic license. Such a set approach characterized the apprenticeship served by draftsmen in the Tower of London during the Revolutionary period.[50] The problem remains, however, that individual plans seldom embody an explanation of color differences, presumably because distinctions were taken to be thoroughly familiar to most users of a plan. For the modern interpreter, they may be less than obvious, and in this context the fortification textbooks are again informative. For British conventions, Muller's *Elementary Part of Fortification* contains a basic color code, reflecting Continental as well as British practice at the time of the Revolution. "It is necessary," Muller wrote, "to use colours in the drawing of plans and profiles of a fortification, in order to distinglish every particular part, and separate, as it were, the one from the other, so as to make their difference more sensible."[51] Muller's list of colors is summarized in table 1:1.

The extent to which the surviving fortification plans of the Revolution follow these conventions varies considerably. Many fortification plans were only crudely executed and made no use of color, even in finished version. This is entirely to be expected insofar as they were drawn neither under textbook conditions nor to illustrate designs and reports in the manner that writers such as Muller had envisaged. A distinguishing feature of the American Revolution, as contemporaries were aware, was that it was not always fought by classic European rules. Its cartography could be equally unconventional. Washington's strategy, apart from West Point, was far less contingent on the erection of major, permanent fortifications than had been normal in eighteenth-century Europe. The French geographical engineers, too, despite their professionalism, were not seriously concerned in North America with the design and erection of major forts.

It is largely in British fortification plans, therefore, especially those produced by trained engineers, that textbook practice is closely reflected.[52] After all, only behind British lines at garrisons such as those at Halifax, Rhode Island, New York, and

Table 1:1. Basic Color Conventions for Fortification Plans
(after J. Muller, 1774)

Color	Features
Blue (a mixture of sea green and indigo)	encampments[1]
Carmine	
crimson	sections of masonry, plans of houses and other buildings, lines in plans to represent walls
paler red	elevations of buildings
Gamboge ("Gum-bouch": fine yellow)	all projected works, unfinished as opposed to completed works. The trenches of an attack in siege plans
Green (mixture of "sap green," a yellowish green, and sea green)	grass, turfed surfaces such as parapets
Indian Ink	
"very black"	all outlines of works
pale black (several applications)	hill shading[2]
Indigo	iron, roofs of buildings covered with slate
Umber (yellowish brown mixed with a little red)	dry ditches, sand, profiles of earthworks wood color
Verdigris	
sea green	wet ditches, rivers, the sea, all "watery places"

1. According to Muller, "to represent the colour of blue cloth."
2. For shading purposes the light entered the top left hand corner of the plan: many plans followed Vauban's practice of taking "left" and "right" to mean those directions as they were seen from the fortress not the countryside.

Quebec, were regular cartographic facilities established. In the drawing rooms at these headquarters, which were presumably not too dissimilar from those maintained at home stations such as Edinburgh, Portsmouth, or Plymouth, cartographic orthodoxy predictably prevailed. Thus color conventions are easily recognized in the work of Abraham D'Aubant, commanding engineer at Rhode Island from 1776 to 1779 and a former draftsman in the Tower of London. No doubt remembering the lessons of his basic training, as well as authorities such as Muller, he noted in his "Plan of Fort Brown" that "Parts coloured yellow are not yet finished."[53] On a plan of Halifax's Citadel Hill, William Spry, the commanding engineer there, made a similar annotation.[54] For the majority of plans made by American, French, and British draftsmen, however, it is necessary to turn to a different part of the classification, and indeed to different textbooks.

Textbooks in the Provision of a Terminology. By the time of the Revolution, fortification was a mature science. In all the major European languages, its literature was massive and reflected continuous growth since the sixteenth century. At different periods, the so-called Italian, Netherlands, German, and French schools or systems of fortification had contributed to the state of the art. The names of classic *fortificateurs,* such as Coehorn, Cormontaigne, Pagan, and Vauban, were almost interchangeable with the designs they had helped to popularize. As an integral part of this technology, a technical language particular to fortification and the military sciences had gained currency. For the historian of cartography, this language offers a ready-made terminology, easily as applicable to the elements in a fortification plan as to the same parts of a fortress on the ground.

The importance attached to terminology, a common language for an international profession, is emphasized by glossaries appended to several military textbooks of the Revolutionary period (see plate 3)[55] and by definitions included in numerous military dictionaries and encyclopedias.[56] Even on a printed plan intended for public information, such as "A Plan of The Town of Boston, with the Intrenchments &c." (1777), compiled by Thomas Hyde Page and engraved by William Faden to illustrate Bunker Hill for the English public, such terms as abatis, bastion, flêches, redoubt, and traverse are encountered.[57] In manuscript plans the terminology may be more abstruse, extending to guns *en barbette,* to breastworks or embrasures, to fascines, lunettes and parallels—to list but a handful of the more common terms. Standard histories of cartography, even the late François de Dainville's *Le Langage des géographes,* contain little or no guidance.[58] Yet for at least two reasons, this terminology needs to be understood. First, technical language is a basic way in which the cartographer communicates the functional significance of the parts of his plans, of various military activities, or of the topography they represent. For the historian of cartography, technical terms thus enter the processes of classifying and interpreting military maps. Second, at a bibliographical level, an agreed and generally understood set of definitions is necessary for consistent recording of the characteristics of military maps.

Throughout the eighteenth century, an immense amount of skill, labor, and capital was lavished on the planning and construction of fortifications throughout Europe and her colonial dependencies. In the training of engineers and in the design stage of actual fortifications, considerable use was made of scale models, two-dimensional plans, relief profiles, and perspective drawings. Scale models of fortifications were used in the instruction of artillery and engineering cadets at the military academy in Woolwich. In Paris, the Galerie des Plans Reliefs contained jealously guarded state secrets. With so much at stake both militarily and financially, once a fortification was approved in principle, the senior engineer usually drafted a memorandum explaining its shape, cost, and properties, together with several sheets of scale plans. When Hugh Debbeig insisted on the submission of detailed plans and careful cost estimates before the construction of any work, he was following a widely held professional consensus.[59] A distinctive portion of the surviving fortification cartography of the Revolution (as of the rest of the eighteenth century) consists of maps and plans made for projects subject to final approval; in some cases they were never constructed.

Intervals between the actual campaigns of the Revolution were long and even leisurely enough to provide opportunities for a fairly orthodox approach to fortification. As a general rule, an engineer would submit his plans for approval to his commander-in-chief. The Marquis de Lafayette, trained in French military methods, wrote to Washington in March 1778 about a minor fort suggested for construction in the back country; he had asked its proposer, he reported, to "send me a geometrical plan of his projected fort with its profiles and dimensions."[60] Similarly, at the very beginning of the Revolution, Bernard Romans, after being ordered by Washington to report on the construction of the defenses at Fort Constitution, prepared five plans of the intended works and enclosed them in a letter to the Committee of Safety of New York, written from the site of the new fort on 14 September 1775 (see plate 4).[61] After an American corps of engineers had been established, Duportail's proposals for fortification were likewise the subject of discussions (with the help of draft plans) between Washington and other general officers at head-

Engineering "Blueprints" and Reports on Fortifications

quarters.[62] So deeply imbued was military thinking with the value of such plans that even when an earthwork was being leveled, there was a case for keeping a cartographic record. In May 1781, Major General Nathanael Greene wrote from his camp at McCord's Ferry on the Congaree that upon the evacuation of the British from ground near Camden, "we immediately took possession of the place, and the works are leveling, a plan of which is herewith inclosed."[63]

Several series of projected fortifications plans also survive in the cartographic archive assembled at Clinton's headquarters. Those surveyed and drawn by the engineers of the Rhode Island garrison from 1777 to 1779 sum up the methodical and often meticulous nature of fortification cartography, with their makers showing off theoretical knowledge in the light of local topography. In "Report of the Service performed at Rhode Island by the Engineer Department . . . accompanied with a general Plan of the Islands in Narraganset Bay, and three particular Plans of Works," D'Aubant itemized: "Taking a plan of the Island, and Plans of the Works which had been erected on it by the Rebels. making fair drawings for the General. Preparing a plan and Project for the defence of Howland's neck."[64] The survival of a written report accompanying these plans is a reminder that just as the engineers performed many tasks other than purely cartographical ones, so too, fortification plans were but a graphic element in a larger written account. They were, however, an essential element, and neither plans nor written reports are fully intelligible without reference to each other—a point that is especially apposite to any consideration of the relative role of maps in military decisions. Six months later, in November 1777, D'Aubant submitted another plan, "Project for the Defence of the Town of Newport," with proposals for various works identified on his "general Plan of the Island."[65] This plan, at a scale of 500 feet to an inch, is a good example of a general fortification plan designed to locate a related series of field earthworks (see plate 5). Its elaborate "explanation" uses letters (an almost standard convention) to key in about forty earthworks, either built or projected, including batteries, sea batteries, counter batteries, flèches, and redoubts. Detailed drawings in both plan and profile of many of these smaller earthworks accompanied the report, and at large scales, such as 10 or 15 feet to an inch. Such a series of plans can almost be described as a military engineer's specimen book for these types of fortification. Their distinctiveness justifies their separation within the general category of fortification cartography (figure 1:2).

Detailed plans were also an integral part of the periodic reports or inspections ordered for most fortifications in North America as elsewhere. They were usually executed by military engineers. In the orderly books of Lieutenant James Hadden of the Royal Artillery, kept in Canada and on Burgoyne's campaign in 1776 and 1777, it was noted that Engineer Wade had been directed "to take such plans, and make such inspection of the works at Quebec, as may be necessary to form a report for the General, of the present situation of the place, so that arrangements may be taken to put it into that state of defence as may be thought proper."[66] This instruction was typical of many given during the Revolution. A group of fortification plans relating to Halifax, surviving in the Clinton collection, was originally surveyed and drawn to fulfill this function by engineers under the command of William Spry.[67] At Halifax, a station removed from active conflict during the Revolution, the relatively undisturbed traditions of British military engineering were again strongly reflected in the types of plan produced.

Elsewhere, especially under campaign situations, fortification plans had to be radically adapted to meet immediate, technical constraints. The basic design stage was particularly subject to abbreviation. In May 1780, Duportail, Washington's chief engineer, noted: "M. de Laumoy and the engineers whom he has under his orders, have been so busy constructing the fortifications of Charlestown, both before and during the siege that there was no time to make a design of the plans—this deprives me of the satisfaction of sending them to Congress—supposing indeed the enemy would permit it."[68] Moreover, with hastily constructed minor field fortifications, plans were not always regarded as necessary. Extemporary methods, bypassing geometrical surveys with theodolite and chain, were advocated in some textbooks. The distinction was clearly made in *The Field Engineer of M. le Chevalier De Clairac*: "A project of fortification is commonly the result of a long meditation; the engineer plans, digests, and examines it in his closet; compares at leisure his different ideas, and, provided the work be solid and durable, he is not anxious about time, materials, or any other necessary means, which he knows are to be had in the execution. In the field it is otherwise, no regard is to be had to the solidity of the works; every thing must be determined on the spot; the works are to be traced out directly, and regulated by the time."[69] Roger Stevenson in his *Military Instructions for Officers Detached in the Field* (published in Philadelphia in 1775, and the first book to be dedicated to George Washington) went even further in asserting that, instead of the surveyor's usual instruments, "a piece of whip-cord twenty yards long, may be made to answer every purpose that an officer on detachment has occasion to ask for."[70] To the impoverishment of the cartographic record, this advice was of necessity heeded on many occasions.

If the attack or defense of a fortified place could provide either a climax or an epitaph to an engineer's career, it could also give rise to a crop of plans, distinctive in their function, content, and physical format. The representation of the events of a siege presented a cartographer with complications additional to those involved in the straightforward depiction of a ground plan or profile of a fort. This had two aspects. First, there was a need to show the positions of the attacking and defending forces— that is, the regimental units engaged—as well as the topography of the fortifications. Second, in some cases there was also a need to show these positions in successive stages, from the beginning of an attack to capitulation. In studying the cartographers' response to these problems, we are fortunate that important sieges tended to be well-mapped events. For the siege of Yorktown, Coolie Verner in his checklist was able to locate over thirty eighteenth-century printed plans relating to the events and over a hundred in manuscript.[71] Although the mapping of Yorktown had a bias toward the work of French cartographers (of the surviving manuscript plans, over thirty of French origin have been located—more than twice the number produced by the British and American cartographers together), the sample is still adequate to illustrate most of the conventions used in Revolutionary siege cartography. Indeed, some of the French plans have an almost textbook quality, perhaps because for some of their cartographers Yorktown was a first chance to put into practice lessons learned at the engineering school at Mezières, near Paris. Moreover, Yorktown was the only major engagement in which Rochambeau's army participated: for purely commemorative reasons, the contemporary French record is particularly full.

In the mode of its conduct as well as in its mapping, Yorktown was also something of a textbook affair. In the classic manner of Vauban, first and second parallels (the attacker's line of trenches for approaching the fortification) were duly opened and

Siege Cartography

are represented on a number of plans. To portray these dynamic aspects of the operational development of a siege on the same plan, several cartographers employed an overlay, or hinged flap. This flap shows the same piece of terrain (at an identical scale) as that part of the main map directly beneath it but with troop or fortification positions recorded in an earlier stage of the siege. A good example of this adaptation of cartographic format to display movement, rather in the manner of an embryonic film strip, is found in the "Plan of the Siege of York," drawn by the topographical engineers, the brothers Louis-Alexandre and Victor-Léopold Berthier. Although their plan is annotated as "figuré à vue" ("drawn freehand"), it employs the device of a hinged flap to depict two stages of the siege. The overlay shows the first parallel, established on 6 October 1781; the same area beneath on the main plan shows the second parallel, established on 15 October.[72] The technique was not unique and was probably understood by many officers capable of making a plan. This is confirmed by its use in the works of Edward Fage, a cartographically minded officer in the Royal Artillery. Fage's "Plan of the Posts of York and Gloucester . . . with The attacks under Operations of the American & French Forces Commanded by General Washington and the Count of Rochambeau . . ." was published on 4 June 1782 as part of *The Atlantic Neptune,* compiled and engraved by Joseph F. W. DesBarres. In this case the overlay was used to show "the position of the army between the ravines on the 28th and 29th September 1781."[73]

To display the position of regimental and other units during the course of a siege, special symbols, color systems, and also letters and numbers on the face of the plan (usually explained in a marginal key) were used in various permutations. It is these specialist conventions that are the essence of military cartography. It follows that a detailed comparative explanation of these conventions in a European context would be an important contribution to both the history of military mapping and the interpretation of military maps by historians. With symbols as with terminology, however, François de Dainville's pioneering study contains only a few examples used by Revolutionary cartographers. It is necessary to turn to authorities contemporary with the plans.

As an introduction to this important subject, which requires fuller exploitation, it may be noted that a number of military textbooks contain descriptions and illustrations of the conventions that had developed to distinguish the component regiments and units within a field army. Such symbols occur in texts published during the Revolution.[74] In the *Mémorial topographique et militaire,* edited at the Dépôt Général de la Guerre at the beginning of the nineteenth century (and incidentally, signed and approved by Louis-Alexandre Berthier, Rochambeau's cartographer, by then minister of war), there is a useful codification of eighteenth-century practices.[75] The relevant sections of the *Mémorial,* together with the pages of *Signes conventionnels pour l'armée de terre,* although far too elaborate for convenient use under combat conditions, were invariably added to fair drawings of siege plans. They offer a basic starting point for deciphering the military content of Revolutionary plans. By comparing the symbols on the actual plans with those in the textbooks, some broad principles and their application can be worked out.

Two main groups of symbols can be identified. First, a relatively small number of special symbols were used for supporting arms such as the artillery park (realistically represented by small guns grouped together), the wagon train of an army, or, on a river, provision *bateaux,* such as those sailing with Burgoyne's fateful push to Albany.[76] Lines of movement across a siege or battle plan were invariably shown by dotted or pecked lines. Second, a family of symbols was derived from the basic flag or rectangle used to depict the various detachments constituting an army. Reflecting tactical theory, a distinction was preserved between infantry and cavalry. For infantry, the rectangle was usually narrower and shorter when representing—in turn—brigades, half brigades, battalions, and small units such as advanced corps. For cavalry, the rectangle was frequently broader and squarer, and it could also vary in size. In another refinement, small flags were added above the upper edge of these symbols: this was either to identify the type of regiment or, where the small flag was either attached or detached and raised a little, to indicate whether a unit was engaged or encamped.[77] Where rectangular symbols were given a dotted or pecked edge, this indicated old positions no longer occupied. [78] Various diagonal divisions of rectangles, accompanied by selective shading or blocking out, could further define the regimental unit. Some differences in the use of rectangular symbols can be discerned among the mapmakers of different national armies. Although all plans—regardless of national origin—employ rectangular symbols, French cartographers in particular tended to add elaborate superscript symbols to the main rectangles. British mapmakers, on the other hand, usually relied on unadorned rectangles distinguished by size, shading, or color. (See plate 6.)

Color was essential to the convention system of most polished siege and battle plans. A basic task of the cartographer was to ensure that the locations of different armies, whether enemies or allies, were clearly distinguished. This was sometimes accomplished by shading different halves of diagonally divided rectangles, but color was almost universally applied for this purpose on both manuscript and published plans (the latter were printed from engraved copper plates and then hand colored). These colors are usually self-explanatory, but they were not necessarily employed consistently from plan to plan. On Faden's "Plan of the Siege of Savannah," the American units were shown in yellow and white, the French in yellow and blue, and the British in red and white.[79] On the Berthier plan of the siege of Yorktown, American positions are colored green, although the French units and those of the besieged British were again respectively colored in yellow and red.[80] Ambiguities in the use of color were often removed by the addition of a key using letters or numbers to identify the opposing regiments.

The choice of color often bore a relationship to the color of the troops' uniforms. The most elaborate development of this form of association was made by French cartographers, who sometimes used colors to differentiate regiments within one army. One such plan, while not specifically of a siege, was drawn by Henri Crublier d'Opterre, a captain in the French engineers accompanying Rochambeau. On his "Plan de la Ville, Rade, et Environs de Newport, avec le Campement de l'Armée Françoise . . . ," the colors infilling the rectangular symbols corresponded to the uniforms of the various regiments deployed around Newport.[81] Numbers were also added to avoid ambiguity, as Rice and Brown explain:

No. 47 on the map is the Saintonge Regiment, whose white uniforms had green cuffs and piping; 46 is the Soissonnais, white with crimson lapels and cuffs; 45 is the Royal Deux-Ponts, who wore light blue uniforms with yellow lapels and cuffs; 44 is the Bourbonnais, white with black cuffs and piping. No. 43 designates the Auxonne artillery, whose uniforms (like those of other artillery regiments) were dark blue with red collars, cuffs, and tail facings . . . . Lauzun's Legion of Foreign Volunteers, stationed near Castle Hill on the Neck, 48, is tinted light blue and yellow, denoting the uniform color of its hussars.[82]

In this description of siege cartography, the central core of established convention has been emphasized. It must also be recognized that this sort of treatment inevitably obscures the range of variation in individual plans. It is helpful, in understanding these variations, to consider the variety of operational circumstance under which siege plans were made. At one extreme, the mapmaker could have been actually in the line of fire, with little opportunity to implement normal practice. Not surprisingly, for example, François de Fleury, a volunteer engineer with the Continental Army, was forced at the time of the British attack on Fort Mifflin to annotate his "Figuré Aproximatif du Fort Mifflin des Ouvrages des Assiègeans 9th 9bre 1777" (see plate 7) with the note, "the engineer officer of this imperfect draft begg indulgence for it; Considering he has not paper, pen, rule neither cercel, and being disturbed by good many shells or Cannon's balls flying in the fort."[83] It is remarkable that he was able to make a plan at all. The fact that he did is a telling aside on the importance French engineers attached to a cartographic record of events. An even more unusual example of improvisation under siege conditions was recorded in the diary of Lieutenant Frederick Mackenzie of the Royal Welch Fusiliers. During the siege of Rhode Island he reported, "The distance of the Enemy's battery N° 2, from the Barrier Redoubt taken from repeatedly observing the flash of their guns and the report, by a stop watch, is calculated to be 2855 Yards. . . ." Even so, the location of other batteries had been "Measured along the Ground" by Edward Fage of the Royal Artillery.[84]

At the other extreme were siege plans—perhaps the majority—made after the event. To give one example, Captain Johann Henrichs, a Hessian officer with the Jäger corps, who was probably employed as an engineer, noted in his diary after the siege of Charleston in 1780, "As regards the enemy's fortifications and their defense, as well as our attack upon them, I shall wait till I have drawn my plan, which I have so far found no time to do."[85] From the routine nature of this entry it would appear that a staff officer regarded the delayed execution of such a plan as normal rather than exceptional.[86] Post-battle siege plans were made for a variety of purposes. Some were designed to accompany official reports ordered by commanding officers to be sent to ministers of war or presented to the crown; others were solely the personal record of a professionally minded soldier; and it is possible that one or two officers contemplated publication as they undertook their surveys.

In helping to explain that all Revolutionary armies tended to record important events in plan form as well as by written reports, it is relevant to observe that just as one army was keen to commemorate its success, so, too, another used plans to help rescue its tarnished reputation. Indeed, the cartography of defeat had to be at least as meticulous as that of victory: military scientists would pore over these dispositions for years to come. After the siege of Savannah, for example, the French engineer, Captain Antoine O'Connor, was apparently just as careful in mapping the French retreat as he would have been with an advance, and his plans were deposited, alongside those of more successful engagements, in the collection of the Service Hydrographique de la Marine.[87] Sir Henry Clinton, following the debacle at Charleston in 1776, was still concerned several years later with fresh surveys to reconstruct the ground where a combination of tactical error and topographical ignorance had helped to defeat the British.[88]

As a final example of the variety of siege cartography, the splendid and ornamental map of the siege of Yorktown by Sebastian Bauman may be noted. The fact that it was boldly dedicated "To His Excellency Gen[e]. Washington, Commander in Chief of the Armies of the United States of America," suggests that the mapmaker, as well as the allied army at large, was in a celebratory mood. The cartouche of the plan, flanked by the American and French flags and embellished by cannon and drum, epitomizes martial glory in a cartographic idiom.[89]

One of the distinguishing features of the Revolutionary War, as contemporaries noted, was that it was not primarily concerned with the methodical investment of fortified strongholds, or even with the outcome of great, set piece battles; it was a war of movement. The continental scale of the confrontation insured that this would be so. All the major strategies—American or British, successful or unsuccessful, local or continental in scope—involved movement. On a continental scale, the British objective (to retain all thirteen colonies, rather than to keep a mere toehold in a few coastal fortresses) demanded long-distance movement, as did the strategic aim of trying to control the Hudson from New York to Canada in order to isolate New England from the other colonies. At a regional level, as in the south, mobility was also a primary logistical consideration: the essence of Major General Nathanael Greene's campaign with Lord Cornwallis lay in evasion and in maneuvering in a difficult and broken countryside. Locally the same considerations were operant, especially when the dominant tactic was *petite guerre:* harassing and skirmishing with the enemy but usually avoiding major confrontations. That maps could play a significant role at all levels in such a war of movement will be obvious. The measure of this significance depends both on the characteristics of the maps and on the specific uses to which they were actually put by military commanders.

The maps associated with military movement, unlike fortification plans, have little in common. The simple fact is that any map relating to an area of military operations —whether crude or sophisticated, and however it was defined cartographically—could have contributed to the mental picture of terrain being built up by a Revolutionary commander. The historical identity and significance of maps of movement is therefore derived from their common military functions, and these functions provide the main unifying concept. Given such an approach, it will be seen how a marine chart of a major estuary, though dissimilar in physical format and convention, was similar in purpose to a map of an important land route: both were vital to the safe movement of troops and supplies in a campaign; both played comparable roles in the Revolution. Under this broad umbrella, a number of distinctive subgroups related to particular military activities can be recognized. Three such groups are described below.

Reconnaissance or reconnoitering, although it tended to be an omnibus concept, was an essential preliminary to most military actions, whether they involved the movement of an army in the field or the planning of a battle or siege. At the time of the Revolution, there was not only broad agreement on its importance, but also unanimity about the value of maps in recording information acquired during military reconnaissance. Thus, in 1775, Roger Stevenson in his *Military Instructions* had

THE CARTOGRAPHY OF
MILITARY MOVEMENT

Reconnaissance Maps

written a section on "reconnoitring" that contained the following advice: "Parties ordered to reconnoitre, are to observe the country or the enemy; to remark the routes, conveniences and inconveniences of the first; the position, march, or forces of the second. In either case, they should have an expert geographer, capable of taking plans readily: he should be the best mounted of the whole, in case the enemy happen to scatter the escort, that he may save himself more easily with his works and ideas."[90] These "works and ideas" were presumably the raw materials of sketch plans which, Stevenson noted, were "chiefly useful, not to say necessary, for a commander of a party, who can give more ample and precise instructions to his officers, by accompanying them with a copy of the routes marked out, which they can consult even in the night, if it happens to be clear; by which they will be guarded against being deceived by ignorant or treacherous guides, which occasions the mistakes of so many who go unprovided with such helps."[91]

The extent to which these maxims represented a military concensus, in theory at least, can be confirmed by reference to many of the other contemporary textbooks. In John Count O'Rourke's *Treatise on the Art of War,* published in 1778, the advice was quite explicit in an article on "knowing or reconnoitring the country." An officer, he asserted, must first study "exactly the map of the province which is to be the seat of war; and to remember perfectly the names of the chief cities, rivers, and mountains."[92] O'Rourke went on to stress, "After acquiring a general notion of the country, you must proceed to the attainment of a more particular knowledge." This included a "perfect acquaintance with the chief roads"; with the "situation of the towns" (plans of all fortified places were essential); with the "course of the large rivers, and their depth; how far they are navigable, and where they are fordable." It was also necessary to know which rivers were impassable in spring or dry in summer, and such information ought to "extend even to the chief marshes in the province." The good officer should reconnoiter with "map in hand, and ascend the hills," and he must end up with "a proper idea of the nature of the passes, defiles, and advantageous positions of a whole province."[93]

The textbooks are indeed full of these exhortations. The problem for studies of Revolutionary cartography is that the majority fail to provide anything approaching a specification for reconnaissance mapping. Quite frequently, as is the case with O'Rourke and Stevenson, they list the features or "interesting particulars" to be mapped, "forgetting nothing, even to mills, bushes, gibbets, gullies," but then say little about how this was to be accomplished.[94] One point, however, seems to have been agreed: methods of reconnaissance survey were permissibly less accurate and detailed than those required in either fortification or regular military topographical surveying. Stevenson, for example, believed that "the best time for the geographer is by day in a mountainous country, where they may flip along from one mountain to another," and presumably he had in mind a form of rapid survey without instruments.[95] Such reconnaissance sketching was already a recognized technique by the time of the Revolution. In some European military academies, it was taught as a separate subject. In 1775, J. D. C. Pirscher, a captain in the Royal Prussian engineers, published a digest of contemporary practices in his *Coup d'oeil militaire.* This is almost exclusively concerned with military topographical sketching without normal surveying instruments; it is, for reconnaissance, a counterpart to the detailed textbooks on fortification cartography. Some of the recommended symbols (see plate 8) had been derived from general topographical survey, but emphasis was placed on techniques required to carry out a survey by eye, aided only by a simple hand-telescope, level, and squared paper.[96]

Such ideas had also reached England. John Burgoyne, vanquished at Saratoga but more successful as colonel of the Sixteenth Light Dragoons, had already incorporated the principle of field sketching in his "Code of Instructions" for "Burgoyne's Light Horse" by the 1760s. In stressing the role of cavalry in geographical reconnaissance, his ideas match Stevenson's plea for a mounted geographer—both were expected to take quick topographical sketches in the field. As Burgoyne observed, "If a man has a taste for drawing, it will add a very pleasing and useful qualification; and I would recommend him to practise taking views from an eminence, and to measure distances with his eye. This would be a talent particularly adapted to the light dragoon service."[97] It was also a quite different talent from the more precise skills required in a fortification survey. This was a point taken up by Lieutenant-Colonel Charles Vallencey, director of engineers and in charge of the survey of Ireland, who in 1779 wrote "Essay on Military Surveys accompanied with Military Itineraries." Referring to quick reconnaissance surveys during campaigns, he noted how "the Engineer, from the nature of his studies in our service, is a stranger to the movements and manouvres of an Army, and ill qualified for a duty of this kind; confined also to mathematical exactness, he moves too slow with his Instruments to get over the ground with sufficient speed for a military survey of this sort."[98] Leaving aside the accuracy of his assertion, Vallencey did make a clear distinction in function and probable specification between fortification and reconnaissance cartography. What he believed was required, as a "great utility," was "a number of officers . . . expert in the art of sketching and reconnoitring a Country." These cartographic specialists, he envisaged, would be sent in advance of the main army and would work "under the command of one Principal Director, who collects the sketches made by his party, & forms one Cart of the Country *en gros,* preparatory to the Generals arrival with the Army."[99]

Turning from the textbooks to actual examples of reconnaissance mapping, practice is sometimes difficult to reconcile with contemporary theory. The problem is not in lack of examples. If the citation of the terms *reconnaissance* and *reconnoitre* in the records is any indication, then the act was routine. On most days when the armies were not completely immobilized, even during battle and siege operations, reconnaissance in one form or another was in progress. It was a continuous process of probing enemy defenses, weighing up the alternatives for defensive positions, securing the vanguard and the flanking columns of an army on the march, and foraging for supplies. The detachments so engaged ranged from a brigade to a dozen or so mounted troops. It is, therefore, the very ubiquity of reconnaissance, as well as its diversity, which makes the study of the maps it produced far more than a simple exercise in equating function with cartographic form. Many reconnaissances did not result in maps at all, but in oral and written reports or in the instant mental mapping of terrain. Even when maps from independent documentary sources unambiguously designated as "reconnaissance" have been grouped together, they make a heterogeneous bunch. Examples range from crude and local sketch maps to detailed plans of several square miles, more akin to the topographical cartography described below than to reconnaissance sketches as understood by writers like Stevenson and Vallencey.

A number of European cartographers managed to retain the orthodox terminology of their training even on active service. Reinhard Jacob Martin of the Hessian engineers used the term *levé à coup d'oeil,* after Pirscher, to describe his "Plan des environs de Brookland & de Bettford," illustrating the American line of defense at Brooklyn.[100] Similarly, a number of French topographical engineers, employed to reconnoiter and survey terrain in advance of the army, were careful to distinguish between freehand maps (*figuré à la vue*) and those surveyed (*levé*) or based on triangulation (*déterminé géométriquement*).[101] In any case, only a small minority of sketch maps made in the Revolution specifically identified the mode of survey. For the rest, a lack of instrumental control in situations of active reconnaissance has to be assumed.

An awareness of the distinctive contribution of reconnaissance mapping in military operations was evident in British thinking from the beginning of the Revolution. In a set of instructions from Thomas Gage, the commander-in-chief in America at the time of Lexington and Concord and Bunker Hill, an operational specification for this type of rapid thematic survey has been preserved. Early in 1775 the British army headquarters in Boston was becoming increasingly alarmed by portents of insurrection in the surrounding countryside. On 8 January 1775, Lieutenant Frederick Mackenzie of the Royal Welch Fusiliers (who was already showing an enthusiasm for military science that was to mark him as a future staff officer) wrote in his diary, "It has been signified to the Army, that if any Officers of the different Regiments are capable of taking Sketches of a Country, they are to send their names to the Deputy Adjutant General."[102] The immediate problem, as he explained in words similar to those of Vallancey, was that "not many Officers in this Army will be found qualified for this Service. It is a branch of Military education too little attended to, or sought after by our Officers, and yet is not only extremely necessary and useful in time of War, but very entertaining and instructive."[103] The sequel to this request and to Mackenzie's aside was that two volunteer officers came forward, John Brown, like Mackenzie a lieutenant in the Welch Fusiliers,[104] and Henry de Berniere, an ensign in the Tenth Regiment of Foot.[105] Gage's instructions for their special duty were:

Gentlemen, You will go through the counties of Suffolk and Worcester, taking a sketch of the country as you pass; it is not expected you should make out regular plans and surveys, but mark out the roads and distances from town to town, as also the situation and nature of the country; all passes must be particularly laid down, noticing the length and breadth of them, the entrance in and going out of them, and whether to be avoided by taking other routes.

The rivers also to be sketched out, remarking their breadth and depth and the nature of their banks on both sides, the fords, if any, and the nature of their bottoms, many of which particulars may be learned of the country people.

You will remark the heights you meet with, whether the ascents are difficult or easy; as also the woods and mountains, with the height and nature of the latter, whether to be got round or easily past over.

The nature of the country to be particularly noticed, whether inclosed or open; if the former, what kind of inclosures, and whether the country admits of making roads for troops on the right or left of the main road, or on the sides.

You will notice the situation of the towns and villages, their churches, and church-yards, whether they are advantageous spots to take post in, and capable of being made defencible.

If any places strike you as proper for encampments, or appear strong by nature, you will remark them particularly, and give reasons for your opinions.

It would be useful if you could inform yourselves of the necessaries their different counties could supply, such as provisions, forage, straw, &c. the number of cattle, horses, &c. in the several townships.[106]

The key phrase is the one insisting that the two officers were not to "make out regular plans and surveys." As envisaged by Vallancey and other writers, this was to be a survey foregoing the leisurely pace and scientific sophistication of a peacetime operation. Results were required quickly; the mapmaker's time scale was one of days or weeks rather than of months or years. It was a military survey: its function influenced its thematic emphasis and was closely related to the requirements of troops moving through and subsisting in unfamiliar terrain. By means of sketches and written notes, only relevant information was to be collected. On the face of it, the instructions should not have presented too much difficulty for trained officers.

The reality of the undertaking was rather different. After their reconnaissance into the Boston countryside, Brown and de Berniere wrote a narrative of their experiences.[107] This account, together with sketches surviving from their mission, emphasizes the extent to which the immediate operational situation, capricious and shifting, could lead to a modification of the most explicit instructions.[108] Indeed, Gage's directions to the surveyors, although they were quite correct according to eighteenth-century military practice (he had given similar instructions to John Montresor to make a reconnaissance map around Boston in 1768[109]), turned out to be overly ambitious. Before Brown and de Berniere left Boston toward the end of February 1775, they had taken almost theatrical precautions to help insure the secrecy of their mission. They set out "disguised like countrymen, in brown cloaths and reddish handkerchiefs round our necks."[110] Although they lodged in the houses of known Tories, they were nevertheless recognized by a Black woman who "said she knew our errant was to take a plan of the country; that she had seen the river and road through Charlestown on the paper."[111] Thereafter they were forced to proceed surreptitiously, losing their way on one occasion; and the account of the actual surveying is extremely sparse. "Some time in sketching a pass that lay on our road," was the extent of their record at one point. At Worcester, Massachusetts, Sunday evening was spent climbing "the hills that command it" and they "sketched every thing we desired."[112] Evenings were occupied with correcting these sketches, which were then sent back in advance of their return to reduce the risk of detection. From similar stray allusions in their narrative and from the maps themselves, an impression emerges of a survey taken largely *à la vue:* without the benefit of surveying instruments (apart from perhaps a surveyor's compass or telescope) and with distances probably estimated by sympathetic countrymen, read from milestones where they existed, or sometimes paced. The result was a map showing only a skeleton of terrain, made hurriedly in a hostile countryside, and without much proficiency on the part of the volunteer mapmakers (see plate 9).

The experience of Gage's surveyors was far from unique. Many Revolutionary maps had this reconnaissance quality and had been subject to constraints that differentiated them from more formal eighteenth-century maps. So much is this so that it is almost necessary to unlearn some of the preconceptions and value judgments about maps derived from a civilian environment. While civilian mapping in colonial America was usually a contemplated, professional activity, military maps were many times a product of the exigencies of the moment. There was (as already noted concerning some fortification plans) a constant need to improvise because of a lack of suitable men, instruments, or materials: several cartographers complained of a shortage of paper and pencils during the Revolution.[113] Normal specifications were often disregarded, and even the more professional military surveyors found they had to accept standards of work alien to their training. Of one map by the American surveyor Benjamin Lodge, Washington's mapmaker Robert Erskine wrote in exasperation, "A most abominably Lazy slovenly performance not to survey such a small piece again or lay it down properly."[114] Other surveyors were as clearly conscious of the inadequacy of their own work. James Straton, a second lieutenant in the British engineers, had completed an "exact survey" of Portsmouth on the Elizabeth River in Virginia, but the result was such that in January 1781 he wrote across it: "This Plan was done in a Great Hurry & partly by Candle Light, It is hop'd there will be some Allowance Made for the Indifferent Drawing."[115] Similarly, on a plan showing Paulus Hook, Lieutenant W. Heymell, a Hessian officer, recorded that it was "drawn by guess."[116]

During a campaign, pressures were so great that many military mapmakers regarded it as unrealistic to aim at the standard of finish expected of the peacetime cartographical craftsman. The clarity of the message was more important than the elegance of the medium. For this reason, reconnaissance cartography was usually thematic and often innovative. Engineer John Montresor, in illustrating the fords across the Schuylkill River for his journal in 1777,[117] produced a diagram that was more topological than topographical: it anticipates a London subway map more clearly than it fits our preconceptions of eighteenth-century military cartography (see plate 10). Similarly, to maintain his communications in 1781, Washington had given instructions to establish a system of express riders. The French part of the chain (see plate 11) was recorded in a simple diagram, prepared by Louis-Alexandre Berthier in his capacity as assistant quartermaster general to Rochambeau's army. Although he had ridden along the route with a wagon train only a few weeks earlier and had made detailed observations, Berthier evidently regarded a simple thematic map as the most effective means of cartographic communication.[118]

Campaign conditions did not encourage unnecessary field surveys. All the armies built up working map collections at headquarters, and they served rather as a topographical data bank might today—frequently updated, with specialist information "recalled" as required. Sometimes information was retrieved by visual inspection, as can be inferred from the "verbal cartography" of some narratives where a writer clearly had a map in front of him, though no map was specified or has survived.[119] On other occasions, quick copies were made of preexisting maps for use in new situations. Some of the maps in Mackenzie's diary, for example, were taken from a master plan at headquarters; these showed only selected details illustrating particular events.[120] The effectiveness of the human eye and a pen as cartographic instruments should not be underestimated: they are both flexible and sensitive in a rapid selection of significant military features.

Even reconnaissance survey was not all sketching and improvisation. A survey was occasionally described as a reconnaissance, but it was far more akin to a military topographical map made in peacetime. Such a survey, indicating a continuum rather than a sharp dividing line in the classification, was the well-documented reconnaissance on Manhattan made by the joint headquarters staffs of the American and French armies in July 1781.[121] At that date, before the decision to march on Yorktown, the principal target of the allied strategy was still New York. On 22 July, Berthier wrote in his journal, "Generals Washington and Rochambeau, with their respective engineers, aides, and myself, made a reconnaissance of all the English works along the Harlem River between Kings Bridge and Morrisania."[122] Detailed surveys were made in the northern part of Manhattan and also in the eastern part, "opposite the junction of the Sound and Harlem River."[123]   Their importance in the intended military operations is implied by the multiple copies made (at least ten) of a map entitled "Reconnaissance of the Works on Northern Part of the Island of New York."[124] Such maps were for operational use, and this is confirmed by one copy accompanied by an "Analise d'un mémoire sur l'attaque de l'Isle de New York et dépendences," keyed directly to the map to address the various factors involved in an attack on New York.[125]

Contemporaries believed the art of reconnaissance to be near the summit of the military commander's skills. Just as Vallancey (following the Continental authorities) had envisaged a general directing the work of reconnaissance, so too, before New York, Rochambeau and Washington went riding with their most skilled technicians. This was no slipshod survey. A baseline was measured, and distances were computed by means of a triangulation. Topographical detail was carefully filled in, and hills were sketched by means of hachures. The result was an unusually complete picture of a landscape, matched only by some of the maps of the cartographers at British head-quarters during the Revolution. These detailed maps really belong to a wider category of military topographical surveys.

Military Topographical Surveys

In one of his more perceptive passages, Charles Vallancey distinguished recon-naissance mapping from topographical mapping: "A military survey of a Country made in time of peace, the angles taken with an Instrument, and The distances mea-sured with a Chain, is of more laborious nature; being performed at leisure, the omission of any material point, would be unpardonable, here the features of the Country are to be carefully depicted and described."[126] The implication of this statement, borne out by other evidence, is that the best work of the military topo-graphical surveyor belonged to times of relative peace. War is regarded as a catalyst in topographical mapping, but its effects were delayed and the notion requires qualification. Much military topographical surveying in the mid-eighteenth century was inspired by hindsight—after events had demonstrated how better maps would have been useful in a particular campaign. This helps to explain surveys of the Silesian borders with Bohemia and Moravia commissioned by Frederick the Great,[127] and it is equally fair comment on the William Roy survey of the Scottish Highlands as a direct sequel to the events of the 1745 rebellion.[128] It was only in peacetime, after all, that military engineers (in Vallancey's words) had the "leisure" required for surveys of such a "laborious nature." With the onset of the Seven Years' War, the engineer surveys in Scotland came to an abrupt halt.

Military Surveys for Civilian Ends: 1763–1775. For North America, a general sequence of war and survey holds true. This was modified in a colonial environment and by the vagaries of British policy, but the interwar years (between the ending of the French and Indian War and the beginning of the Revolution) were characterized by a spate of topographical surveys. These were largely undertaken by military sur-veyors with an engineering background, to military specifications concerning content and style. This group of surveys, however, underlines the need for historians to recognize the actual functions of maps as they were documented in contradistinction to any functions loosely inferred from their provenance or conventions. A distinction also has to be drawn between the functions of the interwar surveys during the peace, when they were agents of social and economic policies, and surveys during wartime, when overnight they became vital tools in the prosecution of a war on land and sea.

The studies of William P. Cumming, Louis De Vorsey, Douglas Marshall, and Nathaniel Shipton have made substantial contributions to an understanding of the activities of military mapmakers in North America from 1763 to 1775.[129] Much more is known about the topographical cartography of this period than of the Revolutionary period. Accurate surveys were essential in the aftermath of war. After the final defeat of the French in North America, England was engaged (as Nathaniel Shipton put it) in an "orderly appraisal of the new domain."[130] Topographical maps were regarded as an integral part of such an inventory; to facilitate their survey, two new offices of surveyor general for the American colonies were established during 1763–1764. The colonies were divided by the Potomac River into a "northern" and "southern" district and the respective chief surveyors appointed were Samuel Holland and William Gerard De Brahm, both military cartographers with an engineering background.[131] Under this administrative umbrella, and with rather desultory Admiralty support for coastal charting, specific schemes included: the "Murray" survey of the Saint Lawrence valley from Montreal to the Island of Orleans (taken under the direction of the military engineer, Lieutenant John Montresor); Samuel Holland's surveys of Cape Breton and Nova Scotia; the De Brahm surveys of parts of South Carolina, Georgia, and Florida; and the coastal charts made under the direction of J. F. W. DesBarres and published in *The Atlantic Neptune*.

All these maps had two faces, and the first was a military one. In their surveyors, conventions, and style, they were military surveys, and they indeed rate among the most competent and extensive of the mid-eighteenth century. In North America these maps made an important contribution to the establishment of scientific cartography and, in their depiction of terrain, represented a mature style, executed with relative consistency in quite discrete areas. As with fortification plans, the recurrent use of standard scales is a symptom of an underlying uniformity of approach. In the survey of the Saint Lawrence ordered by Governor Murray (some sixty-three plans in all), the majority of rural plans were drawn at 2,000 feet to an inch.[132] These can be compared with Holland's work in Nova Scotia, where two-thirds of the thirty or so plans he listed as sending to the government in 1766 were at 4,000 feet to an inch,[133] or with DesBarres's surveys, many of which were drawn at two miles to an inch or slightly over.[134]

The customary British and Continental color conventions and symbols were also common to many of the North American surveys. Following the military objective—depicting features of tactical significance to the movement and deployment of troops as well as to field fortifications—the natural landscape was mapped in much greater detail than in many civilian surveys of the eighteenth century. On finished maps, relief was usually shown by hill shading, with a black or grey to indicate steeper slopes; cliffs and rock faces were drawn in a natural style. Variations in woodland cover included distinctions between deciduous and coniferous forests, with trees spaced according to relative density on some maps; cut over woodland was given its own symbol. Water features were invariably colored blue or a bluish green, with a special symbol for marsh. Particular attention was paid to any military features of the man-made landscape, often keyed by numbers or letters to an explanatory legend. Settlements were shown in red, either by dots or in plan. Roads were indicated by double or single lines and often colored buff; on cleared ground, diagrammatic field boundaries with an impression of cultivation or pasture were often included. Many of the surviving examples are carefully finished and neatly colored. The symbols used in military topographical mapping were usually so well known, through either training or experience, that the actual maps seldom carry any explanation, although DesBarres included an elaborate key to coastal conventions in his *Atlantic Neptune* (see plate 12).

The other face of the interwar topographical surveys was a civilian one. Military mapmaking tended to undergo a process of "civilianization," characterized by subtle adaptation, conscious or unconscious, of military objectives, surveyors, and technical skills to serve the wider needs of colonial government. The emphasis of the general surveys is confirmed by their administration; they were supervised neither by a cabinet secretary of war nor even by the Board of Ordnance (the department of state that controlled the engineers' activities) but by the Commissioners for Trade and Plantations. Samuel Holland's civilian bias is suggested by his wish that a uniform for his surveyors in 1766 should have embossed "in the Front of the Caps . . . the Emblem & Motto of Trade & Plantations."[135] The role of the surveys in colonial development was summed up by De Brahm's instructions for the mapping of the Florida peninsula: it was to provide a "guide, by which His Majesty and his servants are to form their judgements upon the different proposals that shall be offered for making settlements upon these coasts."[136]

Although the surveys were military in conventions and style, when their specification is examined in more detail we see that it could hardly have been put into practice under campaign conditions over an extensive area. Holland's proposals for a general survey of North America east of the Mississippi, which he submitted as a "memorial" to the Lords Commissioners for Trade and Plantations in 1764, forcibly illustrate this point.[137] His long-term aim was no less than "an Accurate and just Survey . . . upon . . . a General scale and uniform Plan" to be made of all America.[138] It was clearly a survey conceived by Holland (and approved by his superiors) as falling within the mainstream of a European scientific culture in which geodesy and cartography had a recognized place. It was a far cry from the reconnaissance surveys advocated by Gage and from many of the topographical surveys of the Revolution, and this is shown by a request for instruments included in the memorial:

For making the Survey with a proper Degree of Exactness the following Instruments will be necessary, the price of which is annexed to each

	£		
An Astronomical Quadrant	21		
A Mecrometer	5	5	
A Theodolite with Vertical Arch & Telescope divided to every Minute	30		
Three Pocket Theodolites at 1 10s each	4	10	
One Large Theodolite divided to every Minute	20		
One Azimuth Compass	4	14	6
One Twelve Inch round Protractor with Index & Nones to every Minute	2	12	6
One Hadley's Quadrant 18 Inches radius	4	14	6
One Telescope and Rule	5	5	
Mr Short's reflecting Telescope 24 Inches Focal Length Rockworth Stand	36	15	
Skeltons Clock or Time piece for Astronomical Observations	40		
A Pair of Globes 17 Inch	6	6	
A Copying Glass	2	2	
Three Brass Chains 50 feet each	3	3	
Stationery Wares Drawing Paper	15		
	201	7	6[139]

Thus equipped, Holland was to produce maps based on geodetic control, "with the Longitudes and Latitudes ascertained by Astronomical Observations."[140] The general scale of the survey was to be one mile to an inch, but with "the Places of Note Channels & Harbours" at four inches to one mile. All channels and harbors were to be properly sounded, and the maps and charts were to be accompanied by "natural and Historical Descriptions of the Countries the Rivers and Lakes and whatever other Remarks shall be thought necessary."[141] Indeed, the whole proposal had more in common with a scientific survey sponsored by the Royal Society or the Paris Academy of Sciences than with a military operation.[142]

The scientific work accomplished under Holland's direction included the keeping of a meteorological journal, observations of solar eclipses and of the eclipses of Jupiter's satellites (to estimate longitudes), the observation of the transit of Venus in 1768,[143] and the collection of extensive notes on the economic geography of the territories being surveyed. It was entirely in character with such an approach that in 1768 Holland should have communicated "Observations made on the Islands of Saint John and Cape Breton, to ascertain the Longitude and Latitude of those Places . . ." to the *Philosophical Transactions* of the Royal Society.[144] In the same volume of the *Transactions,* Charles Mason and Jeremiah Dixon reported their "Observations for Determining the Length of a Degree of Latitude in the Provinces of Maryland and Pennsylvania . . ." and making "Astronomical Observations . . . in the Forks of the River Brandiwine in Pennsylvania, for determining the going of a Clock sent thither by the Royal Society, in order to find the Difference of Gravity between the Royal Observatory at Greenwich, and the Place where the Clock was set up in Pennsylvania."[145] Such was the intellectual climate, reflecting a wider ethos of scientific thought, in which regional cartography was being developed in colonial North America on the eve of the Revolution.[146]

Holland's survey was not in any sense unique. De Brahm's surveys in the "southern district" embody similar economic and scientific concepts and were discharged with similar systematic thoroughness over a number of years. A survey tradition had taken root in North America by the mid-eighteenth century: accurate mapmaking was combined with observation of natural phenomena. It was a blend of activity that would reach an apogee in the nineteenth-century army surveys of the American West, and the Revolution interrupted rather than destroyed its development.[147] Military surveyors did not passively reflect what had become scientifically fashionable in the Age of Reason; they were deliberately encouraged by official policy to undertake wide-ranging surveys to collect information necessary for the economic control of the interior and for the westward expansion of the seaboard colonies. As commander-in-chief during this period, Thomas Gage was almost forced to allow the relatively few officers with surveying skills to be employed in a whole variety of tasks ranging from civil engineering to exploration. In connection with the Iberville Canal project in West Florida, for example, Gage sent two officers of the Thirty-fourth Regiment, Lieutenant Philip Pittman, engineer, and Captain-Lieutenant James Campbell, to survey the river Iberville. This produced but one of a succession of "military" engineering surveys providing a full cartographic record of an abortive scheme.[148]

As this example suggests, it was those officers with engineering skills (often the best mapmakers) who were most in demand. There were, of course, numerous orthodox surveys of fortifications and barracks made by engineers stationed in various parts of America between 1763 and 1775, but probably as many were the incidental byproducts of nonmilitary activities.[149] The career of John Montresor in North America, where he served from 1757 to 1778, becoming chief engineer at the outbreak of the Revolution, provides a well-documented case study of the general tendency. In Montresor's journal, a principal source for his activities, there is ample evidence not only of his drawing maps and plans as a fortification expert but also of his being ordered to make other types of survey.[150] These included the exploration of the frontier, the general survey of the Saint Lawrence from 1760–1762, and the 1769 survey of the boundary line between New York and New Jersey. Like some of Holland's work, this was a fully scientific operation, undertaken in the company of David Rittenhouse, with locations determined by astronomical observations. On the eve of the Revolution, Montresor had just started work on another survey of the New York and Pennsylvania boundary. Samuel Holland and one of his surveying deputies, Thomas Wright, were also employed on similar boundary disputes.[151]

The evidence for such civilianization is substantial and convincing. It was with Gage's approval that Harry Gordon (then chief engineer in North America) was granted what might be described as a military sabbatical in 1766 to accompany the Indian agent George Croghan down the Ohio and Mississippi rivers.[152] Thomas Hutchins, a lieutenant in the Sixtieth Regiment, who had worked under De Brahm in the Southern colonies and during the Revolution was to be appointed geographer to Washington's southern army, was likewise seldom confined to narrow military instructions for his surveys. As an assistant engineer, Hutchins had orders "to go down the Mississippi from the Illinois . . . to survey the Rivers and Country;" he was to make "Remarks and Observations on every Object worthy Notice."[153] On his "many reconnoitring tours" he was encouraged to compile data to be incorporated in a general topographical map of the frontier. In 1778, still holding his commission, in the British army, Hutchins published *A New Map of the Western parts of Virginia, Pennsylvania, Maryland and North Carolina*, accompanied by a topographical description.[154]

The surveying skills of the military engineers were thus in general demand during the interwar years. Their specifically military training was far less significant than the fact that, in colonies crying out for technical specialists, they were highly skilled, experienced, and sufficiently captive in the public service to be directed to all manner of assignments. Under Gage's administration, there was a dovetailing of civil and military activities in 1774. With such sponsorship of cartography (as in all aspects of colonial development in which the crown had made an investment), both maps and surveyors were certainly expected to provide multiple rather than single benefits. This helps to explain both the patchiness of geographical coverage and the cartographic characteristics of the topographical surveys that had been completed by 1775. It is interesting to speculate how much of eastern North America would have been surveyed had it not been for the Revolution.

Military Topographical Surveys during the Revolution. The onset of hostilities in the spring and summer of 1775 quickly destroyed the rationale, the pattern, and the means of topographical surveying that had been developing in eastern North America. The actual surveys rapidly came to a halt. DesBarres, engaged on the hydrographic survey of the New England coast, had already by 1775 transferred his energies to the preparation of manuscript drafts for engraving in London.[155] In the southern district, De Brahm, returning from England to Charleston in September

1775, found it seething with insurrection. His surveying ship, the *Cherokee,* was quickly impressed for military duties and was never restored to his use.[156] In the northern district, the surveys of Samuel Holland suffered a similar fate. By 1774, some of his surveyors had already been exposed to the suspicions of "an Ignorant Populace,"[157] and his surveying ship, the *Canceaux,* was taken off hydrographic duties for service in the blockade of Boston. As a result, the sounding work in coastal waters fell badly behind the mapping on shore. In December 1774 he was still hoping that by next season his surveys would reach "Hudson's river including Long Island."[158] The Revolution was to dash these hopes, and by 1776 he was writing in a very different vein: "That the present Rebellion in America and the Disorders thence ensuing, have for the present diverted him and his Associates from the Prosecution of the Survey which he thinks might otherwise have been completed in the Course of the next Season or at most in one Year more."[159] The "for the present," as with other major surveys, turned out to be "never" for the extension of Holland's work to the south. Such was the negative impact of the Revolution on topographical mapping in eastern North America.

On the positive side, the importance of topographical mapping to the military commanders was sufficient to insure some continuation. The value of a knowledge of terrain (and thus of maps) had been emphasized by Frederick the Great in several essays, and some of the Revolutionary generals had doubtless read his stern warning: "Tactics become a useless art if it is not adapted to the terrain. A correct knowledge of the terrain gives one amazing resources in time of adversity. On this foundation rests true success. . . . The land is to the soldier what a chessboard is to a chess player who wants to make moves with his pawns, castles and so forth."[160] In practice, the commander's "chessboard" was frequently a topographical map. Even more than in peacetime, military topographical surveyors were required to emphasize those features of immediate importance to tactical planning. By 1775, distinctive military perception of landscape had developed, and this permeated the topographical content of maps produced by surveyors in all the Revolutionary armies.

The most obvious expression was the attention paid to roads and other routeways. Topographical maps were primarily an aid to military movement (or to the planning that preceded it), and contemporaries believed that it was "impossible to be too minute" in the description of roads.[161] Some reconnaissance sketches were little more than route diagrams, and on many topographical maps—at a higher level of technical sophistication—roads dominated the military landscape. Together with the river network and settlements, roads were often drawn in first when a map was being laid down from survey data. Under campaign conditions, maps often passed into operational use once they reached this stage of completeness. Such outline topographical maps—primarily route maps—were included by Lieutenant John Hills, a cartographer at British headquarters under Clinton, in his manuscript atlas of New Jersey.[162] Six of the twenty maps in the collection showed only roads, rivers, and principal settlements. On those maps with any pretensions to being finished, roads were often colored buff, and mileages were sometimes added to indicate distances between settlements.[163] On other maps, separate tabulations of mileages, including a few triangular tables of distances, were also inserted.[164] Nor was such an emphasis confined to British cartography. One of the principal arguments for the appointment of a geographer to the staff of Washington's army was that he would be able "to Survey the Roads."[165] This is borne out by the wording of the commission the geographer received from Congress, by his subsequent orders, and by the format—in a series of road traverses—in which many of his surveys have survived.[166] (The origin and organization of the American geographers as a specialist cartographic unit is discussed in chapter 2.)

Other features equally reflected the needs of a field army. Apart from their general topographical importance, the locations of farmhouses and villages were also required by a quartermaster general's department faced with the billeting of troops. Watermills, carefully marked on British headquarters maps around New York, were also regarded as strategically vital for supply and subsistence, offering as they did the provision of flour and (with water-powered ironworks) the repair of weapons.[167] In the countryside, however, natural features had the greatest potential for influencing tactical decisions. Marshy ground on the flank or rear could make or break a position, and wooded country also called for special tactics or invited skirmishing.

The contours of the land could be even more critical. "Strong" ground to a military eye was that capable of easy defense, and a knowledge of "defiles" and "holloways" could lead to their use in an ambush. Whenever time permitted, hills were sketched in by eye, and even during campaigns they could be fair drawn at headquarters in either pen or color wash. The distribution of such areas influenced many important military decisions, including the selection of sites for fortification and encampment, the choice of ground for a battle, and the location of artillery. In such ways, eighteenth-century warfare made specific demands on the skills of a cartographer.

A range of "topographical" scales can also be identified in Revolutionary mapping. There was probably less standardization than in peacetime, but a number of scales were nevertheless regarded as fairly normal among professional mapmakers. Figure 1:4 shows the frequency of scales for maps in the topographical range (including reconnaissance maps) in the British headquarters collections.[168] The pattern tends to be complicated at the overlap with the fortification range of scales (figure 1:3), but the popularity of one mile to an inch and two miles to an inch for topographical mapping stands out clearly. Both scales were favored by mapmakers employed by British army headquarters in New York. They were used, for example, by John Hills in mapping in New Jersey, by Charles Blaskowitz in the New York district, and by George Taylor and Andrew Skinner, who worked behind the British lines in New York.[169] It is likely, moreover, that they had more general currency in Revolutionary America. Washington's geographer frequently employed one mile to an inch in original mapping, although such field surveys were subsequently reduced into more general maps ranging from two to eight miles to an inch. Nor can French cartography be considered exceptional to these tendencies. After conversion of the linear measure (from *toises* to feet), there are significant comparisons in the range of natural scales employed for similar military purposes. The scale bar of the American–French reconnaissance map of New York, for example, was graduated in an *"échelle de 600 toises"* ("scale of 600 *toises*").[170] A *toise,* of which there were 300 to the inch on this map, was equivalent to 6.3945 feet, giving a scale of approximately nineteen hundred (1,918.35) feet to an inch, which fell in the range of the British topographical scales (figure 1:4). A reduced map derived from this survey was drawn at a scale of approximately two thousand *toises* to an inch,[171] which converts to 2.424 miles to an inch—a scale similarly favored by British military surveyors.

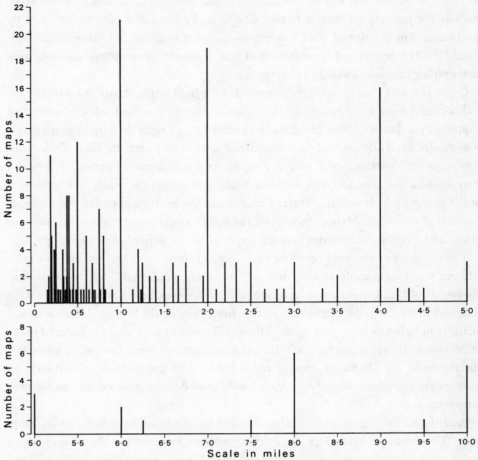

Figure 1:4 Frequency distribution chart of topographical scales of British maps of the Revolution.

The argument is not that exact coincidence is to be expected (different national measures, instruments, and so forth, introduced too many variables), but that similar military functions elicited a similar scale response from mapmakers of different nationalities. Evidence of an international approach to topographical mapping is also suggested by the fact that some French cartographers employed scales calculated in miles (*milles*).[172] A map showing the position of the French army at Philipsburg was drawn at "Echelle de deux miles Anglais,"[173] although this may merely reflect a lack of original survey or failure of a French mapmaker to convert measures derived at second hand. Even so, it suggests that many military mapmakers were at least aware of the main linear measures of the principal European nations.[174]

American Topographical Mapping in the Revolution.

In the approach of the American geographers to topographical mapping during the Revolution, there can be detected different aspirations and possibly different policies from those of British and French mapmakers. The main French army did not arrive in America until the summer of 1780. Although French cartographers mapped Rhode Island and the route to Yorktown with great professionalism, their contribution to the mapping of eastern North America was relatively minor. The British, though they maintained a mapmaking organization at their headquarters throughout the war, after their withdrawal from Philadelphia in 1778 were largely confined behind fixed lines in a few garrisons, most notably New York. These areas were mapped in considerable detail, but the results can hardly be compared with the scope of British pre-Revolution cartography.

The broader challenge of producing general maps was met by American geographers during the course of the Revolution, and the resulting surveys have had a lasting, practical significance. A distinguishing mark of American surveying, even before Yorktown, was that it was undertaken partly with an eye to the future and to the place of maps in an independent United States. Such hopes seem to have colored the surveying strategy of Robert Erskine, the first geographer to the Continental Army. Although Washington's orders relating to maps usually reflect short-term objectives—such as the need to map the environs of a new encampment, to survey terrain through which movement was to take place, or merely to update his "pocket map" in a particular area—Erskine harbored grander designs.[175] Soon after his appointment in 1777 he was writing to Washington about his concept of the job:

In planning a country a great part of the ground must be walked over, particularly the banks of Rivers and Roads; as much of which may be traced and laid down in three hours as could be walked over in one; or in other words a Surveyor who can walk 15 miles a day may plan 5 miles . . . six attendants to each surveyor will be proper; to wit, two Chain-bearers, one to carry the Instrument, and three to hold flag staffs. . . . Young gentlemen of Mathematical genius, who are acquainted with the principles of Geometry, and who have a taste for drawing, would be the most proper assistants for a Geographer.[176]

Out of context, it would be easy to conclude that this appointment had little to do with warfare. Indeed, one of the subtler influences in American Revolutionary mapping was that Erskine had been trained, not at Mézières or Woolwich but at Edinburgh University, in the practical manner of a British civil engineer and land surveyor.[177] This influenced his methods, especially the use of the chain and plane table, which were more cumbersome than military topographical surveying allowed in many situations.[178] The "unfinished" and largely functional character of his surveys (in pen-and-ink rather than in color) should not necessarily be taken as a sign that they were less accurate than the more colored productions of the British and French cartographers. Erskine, who became a Fellow of the Royal Society before his departure for America, was just as conscious of the scientific basis of cartography as either Holland or De Brahm were before 1775, and he was equally aware of the long-term potential of his work to aid in the development of the United States. By February 1780, less than three years after his appointment, he was able to report that his surveys filled "upwards of two hundred and fifty sheets of paper." The areas covered, he informed Washington, included:

both sides of the North River, extending from New Windsor and Fishkill, southerly to New York; eastward: to Hartford, Whitehaven, etc., and on the west to Easton in Pennsylvania . . . the principal part of New Jersey, lying northward of a line drawn from Sandy Hook to Philadelphia . . . a considerable part of Pennsylvania . . . the whole route of the Western army under Genl. Sullivan . . . from New Windsor and Fishkill northward, on both sides of the River, to Albany, & from thence to Scoharie.[179]

With these materials, which he maintained gave clear expression to his wider cartographical ambitions, he "could form a pretty accurate Map of the four States of Pennsylvania, New Jersey, New York and Connecticut." Although "Astronomical Observations" would be required to fix some latitudes and longitudes, and suitable corrections for local magnetic variations in the field drafts were also necessary, he was still confident that his surveys could be developed beyond their *ad hoc* military origins. Among the surviving Erskine maps, the majority of which are in the collection of the New-York Historical Society,[180] some steps in his production of more general maps can be traced. There are various "contractions" (maps reduced to smaller scales) in Erskine's hand, as well as maps described as "rectified" (corrected). Some maps were drawn on grids to facilitate their reduction, and these survive in a relatively finished state with borders added (see plate 13). A number of drawings also confirm that Erskine was experimenting with a suitable projection on which to plot his surveys.[181] The whole group of maps awaits a proper study of its technical significance.

After Erskine's untimely death in October 1780, he was succeeded by Simeon De Witt, an assistant geographer since 1778, who carried on the attempt to synthesize the surveys accumulating at American headquarters. The need for proper geodetic control to assist in fitting surveys together on a proper graticule, remained a major stumbling block. In August 1781, De Witt tried the rather optimistic expedient of advertising for information in the *New York Packet:*

Any Mathematical Gentleman who can furnish the subscriber with the correct variation of the needle in any places in Connecticut, New-York, New Jersey and Pennsylvania, shall have their services gratefully acknowledged; as many observations of this kind as can be collected will be of use in perfecting maps formed of those parts of the country, for His Excellency General Washington. N.B. It will be necessary to mention the times and names of the places (also their latitude if ascertained) at which the observations were made.[182]

The response to this request is not recorded, but De Witt seems to have persevered in his attempt to produce general topographical maps out of the diverse materials of war. After the conclusion of the Yorktown campaign in October 1781, when the surveyors were largely released from operational duties, more time was devoted in their Philadelphia headquarters (presumably including a drawing room on the British or French model) to working up rough drafts and to compiling general maps. As in Erskine's day, some progress was made. One map of northern New Jersey and parts of eastern Pennsylvania, for example, was partly completed at a scale of eight miles to an inch. It was related to a prime meridian running through Tappan near New York City and was plotted on a form of conic projection, with latitude and longitude graduated along its borders.[183] By the year 1783 De Witt believed his contractions were sufficiently promising to merit publication. In June of that year, he put a scheme before Washington "for publishing a Map of the State of War in America."[184] This, characteristically where cartography was concerned, met with Washington's "full Approbation," but a committee of the Continental Congress was less enthusiastic and ruled that "though a map of the principal theatre of war in the middle states from actual surveys on a large scale is much desired, such a work cannot in prudence be undertaken at the public expense in the present reduced state of our finances."[185] There the matter rested. Although De Witt resubmitted his scheme in the following year, it was again rejected on grounds of postwar austerity.

A fuller use of the American military surveys of the Revolution was to be made by Christopher Colles in his *Survey of the Roads of the United States* published in 1789.[186] The role of the geographers in the long-term development of topographical mapping in the United States was thus a complex one, emphasizing in yet another context that the relationships between war and cartography were seldom a matter of simple cause and effect. Despite the farsightedness of both Erskine and De Witt, the military topographical surveys of the Revolution were largely a false dawn in the mapping of the new nation.

After long scrutiny of topographical maps and careful assessment of reconnaissance and intelligence data, a stage was reached, in theory at least, when a commander in chief could put his army in motion. As a generator of cartographical by-products, such troop movement was a formal activity that had more in common with fortification planning than with reconnaissance. Some of the maps produced by an army on the march were almost as predictable as those associated with the construction of a fort. In the military textbooks, the order of marching and encampment, and indeed of battle, ran closely together, as summed up by the early eighteenth-century maxim that "an army marches as it camps and camps as it fights": a reference to the tactical deployment of infantry, artillery, cavalry, and the like in conventional positions.[187] In North America, however, departures from orthodox European practice existed before the Revolution. Some of the rigidity of the classic marching formations had to be rethought on the frontier during the French and Indian War. Particularly after General Edward Braddock's disastrous defeat in the Battle of the Wilderness (Monongahela, 1755), light infantry tactics were progressively adopted. Several light infantry regiments, including "The Sixtieth Royal Americans" (which provided a number of cartographers),[188] were raised for the American service and trained to combine "the qualities of the scout with the discipline of the trained soldier."[189] The effect of these tactical changes, however, merely altered the content rather than the function of the group of maps associated with the army on the march. As in eighteenth-century warfare at large, five main subtypes can be recognized: (a) route maps made before the march; (b) maps of the order of the march; (c) route maps made during the march; (d) overall maps of lines of march made as a record of a campaign; and (e) maps of encampments.

Route Maps Made before the March. By 1775 it was widely agreed that before an army marched, there ought to be careful preparation—if possible with a survey or description of the route prepared by the quartermaster general's department. As far as theory was concerned, it was probably the French, as Vallancey implied, who had most perfected the applications of cartography to the logistics of an army in movement.[190] There was even a special textbook, *Les Connoissances géométriques, à l'usage des officiers employés dans les détails des marches, campements & subsistances des armées* by Dupain de Montesson,[191] and in the same author's *L'Art de lever les plans* a chapter was also devoted to the compilation of itineraries and the rules to be observed for order of march (plate 14). In the 1775 edition of *L'Art,* Dupain de Montesson observed that the engineer marching at the head of the column must "note down, as he comes to them, the successive places along the road, the ascents and descents, the woods, the defiles, the rivers, the brooks, the marshes, the bridges, the fords, the nature of the countryside through which the column is proceeding, and finally the different landmarks that he passes on the right- and left-hand sides of the road."[192] This passage implies that itineraries were made while the army was actually marching. From such field observations, maps as well as written descrip-

The Army on the March

tions could be made up at leisure. Six years after the publication of this book, however, when the French army was planning its overland march from Rhode Island to Virginia in the summer of 1781, staff officers of Rochambeau's headquarters prepared itineraries before the march took place, at least for the section of the route from Providence to the Hudson. They prepared not only a short schedule or timetable of the march (and possibly rough sketches of the route which have not survived) but also a detailed itinerary. Of the third day's intended march, from Plainfield to Windham, it was noted:

The left of the Plainfield camp adjoins the Windham road, which you take on leaving. The road then becomes more wooded. You reach a fork in the road. The left fork goes to Norwich. You take the right fork, which leads into a rather broad valley through which flows the Quinebaug River. Then follow along the river, which flows a short distance to your left, passing some wooded heights on the right. Then turn left to cross the river on a good but narrow covered wooden bridge. You ascend the opposite slope into Canterbury, a little town on a rather pleasant plateau. Through Canterbury runs a high road that crosses at right angles the one by which you have come. This is the road from Norwich to Boston via Pomfret. The church is on the left, also two taverns, the White Ship and the Black Horse.[193]

In such a manner—with meticulous attention to local topography—the quartermaster's staff of the French army planned its route and selected the most suitable sites for encampment. The extent to which such planning was undertaken by other Revolutionary armies will now be examined.

For the Americans, the evidence is fairly clear cut. The duties of the quartermaster general in the Continental Army, as set out in new rules adopted in February 1778, included "the regulating of marches, encampments, order of battle, etc., as described in the books of the profession."[194] That such duties were carried out in this manner is made clear by the correspondence of Nathanael Greene after he had been appointed quartermaster general in 1778. In February 1779, he was directing the planning of an intinerary for the march of Pulaski's legion from Philadelphia to Georgia.[195] In the same year he was systematically collecting information about a variety of routes of potential importance to the army.[196] Elsewhere, Washington's general orders stipulated that "the Quarter master General will furnish the route and order of march,"[197] although on many occasions Washington himself supplied a route—usually in the form of a simple list of places, as if read from a map.[198]

Maps were obviously used directly in route planning, but it is unlikely that many routes were surveyed in detail before a particular march. The geographers, as already noted, were mainly engaged in road traversing, but this often proceeded independently of other events. One exception was the march to Yorktown. At this time Washington was presumably especially open to French influence; his orders of August 1781 to Simeon De Witt for the survey of part of the intended route to Virginia were a direct complement to the French itineraries further north. The precise instructions, issued from Washington's headquarters in New Brunswick, New Jersey, read:

Immediately upon receipt of this you will begin to Survey the road (if it has not been done already) to Princeton, thence (through Maidenhead) to Trenton, thence to Philadelphia, thence to the head of Elk through Darby, Chester, Wilmington Christiana Bridge.

At the head of Elk you will receive further orders. I need not observe to you the necessity of noting towns, Villages and remarkable Houses and places but I must desire that you will give me the rough traces of your Survey as you proceed on as I have reasons for desiring to know this as soon as possible.[199]

Even if De Witt did not compile written itineraries in the French manner, his objective was precisely the same. The surviving maps have a precise functional significance in the planning of the march.[200]

The quartermaster general's department of the British army had been instituted in 1689. Among other duties, it had inherited some reconnaissance functions formerly carried out by the scoutmaster general.[201] It also had responsibility for both encampment—as in European practice in general—and the planning of routes. This was the view of Thomas Simes in his *Treatise on the Military Science* published during the Revolution: "The Quarter-Master General, his Deputy, or an able Engineer should sufficiently reconnoitre the country and navigable rivers, to obtain a just knowledge of them and the enemy, before he ventures to form his routs."[202] This statement suggests a blurring of function (with reconnaissance in general) and of responsibility (with some engineers engaging in route planning) not reflected by the contemporary French textbooks. This may be a fair reflection of British practice during the Revolution. It is interesting to note that only two decades later, in the Peninsula War, it was the cartographic and geographical branches of the quartermaster general's department that were regarded as being particularly in need of reform.[203] Between 1775 and 1783 there is certainly no map evidence for a careful advance survey of routes characterizing the march to Yorktown. Although the British headquarters doubtless planned routes as carefully as possible from maps and intelligence reports (aided by the corps of guides and pioneers, whose cartographic significance is discussed in chapter 2), they often could move freely only behind their own lines. When they marched beyond these defended areas, it was often into hostile territory where they could penetrate only in force; the advance preparation of a route, with itineraries and maps, was impossible. In a negative sense, this could still be of immense significance, as was the case with Burgoyne's disastrous march to Saratoga: whatever his merits, Burgoyne seems to have been classically inept in his failure to recognize the logistical implications of a lack of route planning.

The Order of March. Such arrangements, based as much on seniority of regiment as on tactical theory, dominated the deployment of eighteenth-century armies on the parade ground,[204] in camp, on the battlefield, and during a march. Many textbooks advocated fixed orders of march. When developments in tactics occurred, as in the introduction of light infantry in North America, new orders of march, illustrated by modified diagrams, were advocated.[205] Washington, as colonel of the Virginia militia, had designed an order of march appropriate to movement in the American back country.[206] Later, his contribution to this subject was carried over into the Revolution, as in June 1778 when his general orders contained "a standing Model for the Order of March, whether of the whole Army, a Division, Brigade or Battalion."[207] There was a varied cartographic expression of such arrangements—model or otherwise. In some cases the order of march was given only in written form.[208] In an interim form, the writing was arranged to correspond roughly to troop positions but without topography or symbols; where an approximate scale was preserved, it warrants classification as a thematic map.[209] In other examples, as in the order of march of St. Leger's troops from Oswego in 1777, a recognizable though pictorial plan of the positions had been drawn.[210] Similarly, officers who thought cartographically sometimes translated verbal or written instructions into simple maps for their own use. One such officer was Lieutenant James Hadden of the British artillery, who was trained at Woolwich and who accompanied Burgoyne's army to Saratoga. Hadden noted in his journal for Wednesday, 17 September 1777:

The Army marched to Sword's Farm (3½ Miles). The order of March was *Frazer's Corps* and the *Right Wing* with their Artillery & Baggage upon the heights to the Right of the main Road, (as reconnoitred yesterday) forming the *Right* Column. The Park of Artillery & Baggage of the Army on the main Road formed the Centre Column: and part of ye Left Wing moved on their left, being the left Column. The Provisions were floated down the River under the 47th Reg't.[211]

There was nothing particularly remarkable in these jottings, except that on the facing page of his journal Hadden drew the same positions in the form of a rough diagram, employing rectangular symbols in order to distinguish various units. Although the surviving examples are not numerous for the Revolution (and they were rarely printed by contemporaries), such maps are nevertheless sufficiently distinctive in purpose and content to warrant separate discussion in any classification of eighteenth-century military maps.

Route Maps Made during the March. The mapping of a route during a march was also accepted practice, and its most formal expression in Revolutionary America was again in the work of Rochambeau's cartographers on their march from Rhode Island to Virginia. In addition to the advance survey of the northern part of the route, the French mapmakers were responsible for a series of route maps and written itineraries relating to the actual march undertaken by the French army to Yorktown and back to Boston in 1781 and 1782. The maps, though surveyed during the march, survive in the form of carefully finished and colored drawings. They were made after the campaign and probably were designed to accompany written reports submitted to various administrative officials in France. A similar scale was maintained throughout, and standard color conventions, such as yellow for regimental positions and pink for artillery locations, were matched along the whole route. On the return march, the regimental positions occupied in 1781 were shown by rectangles with dotted perimeters.[212] Each map sheet accommodated a route for one day's march, usually covered on four successive days by four divisions, and the maps topographically duplicated the content of the written itineraries. Such linear maps of roads had characterized both British and French cartography for well over a century before the Revolution.[213] Confined as they were to a narrow strip of landscape along the immediate line of the march and its encampments, these maps display a close adaptation of format to function.

As the work of Rochambeau's cartographers in the Revolution was closely modeled on French textbooks, their maps are sometimes regarded as exceptional. Rice and Brown inclined to the view that they were unique. "To the best of our knowledge," they write, "the British produced no series of maps like those of the 'camps and marches' of Rochambeau's army—possibly because such a concept was peculiar to the French."[214] The wider evidence does not lend support to such a view. Although no other maps directly parallel the so-called French strip maps in distances covered and consistency of style, evidence shows that the concept of the military route map was widely understood outside French spheres. For cartographers attached to an army on the march, it was an obvious operational priority to survey the immediate route before engaging in other tasks. Well before the Revolution, such maps had been produced by British military cartographers in North America. Thomas Hutchins, when he accompanied Colonel Henry Bouquet as an assistant engineer on a march through the Ohio country in 1764, had made a linear map of the route, with the locations of encampments numbered in a way comparable with French practice.[215]

Perhaps the nearest British equivalent to the French maps of the Yorktown march were those surveyed on the march from Philadelphia to New York in June 1778 by Lieutenant John Hills, a mapmaker attached to Clinton's headquarters. Of military necessity this march was a less regulated affair than Rochambeau's progress to Yorktown, but the route was surveyed in some detail. The surviving copies were again made after the event (they were incorporated in Hills' New Jersey atlas), but they still reflect the rapid nature of the traverse: distances were measured by pacing, direction was established by a surveying compass, and hills and woodland were largely sketched in freehand.[216] Apart from the absence of troop positions on some of the maps, there is little to distinguish them in either function or content from the work of the French cartographers in the Revolution.

The same holds true of the route maps of the American geographers. Even before the American and French armies were engaged in a joint strategy in 1781, mapmakers had been detached to record the routes of particular military expeditions. In 1778, William Gray—a captain in the Fourth Pennsylvania Regiment, acting under the orders of Robert Erskine—mapped Colonel William Butler's line of march against the Iroquois at Unadilla.[217] In the following year, a similar series of maps was made by Benjamin Lodge to record the "Route of the Western Army under Gen'l Sullivan."[218] On the western frontier, however, the purity of the simple route map was sometimes diluted by Erskine's desire to have observations of wider cartographic relevance made in the unknown country. Lodge accordingly extended his surveys beyond the immediate route to lay emphasis on the river system of the whole region.[219] Judging from a passage in Gray's letter to Erskine, dated 28 October 1778, Gray had evidently been asked to determine magnetic north: "As to my finding out the Varyation at this place I imagine that it will be very Difficult as sun is not to be scene for at least one hour after he Rises & an hour before he sets However I will try my best."[220] Although both surveyors set out to produce a fairly standard type of military map, this goal had been modified by wilderness conditions. Gray complained, "I had Neither pencil or Indian Ink to shade the Hills which are Very Numerous as there is nothing Else after you Quite the Waggon Road."[221] This *cri de coeur* could well have reflected a more general difference between the Americans and the well-equipped cartographic unit that was later to accompany Rochambeau on his marches.

General Maps of Lines of March. General maps were also made to summarize for a period of up to several years the total marches of an army in a theater of warfare. They usually took the form of military details—locations of engagements and lines of movement—superimposed on a small-scale base map. Such summary maps of campaigns, often termed "general maps," were prepared by British, French, and Hessian mapmakers; they constitute another distinct subtype in the cartographic record of the Revolution. Indeed, the group contains some of the largest and (in the sense of their military information) most detailed maps prepared by Revolutionary mapmakers as a postwar record of events. Such was the large manuscript map in three sheets, extending its representation from New York to Salisbury, Delaware, and "Showing the Operations of the British Army Against the Rebels in North America from the 12th of August 1776 to the end of the Year 1779." It provides, in the assessment of William Cumming, "the best map of the New Jersey–Pennsylvania campaign," and it records opposing troop movements in color, keyed to a folio reference sheet containing over eighty identifications of military locations.[222] A similar Hessian map, *Plan Général des operations de l'armée Britannique contre les Rebelles dans l'Amérique Depuis l'Arrivée des Troupes Hessoise le 12 du Mois d'Aoust 1776 jusqu'à la fin de l'Anée 1779*, indicates an almost identical approach by the cartographer. It was described by Guthorn as "handsomely and carefully executed in ink, illuminated in red and yellow, by a professional hand."[233] Like the British example, it is a thematic map showing troop positions in color (British in red, Americans in yellow). In the bottom center of the map, we find incorporated a tabular return of the operations: identifying and listing alphabetically and numerically 138 camps, marches, attacks, batteries, redoubts, and positions in which the Hessians participated. These cartographic summaries were regarded as sufficiently important to warrant development into a routine task for headquarters mapmakers at the end of a campaign. Their military content was doubtless carefully vetted by senior staff officers, and this would explain why John André, at the time deputy adjutant general of the British forces, should have prepared a preliminary draft of such a map recording the Long Island and Fort Washington campaign.[224] To accompany the detailed maps of the French marches, a general map was likewise prepared of the "Camps of the French Army Commanded by General Rochambeau, 9 June 1781 to 1 December 1782."[225]

Maps of Encampments. Military theoreticians of the eighteenth century wrote a great deal about the art of castramentation, or the laying out of camps. Frederick the Great, in his "Military Instructions for the Generals," asserted it was "one of the primary studies that a general should make."[226] The textbooks of the Revolutionary period often devoted a chapter or so to the exposition of its principles. Like most other military activities, it required cartographic skills. This was recognized by Dupain de Montesson, and in *L'Art de lever les plans* a chapter deals with the "Mainière de lever le plan d'un camp" using a plane table.[227] Laying out an encampment, normally involving the preparation of a map or sketch, was a responsibility of the quartermaster general's department in European armies throughout the eighteenth century. As early as 1727, Humphrey Bland had written: "A little before the Opening of the Campaign, it is the Duty of the Quarter-Master-General to Draw out on Paper the Incampment of the Army."[228] Such was the continuity of practice that during the Peninsula War the officers of the quartermaster general's department in the British army were still expected to report on the suitability of sites for "encamping or bivouacking troops" with the instruction, "A Sketch of the ground upon a pretty large scale, should always accompany these reports."[229]

There can be little doubt that maps were expected to (and did) play this type of role in the choice and development of new sites for encampment during the Revolution. Where documentary evidence is available, as for the stages in the establishment of the Morristown camp by the Americans in 1779, maps are seen to enter into not one but several stages of site assessment. By the autumn of 1779, the American Army, as in previous years, was casting around to find a suitable location for a winter encampment. The search had evidently been delegated to Nathanael Greene as quartermaster general, because on 10 November he had received a rough sketch in a letter from Colonel James F. Abeel at Morristown, with the explanation that the latter had found a "beautiful place for an encampment," that was "abounding in wood, water and every other necessary."[230] The choice, however, does not seem to have been resolved immediately. A fortnight later, Washington wrote to Greene that he was sorry "you have found the Ground described by Lord Stirling and Colonel Abeel so different from your expectations. It is impossible to decide upon a position, untill you have fully reconnoitred that district of Country, in which we shall be obliged to Canton."[231] The approach to this problem suggests that he was well versed in the principles of castramentation as expounded by Frederick the Great and other eighteenth-century writers. Indeed, so worried was Washington about the lack of progress that he wrote to Greene on the same day, outlining what further qualities of terrain he felt might influence the choice.[232]

Once the new camp had been established, the services of a mapmaker were again required. On 9 December Washington wrote to his geographer, Robert Erskine, that he was "extremely anxious to have the Roads in front and rear of the Camp accurately surveyed as speedily as possible. He therefore wishes to see you immediately at Head Quarters that he may give you particular directions as to the Business which he wants executed."[233] The resulting map of the encampment (see plate 15) can be regarded as another tool to aid Washington in his assessment of the tactical potential of its situation. The careful development of the Morristown site would seem to reflect Frederick the Great's advice: "An army commander must choose his camp himself, since the success of his enterprises depends upon it and often it must become his battlefield."[234] In this spirit, Washington ordered further surveys to increase his preparedness in the event of attack. Nathanael Greene, as quartermaster general, and Duportail, as chief engineer, were to "examine all the grounds in the environs of our present encampment and make a written report to me without delay, of the different spots which appear most proper to be occupied in case of any movement of the enemy towards us."[235] On this occasion, too, a sketch map served to identify the hills and "advantageous grounds" listed in a written report as being suitable for occupation against attack.[236]

Maps were thus required at every stage in establishing the encampment at Morristown: despite differences of format and origin apparent at first sight, they possess a historical unity based on function. They reflect eighteenth-century theories of castramentation, Washington's grasp of them, and his principal staff officers' contributions to the mapping of the camp and its environs. The approach in this example would have been followed by British and French staff officers during the Revolution.

A battle, like a siege, was a climax in a campaign. The extent to which battles were mapped reflects their local importance in the whole military process. More than other types of military map (apart from siege plans), battle maps were familiar to contemporaries (and have become so to modern historians of cartography) because they were frequently published. Their considerable variety is emphasized in a recent bibliography that lists more than two hundred printed battle plans of the Revolu-

BATTLE MAPS

tion published in the period 1775–1795.[237] Their authorship can be attributed to cartographers in all armies, rebels and loyalists alike. They attempted to depict engagements on both land and sea. Land battles were represented by symbols which have already been described, but naval cartographers employed their own distinctive range of symbols.[238] In promptness of appearance, battle maps range from those published a few weeks after an engagement to those that appeared in books after the Revolution had become a matter of history and were designed to rescue the damaged reputations of defeated generals. In format they vary from large, single-sheet maps, engraved in the cartographic workshops of specialist map sellers in London and Paris, to more ephemeral maps in contemporary magazines. Nor were all battle maps drawn in two dimensions. They were a favorite subject of military artist-cartographers (such as the talented Thomas Davies, an officer in the British Royal Artillery[239]) and perspective views of battles can be regarded as a minor subtype within the classification.

Despite these irregularities, some of the patterns common to other military maps can be discerned. Apart from naval symbols, the symbols for military details largely conform to those already described as current in siege cartography, including the occasional use of a hinged flap to indicate a change of position during a battle. On finished battle maps, too, an attempt was almost invariably made to show the basic facts of terrain—slopes, woods, streams, and marsh. The facts of physical geography had an explanatory as well as descriptive value in the analysis of military topography. A study of battle maps in relation to their military functions demonstrates, however, that attributes of individual maps are often less important than the wider military process to which groups of maps contributed. Most of the known examples can be placed in a sequence of events—before, during, and after a battle. In such a context, engraved maps (since they owe some of their character and content to influences after the battle) represent only one part of the subtype as a whole, although the one best known.

Most battles were preceded by careful tactical planning, for which maps were made and used; in some cases, these grade imperceptibly into maps of reconnaissance. In this matter, as in so many others, Frederick the Great had argued that terrain was the "foremost oracle" that ought to be consulted, because "There are as many different kinds of battles as there are types of terrain."[240] This fact no doubt was brought home particularly to commanders in the American countryside, for whom the choice of ground on which to stage a major battle was often a difficult decision. In view of the logistic value of both the sea and major rivers for transportation along the eastern seaboard, land reconnaissance required joint planning with the naval command. In July 1780, shortly after the arrival of the French in Rhode Island, Lafayette had been engaged in such tactical planning for battle. He reported to Washington:

I am going this evening to fix places with pilots, and also to speak of the entrance of the harbour—Dobs and Shaw are here and I will have a full conversation with them and the Admiral both for the entrance of the harbour and Navigation of the Sound—tomorrow I call with as much secrecy as possible a number of pilots for the harbour of Hallifax and River St. Laurens.

. . . After I will have seen the pilots, and made calculations with the Commander of the Artillery and the first Engeneer whom the Count will consult, I shall draw a plan which I will get theyr answer to and repair with it to head quarters.[241]

Scrutinizing maps and charts, interviewing guides and pilots, consulting with technical specialists in the artillery and engineers, and viewing the actual ground where possible—all were an essential and normal part of preparations for battle. Far from being the results of spontaneous decisions, most Revolutionary battles were carefully deliberated and often involved a conference of general officers, with the submission of maps and written memoranda. Washington's plan for an attack on New York in 1780 was explained in the minutest topographical detail, with one paragraph emphasizing the key role of cartography in military planning:

19th. The Plan or sketch which accompanies this with the explanations will give a more perfect idea of the place of debarkation, the Road, the Houses, the March of the Column, the separation of it, first by the detachment that goes to Fort George, and afterwards of the other two, for the Forts Knyphausen and Tryon.[242]

A time was eventually reached when formal troop disposition would be made for a battle. This was a battlefield equivalent of the order of march, and it sometimes reflected the placing of units within their previous encampment. It was also a compromise between the theoretical recommendations of the textbooks (the *Atlas* to the *Oeuvres de Frédéric le Grand* contained a whole series of hypothetical battle orders[243]), the dictates of actual terrain, and the types of regiments and corps available to a commander. During the Revolution, the order of battle was either issued as written orders or (for staff officers at least) expressed in plan form. James Hadden recorded Burgoyne's order of battle for 19 September 1777 in the form of a simple sketch.[244] More commonly, the record of these initial positions was preserved in plans made during or after a battle.

There is some evidence that a few officers attempted to keep a cartographic record while a battle was in progress. Burgoyne, in *A State of the Expedition from Canada*, commented on the difficulty of making plans under such conditions as an apologia for one of the maps published in his account of events (see plate 16). He noted:

the third and fourth positions of the army in the engagement of 19th of September may appear upon a cursory view to want precision. The inequalities of the ground could not be distinctly marked upon so small a scale; and the continual shift of the positions of separate corps, as they were attacked by corps of the enemy, which frequently, from the thickness of the wood, they did not see, made it equally difficult to mark regularly the position of the whole at any one time.[245]

Such drawing of military maps—in the thick of the events they portrayed—was uncommon; maps were usually made after the battle. As with sieges, some of these plans were part of a personal record. Of his pen-and-ink map of the battle of Camden, 16 August 1780, "taken on the spot by Thos. Geoe. Leond. Barrettè, Lt. 23rd Regt. . . . this 22nd August, 1780" (that is, six days after the battle), the cartographer explained in a letter to Henry Clinton:

I am keeping a correct Journal of the Present War, in its Infancy, progress, &c &c, with drawings of Battles, engagements &c. & political remarks for the Conduct on Both sides; —humbly hope at the conclusion thereof, your Excellency will think it worthy, to honor it with yr. countenance & Patronage. I have taken the liberty to enclose your Excellency a Plan of the Battle fought on the 16th. inst. which is pretty correct, you will please to overlook the inelegancy of the drawings having no sort of instrument with me, I was obliged to make use of a Common Pen & Bad ink.[246]

Other mapmakers would have found themselves similarly ill-equipped in the aftermath of a battle. Partly for this reason, as well as to conform to the methodical military habit of report and post mortem, commanders-in-chief often appointed a staff officer to make a proper postbattle survey. Whether from British, French, or Hessian cartographers, many of the large scale and more formal battle plans, including some of those later published, originated in this way. Their official nature is suggested by the fact that they were often signed by surveyors known to have been employed as mapmakers at headquarters; sometimes they were specifically surveyed "by order." By the first of these criteria, the several battle plans attributable to John Hills were given an official hallmark. A map of the action at Fort Washington, engraved by William Faden and published on 1 March 1777, was similarly surveyed by Claude Joseph Sauthier, a mapmaker who had been attached to Howe's headquarters in 1776. The title of the last-named map clearly explained its provenance: it had been surveyed "immediately after" the action and, moreover, "by order" of Earl Percy, who commanded the detachment.[247]

The matter of authority was quite obviously regarded as important in maps that could help to make or break a general's career. As a result, such maps were provided with marks of authenticity—such as the surveyor's name and appointment—as well as the assurance that they were taken "on the spot."[248] On a plan of the battle of Brandywine, also engraved by Faden, this tendency went as far as to identify the source of part of the plan: "The operations of the Column under the command of his Excellency Lieutenant General Knyphausen," the title noted, "is engraved from a plan drawn on the spot by S. W. Werner Leiutt. of Hessian Artillery."[249]

Such were the almost continuous roles of maps in the conduct and study of battles. From the planning stage to the inevitable post mortem (and beyond it, to the time when battles would be restaged as part of a military education), maps were important. Even slight and scrappy maps usually served well defined though ephemeral purposes. These original functions, when properly identified and verified by other evidence, enable any military map to be assigned a place in an overall classication. Ultimately, it is through a reconstruction of the maps' operational uses that their historical significance in the Revolution can be assessed.

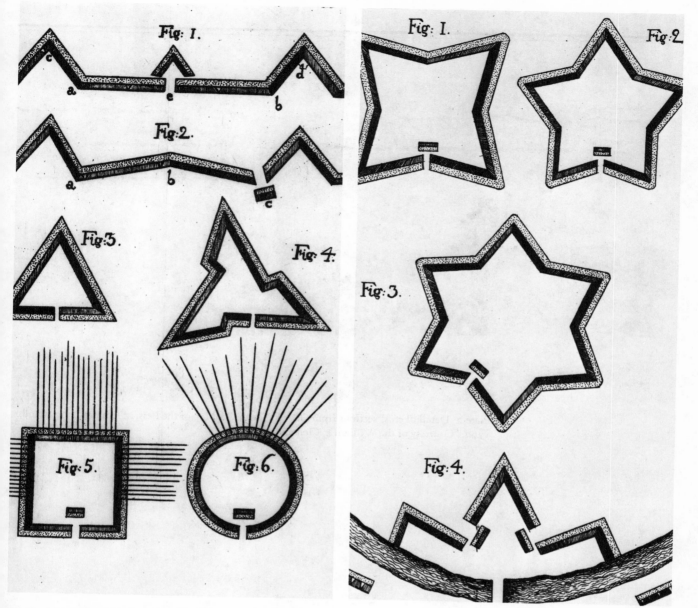

Plate 1 Engravings showing range of eighteenth-century fortification designs. From Peter
Lotharius von Orholm, *Anviisning til Feldt-Ingenieurkonsten* (Kisbenhavn, 1777).

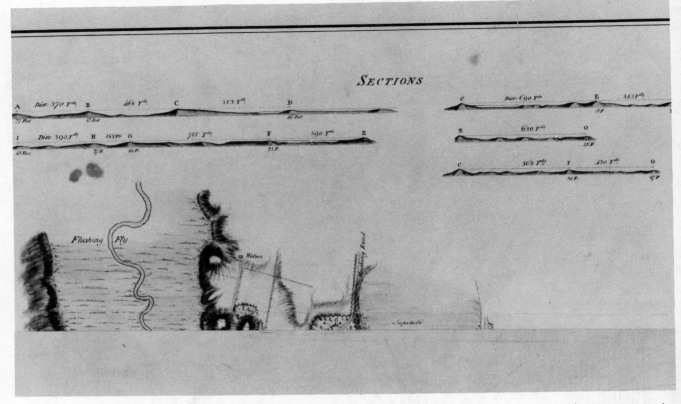

Plate 2 Detail of cross sections from George Taylor, "A Map of the Pass, at Jamaica Long Island, 1782." Courtesy of the William L. Clements Library.

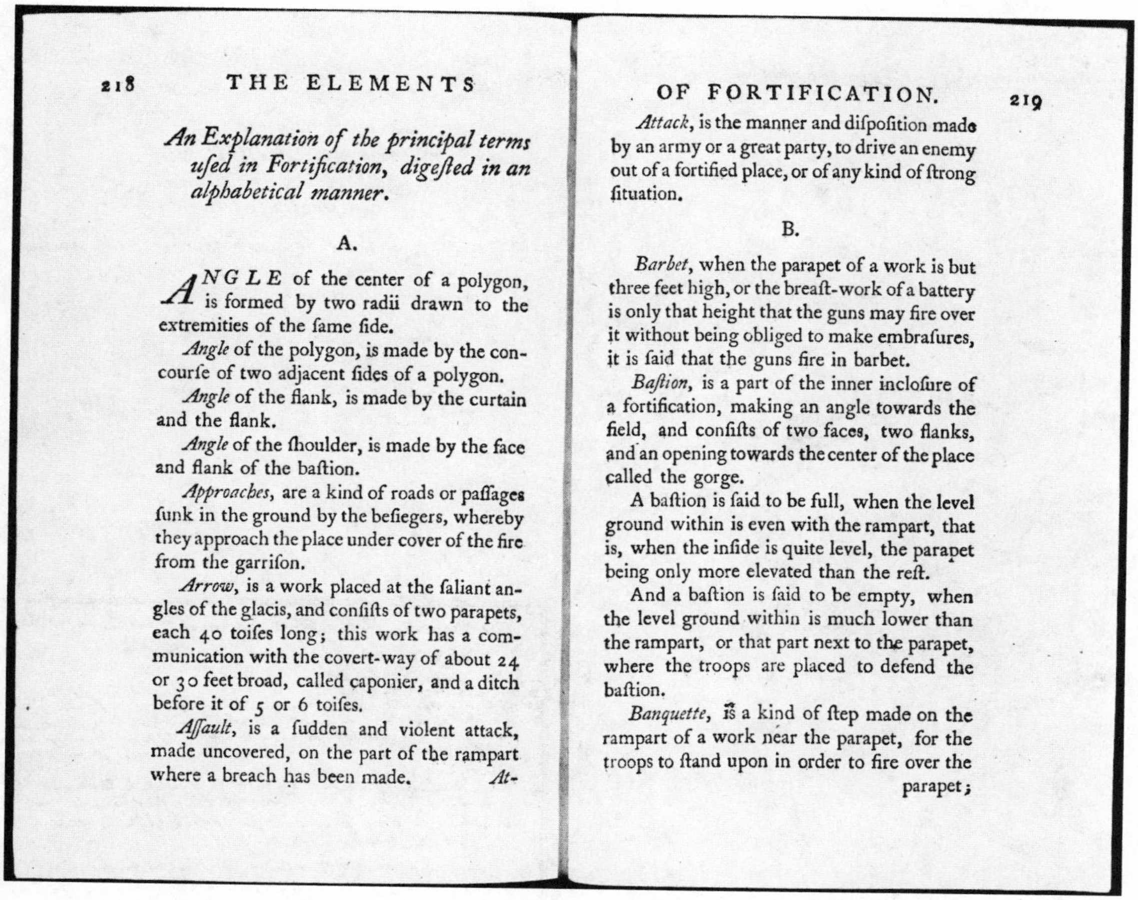

An Explanation of the principal terms used in Fortification, digested in an alphabetical manner.

A.

ANGLE of the center of a polygon, is formed by two radii drawn to the extremities of the same side.

Angle of the polygon, is made by the concourse of two adjacent sides of a polygon.

Angle of the flank, is made by the curtain and the flank.

Angle of the shoulder, is made by the face and flank of the bastion.

Approaches, are a kind of roads or passages sunk in the ground by the besiegers, whereby they approach the place under cover of the fire from the garrison.

Arrow, is a work placed at the saliant angles of the glacis, and consists of two parapets, each 40 toises long; this work has a communication with the covert-way of about 24 or 30 feet broad, called caponier, and a ditch before it of 5 or 6 toises.

Assault, is a sudden and violent attack, made uncovered, on the part of the rampart where a breach has been made.   *At-*

Attack, is the manner and disposition made by an army or a great party, to drive an enemy out of a fortified place, or of any kind of strong situation.

B.

Barbet, when the parapet of a work is but three feet high, or the breast-work of a battery is only that height that the guns may fire over it without being obliged to make embrasures, it is said that the guns fire in barbet.

Bastion, is a part of the inner inclosure of a fortification, making an angle towards the field, and consists of two faces, two flanks, and an opening towards the center of the place called the gorge.

A bastion is said to be full, when the level ground within is even with the rampart, that is, when the inside is quite level, the parapet being only more elevated than the rest.

And a bastion is said to be empty, when the level ground within is much lower than the rampart, or that part next to the parapet, where the troops are placed to defend the bastion.

Banquette, is a kind of step made on the rampart of a work near the parapet, for the troops to stand upon in order to fire over the parapet;

Plate 3 Pages from John Muller, *A Treatise Containing the Elementary Part of Fortification* (London, 1756). Courtesy of The Newberry Library.

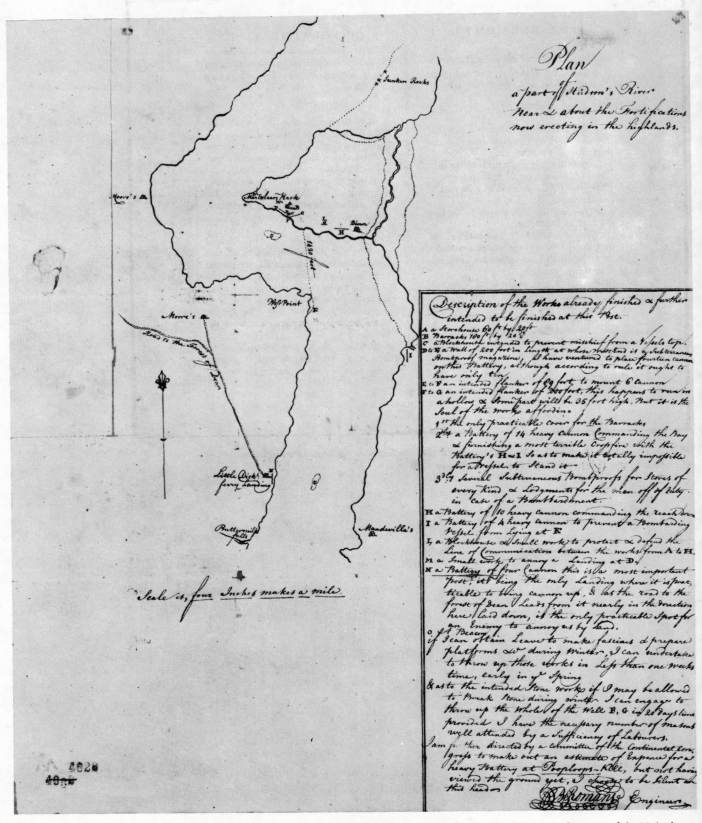

Plate 4 Bernard Romans, "Plan of a Part of Hudson's River" [1775]. Courtesy of the United States Military Academy, West Point.

PLAN of the TOWN and ENVIRONS of NEWPORT
RHODE ISLAND.

Exhibiting its defenses formed before the 8th of August 1778 when the French fleet engaged and passed the Batteries: the course of the French Fleet up the Harbour the Rebel attack. and Such defensive works as were erected since that Day until the 29th of August when the Siege was raised: also the Works proposed to be erected in the present year 1779.

Explanation, in which an Asterisk * preceeds each article
that was performed before the 8th of August 1778.

A Battery, prepared for 10 Guns. finished on the 9th of August in it were planted Six 12 Prs.

B Counter-Battery for four 24 Prs. and three 18 Prs. opened the 25 of August: it bore upon the whole attack of the Rebels. and silenced their two lower Batteries E. F.

C Battery for one 12 Pr. opened the 19th. it enfiladed the right branch of the Approach.

D Battery for two 8 Inch Mortars. opened the 25th.

E* A Redoubt for two 12 Prs. and 70 men.
N.B. on the 8th August Six Cohorns were added to it.

F Counter-Battery for three 18 Prs. against the whole attack opened the 20th.

G Battery prepared for five Guns. finished on the 9th in it were planted three 12 Prs.

H* Redoubt for two 12 Prs. and 70 men.

I* Battery prepared for five Guns. in it were planted two 12 Prs.

J* Redoubt for three 12 Prs. and 70 men.

K* Redoubt for two 18 Prs. one 12 Pr. and 70 men.

L* Fort for one 18 Pr. Seven 12 Prs. and 200 men.

M A fleche with two 6 Prs.

N* A fleche for 50 men.

O* Enclosed Battery for four 24 Prs. four 12 Prs. one 8 Inch and two 5 and a half Inch Howitzers.

P. Q. R. S. * Redoubts for three, four, two. and three 12 Prs. and for 60. 57. 60. 68. men respectively.

T* Redoubt for two 18 Prs. one 12 Pr. and 50 men.

V. U. Redoubts for four 12 Prs. and for 50 men each.

W* Battery for four 24 Prs. with a Redoubt for 150 men.

X* Battery for Five 24 Prs. and Two 18 Prs.

Y* Battery, on barbette for two 24 Prs.

Z + intended Battery for Four 24 Prs.

The works towards the Harbour were improved and put into a State of defense between the 8th of July, and the 8th of August. The Soundings are expressed in Fathoms. The Sunk Vessels coloured Brown. The faint dotted black lines were the Stone walls. The inundation was formed the 18 of April. The Line from A to Tomini Hill was begun the 12th of August. The Rebels broke ground on the fifteenth.

Rebel Batteries { A Two 18 Prs. Two 12 Prs. one mortar. C Four 12 Prs. one Howitzer F one 32 Pr. Three 24 Prs. E Five 24 Prs. one mortar. H one mortar. D, G unfinished B Redoubt.

WORKS PROJECTED FOR THE PRESENT YEAR.

		N° of Men	N° of Guns
I	A Fleche to be added to this Redout and the Work itself enlarged	80	
K	A Sea Battery to defend the South Entrance of the Bason, and the Bason itself, with additional works to support the Battery	140	3
	The pass between I and K to be abbatised		
L	A Redout to defend the pass between I and K, the heads of the ponds and	2	
	and the rest of the right to M and N	100	4
M	A Redout, commanding the ground before it, and that between L and N	100	4
N	A Redout; it will support M and T	60	2
O	A Redout commanding the right, and rear; the ground in front declines in a curved line, and therefore requires Mortars for its defence	140	4 }{ 5 } Cohorns
P	A Redout affording cross-fires of musketry with O and Q	60	
Q	A Redout crossing a fire of musketry with Fort Fanning	80	
R	Enclosed Sea-Battery to defend the passage between Post Island & blue Rock	60	
S	A Redout to strengthen the left between W and X, and to support T	30	
T	A Redout to support R and S	100	
U	A Sea-Battery to prevent Ships from laying in Codington Cove whence they might cannonade our left	32	
W	A Redout to support U	100	
X	A Redout to support W	60	2
	The Redouts Q, R, S of the Town Line, conjunctively with O and Tomini, defend the pass between O and Q	1132	3

Wm. D'aubant
Commanding Engineer.

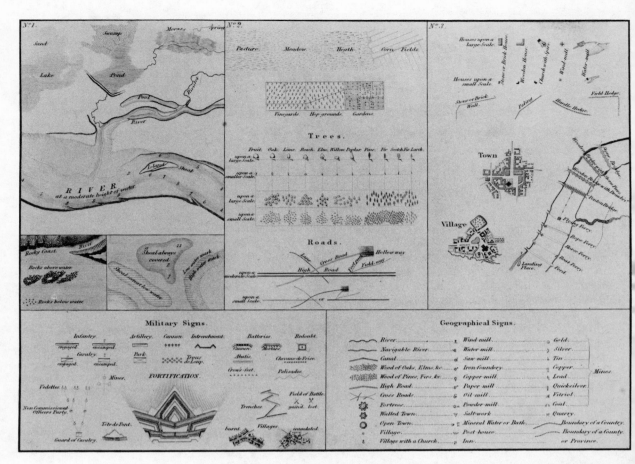

Plate 6 W. Siborne, *Instructions for Civil and Military Surveyors in Topographical Plan-Drawing* (London, 1822), plate 4. Courtesy of the British Library.

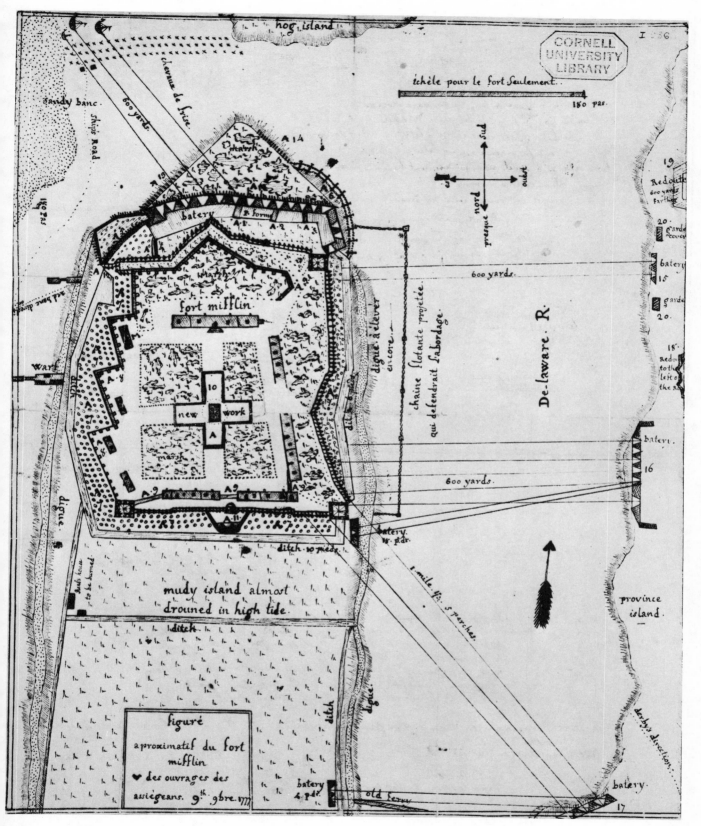

Plate 7 François de Fleury, "Figuré aproximatif du Fort Mifflin, 1777." Courtesy of the Sparks
Collection, Cornell University Library.

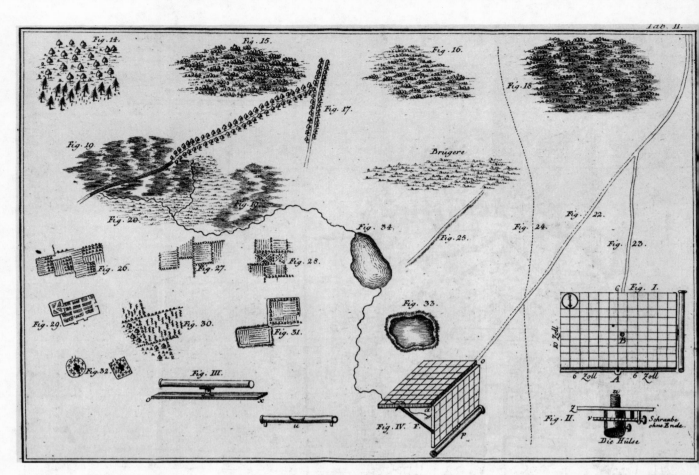

Plate 8 Symbols for topographical survey, from J. D. C. Pirscher, *Coup d'œil militaire* (Berlin, 1775). Courtesy of The Newberry Library.

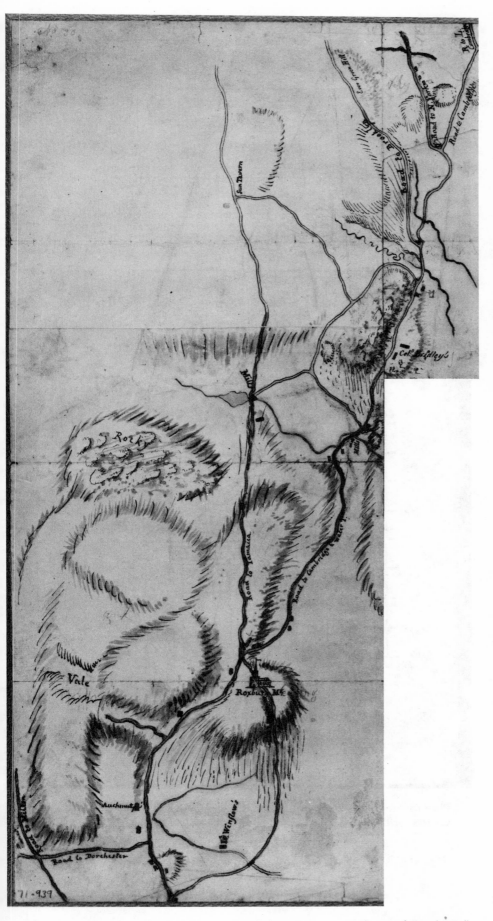

Plate 9 Henry de Berniere and John Brown, [Roads from Boston to Roxbury and Dorchester].
Courtesy of the Library of Congress.

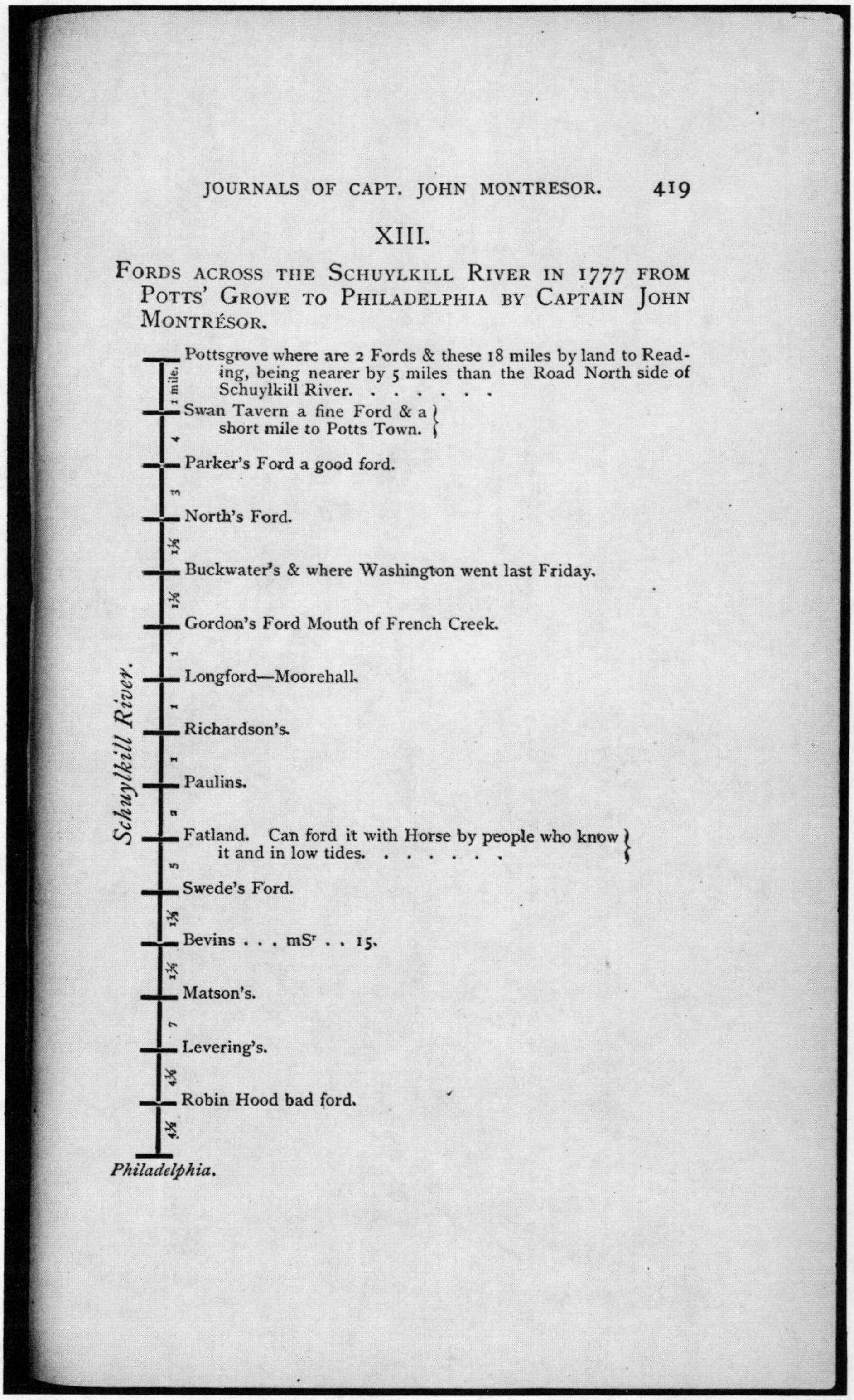
JOURNALS OF CAPT. JOHN MONTRESOR. 419

XIII.

FORDS ACROSS THE SCHUYLKILL RIVER IN 1777 FROM POTTS' GROVE TO PHILADELPHIA BY CAPTAIN JOHN MONTRÉSOR.

Schuylkill River.
Pottsgrove where are 2 Fords & these 18 miles by land to Reading, being nearer by 5 miles than the Road North side of Schuylkill River. . . . . . .
1 mile.
Swan Tavern a fine Ford & a short mile to Potts Town.
4
Parker's Ford a good ford.
3
North's Ford.
1½
Buckwater's & where Washington went last Friday.
1½
Gordon's Ford Mouth of French Creek.
1
Longford—Moorehall.
1
Richardson's.
1
Paulins.
2
Fatland. Can ford it with Horse by people who know it and in low tides. . . . . . .
5
Swede's Ford.
1½
Bevins . . . mS^r . . 15.
1½
Matson's.
7
Levering's.
4½
Robin Hood bad ford.
4½
Philadelphia.

Plate 10 From *The Montresor Journals,* edited by G. D. Scull (New York, 1882), vol. 14. Courtesy of The Newberry Library.

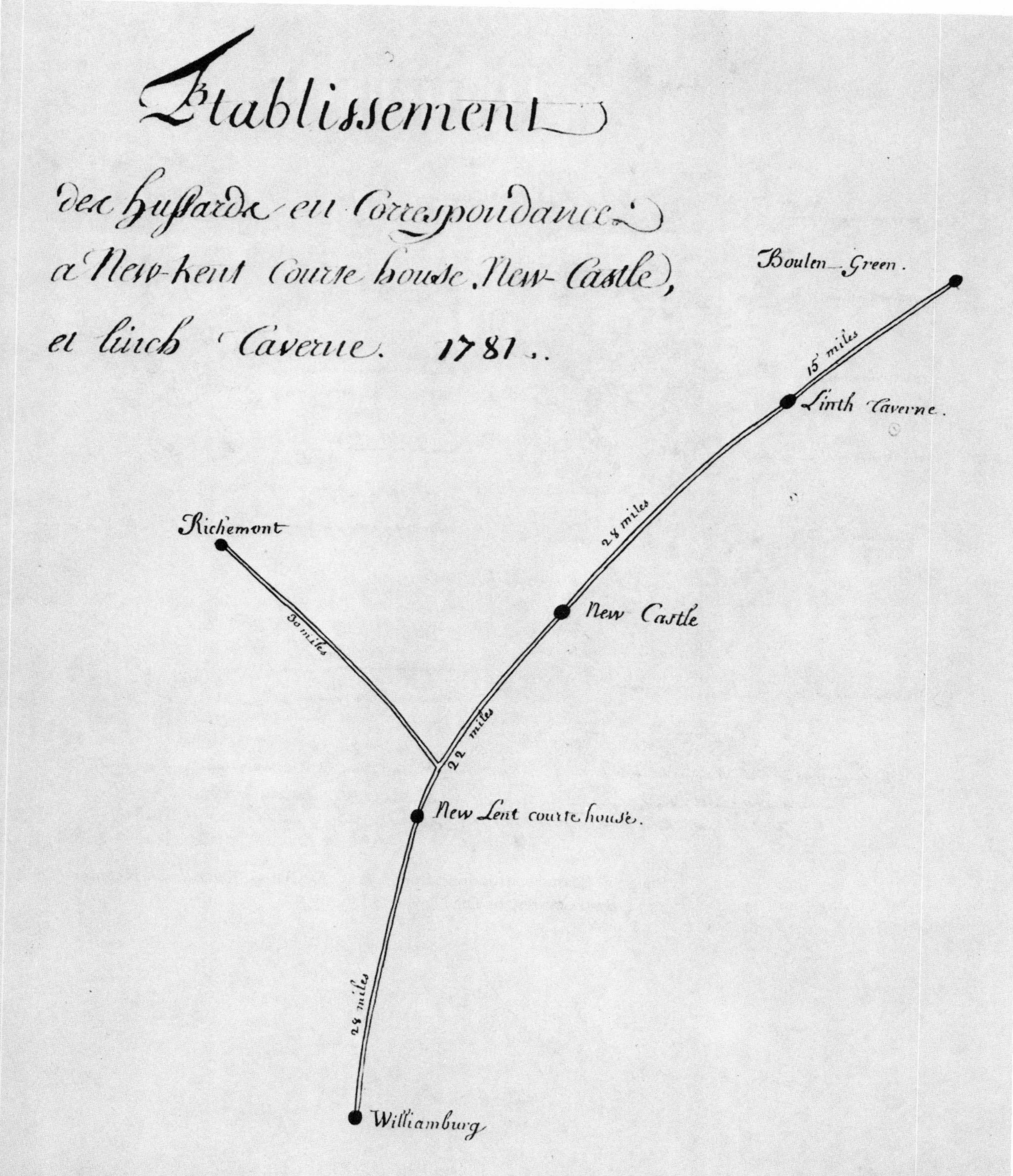

Établissement
des hussards en correspondance
à New-kent Courte house, New-Castle,
et Linch Caverne. 1781.

Boulen-Green.
15 miles
Linth Caverne.
28 miles
Richemont
30 miles
New Castle
22 miles
New Lent courte house.
28 miles
Williamburg

107A CHAIN OF EXPRESSES BETWEEN NEW KENT COURTHOUSE,
NEWCASTLE, AND LYNCH'S TAVERN, 1781

Plate 11 From *The American Campaigns of Rochambeau's Army,* edited and translated by
Howard D. Rice, Jr., and Anne S. K. Brown (Princeton, 1972). Courtesy of Princeton
University Press.

REFERENCES

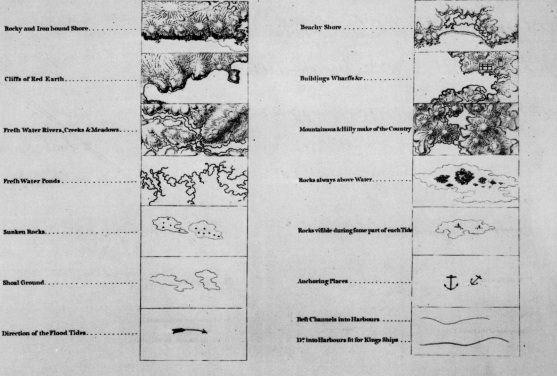

Rocky and Iron bound Shore . . . .

Cliffs of Red Earth . . . .

Fresh Water Rivers, Creeks & Meadows . . . . .

Fresh Water Ponds . . . .

Sunken Rocks . . . .

Shoal Ground . . . .

Direction of the Flood Tides . . . .

Beachy Shore . . . .

Buildings Wharffs &c . . . .

Mountainous & Hilly make of the Country

Rocks always above Water . . . .

Rocks visible during some part of each Tide

Anchoring Places . . . .

Best Channels into Harbours . . . .

Do into Harbours fit for Kings Ships . . .

N.B. The figures express the depth of Water in Fathoms at the time of Low Water. (M) under them denotes Mud, (S) Sand, (Sh) Shells, (Gr) Gravel, (St) Stoney, (R) Rocks.

The time of high Water at the full and change of the Moon, is expressed in Roman Figures & the Vertical rise of the Tide in small figures above, viz: IX signifies that it flows till 9 oclock and the Tide rises 8 feet perpendicular.

Plate 12 Coastal conventions, from J. F. W. DesBarres, *The Atlantic Neptune* (London, 1774–82). Courtesy of The Newberry Library.

Plate 13 Example of a "contraction" by Robert Erskine, "Contraction of the Roads from below Robinson's Mills to Peekskill" (1778). Courtesy of the New-York Historical Society.

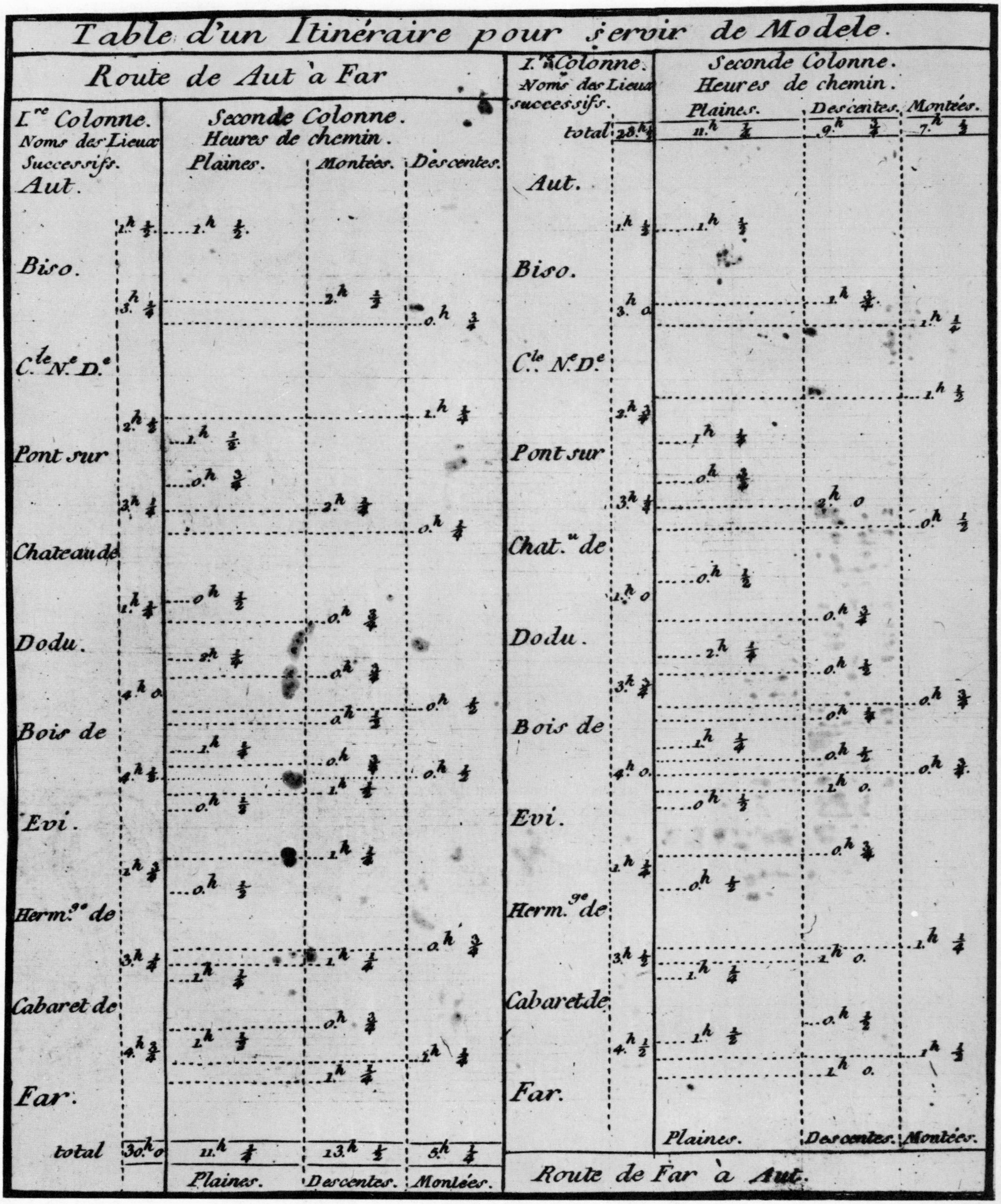

Table d'un Itinéraire pour servir de Modele.

Route de Aut à Far

Ire Colonne. Noms des Lieux Successifs.		Seconde Colonne. Heures de chemin.		
		Plaines.	Montées.	Descentes.
Aut.				
	1h 1/2	1h 1/2		
Biso.				
	3h 1/4		2h 1/2	0h 3/4
Cle N.De				
	2h 1/2		1h 1/4	
Pont sur	1h 1/2	0h 3/4		
	3h 1/4		2h 1/4	0h 1/4
Chateau de		0h 1/2	0h 3/4	
	1h 1/4	8h 1/4	0h 1/4	
Dodu.	4h 0		0h 1/4	0h 1/2
		1h 1/4	0h 3/4	0h 1/2
Bois de	4h 1/4	0h 1/2	1h 1/4	
	2h 3/4		1h 1/4	
Evi.		0h 1/2		
	3h 1/4		1h 1/4	0h 3/4
Herm.ge de		2h 1/4		
	4h 3/4	1h 1/2	0h 3/4	
Cabaret de			1h 1/4	
Far.				
total 30h.0		11h 1/4	13h 1/2	5h 1/4
		Plaines.	Descentes.	Montées.

Route de Far à Aut.

Ie 2Colonne Noms des Lieux successifs.		Seconde Colonne. Heures de chemin.		
total 28h		Plaines. 11h 1/4	Descentes. 9h 1/2	Montées. 7h 1/4
Aut.				
	1h 1/2	1h 1/2		
Biso.				
	3h 0		1h 3/4	1h 1/4
Cle N.De				1h 1/2
	2h 3/4	1h 1/4		
Pont sur		0h 3/4	2h 0	0h 1/2
Chat." de	1h 0	0h 1/2		
Dodu.		2h 1/4	0h 1/4	0h 1/2
	3h 1/4		0h 1/4	0h 3/4
Bois de	4h 0	1h 1/4	0h 1/4	0h 3/4
		0h 1/2	1h 0	
Evi.	1h 1/4		0h 3/4	
		0h 1/2		
Herm." de	3h 1/2	1h 1/4	2h 0	1h 1/4
Cabaret de			0h 1/2	
	4h 1/2	1h 1/2		1h 1/4
Far.			1h 0	
		Plaines.	Descentes.	Montées.

Plate 14 Illustration of the compilation of itineraries, from M. Dupain de Montesson, *L'art de lever les plans* (Paris, 1763). Courtesy of The Newberry Library.

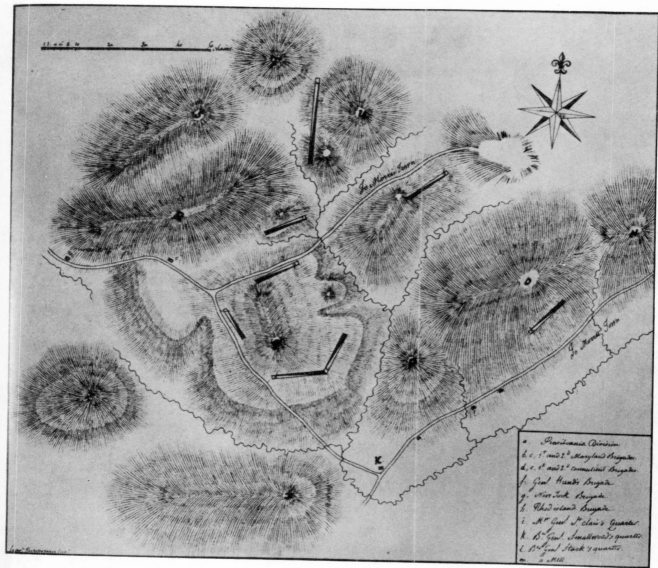

Plate 15 From *The Writings of George Washington*, edited by John C. Fitzpatrick
(Washington, D.C., 1931–44), vol. 17. Courtesy of The Newberry Library.

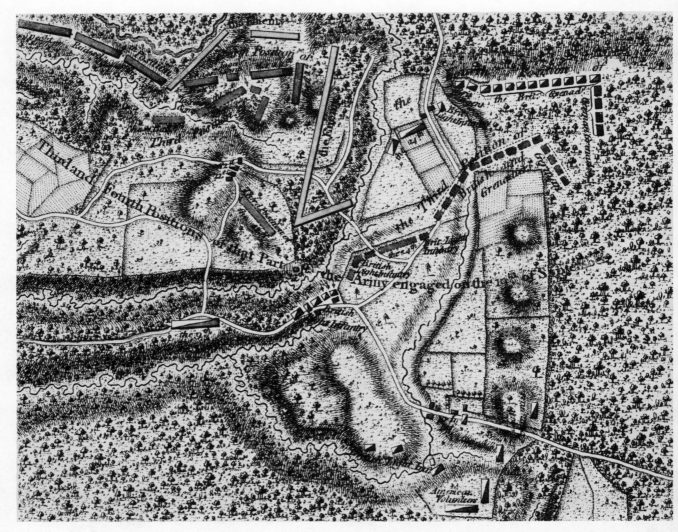

Plate 16 From John Burgoyne, *A State of the Expedition from Canada, as Laid before the House of Commons* (London, 1780). Courtesy of The Newberry Library.

Plate 17   A page from the register in the Tower Drawing Room, showing American maps listed.
Courtesy of the Public Record Office, London.

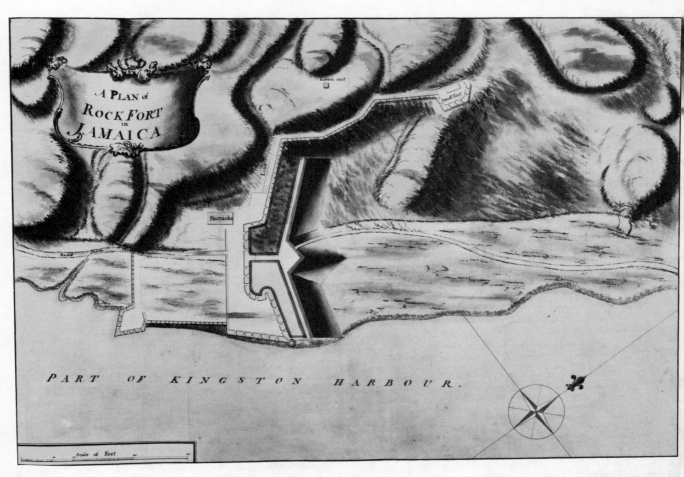

Plate 18 Exercise used by Tower draftsmen. Courtesy of the Public Record Office, London.

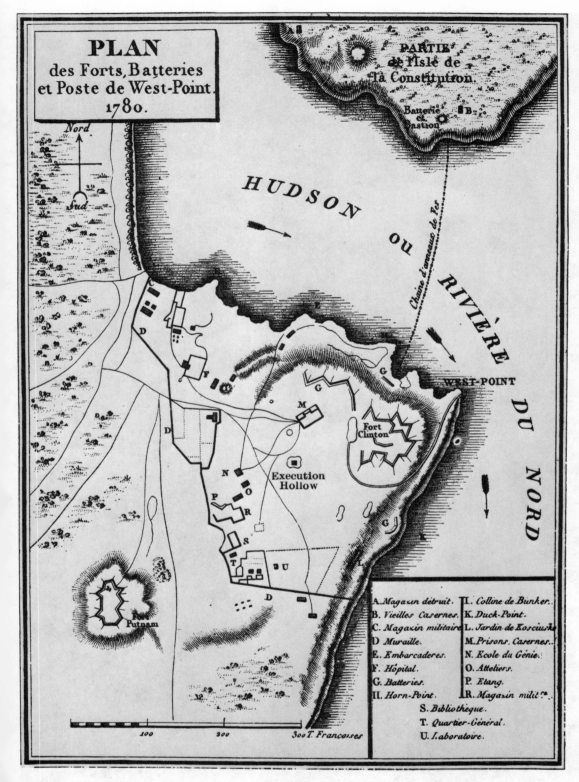

Plate 19 From Edward S. Holden, "Origins of the United States Military Academy," in *The Centennial of the United States Military Academy at West Point, New York* (Washington, D.C., 1904). Courtesy of The Newberry Library.

Plate 20 John Singleton Copley's portrait of John Montresor. Courtesy of the Detroit Institute of Arts.

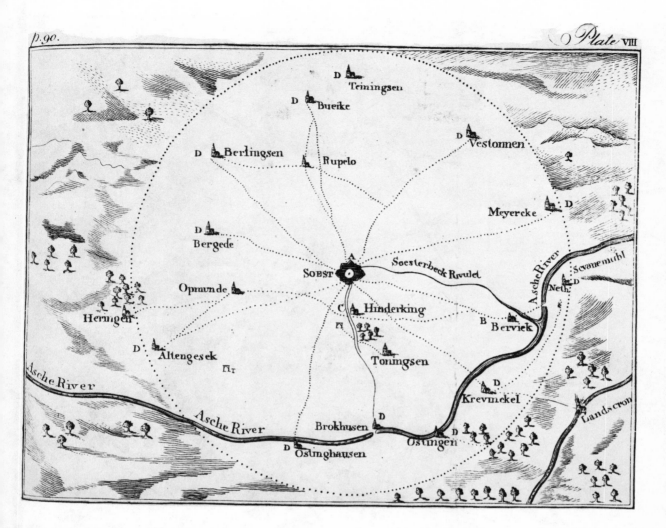

Plate 21 Military surveying and reconnaissance methods, from Roger Stevenson, *Military Instructions for Officers Detached in the Field* (Philadelphia, 1775). Courtesy of The Newberry Library.

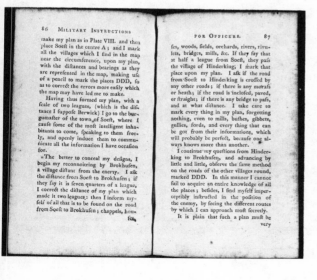

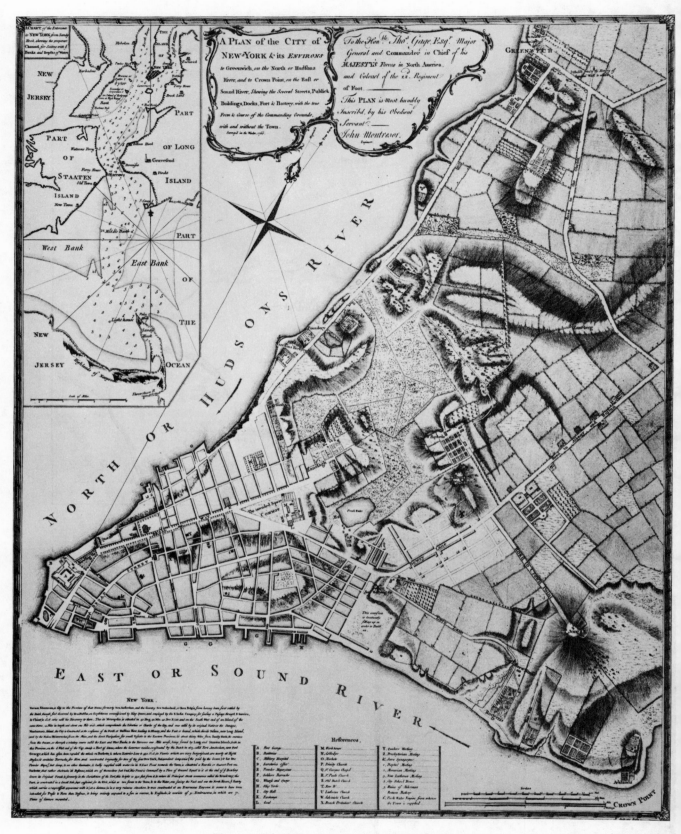

Plate 22 John Montresor, *A Map of the City of New-York* [1775]. Courtesy of The Newberry Library.

Plate 23 Detail from "Boston Harbour." in J. F. W. DesBarres, *The Atlantic Neptune* (London, 1774–82). Courtesy of The Newberry Library.

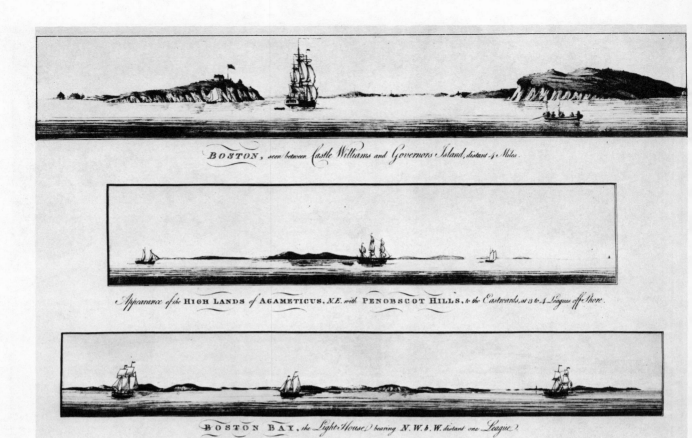

BOSTON, *seen between* Castle Williams *and* Governors Island, *distant 4 Miles*.

Appearance of the HIGH LANDS *of* AGAMETICUS, *N.E. with* PENOBSCOT HILLS, *to the Eastwards, at 3 to 4 Leagues off Shore*.

BOSTON BAY, *the Light House, bearing N.W. b. W. distant one League*.

Plate 24 Views of Boston, from J. F. W. DesBarres, *The Atlantic Neptune* (London, 1774–82).
Courtesy of The Newberry Library.

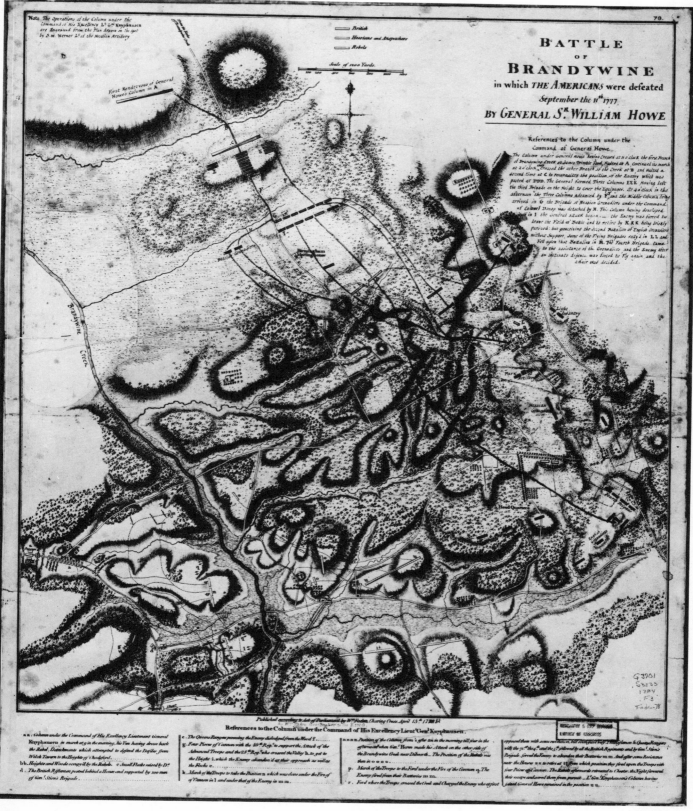

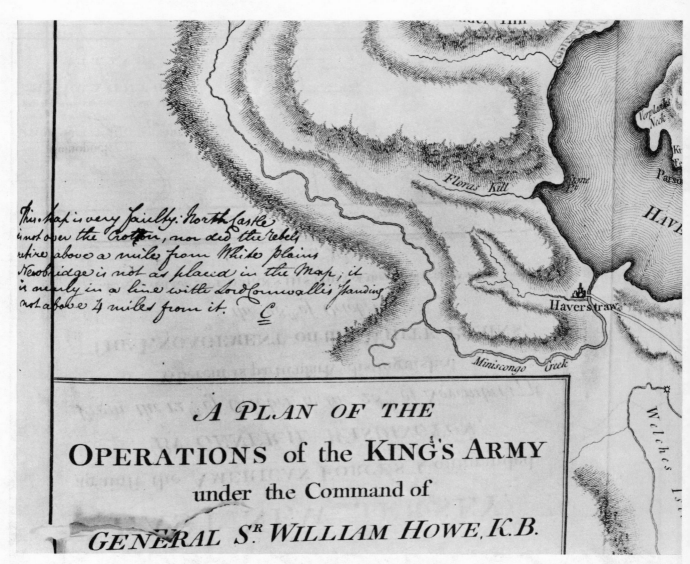

This map is very faulty: North Castle
is not over the Croton, nor did the rebels
retire above a mile from White plains
Newbridge is not as placed in the Map; it
is nearly in a line with Lord Cornwallis's ftanding
not above 4 miles from it. C

A PLAN OF THE

OPERATIONS of the **KING'S ARMY**

under the Command of

GENERAL Sᴿ WILLIAM HOWE, K.B.

Plate 26 Detail from "A Plan of the Operations of the King's Army," showing Clinton's annotations. In Charles Stedman, *The History of the Origin, Progress, and Termination of the American War* (London, 1794). Courtesy of the John Carter Brown Library.

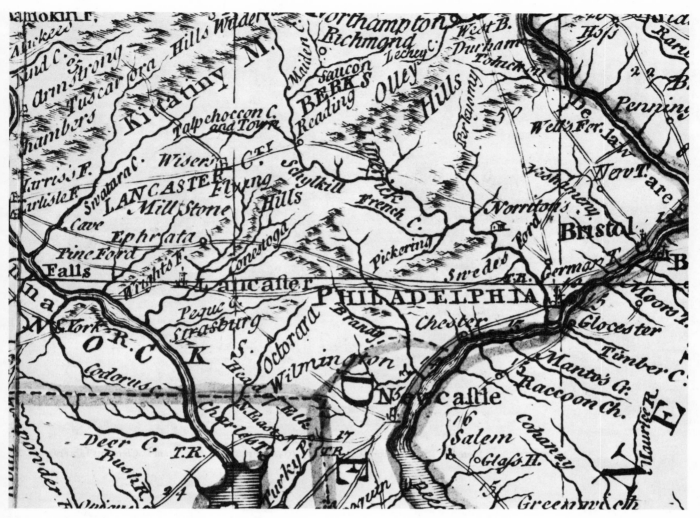

Plate 27 Detail from "A General Map of the Middle British Colonies in America," in
Robert Sayer and John Bennett, *The American Military Pocket Atlas* (London, 1776).
Courtesy of The Newberry Library. The scale of this photograph is 1:746,212.

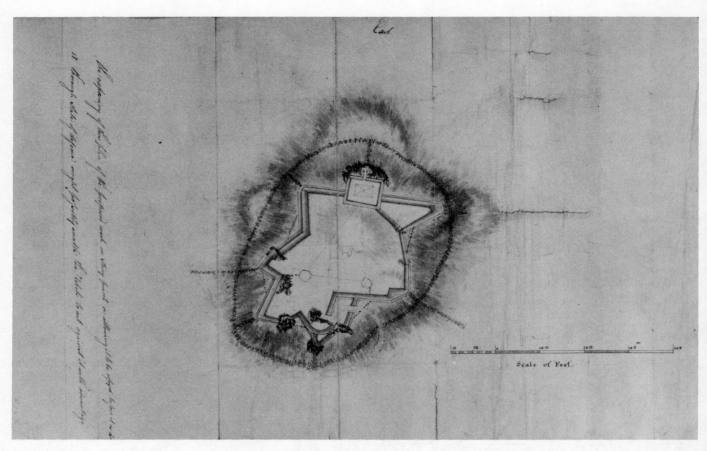

Plate 28 [Stony Point], Clinton map 163. Courtesy of the William L. Clements Library.

2 | The Spread of Cartographical Ideas between the Revolutionary Armies

One remarkable general characteristic of the military cartography of the Revolutionary era was the extent to which different armies took a common approach to the making and use of maps. Whoever the participants, there were important similarities in the roles maps played in the various engagements of the war. Although the diverse national origins of the Revolutionary armies might be expected to inhibit the development of such an underlying uniformity, it is clear that much deeper structural influences were at work: maps reflected not differences in national origins but affinities in eighteenth-century military organization and practice.

To understand the operational environment of Revolutionary War cartography, it is essential to realize that the armies of eighteenth-century Europe shared much more of a common military inheritance than superficial differences might suggest. The successful military leaders of the century—both the thinkers and the generals—were admired as much in Britain and America as they were in Continental countries. On all sides, the training of technical specialists—especially of artillery and engineer officers —was founded on the same widely accepted body of theory and was aimed at inculcating the same practical skills required for the attack and defense of fortified places in varied terrains. These recurrent elements of a common experience, in which the same battles, books, generals, and tactical systems stood out as acceptable models, inevitably led to a similarity of outlook in the making and use of maps. Once the language or style is stripped away, a central core of cartographic practice transcending superficial distinctions is revealed among maps of different national origin.

Such observations will be almost self-evident to those familiar with the events of the Revolution. But beyond this general explanation, we can discern a pattern of particular processes through which cartographical ideas and techniques were spread—a pattern that had been woven into a distinctive military map culture by the time of the Revolution. Thus the aim is to explain the characteristics of Revolutionary period mapping— as described in chapter 1—by considering its formative influences. One of the difficulties of such an explanation arises from the rather inclusive definition of a military map. This term was extended to embrace all maps used for military purposes, of whatever provenance, including those made by military surveyors; but any examination of such a general group of maps would call for a broad history of eighteenth-century cartography. Even a definition narrowed to include only maps made by cartographers attached to the Revolutionary armies would not lessen the problem of devising a time scale long enough to provide an adequate explanation.

As a mere snapshot in the history of military mapping, the cartography of the Revolution, even if narrowly interpreted, can hardly contain the seed of its own characteristics. Indeed, an analysis of the continued geographical and chronological development of military map features of the 1770s and 1780s would have to trace back improvements to at least the dawning of modern military engineering and topographical mapping in sixteenth-century Europe. Such difficulties here lead to the abandonment of an approach through origins. Instead (though as something of a compromise), an attempt will be made to identify and describe some of the mechanisms by which information about maps (rather than on maps) was being spread during the decade or so preceding the Revolution. This will contribute at least a partial explanation and will add some account of contemporary change to an otherwise static picture of Revolutionary mapping.

By the mid-eighteenth century, standing armies were being supported by the state in most European countries. This military world was the essential environment for the spread of cartographical ideas and techniques. Although the organization of national armies differed in detail, they had much in common. Channels of communication, both official and social, were established, and through these, contacts and exchanges of information occurred. It is true, of course, that within this military milieu, maps and mapmaking—as any search of official documents will soon reveal—occupied a relatively tiny place. Yet the position of cartography was well defined and significant enough that it is possible to discuss the means by which cartographical ideas, techniques, and particular types of maps were disseminated among the different armies. Four such influences—(a) individual mapmakers, (b) the content of formal military education, (c) the publication and circulation of military textbooks, and (d) the adoption of similar headquarters' organizations—are examined below. These were not the only factors in cartographical innovation during the Revolutionary era, but they were clearly among the most important.

INDIVIDUAL MAPMAKERS AS AGENTS OF CHANGE

The raw material of the history of cartography is intimately tied up with the individual mapmakers. Quite properly, along with bibliographical studies, the literature has been extensively concerned with their biographies. William P. Cumming, for example, often focuses his narrative on individual mapmakers,[1] and the work of Peter J. Guthorn, in particular, has done much to provide a biographical framework for the American, British, and Hessian mapmakers active during the Revolution.[2] It is a proper assumption of these studies that the background of mapmakers, their education and subsequent careers, often provides a crucial key to the maps they produced. If the value of a biographical approach lies partly in the amount of detail it generates, it can equally be argued that when a sufficient number of biographies of mapmakers is available—as for the Revolution—it should be possible to generalize about the role of the individual in cartographical change.

The Mobility of General Officers

One of the principal reasons for similarities in the provision and use of maps among the Revolutionary armies was the considerable mobility of individuals within the international military system of the eighteenth century. There was a relatively free flow of ideas and cartographers, in which two distinctive currents can be identified. The first comprises the generators and users of maps, who were often (but not necessarily) surveyors and cartographic draftsmen themselves. This group, which made an important contribution to cartographical development, included the politicians (often avid scrutinizers of campaign maps) and the general officers at headquarters, along with their immediate staffs (quartermasters, adjutants, aides, and so forth). All these were responsible for initiating many of the specific orders resulting in the production of new maps and plans. A detailed analysis of the "action space"[3] of such men as individual soldiers is beyond the scope of this essay, but the concept is useful in stressing that many of the principal officers active in Revolutionary America possessed a wide experience in military matters extending beyond their national armies. Among British generals, for example, both Howe and Clinton had campaign experience as staff officers in Europe.[4] The ill-fated Burgoyne was an experienced European campaigner who had, moreover, made a special study of the military methods of Frederick the Great.[5] Cornwallis, as part of his military apprenticeship, had traveled in Europe with a Prussian officer, attended a military academy in Turin, and also served in the allied army at the battle of Minden.[6] It may be relevant to note that the armies of eighteenth-century Europe all relied on recruitment from the aristocracy to fill their officer corps, and this contributed to the ease with which its members moved in European society as a whole. There can be little doubt that by the time of the Revolution, generals such as Rochambeau and von Heister, the veteran Hessian, were just as familiar as were Clinton and Howe with the characteristics of other nations' armies.

Another factor in professional mobility was that the eighteenth century was *par excellence* an age of the mercenary officer. The very nature of such contracts implied movement from army to army. There is no better illustration of its results than in the composition of the French expeditionary force under Rochambeau, which, in Guthorn's words, had a truly international flavor. Rochambeau's principal aide, Count Ludvig von Closen, was Bavarian, and several of the thirteen regiments had non-French officers. There were two units—the Regiment De Dillon and the Regiment De Walsh—whose officers were mainly men with Irish names. The largest foreign contingent consisted of Germans: the Royal Deux Pont, or Zweibrücken, was largely a German regiment; a German battalion from Trier was attached to the Saintonge Regiment; Alsatians and Lothringers filled in the light companies of the Bourbonnais and Soissonais Regiment. So thoroughly did they permeate the whole force, it has been estimated that at the time of Yorktown nearly a third of Rochambeau's army was German or Swiss.[7]

Nor were European military ideas denied to the Americans, even in the early stages of the Revolution. Charles Lee was perhaps exceptional in his direct European experience,[8] but other general officers in the Continental Army either were veterans of the French and Indian War or had picked up ideas as members of British colonial regiments or militia. The Royal American Regiment, founded as a light infantry unit by the Duke of Cumberland after Braddock's defeat, was particularly important in helping to transplant newer European military ideas into colonial North America. Its first lieutenant colonels—Henry Bouquet and Frederick Haldimand—were Swiss officers who had served with the Prince of Orange, and the forty German officers persuaded to join the regiment also confirm its international character.[9] Men with experience in the Royal Americans supported both sides in the Revolution, as may be illustrated by the careers of two of the most notable cartographers of the Revolutionary period—Samuel Holland for the British and Thomas Hutchins, geographer to the southern army, for the Americans—who had both been commissioned in that regiment. It is perhaps a truism to point to the common roots of military science in the British and American camps at the outbreak of the Revolution; nevertheless, these roots were a determining factor in the nature of their cartographic output.

After 1775, the European element in the Continental Army was greatly strengthened. This was partly the result of the deliberate congressional policy of recruiting officers directly from Europe, especially France, to staff its technical corps, and partly the consequence of the flow of adventurers and mercenaries who left Europe to offer their services to the American cause. Between them, men such as de Kalb, Pulaski, Lafayette, and von Steuben had been exposed to most of the current theories of European warfare.[10] They made a vital contribution to the professionalism of the American general staff—one small aspect of which was their understanding of the value, use, and specific roles of maps in warfare. This is not speculation. It is borne out by the evidence of the training these men received in mapmaking, by documented examples of their use of maps, and by their practical ability to survey and draw them. Von Steuben, who served on the staff of Frederick the Great[11] and later became inspector general in the Continental Army, epitomizes the penetration of European ideas into the American headquarters' staff. By the time von Steuben arrived in North America, his commander-in-chief, George Washington, already had a portrait of Frederick the Great at his headquarters,[12] had read Frederick's military writings in translation,[13] and thereafter had a Frederician staff officer in his camp. Whichever way we look at the Revolution, we find armies reflecting not only their particular national influences but also those of other eighteenth-century countries.

The Mobility of Technical Officers

Within this general military society, there were also a few regiments channeling the flow of specialized ideas and men. From a technical point of view, including the development of military cartography, perhaps the most important were the engineer corps of various armies. Although engineers (and the surveyors and draftsmen who sometimes worked under them) were attached to army headquarters during the Revolution, they tended to be independent by virtue of their scientific education and their sometimes separate affiliations, as was the case with the British corps of engineers, administered by the Board of Ordnance rather than by the army. In any case, engineers were usually men of a varied international experience. During the Revolution, French engineers of Huguenot extraction were serving in some of the Hessian units, and German engineers were attached to Rochambeau's expeditionary force. Engineers were regularly posted in times of both peace and war, resulting in frequent contact with specialists in other armies. Maps and plans were captured on occasion, and their detail and style were then assimilated into the professional experience of the victors.[14]

For the British engineers deployed in North America during the Revolutionary period, there is ample evidence of geographical mobility. Hugh Debbeig had served in both Flanders and Scotland before coming to North America.[15] James and John Montresor had both acted as engineers in Gibraltar.[16] Archibald Robertson, also of the engineers, arrived in the New World via the West Indies.[17] Moreover, a North American tour of duty, as Douglas Marshall has shown,[18] usually involved several postings—ranging from Newfoundland to Florida and taking in stations like those at Halifax, Quebec, and New York, as well as a number of less permanent locations. At the very least, engineers and draftsmen were given ample opportunity to become familiar with military maps accumulating in drawing rooms up and down the continent. Nor was it merely a question of the movement of British-born engineers. There was also a tendency for British armies on European campaigns to pick up trained draftsmen and engineers from other armies. North America tended to act as a magnet for the talents of these men. Such adventurous military engineers on the eve of the Revolution included: De Brahm, who had been a captain of engineers under Emperor Charles VI;[19] Samuel Holland, a lieutenant in the Dutch artillery before going to England around 1754;[20] Joseph F. W. DesBarres, who was born in Switzerland, trained in mathematics at the University of Basel, and schooled in military engineering at Woolwich;[21] and Claude Joseph Sauthier, born in Strasbourg, who was successively cartographer to Governor Tryon of New York and then to Earl Percy in the New York and Rhode Island campaigns.[22] The growth of empire had helped to create an environment in which attractive employment was often available to skilled foreigners and in which cartographic ideas and techniques, among many others, could be readily transferred. Developments in North America came to reflect the success and character of projects for mapping in Britain and other parts of her overseas colonies. The mapping undertaken in India, for example, by the engineers of the East India Company, may well have influenced the British headquarters' provision for mapping made during the Revolution,[23] just as William Roy's military survey of Scotland could have served as an initial model for the general surveys in progress after 1763.[24]

The simple fact is that military engineers—much as technocrats in any age—were well qualified to cross national frontiers. In a study of Revolutionary cartography, there is no better illustration of this influence than the manner in which Congress deliberately recruited foreign specialists to build up an engineer corps. At the beginning of the war, as Washington frequently complained, the Americans were desperately short of technical officers capable of drawing and using fortification plans.[25] The few engineers available to the Continental Army either had been trained in America by the British before the Revolution, had been educated in Europe, or had merely picked up their trade on the job. Richard Gridley, the first American chief of engineers, belongs to the first category, having studied under John Henry Bastide, a British military engineer serving in America from 1758–1763.[26] Bernard Romans, born in the Netherlands, was trained in England as a military engineer and was employed by Washington in 1775; he belongs to the second category.[27] In the third, Rufus Putman, largely a self-taught man, was said to have lacked the mathematics to become a first-rate engineer, although he was a competent land surveyor.[28]

Against this background, Congress had given instructions for four skilled military engineers to be engaged in France as early as December 1776.[29] The arrival of suitable recruits in America was delayed until 1777, but the commissioning of Louis Lebègue Duportail as commandant of the corps of engineers, with Radière, Gouvion, and Laumoy under him,[30] marked the successful transplant into Washington's military headquarters of a group of officers trained in French methods and imbued with the scientific approach of the engineering school at Mézières.[31] These officers were soon joined by others with similar backgrounds, including Jean-Louis Imbret, "a gentleman well recommended as an engineer," Thaddeus Kosciuszko, the count of Vrecourt, Louis Fleury, and Pierre-Charles L'Enfant.[32] Even where their qualifications as military engineers were less than impeccable by the elitist standards of Mézières, as military surveyors and draftsmen they offered a welcome infusion of skill into the American service. Thus, in January 1778, when Duportail was entreating Washington and Congress to increase the engineers, he was anxious to see Jean de Villefranche added to the establishment, and ventured: "There is at York Town a French officer who was brought by Mr. Du Coudray and introduced by him as Engineer—for my part I do not give him out as such, because he was not in that character in France and has no such pretensions himself—but he studies with a view to become a member of the Corps—he has studied Geometry, understands surveying and Drawings, and therefore ought to be very useful to us."[33] In a similar category was de Murnan, who, although not trained in the French corps of engineers, "may be very useful here, he possesses sufficient theoretical knowledge to make him an exceedingly good Engineer, and he acquired some practice in Russia."[34] So important were foreign recruits to the American engineers that as late as April 1782, when the corps contained fourteen officers, only one was an American—a Captain Niven, ranking thirteenth in the list.[35]

Up to this point, we have been concerned with the mobility of officers who were often either initiators of new surveys or makers of decisions by means of maps, rather than actual surveyors and draftsmen. The distinction was not, of course, hard and fast. Many senior staff officers in the Revolution (notably Clinton and Washington) could turn their hand when necessary to drawing and even surveying maps. Similarly, in all armies, engineer officers made a major contribution to the total cartographic record of the Revolution. If the argument from mobility is to avoid a heroic approach to the history of cartography, it needs to embrace a wider population of Revolutionary map-makers. This has been made possible by the pioneer biographical work of Guthorn. Figure 2:1, based on his data, portrays the national origins of all Revolutionary map-makers he was able to identify. This must be regarded as a sample rather than a defini-tive listing. For one thing, Guthorn's definition of who should be included has not been accepted.[36] For another, whatever our terms of reference, many manuscript maps of the Revolution remain anonymous. In other cases, the biographies of identified cartographers lack information on their birth and education. Figure 2:1 is based on the assumption that the country in which a mapmaker was born and educated was a major formative influence on the cartographical ideas subsequently carried to America. Yet there were exceptions. Bernard Romans, for example, could have been influenced as much by working for De Brahm on the survey of the southern colonies as by his military education in England.[37] Many contemporary cartographers could likewise have developed attitudes and skills as mapmakers through work in North America. Even with such caveats entered, figure 2:1 provides an adequate summary of the potential role of migration in the cartography of the Revolution. "British" and "American" mapmakers (in the sense of the armies to which cartographers were attached) are distinquished, with the upper part of the diagram locating the European origin of mapmakers and the lower, their North American origins. Regarding the former, the overwhelming contribution of Great Britain to the supply of "British" mapmakers is perhaps predictable, but British military mapmaking was hardly an insular activity. Otherwise, figure 2:1 emphasizes how both British and American mapmakers had their origins in several Continental countries, with the predominance of the French in the American camp largely attributable to the migration of trained engineers, as already noted.

These facts illustrate the danger of making sharp distinctions in the history of cartography on the basis of national labels. In mapping, as in other aspects of the con-flict, the sympathies of men with particular military skills were frequently divided between the Revolutionary and the Loyalist cause. Loyalists of diverse background

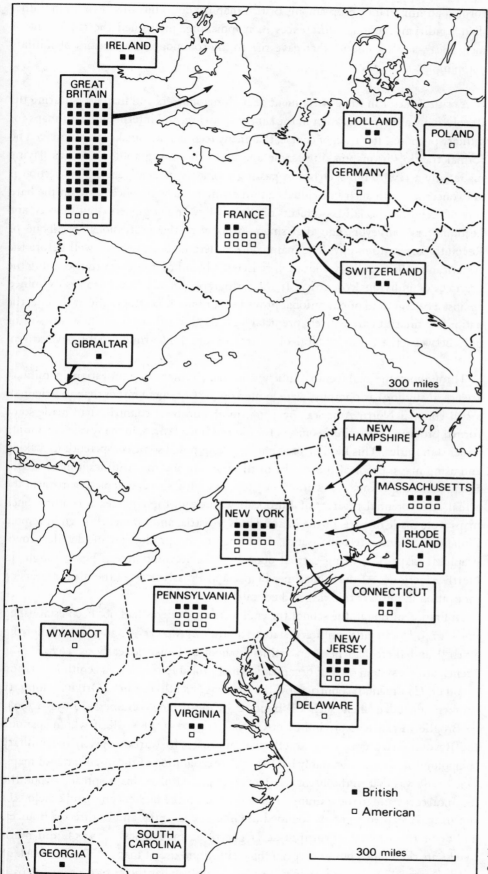

Figure 2:1 The national and state origins of Revolutionary mapmakers, based on Guthorn.

formed an important group among British mapmakers. Thus the Revolution, rather than rigidifying national differences in mapmaking, intensified the movement of men, ideas, and techniques that gave rise to the common characteristics of military mapping.

MILITARY EDUCATION
AS A MEANS OF SPREADING
CARTOGRAPHICAL IDEAS

A critical factor in the environment of both mapmakers and map users during the Revolution was their education in the survey, drawing, and interpretation of maps for military purposes. It is true, of course, that many recorded mapmakers had received no formal training in mapmaking; some appear in the cartographic record as having made only a few rough sketches in passing moments of emergency. This section is not concerned with such individuals and their maps; it will concentrate on the hard core of technical specialists—officers of the artillery and engineers, staff officers, and headquarters' surveyors and draftsmen—who were the professional backbone of Revolutionary cartography. The main concern here is to show how, well before the American conflict, military education reflected a blend of influences transcending the practices of individual countries. If the cartography of the Revolution is examined against a background of educational provision for military cartography in Europe, the national similarities are entirely predictable. Indeed, it is hard to see how any sort of gulf between the cartographical objectives of different armies could have arisen.

Developments in
France and Prussia

Throughout the eighteenth century, the main centers of innovation in military science, including cartography, were located on the Continent rather than in Britain or a still colonial North America. By 1775, most European countries had made some formal provision for training officers for their technical corps, in many cases including wider staff duties. This kind of preparation presupposed some competence in making and using maps. Proof of the quality of this training and the attitudes it inculcated is found in the impressive series of military topographical surveys, depicting many of the actual and potential theaters of European warfare in the eighteenth century. Such maps were made of parts of the Netherlands, Austria, and Sweden.[38] Even in remote Finland a military reconnaissance, resulting in the production of detailed topographical maps, was being carried out while the Revolution was being fought in North America.[39] At the same time, France and Prussia boasted the main centers of innovation in military thinking and education.

In France, although the school for engineers at Mézières had not been established until 1749,[40] a regular military status for the *ingénieurs géographes* dated from 1716,[41] and there had been an artillery school at Douai as early as 1679.[42] The French army's system of staff organization had probably reached its zenith in relation to other Continental countries by the mid-eighteenth century. Original military thinkers included men such as Bourcet (1700–1780), Guibert (1734–1790), de Broglie (1718–1804), and Saint-Germain (1707–1778), all of whom spanned the Revolutionary era. Their intellectual approach to warfare, given the military technology of the age, inevitably led to a wider recognition of the importance of maps. One result was that in the French system an appreciation of maps spread beyond the technical corps and to the training of general staff for the higher command echelons of the army. A staff college was founded in Grenoble in 1764, and its director Bourcet, author of the seminal "Principes de la guerre de montagnes" (1775), did·much to educate the French officer corps in the making and use of maps.[43] The first book of the *Principes,* "De la connaissance du pays," implies that the critical use of maps is an essential preliminary to all military planning.[44] That this is no mere theoretical textbook exhortation is indicated by the impressive number of military surveys and maps listed by Berthaut in *Les Ingénieurs géographes militaires*.[45] These were undertaken not only by the geographical engineers but also by staff officers such as Bourcet. In the course of the eighteenth century, they came to cover many of France's borderlands and the adjacent territories over which war had been waged.

These observations are also generally true of Prussia. Although it produced fewer original military thinkers than did France, Prussia's military ideas were copied both by Britain and by the fledgling Continental Army. Prussia was far more of a military state than was France. With the exception of the academy of sciences, all Prussian educational institutions served mainly military purposes: the Ritterakademie, cadet schools designed for the education of the nobility; the Militärakademie; and the Ingenieurakademie, specializing in the training of military engineers.[46] A national school for military engineering was founded in the first decade of the eighteenth century.[47] Under Frederick the Great, engineer officers were frequently assigned to cartographic projects. As early as 1741, Frederick had commissioned a military map of Silesia on a scale of 1:200,000; subsequently, Major von Wrede was ordered to compile a detailed map of the Silesian borders with Bohemia and Moravia.[48] The cartographic component in military education and staff duties attained major importance only after the Breslau instructions of 1758, however, when the Prussian field engineers were ordered to concentrate on ground surveys, finding and establishing roads for troop movements, and reconnoitering enemy camps and positions.[49] It has been said that Prussian military cartography attained a high point in the work of Dietrich de Haas, who drew three maps of the theater of operations of the Russo-Turkish campaign of 1770.[50] As in France, an educational provision for cartography was thus not confined to engineers and artillery cadets but also included the general staff. Frederick's quartermaster general's department included twelve elite officers selected for their special aptitude and instructed in surveying, reconnaissance mapping, laying out camps, and placing villages in a state of defense.[51] One of Frederick's teaching maxims, as we have already noted, was "The land is to the soldier what a chessboard is to a chess player."[52] The place of maps in such a military philosophy can hardly be in doubt.

Europe's political boundaries offered relatively free movement of such ideas through academies and textbooks. The Prussian engineering service, for example, had been built up largely through the imported knowledge of a succession of foreign technicians, beginning with the Dutch-born engineer Cornelius Gerhardt von Walgrave (1692–1773).[53] When Frederick established the Académie des Nobles in 1765, it was partly staffed by French officers trained in the methods of Bourcet and other leading military scientists.[54] Indeed, many of Frederick's writings, widely read in other countries, were a digest and codification of ideas originating as much in France as in Prussia. It is clear, then, that the eighteenth century saw significant development of innovations in the theory of warfare, and that these innovations, once defined, spread rapidly among Continental armies.

Against a background of European armies rapidly accepting topographical maps as an integral part of tactical planning, the military training for cartography in both Britain and America (the latter after the Declaration of Independence) may be examined. At first sight, the British system lagged far behind that of either France

Educational Provision in Britain

or Prussia. Eighteenth-century Britain produced no major theorist of the stature of many Continental writers; not until the end of the century was a military college founded (apart from Woolwich) in which military surveying and other aspects of cartography were compulsory in the training of officers.[55] On the other hand, the British army was not entirely cut off from military thought on the Continent. When the training received by the professionals among the British mapmakers of the Revolution is considered, the extent to which it had been penetrated by other European influences is surprising. To a certain extent, therefore, the cultural lag applied only to formal institutions in which military mapping was taught. The actual maps— despite characteristic British scales and established conventions in drafting and coloring—gave little support to the idea of an exclusive national school of mapmaking. If anything, the British approach can be best interpreted as a provincial variant of practices entrenched in countries like France, the Netherlands, and Prussia. It is, however, misleading to talk about the education of mapmakers as if it were a specialized, monolithic teaching system. Military training was generally directed at wider objectives, and maps and plans (as chapter 1 indicated) were often the incidental by-product of other activities. For this reason, a useful distinction may be drawn between the education, on the one hand, of those cadet officers destined for the artillery and engineer corps, who sometimes made maps and, on the other hand, of a much smaller number of surveyors and draftsmen for whom mapmaking was largely a full-time activity.

The Woolwich Academy. In the training of British artillery and engineer officers, it is possible to piece together some Continental influences. Although the two corps were formally established under the Board of Ordnance only in the second decade of the eighteenth century, the beginnings of systematic technical training can be discerned as early as 1720.[56] The Royal Military Academy at Woolwich was founded by royal warrant, dated 30 April 1741.[57] From that date until the Revolution, there is ample evidence for the presence of a Continental approach in the basic instruction given to these two "scientific" corps being developed by the Board of Ordnance.

As with mapmakers in Revolutionary America, so too with some of their teachers: the migration of skilled specialists, in this case to Britain, was a critical factor in the spread of ideas. There is no better illustration than the career of John Muller, at first deputy headmaster and later professor of fortification and artillery at the Woolwich academy until his retirement in 1766. With some justification, Muller was described by a contemporary as "the scholastic father of all the great engineers this country [Britain] employed for forty years."[58] Born in Germany in 1699 (in 1755 he still wrote of his "want of being thoroughly acquainted with the *English* language"[59]), Muller was first employed at the Drawing Room in the Tower of London. During this period, he established a reputation as a writer of textbooks on mathematical subjects.

Muller's greatest contribution to British military engineering and its cartographic by-products may have been as translator and editor of a number of Continental works, including: *The Attack and Defence of Fortified Places* (1747); *A Treatise containing the Practical Part of Fortification, for the Use of the Royal Military Academy, Woolwich* (1755); *A Treatise on Fortification, Regular and Irregular: With Remarks on the Constructions of Vauban and Coehorn* (second edition, 1756); *The Field Engineer: Translated from the French of De Clairac* (1759); and *A Treatise on Artillery* (1757; supplement, 1768). All of these texts offer pragmatic explanations of the fortification systems of such classic European engineers as Coehorn, De Ville, Pagan, and Vauban. Through these works, Muller made an important individual contribution to the spread of Continental methods at Woolwich and elsewhere.

One effect of Muller's teaching was to help make military maps a *lingua franca* by the time of the Revolution. In one of his writings, *The Elements of Fortification*, Muller included an international comparison of the linear "measures and scales used in Fortification":

The French make use of a measure called a *toise*, which is six feet, and therefore, is what we call a *fathom* here in *England*.

The *Dutch*, and most of the Germans make use of the *Rhinland rod*, which is 12 Rhinland feet.

The *French* royal foot is to the English foot, as 114 to 107, or as 16 to 15 nearly, in smaller numbers.

The Rhinland foot is to the *French* foot, as 1033 to 1068, or as 29 to 30 nearly, in small numbers; and therefore, half the Rhinland rod is to a *French* toise, as 29 to 30 nearly.[60]

The value of such an explanation was to demonstrate a broad compatibility between different national measures. Even to a dull student, wrestling with his arithmetic, it would be obvious that in a rough and ready way a *toise*, or half a Rhineland rod, could be easily converted as a fathom; and the French and Rhineland feet were not too different from their English counterpart. A knowledge of the underlying similarity encouraged a freer exchange of cartographic information, through textbooks as well as on working copies of maps and plans used in campaigns.

Muller was not the only emigré teacher to be recruited as an instructor at the Woolwich academy. In 1744, Gabriel Massiot had been appointed as a drawing master, and several of those who came to teach French to the cadets were of French origin. In 1777, Isaac Landmann, an experienced French staff officer and formerly of the Ecole Royale Militaire in Paris, was appointed professor of fortification and artillery.[61] Moreover, when the diplomatic relations were cordial enough, contacts between France and England (as later between France and America) could be even more direct. In 1766 the master general of the ordnance had sent James Pattison, the lieutenant governor at Woolwich, "to visit the Royal Military Academy at Paris, in order to get the best information . . . concerning the government, regulations, &c." Pattison reported how he had made himself "master of the whole establishment, civil and military, together with a detail of rules and orders now in force relative to the education, discipline, and economy."[62]

Some of these ideas, transmitted in various ways, were actually put into practice, as is confirmed by the Woolwich syllabus. The original warrant for the academy's educational requirements was fairly general, calling for "instructing the raw and inexperienced people belonging to the Military branch of this office, in the several parts of Mathematics necessary to qualify them for the service of the Artillery, and the business of Engineers."[63] In a subsequent series of "Rules and Orders" for its conduct, the curriculum was itemized in detail, specifying both subjects and books. French, the international language of military science, was compulsory (as it had been since the founding of the academy), "both as to speaking it fluently, and writing it with accuracy."[64] The main technical subjects were classified into four groups: fortification and artillery; mathematics and geography; drawing; and classics, writing, and common arithmetic. Neither surveying nor map drawing were taught as principal subjects; in the manner of the European textbooks, they were an integral part of several other topics. By 1776, they were a recognizable component in three of the major subjects just mentioned; only classics and writing lacked a cartographical element.

It was specified that the professor of fortification and artillery would teach "Practical Geometry, and Mathematics" and the "Arts of Surveying and Levelling." He also would give instruction in the "Rudiments of Military Architecture, particularly the Method of making Plans, Elevations, and Sections of Powder Magazines, Guard Rooms, Barracks, Store-Houses, and other Buildings that may be necessary in fortified towns."[65] This was a key part of the engineers' training from a cartographical standpoint, and the Woolwich syllabus was clearly impregnated with Continental practices. The recommended texts provide one measure of this: they consisted of four of Muller's books cited above, as well as Vauban's *Fortification* and Coehorn's *Fortification*.[66]

In 1768 Paul Sandby, who had been employed on William Roy's military survey of Scotland,[67] was appointed chief drawing master at the academy.[68] Although it cannot be said that his approach to map draftsmanship was specifically Continental, his emphasis on the depiction of terrain features aiding the logistics of troop movement was certainly in line with cartographical teaching in the French and Prussian academies. Among other stipulations, it was laid down that Sandby should teach "the best Method of describing the various Kinds of Ground, with its Inequalities, as necessary for the drawing of Plans".[69] A bold portrayal of relief, as chapter 1 indicated, was a characteristic of many finished maps throughout the Revolution.

One of the responsibilities of the professor of mathematics at the academy was to teach "Geography, and the Use of Globes,"[70] but his primary contribution to the training of future military mapmakers lay in grounding them in basic trigonometry and geometry. These were subjects vital to a grasp of fortification, topographical mapping, and, to a lesser extent, the theory of perspective. Through these studies, the teachers of mathematics at the academy, notably John Lodge Cowley and Charles Hutton, did much to enhance its scientific reputation.[71] They entered its service as civilian philomaths, but their influence became particularly beneficial in military mapping projects staffed by the engineers, including the general surveys of North America brought to a halt by the Revolution. Conducting the surveys had involved observations of latitude and longitude to provide coordinates for triangulation. In several such ways, the academy's teaching was an essential though unspectacular precondition for the development of British military cartography in the second half of the eighteenth century.

The existence of a syllabus was of course no guarantee of the academy's overall effectiveness in training cartographers. The evidence on this score points to some deficiencies. For one thing, the particular branch of military cartography must be specified. A number of British engineers may have been competent as designers of fortification blueprints, or even as mathematicians, but their skills, as Vallancey pointed out, did not always include rapid military surveying.[72] In any case, the training in basic surveying received by the cadets seems to have varied. Although "orders" in 1776 referred to cadets being sent out of the academy "to practice the Arts of Surveying and Levelling"[73] (and some cadets were attached to private surveyors[74]), in 1774 it was reported that one class had "received no instruction either in Practical

Geometry or in the art of Surveying."[75] Nor was the mode of instruction designed to foster versatility—it often consisted of writing out textbooks and mechanically copying the existing plan models. It is true that from 1770 some practical work had to be presented in a portfolio at the time of a cadet's final examination, but the oral nature of that review may also have lacked rigor.[76] All that can be said is that the eminence of some of the examiners pointed to the aspirations if not the achievements of the academy. In 1765, for example, the reviewers included "the Earl of Morton, President Royal Society" and "the Reverend Mr Masculine, Astronomical Observator at Greenwich."[77] Such links with the wider scientific community exerted a progressively important influence on the content of the academy's syllabus during the rest of the eighteenth century.[78] As a footnote to the 1765 examination, the gold medal winner in the fortification class was Thomas Page, later to be wounded at Bunker Hill and also one of its cartographers.[79]

The Drawing Room in the Tower of London. Another point for Continental ideas to enter British military cartography was through the Drawing Room of the Tower of London. In three main respects, this establishment played a significant part in the development of British military cartography. First, it predated the Woolwich academy by at least half a century. The origins of the Drawing Room are obscure but it was probably in existence as part of the headquarters of the Board of Ordnance in the Tower at the time of the reorganization of the engineering service in 1683.[80]

Second, as a part of this specialist engineering center maintained by the Board, the Drawing Room required the importation of Continental technicians. In this respect (as with Muller for the academy), the tenor was set by Bernard De Gomme, who supervised the royal fortifications after the Restoration. A Dutchman born at Lille in 1620, De Gomme had served in the campaigns of Frederick Henry, prince of Orange, before acting as engineer and quartermaster general to the Royalist army in the English Civil War.[81] After his death in the Tower in 1685, he was succeeded as chief engineer by his former deputy, Captain Martin Beckmann, also a naturalized foreigner.[82] During the eighteenth century there were others like Muller who helped to maintain the links between ordnance headquarters and developments throughout Europe.

Third, it was through its practical function as a cartographic workshop that the Drawing Room contributed most to the character of British Revolutionary mapping. Few of the military engineers known to have been associated with the Tower failed to make a map, plan, or chart.[83] De Gomme, for example, was a fairly prolific draftsman. During the first half of the eighteenth century, the Drawing Room gained a reputation as a source of skilled military cartographers. Such a specialist and a founder of the Drawing Room style of cartography was Clement Lempriere, whose obituary in the *Gentleman's Magazine* described him as "an ingenious gentleman, draughtsman to the office of Ordnance, and Capt. of a marching Reg. of foot."[84] At least a score of his manuscript maps have survived, and he was the designer and draftsman of Henry Popple's great "Map of the British Empire in North America."[85] In the late 1740s, it was from the Tower that surveyors and draftsmen—including Paul Sandby and his elder brother Thomas—were posted to work under Roy on the military survey of Scotland.[86] Throughout the eighteenth century, such engineer-draftsmen were recorded at the main engineer stations in Britain and in North America; they tackled a variety of assignments concerned with both fortification and mapping.

In two other respects, the Drawing Room at the Tower had by 1775 become an important center for military cartography. First, the Board of Ordnance had pursued a policy of systematic collection of maps and plans relating to its main areas of geographical interest. Items were classified according to area (American maps were placed in the eighth division) and listed in a large folio volume, the "Register of Draughts in the Drawing Room," which by the mid–eighteenth century contained many hundreds of entries (see plate 17).[87] Second, the Drawing Room developed as an establishment to train boys as draftsmen and surveyors to complement the engineers in the field and to help with the compilation, drawing, correction, reduction, enlargement, and copying of plans. These Tower draftsmen held civilian status, although a few were commissioned into the engineers.[88] Even in the early eighteenth century, several of the clerks and draftsmen in residence were probably undergoing instruction.[89] Later, the number of both apprentices and qualified craftsmen in the Drawing Room increased from around a dozen in the 1750s to nearly fifty in the early 1780s.[90] This growth trend reflects the demand for cartographic skills during the Revolutionary period.

Information on the training of Drawing Room apprentices is somewhat patchy, but boys seem to have been taken on from the age of eleven or twelve.[91] They were instructed by the chief draftsman and by mathematical and drawing masters in elementary mathematics, drawing, and in the drafting and copying of fortification plans and military topographical maps. Although the actual syllabus has not been located, doubtless a watered-down version of the views current at Woolwich was offered, and some masters taught at both. On the practical side, there were opportunities for surveying in the field,[92] but the most important element in the draftsman's training consisted of copying a standard range of plans until a suitable level of proficiency was reached. Surviving specimens of the 1780 drawing exercises describe a plan of the Tilbury area (at a scale of fifty feet to an inch), a road survey, and drawings of garrison buildings and fortifications in the Isles of Scilly, Portsmouth, and Jamaica (see plate 18).[93] As each successive class of trainees copied the same models, some of which originated from plans over twenty years old, Tower drafting from the days of Lempriere largely became standardized in the so-called British style of military mapping, especially in the application of color to finished plans.[94]

As with the Woolwich academy, it is impossible to gauge the exact influence of this training; its effectiveness was certainly variable. Reuben Burrow, who had been appointed mathematical master in the Drawing Room in 1776, was clearly dissatisfied with some of his pupils, whom he reported as "idle," "very idle," "very indifferent," and "scarce any good."[95] Nor was the Board of Ordnance convinced that the Tower played an efficient part in the sort of military technical education it wished to develop. In 1782, a warrant was issued "for reducing the Establishment of the Drawing-Room" on the grounds that it seemed "ill calculated for instruction, and might be considerably reduced without any inconvenience to our service."[96] Perhaps the resources thus saved were to be used to augment the artillery and engineer cadets passing through Woolwich. This decision may well indicate a failure on the part of British authorities to recognize the wartime value of men trained primarily as surveyors and draftsmen. Not until 1787 was the Drawing Room reorganized to provide a field surveying unit—too late for service in the Revolution.[97] In actual mapmakers (and maps produced), the contribution of the Tower draftsmen to the mapping of the Revolution was relatively small. Yet, whenever they were able to work under suitable conditions in North America, they introduced—through such cartographers as Blaskowitz and D'Aubant—a touch of Continental professionalism to British military mapping.

Educational provision for the Continental Army was probably introduced too late to have a major effect on the quality of maps produced by the Americans in the Revolution. It nevertheless furnished another illustration of the way in which academies and schools were primary agents for the spread of military ideas. One of the first advocates of an American military academy was Henry Knox, Washington's chief of artillery, and this points to a British contribution to American military thinking. Knox, born in 1750, had joined the militia at eighteen. As owner of the London Book Store in Boston, he had read extensively on military matters. He was, moreover, an active member of the artillery company in that city.[98] Before the Revolution, Knox had obviously been exposed to British ideas. Thus it was natural that, initially at least, he should favor a British approach to technical training. As early as 1776 he was corresponding with John Adams, a member of the Board of War, about the desirability of founding academies for "educating young gentlemen in every branch of the military art."[99] In September 1776, Knox's "Hints to Congressional Committee now in Camp, Headquarters, Harleem Heights" contained the suggestion, "As officers can never act with confidence until they are Masters of their profession, an Academy established on a liberal plan would be of the utmost service to America, where the whole theory and practice of Fortifications and gunnery should be taught; to be nearly on the same plan as that of Woolwich making allowance for the difference of circumstances."[100]

The subsequent history of this proposal is a neat demonstration of how the military systems of different countries were blended during the Revolution. Congress appointed a committee to prepare a plan for "a military academy at the Army" in October 1776, but the resulting resolution of June 1777 abandoned the Woolwich model in favor of a "Corps of Invalids" (that is, veterans) as the means of educating young officers serving with their regiments.[101] The corps was to be directed by Colonel Lewis Nicola, a typically cosmopolitan figure. Nicola was born in France, educated in Ireland, and had reached Philadelphia from Dublin in 1766 with some twenty-six years of service as an army officer.[102] This meant that a French rather than an English influence came to predominate. The plan adopted by Congress was for a "school propagating military knowledge and discipline." Subaltern officers were to "be obliged to attend a mathematical school, appointed for the purpose, to learn geometry, arithmetic, vulgar and decimal fractions." The officers of the Corps of Invalids were to contribute one day's pay a month "for the purpose of purchasing a regimental library of the most approved authors on tactics and the petite guerre."[103] It was part of this corps that Washington transferred in 1778 to West Point, where it was consolidated in 1781. No doubt its teaching was intermittent and often hybrid, but when a French officer visited West Point in 1780, he was able to draw a detailed map of the fort, depicting, among other buildings, an *école du génie* and a *bibliothèque*. (see plate 19)[104]

The Establishment of a Military Academy by the United States

The Corps of Invalids made no significant contribution to the supply of technically trained officers during the Revolution, but it was extremely important in the sense that the corps constituted yet another institution encouraging the Americans to base their military practices (including the use of maps) on those of the Europeans. The American situation demanded that much of the officers' training be fitted in between spells of active service. Even so, the theoretical needs of the technical corps seem to have remained in the front of Washington's mind, and in 1778, in connection with setting up a company of sappers, he wrote:

Three Captains and nine Lieutenants are wanted to officer the Companies of Sappers: As this Corps will be a school of Engineering it opens a Prospect to such Gentlemen as enter it and will pursue the necessary studies with diligence, of becoming Engineers. . . . The Qualifications required of the candidates are that they . . . have a knowledge of the Mathematicks and drawing, or at least be disposed to apply themselves to those studies.[105]

It has already been shown how this conviction concerning the need for professional training was shared by a number of other senior officers. In 1783 both Duportail and von Steuben went as far as to draw up a more detailed plan for a military academy.[106] It was not, however, until 1802 that the United States Military Academy was permanently established at West Point.

MILITARY TEXTBOOKS AS CARRIERS OF CARTOGRAPHICAL INFORMATION

Much has been said about the importance of military textbooks as a key to the maps of the Revolution and as essential tools in educating the Revolutionary armies. So numerous and important were the textbooks as mediums of dissemination of cartographical ideas and techniques that they warrant separate study in this regard. Their particular importance was in carrying information far beyond the confines of military academies, thus making a special contribution to the professionalism of an American army in which formal military instruction was only beginning to take root by the end of the Revolution. The lack of a modern descriptive bibliography of eighteenth-century military textbooks precludes the much needed interpretative study of their cartographic content. There are limited bibliographies of the military sciences, including works in French, German, Italian, and Spanish, published before 1800.[107] These are supplemented by bibliographies of collections in various libraries, but even taken together they are unsuitable for an analysis of the spread of textbooks as artifacts.[108] Against this background, one of the more useful early bibliographies is Heinrich Friedrich Rumpf's *Allgemeine Literatur der Kriegswissenschaften,* published in 1824.[109] Rumpf may be used to sample some of the characteristics of the period's military textbooks as they relate to the spread of cartographical ideas.

A simplified interpretation of the mechanisms involved in the spread and adoption of military textbooks is given below. In Europe, in the British Isles, and in North America, three idealized stages have been recognized. While there were exceptions to this sequence, and not all textbooks passed through all stages, isolating some of the necessary and sufficient conditions nevertheless helps to demonstrate that textbooks did in fact exert a significant influence on Revolutionary cartography.

1. Origination in Europe

Rumpf provides useful data for the study of the salient characteristics of the military literature published in Europe during the seventy-five years or so leading up to the Revolution—literature that could have influenced the character of mili-

Table 2:1. Selected Military Tactics Textbooks, 1700–1783

Category (Classified under Tactics by Rumpf, 1824)	French	German	English	Other Languages	Total
1. Tactics in general	72	29	10	9	120
2. Elementary tactics[1]					
a. Infantry	20	35	8	5	68
b. Cavalry	14	12	2	10	38
c. Artillery	3	3	—	—	6
3. Sciences dealing with terrain[1]					
a. Preparatory sciences: land surveying, measuring, drawing plans, etc.	40	61	27	7	135
b. knowledge of terrain, military geography[2]	8	6	3	6	23
c. Fortification:					
Permanent	114	146	17	57	334
Temporary	8	22	2	1	33
4. Grand tactics[1]					
a. Infantry	7	5	1	—	13
b. Cavalry	9	8	—	2	19
c. Artillery	5	5	—	1	11
d. Engineers[3]	50	32	5	5	92
e. Marches and encampments	5	4	2	—	11
f. Light Infantry & *petite guerre*	10	11	1	—	22
Totals	365	379	78	103	925

1. The division is Rumpf's.
2. Excluding military maps and plans (that is, any published maps of potential value in campaigning), which are listed separately.
3. The division includes engineers, sappers, and pioneers.

tary mapmaking. Table 2:1 is an analysis by subject and language of publication of the works listed in the eighth part of his bibliography, relating to various aspects of tactics.[110] This table is based on the assumption that the tactics section, although its subdivisions overlap and there is some duplication of titles, contains at least a core of books of cartographic relevance.

Four general characteristics stand out. The first is the large number: almost a thousand relevant texts were published in the period 1700–1783. This may be regarded as a crude measure of the potential "population" of textbooks that could have influenced Revolutionary practice, although the total is almost certainly an underestimate. Many titles in earlier sections of the bibliography, such as those relating to the military art in general and to army administration (including some of the entries in military dictionaries and encyclopaedias), also contained material relevant to a study of military cartography in one of its several forms. On the eve of the Revolution, almost every important text had been published. There were exceptions, such as Bourcet's "Principes de la guerre de montagnes," which was still circulating in manuscript.[111] Yet even "secret" works found their way into print: the first essay of military importance by Frederick the Great, *Military Instructions for the Generals,* was written in 1747 and limited to his staff's use until the capture of one of his generals in 1760 led to its publication.[112]

A second point is that most textbooks were published in continental European countries: by comparison with Paris, even London was a relatively minor center in this trade. A third characteristic of the literature is the extent to which it was dominated by titles in French and German. Well over four-fifths of the titles included in table 2:1 originated in one or the other of these two languages, though the proportion varied among subjects. Moreover, when significant works were written in French or German, initial publication in one language was usually soon followed by translation into the other. Translation into other European languages was far less frequent. The textbooks confirm that throughout the Revolutionary period France and the German states were the leading centers of innovation in the teaching of those military sciences requiring the use of maps and plans.

A fourth characteristic is the extent of specialization within the literature. Many of the contemporary bibliographies, as well as Rumpf, were classified to take account of these divisions. In this respect the texts confirm the evidence of the surviving maps: the historian of military cartography is concerned with not one but several distinct mapmaking traditions.

The specializations within the literature also suggest that textbooks, as carriers of cartographical information, adopted a number of distinct geographical and chronological patterns in the course of the eighteenth century. This theory remains to be tested in a fuller study. For the present, Rumpf's titles can be simplified into two main categories: the great majority of texts that included material which may have affected mapping; and a mere handful of titles exclusively concerned with cartography.

In the first category fall most of the titles in Rumpf dealing with tactics in general, elementary tactics, and grand tactics, together with most works concerned with fortification. Throughout the Revolution, these more general works exerted the greatest influence on the British and American armies' approach to mapping.

Only a few textbooks were devoted primarily to military cartography. As might be expected, they fall within the "preparatory" sciences classification as defined by Rumpf, but the total in table 2 greatly exaggerates the number of cartographical works that can be classed as military by the time of the Revolution. Rumpf does indeed include many works on general land surveying in all languages, but this should serve to remind us that the military surveyor drew on the same basic mathematical and topographical skills as did his civilian counterpart.

If military cartography had been merely a specialized application of a general science, its detailed adaptation had already begun in France by the beginning of the eighteenth century. As early as 1693, Jacques Ozanam's *Méthode de lever les plans et les cartes de terre et de mer* had been published; it was reissued several times during the eighteenth century, and a completely revised edition was brought out in 1781.[113] Such textbooks were used by the two branches of the French service concerned with mapmaking—the *Corps Royal du Génie* and the *ingénieurs géographes.* Dupain de Montesson, an officer instructor in the latter corps, had become a leading writer on military mapmaking by 1775. In 1750 his *La Science des ombres* (containing a section on "Le Dessinateur au cabinet et à la armée") was published, but *L'Art de lever les plans* (1763, revised edition 1775) was especially designed to assist recruits training under the topographical engineers.[114] Among Dupain de

Montesson's pupils were the Berthier brothers (Rochambeau's cartographers in the American campaign), some of whose maps, as Rice and Brown point out, closely reflect methods set out in the textbooks by which they were taught.[115]

As table 2:1 suggests, the role of German writers in formalizing methods of military mapmaking during this period should not be underestimated. It is possible that in the art of rapid reconnaissance sketching (done "by eye") they led the field. Some German military cartographers were developing independent methods, and their textbooks reflected those field practices. An example of such a work was entitled *L'Ecole de l'officier, contenant une méthode de lever un plan sans l'usage de la géométrie ordinaire* (Paris, 1770). It is significant that, in a period when French writers often dominated the literature on military mapmaking, this was translated from the German.[116] In the same way, Pirscher's *Coup d'oeil militaire* (Berlin, 1775) serves to indicate the growing importance of German practice in the development of reconnaissance mapping.[117] Nevertheless, it was matched in the same year by the publication of a text of similar scope in Paris.[118]

In the description of the curriculum at the Woolwich academy, it has already been implied that British military theory leaned heavily on Continental ideas. From the more extensive evidence of the textbooks, it is clear that this had been the case since the sixteenth century.[119] English authors seldom disguised the foreign origin of their material—indeed it was often a hallmark of topicality to stress it—and even ostensibly original English books were almost invariably a digest of Continental authorities. Apart from their role in such summaries and reviews, Continental textbooks directly penetrated British military education as they were read in Britain, either in their original languages or in translation. That they were read in their original language is shown by the contents of several eighteenth-century British libraries.[120] Among the foreign authors consulted by Charles Vallancey in compiling his "Essay on Military Surveys," were Faesch, Feuquières, Folard, Frederick the Great, Saxe, and Turpin, as well as a volume of an unspecified *Cyclopaedia*.[121] It is, however, worth pointing out that Vallancey was born in Flanders of French parents.[122] He was probably better equipped linguistically than most British officers.

British students were also reached through translation of these texts into English. London was the main center for the publication of the translations, but Dublin, whose booksellers had direct links with the North American colonies, also shared in the trade. By the time of the Revolution, most of the classic European works on fortifications or tactics, in one recension or another, were available in English. These were the texts, in the distinction drawn above, that dealt with military mapping only incidentally to their main purpose. It may be equally significant that those titles dealing with cartographical matters exclusively were *not* translated into English in the Revolutionary era; they remained relatively unknown in British circles. Vallancey, perhaps the only British engineer of the period to attempt a treatise on military mapping, failed to refer to either Dupain de Montesson or Pirscher in his "Essay," and his knowledge seems to have been drawn from more general sources.

The effect of the Continental manuals on the British military cartography of the Revolutionary era was substantial. Military textbooks containing printed lists of subscribers suggest that though few titles were best sellers, a vital role of the textbook was to reach students outside the specialist courses at the academy in Woolwich.[123] After all, of the British corps of engineers in the period 1741–1781, barely more

2. Adaptation and Translation in the British Isles

than a third of the recruits were trained at Woolwich.[124] Add to these the handful of men passing through the Drawing Room of the Tower into the engineers, and still a majority remains who acquired their knowledge by other means. Many engineers were trained by apprenticeship in the field, and in this situation textbooks would have provided at least a smattering of theory for would-be practitioners. It is symbolic of the place of these texts in the career of many engineers that John Singleton Copley's portrait of Captain John Montresor, sometime chief British engineer during the Revolution, shows him holding a treatise on field engineering (see plate 20).[125]

Nor were the engineers the only officers to acquire professional skills through this medium. Subscribers to British military manuals often included officers of line and cavalry regiments, as well as senior staff administrators at army headquarters.[126] Finally, translations and digests of non-English works circulated in private military academies and in other schools that included military subjects in their curriculum. The mathematical foundations required for survey, navigation, and fortification were widely taught in eighteenth-century Britain.[127] There were, however, relatively few specialist schools to train young gentlemen for naval and military careers. One of the better known establishments was Lewis Lochée's military academy in Chelsea.[128] Lochée himself was a fairly prolific editor and translator of military texts originating on the Continent.

3. The Use of Textbooks by the Americans

By 1775, European textbooks had reached Revolutionary America through several channels. Some were imported directly from Europe; more often than not, the information they carried was filtered through English editions and translations. Their availability is revealed in the catalogues of colonial libraries.[129] After the start of hostilities, however, the supply of imported books tended to dry up and was supplemented by editions (including new digests and translations) from American presses. Even textbook writers were enlisted into the American cause. Lewis Nicola wrote *A Treatise of Military Exercises* (1776); he also produced new translations from the French of de Clairac's *Field Engineer* (previously translated into English by Muller) and of Grandmaison's *Treatise, on the Military Service, of Light Horse and Light Infantry* (1777).[130] For a time, Philadelphia was a center for such publications, and it was from there that Robert Aitken issued Roger Stevenson's *Military Instructions for Officers Detached in the Field* (1775), as well as Nicola's translation of de Clairac. Among other Philadelphia publishers of military works were Styner and Cist, who in 1779 ("According to the second London edition") pirated John Muller's *Treatise of Artillery,* and Robert Bell, who brought out James Wolfe's *Instructions to Young Officers* (1778) just ten years after its first appearance in London.[131]

These titles provide examples of the spate of books about military administration, discipline, tactics, and techniques that helped to make the Continental experience almost as freely available to the Americans as it was to their British opponents. Indeed, taken as a whole and considering that there were fewer titles, the literature published in America was not dissimilar to that then circulating in the British Isles. Some of the more important works were the same, and there was also a similar absence of manuals specifically dealing with military mapmaking. The Americans thus picked up part of their approach to the making and use of maps and plans from general tactical works, such as Stevenson's *Military Instructions,* which dwelt more on the role of maps than on minor technicalities of survey and drawing.

The Stevenson work also exemplified part of a process by which European ideas were adapted in an American context. What was remarkable, however, was the degree to which a European approach was retained in the new environment. In its preliminaries, at least, this was an American book designed to instruct new patriots. It was, symbolically enough, dedicated to George Washington, and the title page explains that it contains "A Scheme for Forming a Corps of a Partisan. Illustrated with Plans of the Manoeuvres necessary in Carrying on the *Petite Guerre.*" A reliance on *petite guerre* (to the avoidance of major confrontations and formal set pieces which had characterized the battlefields of eighteenth-century Europe) was, as military historians have noted, a major plank of American strategy in the Revolution. It should be clearly stated: this was an essentially European idea, for which North America provided a testing ground. The same was true of the cartographic support required for this type of warfare. Most of Stevenson's ideas, as illustrated in chapter 1, derived directly from European writers,[132] but either through haste or lack of finesse as a textbook writer, he neglected to tailor his advice to an American audience. A passage concerning the use and making of campaign maps quotes from the "method of Mr. Jeney for getting intelligence without approaching [the enemy], and taking plans and observations."[133] Stevenson's carelessness resulted in a bizarre passage in which an American user would have to transplant himself mentally to Europe where, finding himself in the Westphalian countryside, he is told how to make a plan extending into enemy territory (see plate 21). The essence of the method was that a tracing was first made from the best available printed map, after which details were verified and amplified by field observation and inquiry. In this Westphalian example, the officer had been advised to "go to the burgomaster of the town . . . [and] cause some of the most intelligent inhabitants to come, speaking to them freely, and openly to induce them to communicate all the information . . . [you] have occasion for."[134] In their own theater of war, such advice was heeded by some of the American staff officers, though it is impossible to say whether this was because they had read Stevenson or just the exercise of plain common sense. Washington intermittently maintained a pocket map, traced from printed maps available to him, on which he made his own annotations.[135]

From fragmentary examples such as this and from surviving maps, it is possible to assert that the textbooks did contribute materially to the Americans' use of maps. Their importation into America and consequent republication (in some cases during the Revolution) established that texts were potentially capable of transmitting information into a new theater of war. In order to show that this actually occurred, it would be necessary to prove that the texts were indeed read and used by those involved in making military decisions about maps. Naturally enough, Stevenson would have had it so. In his preface, he informed potential American readers that, "In a country where every gentleman is a soldier, and every soldier a *student* in the art of war, it necessarily follows that military treatises will be considerably sought after, and attended to."[136] What is more valuable is some independent corroboration that his fellow revolutionaries had taken the advice to heart. One such piece of evidence comes from the postwar pen of Captain Johann Ewald of the Jäger Corps, writing after he had made a special study of American tactics. The Continental Army's attention to theory had made a deep impression on him:

I was sometimes astonished when American baggage fell into our hands . . . to see how every wretched knapsack, in which were only a few shirts and a pair of torn breeches, would be filled with such military works as "The Instructions of the King of Prussia to his Generals," Thielke's "Field Engineer," the partisans Jenny and Grandmaison. . . . This was a true indication that the officers of this army studied the art of war while in camp, which was not the case of the opponents of the Americans, whose portmanteaux were rather filled with bags of hair powder, boxes of sweet-smelling pomatum, cards (instead of maps), and then often, on top of all, novels or stage plays.[137]

This testimony could be regarded as a little biased, as Hessian memories of the war were often bitter. Yet other sources also describe the great extent to which the senior American officers were often self-taught, with the help of European texts. It was certainly true of Henry Knox, whose Boston store was a point of entry for European books. One of Knox's biographers wrote, "By conversing with the British officers who frequented his bookstore, by earnest study of military authors and by careful observation of the soldiery in Boston, he soon attained great proficiency in the theory and practice of the military art."[138]

He was indeed well read enough to be regarded as an authority. John Adams wrote to him from Philadelphia in November 1775 to inquire: "What is comprehended within the term Engineer? and whether it includes skill both in fortifications and gunnery. . . . I want to know if there is a complete set of books upon the military art in all its branches in the library of Harvard College, and what books are the best upon those subjects."[139] Another general officer who could have answered the last part of this question was Nathanael Greene. He was a particularly assiduous student of military writings, including Sharp's *Military Guide* and the works of Saxe and Turenne.[140] As both quartermaster general and commander-in-chief of the southern campaign that led to Yorktown, Greene demonstrated his detailed grasp of tactics involving the commissioning or use of maps.

It is, however, the career of Washington that provides the best documented (and from a cartographic standpoint, probably the most significant) illustration of the absorption of European ideas into American strategic thinking and organization. As a headquarters aide in Braddock's army, Washington was even then attempting to adapt European tactics to the American environment; he was modeling himself on the best textbooks of his day, as is shown by his "Plan for a Line of March in Forest Country" (1758), which summarized the tactics in a diagrammatic map.[141] Later Washington gave what support he could to proposals for new texts. In August 1777, for example, he wrote to Baron de Holtzendorff about a "plan of a military work" with the observation that if it were "well executed . . . few good books we have circulating in this Country on the Military art, afford a favourable prospect of the publication being attended with success and utility."[142] Equally suggestive of Washington's zeal for military knowledge were the contents of his library. Among the books he had collected were the Dublin edition of de Clairac's *Field Engineer,* the two volumes of Le Blond's *The Military Engineer,* John Muller's *Treatise on Artillery* and his *Treatise on Fortification,* Count Saxe's *Plan for New-Modelling the French Army,* Thomas Simes' *The Military Guide for Young Officers* (the Philadelphia edition, dedicated to Washington), and Roger Stevenson's *Military Instructions.*[143] All these titles had a strong European flavor and contained explicit cartographic advice. It is perhaps ironic that, while cadets at Woolwich were studying translations of European texts, Washington, as an officer in the Virginia militia, was digesting much the same lessons. Textbooks undoubtedly helped to form his approach to military mapping, just as they did that of his fellow officers and their English, French, and Hessian counterparts in the Revolution. Indeed, such importance did Washington attach to textbooks that in 1777 he opened his "General Instructions for the Colonels and Commanding Officers of Regiments in the Continental Service" with the order: "As War is a Science, and a great deal of useful knowledge and instruction [is] to be drawn from Books, you are to cause your Officers to devote some part of their time to reading Military Authors."[144] A full study of the textbooks as carriers of cartographical ideas, attempting an analysis of their content as well as an assessment of their impact, would make a valuable contribution to the history of military mapping in the eighteenth century.

The provision made for surveying and copying maps within the two main Revolutionary armies was a critical part of the environment of military cartographers, and one which provided an organizational framework for important sectors of the mapping accomplished during the Revolution. In 1775, neither the American forces nor the British army in North America had developed headquarters units specialized in making maps for tactical movement as opposed to plans for fortification. The development of such units as additions to existing headquarters staff was an important aspect of cartographical change. It was, after all, only through regular employment of trained mapmakers that military teaching about maps could finally and properly be put into practice. There was no exact equivalence between the arrangements for mapmakers attached to British and to American headquarters, and both sides continued to employ amateurs as well as professionals in many situations. Nevertheless, despite the survival of a great deal of improvisation, there was a tendency for more formal arrangements to arise during the course of the Revolution. It is this growth of a cartographic professionalism—its origins, characteristics, and consequences—which will now be assessed.

MILITARY ORGANIZATION AND MAPMAKING

One of the more interesting specialist cartographic units to be set up as a direct result of the Revolution was the tiny group of mapmakers known as geographers who were attached to the Continental Army. The steps leading to the establishment of this subcorps (initially within the Corps of Engineers but later affiliated with the quartermaster's department[145]) have been described by several authorities.[146] It is well known that it arose from the difficulties Washington experienced in trying to obtain adequate maps with which to plan his campaign. In November 1776, he wrote to John Augustine Washington, "It is not in my power to furnish you with so extensive a Draft as you require, as I have none but printed Maps of the Country you wish to see deleneated, and have no person about me that has time enough to Copy one, but a rough sketch of the Country in whc. we have been Manourvreing, and which I had taken off to carry in my pocket, I enclose you [the latter] as it will afford some Idea of the parts adjacent to New York."[147] At this date apparently even the commander-in-chief was forced to control his army's movements with only the aid of inadequate sketch maps—these he may even have traced himself from small scale printed maps lacking much of the necessary terrain detail.

It was against such a background that, in January 1777, Washington wrote from his New Jersey headquarters to draw the attention of Congress as forcefully as pos-

Mapmaking at American Headquarters

sible to his problem: "The want of accurate Maps of the Country which has hitherto been the Scene of War, has been of great disadvantage to me. I have in vain endeavoured to procure them, and have been obliged to make shift, with such Sketches, as I could trace out from my own Observations, and that of Gentlemen around me."[148] He went on to make a specific proposal that "if Gentlemen of known Character and probity, could be employed in making Maps (from actual Survey) of the Roads, Rivers, Bridges and Fords over them, the Mountains and passes thro' them, it would be of the greatest Advantage."[149] There is no record of any immediate response to this request. As the likelihood of a British attack grew greater in the summer of 1777, Washington also tried to enlist the support of individual states. On 9 July he wrote to "President Thomas Wharton, Junior, and the Pennsylvania Council," entreating them to find "accurate Draughts or Maps of the Country which is or may be the Seat of War, so essentially necessary, that I must beg leave to recommend such a Measure with all possible Expedition, so far as regards the Shores of the Delaware, where the Enemy may probably land and March. . . . In the execution of this Work I could wish the Eminences, Distances of Places, Woods, Streams of Water, Marshy places and passes may be particularly noted. And that it be done on as large a Scale as is tolerably convenient."[150] Later in the same month he was still pressing Congress to appoint "a good Geographer to Survey the Roads and take Sketches of the Country where the Army is to Act," and his proposal was sufficiently developed for him to have in mind a suitable candidate for the appointment. This was Robert Erskine, who was "thoroughly skilled in this business" and had "already assisted us in making Maps of the Country."[151] On this occasion, Congress acted with unusual speed, and on 25 July it was resolved: "That General Washington be empowered to appoint Mr. Robert Erskine, or any other person that he may think proper, geographer and surveyor of the roads, to take sketches of the country, the seat of war, and to have the procuring, governing and paying the guides employed under him."[152] Three days later, Washington wrote to Erskine offering him the appointment and inquiring about "the conditions on which it will Suit you to undertake it."[153]

A formal mapmaking unit was thus set up in the Continental Army at Washington's request, and it was operational by the late summer of 1777. The idea arose from both his military planning experience in the first two years of the war and his bookish acquaintance with the best practices of European warfare. Indeed, some of Washington's orders on mapping read like half-digested textbook passages. His didactic bent surfaces in a letter written shortly after Erskine's appointment in August 1777:

As an accurate knowledge of the Country is essential to a good defence, and as the Enemy's approach may be sudden and we may be called to act, without having time . . . it would answer a valuable purpose, to have it immediately carefully reconnoitred, and sketches taken of all the landing places, great roads, and bye-paths, encamping grounds, heights, Rivers, creeks, morasses, and everything that it can be of any importance to know.[154]

The appointment of a geographer to the army can thus be regarded as a modest American counterpart (in fact, not fully implemented until 1813) of the French *ingénieurs géographes* or some of the *Quartermeister* staff in the Prussian army.[155] The very selection of Robert Erskine, a surveyor of British civilian background, as the first appointee to this post is proof of Washington's gift for improvisation and neatly points to the hybrid character of much of Revolutionary mapmaking.

In some respects it is hard to assess the military significance of this post. Erskine's appointment in 1777 did not represent an entirely novel departure in Washington's view of his headquarters staff. As with many administrative acts, it partly represented a formalization and extension of an existing practice. Washington's statement in recommending Erskine to Congress that the surveyor had already assisted him is confirmed by other records.[156] Erskine was not the sole officer to be so employed. Before the staff position of geographer had been created, it was accepted that wherever possible a surveyor ought to be attached to military expeditions. It was to undertake such duties that John Pierce accompanied Arnold's otherwise ill-prepared party on the march to Quebec.[157] Even in its embryonic period of staff organization, the Continental Army was making an effort to recruit men with map-making skills.

Since much of the essential work of the geographer was already being carried out before 1777, it is understandable that the newly created corps did not immediately establish a monopoly in the making of American military maps. The geographer's staff in the remaining years of the Revolution consisted of little more than twenty recruited individuals, not all of them working at once.[158] The corps was never large enough to satisfy all the map demands of Washington's headquarters. This was true even after their strength had been increased in July 1781 by the appointment of Thomas Hutchins as geographer to the southern army.[159] The small size of the unit as late as November 1782 was implied by the rather meager provision made by Congress in its resolution that:

The geographer to the main army and the geographer to the southern department be each of them allowed 60 dollars per month, three rations per day, forage for two saddle horses, one two-horse covered wagon, 6 2/3d dollars per month for a servant, for whom they shall be entitled to draw one ration per day and the clothing allowed to a private soldier.

That the assistant geographer, if such officers shall be judged necessary by the Commander in Chief, be allowed 30 dollars per month, one ration per day, and forage for one saddle horse.[160]

This would seem to confirm that the arrangements secured by Washington fell far short of his needs. Notwithstanding the long-term and rather grandiose cartographic ambitions of both Erskine and De Witt, they clearly remained very much at the beck and call of their commander-in-chief. The nature of eighteenth-century warfare, alternating between a summer campaign and a winter season spent largely in camp, meant that surveyors were often diverted at short notice to new assignments. In August 1779, Washington was writing to Erskine from West Point, "Are the cross roads between the Sussex and Morristown Roads Surveyed? If they are I wish to have them laid down on my pocket Map as soon as possible; If they are not, no time should be lost in the completion of this necessary work."[161] Although they were sometimes placed under the command of other officers (such as the quartermaster general) or sent on surveys far from headquarters, the geographers were an integral part of the personal staff of the commander—both under Washington and under Greene in the southern army.

The other factor that made it impossible for Erskine, and later De Witt and

Hutchins, to provide enough of the new maps needed by the Americans was the immense area over which the war could range. Geographical distance, as much as anything else, forced Washington to supplement the geographers' activities in three main ways. First, with some regularity, he was able to call on the engineers, who were trained to make maps of the surroundings of fortifications, to help in the production of topographical maps. In June 1779, Washington had given an order from his headquarters at Smith's Tavern, New York: "The Chief Engineer will furnish the General with a draft of West Point and its environs, including the communications with this Camp. The roads leading from June's and the Widow Van Ambra's to the Furnace of Deane are in the first instance to be ascertained. The Geographer's will assist in this business."[162] With these maps, as with others, engineers and geographers were working in tandem, and their respective contributions as cartographers would hardly have been distinguishable.

Washington's second method of supplementing the geographers' activities was to attach to army headquarters those line regiment officers known to be skilled as mapmakers. This was the case with Benjamin Lodge, who was on the rolls of various units of the Pennsylvania Regiment,[163] but who in 1779 and 1780 was largely employed as an assistant on cartographic duties—under Nathanael Greene,[164] and later when he accompanied the western expedition of Major General John Sullivan.[165]

Third, Washington frequently had to rely for better or worse on more distant correspondents to supply him with maps, especially when he was planning activities on the periphery of the main theater of war. Thus in July 1780, he wrote to Jonathan Trumbull, governor of Connecticut:

It is a matter of great importance for me to be acquainted with our several Harbours, their depth of Water within and leading to them, and all the difficulties and circumstances attending their navigation. At present this knowledge is more peculiarly essential with respect to the Eastern Ports and particularly in the instance of New London. . . . I have therefore to intreat the favor of Your Excellency to furnish me by the earliest opportunity, with a correct map of that Harbour, in case you have one, describing in a particular manner the Channel leading to it, from the Sound, with its depth and width and such obstacles and Shoals as may attend the navigation. If your Excellency should not be in possession of a map that will answer, I request that you will be so obliging as to procure me one as soon as it can be done . . . even by an actual survey and sounding.[166]

By such means—a small corps of professional mapmakers and a handful of other surveyors drafted for some assignments, and the help of maps begged and borrowed from his many correspondents—Washington gradually built up an operational archive of maps at his headquarters. It included maps sent to him on request, the printed maps to which he refers from time to time, and also copies of the manuscript surveys of the geographers and of other Continental Army officers. There can be no doubt that Washington considered the acquisition of these maps a matter of major importance. Many of his orders to his aides must have been dictated with map in hand. The headquarters map collection was also a source of supply for the maps required by other general officers for campaigning purposes. In May 1779, Washington sent to Sullivan, in connection with the Indian expedition, "the best maps I have of the country."[167] Writing to Major General Arthur St. Clair during the following month, he enclosed "a little sketch that will serve to give you an idea of the country you are in."[168] To Colonel Richard Butler, he explained later in the same month that "the inclosed map is from actual survey and is intended for the use of the Commanding Officer at the post."[169] This map was annotated by means of letters to indicate a suitable site for encampment and the probable spot where the enemy forces would land. It was to provide such terrain and intelligence maps that Washington, modeling himself on European practice, had created a small mapmaking organization at his headquarters, one that he clearly used on many occasions.

Mapmaking arrangements at British headquarters in North America during the Revolution give the initial impression of greater sophistication than the American camp had achieved. One or two writers have argued that the British were better served with maps, especially at the beginning of the Revolution.[170] Coupled with this view, there is the impressive evidence of the large surviving corpus of maps from British headquarters. Recently, on the basis of maps found in Sir Henry Clinton's papers, it has even been suggested that a collection of perhaps some twenty thousand British maps once existed.[171] The impression, in any event, is that the British working archives may have exceeded the cartographic resources of the Americans, though there is little firm evidence of this. These are perhaps only superficial comparisons. A closer examination of the organizational framework of British Revolutionary mapmaking reveals that the main features are often those already described for Washington's army. Moreover, so strong were the common threads in the military tradition that, if some differences in nomenclature are ignored, the same elements can be detected—modeled on the organization of general staffs in other European armies.

The British also regarded mapmaking as an activity to be carried on by a specialist staff, usually located with (and closely controlled by) army headquarters. A partial exception to this formulation, however, was the detachment of mapmakers to regional headquarters, below the organizational level of the main army. It would have been surprising if an army as well drilled in European methods as the Hessian organization had not brought some mapmakers with them to North America. Guthorn has identified several cartographers attached to the Hessian headquarters. They included Captain Reinard Jacob Martin of the Engineers, thirty-four of whose maps have survived, and de Gironcourt, who seems to have succeeded him in maintaining a map record of the Hessian part in the war.[172] Even small units tended to parallel the staff structure of the main army. British expeditionary forces during the Revolution were, as a result, usually accompanied by a mapmaker or two.[173] Even a provincial corps, such as Simcoe's Queen's Rangers, had a rudimentary staff organization to delegate the making of occasional maps to a competent officer and to insure that there was also a register of experienced guides to serve in areas where adequate maps were lacking.[174]

The British, like the Americans, decided that some of their map needs would best be met by setting up a specialized unit. This was the so-called Corps of Guides and Pioneers which, as its name suggests, also mustered men to construct roads and for duties such as mending bridges and felling trees when the army was on the move. It was however, not dissimilar in conception to the American geographers. What is of equal interest is not that the British should have created such a unit but rather that at the start of the Revolution they possessed no professional mapmaking organization—as the *ingénieurs géographes*—ready for service at army headquarters. As we have seen, Vallancey and Mackenzie had commented on this deficiency, and

Mapmaking at British Headquarters

Gage was hard put in 1775 to find men capable of making maps in the countryside around Boston.[175] Moreover, when the Corps of Guides and Pioneers was established, it was an *ad hoc* unit—it might even be termed an amateur solution—rather than an attempt to make a fully regular addition to the military machine at headquarters. In this matter the British were perhaps less in touch with the best Continental practice than were the Americans.

Guides and pioneers were widely employed in European armies throughout the eighteenth century, but the Corps of Guides and Pioneers may have developed from the British experience of military mapping in other colonial territories. It could be coincidence, of course, but in May 1773 a similar corps had been formed in India: the local commander-in-chief in Madras, General Joseph Smith, had put forward a scheme for raising a corps of guides under the quartermaster general. His main object was "to procure or form as accurate a Chart as possible of all the principal places in the Country their situations & Bearings from each other, with the nature of the Roads between, and their distance; . . . to form a compleat Military Chart."[176] What may be slightly more than coincidence, however, was that a Captain Henry Amand Montresor of the Madras engineers was appointed by the directors of the East India Company to oversee the survey and the guides. He was the brother of John Montresor, the chief engineer in North America, who served on Howe's staff at the beginning of the Revolution.[177] Although Henry died in 1773 before he could take up his appointment, this illustrates one possible channel, within a network of the British empire and a family of engineers, by which an idea could have reached North America. Its main advantage lay in harnessing local ability among the loyalists, while simultaneously economizing on skilled manpower—especially that of engineers, who were also required for fortification duties.

Whatever the truth about the corps' model, an apparently authoritative statement on its formation occurs in a report of 1782 made by Alexander Innes, inspector general of provincial forces, to Sir Guy Carleton, who had succeeded Clinton as commander-in-chief in North America. The report asserts: "The Corps of Guides & Pioneers were originally formed by the Orders of Sir William Howe, by the Quarter Master General, attached to his Department, and paid by him till the 24th December, 1777, after which period the detachment of that Corps that accompanied Sir William Howe to Pennsylvania were ordered to be paid by the pay Master of Provincial Forces and commenced accordingly."[178] The main implication of Innes's account is that the corps had a double administrative origin. Initially, it was a unit under the direct control of the quartermaster general's department, but later it was transferred to the establishment of the provincial regiments.

It was the establishment of the corps within the quartermaster general's department that provided a precedent for including trained cartographers among its officers. In some respects the staff organization at British army headquarters was more inchoate than that of either the French or Prussians. Mapmaking nevertheless formed an essential part of reconnaissance, route finding, and encampment; it had long been regarded as within the province of the quartermaster general's department.[179] It was Colonel David Watson, as deputy quartermaster general in North Britain, with William Roy as an assistant, who had undertaken the seminal military survey of Scotland in the mid-eighteenth century.[180] Later, Watson had also organized military reconnaissance maps executed in southern England, and these were similar to some made by the British headquarters during the Revolution.[181] It may also be significant that in 1775 there were a few officers in the quartermaster general's headquarters in London who possessed cartographic experience. Notable among them was Daniel Paterson, veteran cartographer of the 1745 Rebellion,[182] who had been stationed in New York in the 1760s[183] and was better known as compiler of a roadbook of Britain.[184] (In part this can be interpreted as a civilian counterpart of a common type of military map.) Against such a background, it was predictable that the army in North America should try to establish a unit capable of discharging some of the recognized campaigning functions of the quartermaster general's department. The precise way in which it was established and developed reflected conditions in North America, as well as an evident shortage of trained military surveyors.

Thus, factors particular to North America influenced the 1777 decision to transfer the corps to the establishment of the provincial regiments. This probably had no cartographic significance and was no more than an administrative device to give satisfactory commissioned rank to skilled mapmakers and loyalist guides who lacked a formal regimental or engineer background. This presented a problem of establishment to which Clinton alludes in a letter to Germain.[185] If this was the case, it was a compromise reflecting a lack of conviction that the principal mapmakers to the army ought, in the French and American manner, to be a fully established part of the headquarters' staff.

A shortage of suitable recruits was manifest in the diverse background of the cartographers in the corps, including a reliance on men already established as mapmakers in North America before the Revolution. Among these, though his appointment was shortlived, Samuel Holland, veteran of the general survey in North America, was probably the most experienced. In 1775, he was still employed under the Board of Trade in surveys of New England, but from 4 March 1776 he was appointed as a major in the guides and pioneers.[186] Commissioned into the corps doubtless to strengthen its ability to carry out surveys, very few maps attributable to Holland can be dated to the period of the Revolution.[187] He soon disappears from the muster rolls of officers in the regiment.[188] A likely explanation is that Holland left the corps when it was reformed as a provincial unit and was thereafter engaged in other headquarters duties.

Nothwithstanding Holland's departure and the lessened role of the quartermaster general's department in the affairs of the corps (though the department could have largely continued to direct activities), it was still staffed after 1777 by a small number of trained surveyors and draftsmen. Charles Blaskowitz and Pierre Nicole, it was claimed, "Served as Surveyors all the war."[189] Like Holland, Blaskowitz had previously worked on the coastal survey of North America, passing through the grades of "volunteer surveyor," "assistant surveyor," and "deputy surveyor,"[190] before being appointed a captain in the guides and pioneers on 3 May 1777, a rank he retained until 1783.[191] Nicole, of Swiss origin, also held the rank of captain, but in addition to being a mapmaker and draftsman (his drafting skill was praised by Montresor[192]), he was employed on intelligence duties in liaison with the loyalists. Later in the war, probably in 1780 or 1781, the cartographic strength of the corps was again increased by the arrival of George Taylor and Andrew Skinner, both experienced land surveyors. Their road surveys before coming to America—of the roads between London, Bath, and Bristol; of Scotland; and of Ireland[193]—were so similar to Paterson's contemporary roadbooks that it is tempting to believe that it was Paterson, as an assistant quartermaster general in London, who recommended them for service in America.

As far as mapmaking was concerned, these five officers—Holland, Blaskowitz, Nicole, Taylor, and Skinner—were the real professionals of the unit. A few other officers, including Abraham Close and William MacAlpine, sometimes made maps, but together with the rest of the corps they worked mainly as guides and on other intelligence duties. On such occasions, the corps as a whole moved with the army. When the army was divided, a detachment of the corps (never large in number[194]) went with it. According to the "Memorial" of Major John Aldington, the officer commanding the corps for much of the war, it had "constantly been on service from the year 1776 to the Capitulation of New York, Vitz at Danbury in the Jerseys, from the Head of Elk to Philadelphia, at the Reduction of Forts Clinton and Montgomery, at Rhode Island, Bedford, and Marthas Vineyard—at the reduction of Charlestown and through the Southern Provinces—at Cape Fear with General Leslie, and in Virginia with General Arnold."[195] This testimony explains the presence of map-makers at a number of actions. For example, Charles Blaskowitz, even before he was commissioned in the guides and pioneers, had made surveys of "Frog's Neck and the Rout of the British Army to the 24th. of October 1776, under the Command of . . . William Howe" and of White Plains.[196] Thereafter, he seems to have continued in the role of official cartographer at a number of major actions. In November 1777 he was at the Siege of Fort Mifflin and in 1780 at the Siege of Charleston. On plans of both these actions, he described himself as "Captain of Guides & Pioneers," and he tells us that the plan of Charleston was "surveyed during & after the Siege."[197] Later, still with Clinton, he returned to New York, where his colonial experience as a coastal surveyor evidently stood him in good stead: he compiled the hydrographic detail off Sandy Hook for his map of New York and Staten Island.[198]

A third way in which the British organization of mapmaking paralleled that of the Americans was in the practice of attaching surveyors and draftsmen, whatever their formal regimental affiliations, to the personal staff of the commander-in-chief. In an age in which generals often regarded their headquarters maps and papers as their own personal property (rather than as belonging to the official record), such an approach was a normal one. Indeed it could be argued, to a certain extent, that the organization of headquarters into different units was more a matter of mustering men on paper than a practical reality, and that the assignments of corps with complementary functions were often blurred. As a result, men from the engineers and the guides and pioneers were seconded from time to time to undertake surveys for the commander-in-chief. Just as Duportail and other French engineers were detailed by Washington to mapmaking rather than strictly to engineering duties so, too, Montresor and the British engineers stationed in North America were often given staff duties—some of a cartographical nature.[199] At one moment, Montresor, who had been attached to the headquarters' staff of Sir William Howe, was moved to complain of the "despotic Power of Commanders in Chief abroad."[200] Such was the fluidity of headquarters arrangements that his situation was in no sense unique. Among the guides and pioneers, Taylor and Skinner worked largely around and within the New York headquarters of the British Army. At one point, Skinner was employed as cartographer by the adjutant general, whose responsibilities included direction of military intelligence, and maps obviously played a vital part in the collection of information about terrain under enemy control, fortifications, and troop dispositions.[201] Taylor also surveyed under Clinton's eye. On at least one map, Taylor and Skinner describe themselves as "Surveyors to his Excellency The Commander in Chief."[202]

This last type of appointment may be closer to the heart of the cartographic arrangements at British headquarters than its formal organization plan would indicate. At least five or six cartographers are known to have worked in a personal capacity for British generals. The fact that some topographical maps were made, as their titles inform us, "by order," presupposes that such personnel were available at headquarters and that there was a drawing room and suitable map store in New York. There is no better testimony to these policies than in the impressive collection of maps, plans, and sketches accumulated in Clinton's headquarters during his period of command in North America.[203] Most of them were the working tools of his tactical maneuvering, his battles, reconnaissances, and defensive arrangements from the New York headquarters and elsewhere. Among the men who worked mainly at headquarters to produce such maps were Samuel Holland (after he left the guides and pioneers); Claude Joseph Sauthier, employed on Howe's staff after the landing on Staten Island in 1776 (and later on detachment from the main army with Earl Percy, with whom he returned to England[204]); Thomas Wheeler, an engineer draftsman transferred to Howe's personal staff in June 1777;[205] and Taylor and Skinner.

Certainly one of the most interesting of the "personal" cartographers was John Hills. He was variously designated as an "extra draftsman," an "assistant engineer," a "surveyor and draftsman," "Lieutenant in the 23rd Regiment," and finally, in a 1782 map of part of eastern New Jersey, as "Private Surveyor and Draftsman to his Excellency the Commander in Chief."[206] Hills's elusiveness in the documents may merely reflect a lack of formalization in Clinton's arrangements. Men were simply seconded if they had the necessary skills. In New York, for example, Montresor, an engineer, was an active mapmaker, and in the Rhode Island garrison, Captain Abraham D'Aubant of the engineers and Edward Fage, an artillery officer, drew several of the more important surveys of the garrisoned territory around Newport.[207]

It is now possible to generalize about the mapmaking arrangements that either existed or were developed during the course of the Revolution. Although the component parts of the headquarters staffs of the various armies had different names and varied relative strengths, their underlying command structure and breakdown of specialist duties were much the same. This structure is summarized in figure 2:2, emphasizing the main operational contexts in which maps were made— by the personal staff to the commander-in-chief, in the quartermaster general's and adjutant general's departments, and within specialized units such as the engineers, the geographers, and the guides and pioneers. The diagram is accordingly a key to the organization of mapmaking in the headquarters of all the Revolutionary armies and demonstrates the widespread common approach to cartographic provision throughout the Revolution.

At the same time, figure 2:2 is an idealized structure. It could be argued that the extent to which the actual organization within a particular army matched these arrangements (as measured by the regimental or other affiliations of its recorded

General Characteristics of Headquarters' Mapmaking

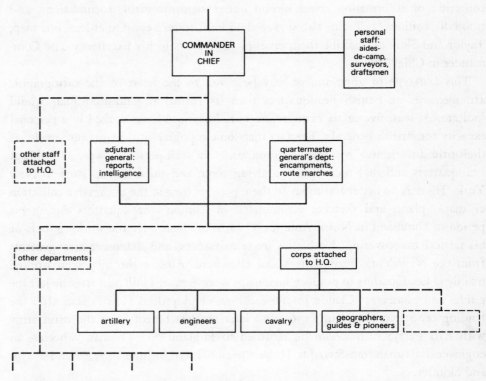

Figure 2:2 Organization chart summarizing the hierarchy of headquarters' staffs of the Revolutionary armies.

mapmakers) is one index of its professionalism, and whether or not it conformed to the teaching of contemporary military scientists. Another advantage of setting the evidence of the surviving maps against the administrative structures identified in textbooks and other sources is that the former provide an independent measure of the relative importance of groups (such as engineers or geographers) who have already been identified in a qualitative manner as making significant contributions.

Mapmaking as practiced by the French during the Revolution can be relatively easily dealt with, since it was largely carried out under one or another of the units identified in figure 2:2. Although Rice and Brown have divided the output of the French cartographers into maps produced by "amateurs or semi-professionals," the corps of Royal Engineers, and by the Topographical Engineers,[208] they can all be classified as headquarters staff. In the absence of any study of French Revolutionary cartography in the manner of Guthorn's enumeration of American and British mapmakers, it has not been possible to quantify the relative contribution of different groups of mapmakers. The impression is of a high degree of professionalism, with the trained manpower at headquarters being sufficient for the demands made on it by the American campaigns. When the French arrived in North America, however, the Revolution was already two-thirds over. They operated in a relatively limited theater of war (the Yorktown campaign) so that their resources were not particularly stretched and their problems were not representative of those faced by the mapmakers of the main combatants.

Guthorn's data shows the extent to which mapmaking was carried out by headquarters staff and, among that staff, the balance between different groups of cartographers. The results of looking at the evidence in this way are summarized in

Table 2:2. Regimental Attachments of American and British Mapmakers
in the Revolution

Type of attachment[1]	Numbers of Cartographers				Numbers of Maps[2]			
	American		British		American		British	
	No.	%	No.	%	No.	%	No.	%
Headquarters mapmakers[3]	5	10.2	9	10	11	3.7	143	26.9
Mapmaking corps[4]	6	12.2	5	5.5	157	53.2	30	5.6
Engineers[5] and Artillery	17	34.7	23	25.5	65	22	140	26.4
Line Regiments and Cavalry	8	16.3	33	36.6	41	13.8	133	25.1
Civilian and others[6]	13	26.5	20	22.2	21	7.0	84	15.8
Totals	49	100	90	100	295	100	530	100

SOURCE: Based on Guthorn (1966) and (1972)
1. Individuals have been classified under the duties they were performing when they made maps rather than their training or original affiliation.
2. Parts of the same map (as with the Erskine-De Witt maps) have not been enumerated separately.
3. Includes staff officers working as aides, general officers in staff appointments, and "personal" cartographers attached to the commander-in-chief.
4. The geographers and the guides and pioneers, respectively, for the British and the Americans.
5. Includes men designated as "assistant engineers."
6. The British figures include inshore maps and charts by naval officers.

table 2:2, and that can form the basis for three main conclusions—despite considerable imperfections in the data.[209]

When the regimental affiliations of mapmakers are analyzed, they confirm the danger of confusing administrative symmetry on paper with the reality of the day-to-day running of a campaign. It is clear that both the Americans and the British had to rely on some nonprofessionals which is perhaps a measure of the failure of their staff organization to meet all the cartographic needs of the Revolution. Even where men were attached to headquarters, sometimes for only short periods, some officers served in more than one capacity: Benjamin Lodge was recorded both as an infantry officer and was also attached to the geographers; for the British, Thomas Barrette worked as an infantry officer, an aide de camp at headquarters, and an assistant engineer. One surprising feature of table 2:2 is that, looking at the numbers of men recorded as making maps for the British, the line regiments were almost as important as the technical corps. Indeed, one or two regiments built up modest reputations for their ability to supply staff officers capable of performing cartographic as well as other headquarters duties. Such a regiment was the twenty-third, or the Royal Welch Fusiliers—at least five of its officers, Barrette, Brown, Hills, Mackenzie, and Williams—made maps for the British during the Revolution. Civilians who made maps for the British also comprised a relatively high proportion—above one-fifth—of the total of all mapmakers.

If the total number of maps made by each group is examined, then the balance is redressed in favor of the groups of professional mapmakers at headquarters. This was especially true in the American army, in which three headquarters staff units were responsible for about three-quarters of the maps recorded by Guthorn. The figure (59 percent) was somewhat lower for the British, but the difference may be interpreted in more than one way. One factor inflating the nonprofessional tally was that the British had an extensive intelligence service among the loyalists—under the map conscious Beverley Robinson, this was responsible for bringing a number of terrain sketches into headquarters.[210] The reverse, though the evidence is difficult to interpret, may have been that the Americans were relatively unsuccessful in obtaining suitable maps except from a limited number of staff officers employed at their headquarters—although the territory over which they had to operate, the number of trained guides available to them, and so on, were also variables in their cartographic output at different stages in the Revolution.

Despite the variations and the degree of improvisation in both armies, mapmaking was basically a headquarters activity and was confined to a limited number of specialized units. Thus the organization of the military staff reflected a consensus about the operational needs of a field army, including its cartographic requirements. This characteristic serves to sum up the extent to which Continental military thinking had permeated both the British and American armies during the Revolution. The carriers of these constructs—a mobile officer corps, an educational system imbued with common teaching, and a family of textbooks largely common to both Europe and America—are all integral to the history of military cartography.

3 | The Map User in the Revolution

"Maps," wrote the historian J. A. Williamson, "are a dangerous type of evidence; too much study of them saps a man's critical faculty."[1] While he did not specify it, one such pitfall for the unwary lies in inferring the historical significance of maps only from a superficial acquaintance with their titles or contents. The phrase "historical significance" is used in a particular sense. All past maps indeed have significance—either as a record of the technique by which they were made or by virtue of the recorded detail, however scrappy, that a cartographer had reason to include. Only for a much smaller group of maps is it possible to say that they definitely played a role—in the sense that they were the basis of a recorded decision—in events we may wish to decipher. This is a particular problem with the maps of the American Revolution.

At first sight, a definite use is apparent for most maps, and they can be readily classified into sets to reflect the contemporary realities of the war and the way it was fought. How many of these hundreds of maps, however, were actually used for the purpose for which they were designed? How many were involved in a critical decision? It will be necessary, of course, to define "critical," because (within a military hierarchy) decisions were taken at a variety of levels of importance. For many historians (whose objectives are different from those of the cartographic historian), this may be a vital question. That a map shows terrain where a skirmish took place, the route of a march, or the disposition of opposing forces in a battle or siege does not in itself indicate that the map played, or even was capable of playing, a significant part in the events. To argue thus is not to underrate the influence of maps in many military decisions of the Revolution; it is to urge the necessity of attempting a more systematic study of situations in which maps were used, who used them, and with what likely effect. Only then can we arrive at logical conclusions about maps.

The map user in the Revolution is, accordingly, the focus of this chapter. Although in a military context mapmakers and map users are sometimes the same people, the justification for an independent study of map users is that they are the ones who always make decisions with maps in events we may be trying to illuminate. R. A. Skelton reminded us that one historical function of early maps is to reflect for our benefit the "map maker's knowledge, thought and state of mind." It can be asserted that an equal concern should be the *map user's* knowledge, thought, and state of mind, especially as they are conditioned by the maps available to him and by the constraints and opportunities that either encouraged or inhibited his use of maps. If technical and typological studies of maps are pursued in isolation, there is a danger that although much will be known about maps as such and about the mapmaker's art, at the same time they may well become static artifacts, relegated to the footnotes in the process of understanding historical change. If historians of cartography genuinely have the needs of other historians in mind—as they have averred in two recent conferences and in an extensive literature[2]—then they will have to be concerned as much with the elusive task of documenting maps in real situations as with analyzing them as technical objects.

Studies of map use are also made imperative by recent attempts of modern cartographers to develop a body of theory relevant to their subject matter. In examining the map user, the concept of maps as a communication system is particularly useful in defining and justifying the area of study as well as in suggesting new approaches to past maps. Any map, as Arthur H. Robinson has explained, "even a simple straightforward one," is "an extraordinarily complex form of graphic expression because it is an artificial thing embodying, in addition to its own visual complications, several transformations of reality in scale, shape, and symbolism."[3] Conceptions of maps as a particular sort of symbolic system, embodying a process of visual communication,[4] are now widely accepted.[5] For the historian of cartography, this approach has a general value as a unifying concept, linking the technical studies of how maps were made with evidence for their use in past societies. If the theory is valid, as set out in a series of diagrams by which various writers have attempted to illustrate the design of the communication process (fig. 3:1 I, II, and III), then an even more far reaching implication is that the map user is at least as important as the mapmaker.[6] A common element in all these diagrams is an implied symmetry between the two "stages" or "sectors" in the communication process: on the one hand, there is the part relating to the mapmaker (variously described as the "encoder" and "conceptualizer" of the real world); on the other hand, there is that part relating to the map user (variously called the "decoder," "recipient," or "percipient" of the message in the map). Such an implied balance of research effort is not reflected by the literature of the history of cartography, which has tended to emphasize the mapmaker and mapmaking. Even if a future strategy of equality is unrealistic (as much because of the available sources as the preferences of individual scholars), the theoretical advances of our colleagues working with modern maps should not be disregarded: an established place in historical studies ought to be safeguarded for the map user.

Recent work on the map as a communication system also offers ways of approaching the map user of the past. It is a recurrent theme, for example, that although the environments of the mapmaker and the map user often overlap (fig. 3:1 II), each surely has an independent identity. Accordingly, the aim of this chapter is to explore the distinctive part of the map user's environment in the Revolution. Elements in this environment have also been set down in recent studies, and they usually include considerations such as the needs, interests, and aims of map users, their knowledge and experience, and also various external conditions that impinge on the way maps were used. The map user's environment could thus embrace all aspects

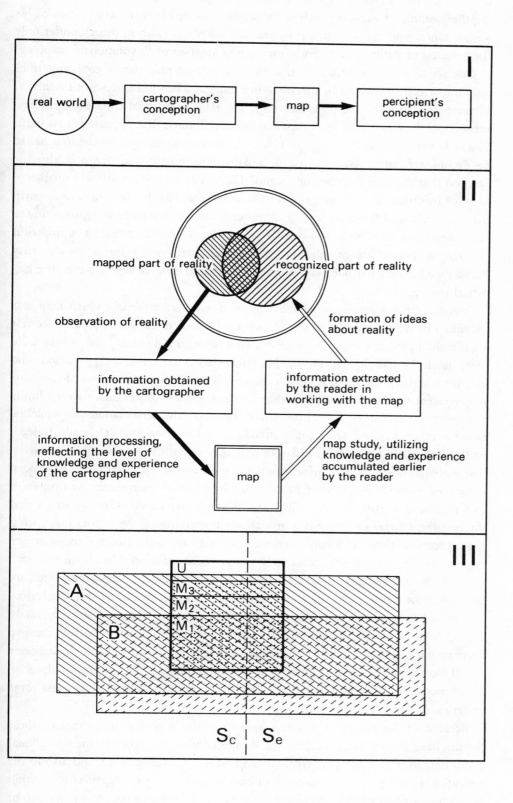

Figure 3:1 The relationship between
the mapmaker, the map, and the map user.
Key from Robinson and Petchenik (1975).

of the real world to which he was exposed. Cartographic theory, as a tool for exploring the past, might suggest which of those aspects were likely to have influenced his actions when working with maps. In practice, however, existing theories offer only the broadest of pathways into an historical investigation of Revolutionary mapping.

One set of problems arises because existing cartographic theory poses questions only imperfectly answered by the surviving sources. Thus Robinson and Petchenik, in their discussion of the map user (fig. 3:1 III), imply that the seemingly new information acquired through a map may be more limited than appears at first sight. Not only that fraction of a map previously known or understood by the user has to be excluded from its contribution in a particular situation but there is also the fraction that the user fails to understand. There may be left a relatively small segment of information, and this can properly be regarded as the increment to the map users' knowledge.[7] It is a commonsense observation that the past use of maps, in the Revolution and elsewhere, was equally subject to this consideration. The historical problem is how to identify the increment—the vitally new information that may have tipped a decision one way or another—so extraordinarily elusive in the historical sources.

It restates the problem to say that, even if we may establish which map was consulted by whom, we cannot be sure what information was actually perceived nor what mental picture of terrain resulted. Maps speak to individuals just as they were often made by individuals. Phillip Muehrcke has commented, "To a person who uses his imagination, a map is greater than itself, for it evokes images and emotions not apparent on the piece of paper that is called a map."[8] By broadening the limits in this way—beyond the factual content of the map—the permutations are stretched in yet another direction from those envisaged by Robinson and Petchenik. Indeed, such is the nature of image formation that the possibilities are virtually limitless. The amount and content of information extracted by the map user could have been influenced as much by preconceptions as by the external, momentary circumstances that regulated a particular use.[9] In many cases, it may be necessary to accept that the best the sources can offer is a general understanding of the factors influencing these preconceptions. If a map user was an assiduous student of the maps of one region, then his mental map was likely to have been influenced by all the previous maps of the area he had consulted. If his experience with maps was unfortunate (not unusual in the Revolution), he would be less likely to absorb and act on the information found in maps but would seek confirmation through other means. By establishing such conditions of individual map use, we at least start to narrow the gap between what Kitson Clark has called the likely guess and the probable deduction.[10]

All that can be attempted, then, is a reconstruction of those aspects of the map users' world in the Revolution that seem to be important and have at least some materials available for their study.

Because of the overlap between mapmaking and map use, a number of these themes have already been touched upon, especially as they relate to the operational conditions in which different types of map were used (chapter 1) and also to the educational background of military officers and the type of organization within which they structured their decisions (chapter 2). This leaves four main topics to be discussed: (a) the availability of maps in situations where they could have exerted a significant influence on course of events; (b) the operational limitations of particular types of maps in relation to their assumed uses; (c) the attitudes of military map users toward cartographical matters; and (*d*) the rationale of single decisions made with maps. These subjects leave many gaps to be filled, but they begin to bridge the gulf between our intuitions about the role of maps during the Revolution and the reality of their true influence.

A very elementary pitfall in some studies that argue the influence of maps in particular events is that the authors fail to establish, from independent historical evidence, whether these maps were available at the right time and place to exert an influence in the manner hypothesized. When reconstructing the maps available to Revolutionary commanders, for example, it is not sufficient to note from the catalogues of major national libraries that there were so many published maps of an area for an appropriate date. This may enable a total population of maps to be examined, but it says nothing about their distribution—a particularly relevant consideration in the eighteenth-century North America. Since many important regional surveys were compiled, engraved, and published in either London or Paris, some may never have reached the theater of action.

ON THE AVAILABILITY OF MAPS

These considerations apply equally to manuscript maps. While it is true that the number of maps made by the British (see table 2:2) seems to have exceeded the number made by the Americans, this fact in itself had little necessary congruence with the ability of either side to wage war. Indeed, the recently stated view that "the British Army's superior cartographic resources are reflected in the more extensive extant collections of British Revolutionary War maps" does not stand up to closer scrutiny—if by "superior" it is meant that they were useful tools available for campaigns that actually took place.[11] The simple fact is that the British maps were frequently of the wrong area. Some of the finest manuscript surveys made by the British in North America before 1775 might as well have been of South America as far as the effective prosecution of the Revolution was concerned. This was true of the surveys of Nova Scotia, of parts of northern New England, and of the elegant survey of the Saint Lawrence valley made between 1761–1763, which seems to have played little or no role in Arnold's siege of Quebec. The British interwar surveys were conceived in a very different strategic climate—at the end of the French and Indian War—with peaceful colonial objectives as much as military conflicts in mind. The center of gravity of the Revolution lay much further to the south and east than the old frontiers with France. One symptom of this lack of coincidence between the cartographic needs of 1765 and 1775 was, as we have noted, that the British were ill prepared with suitable maps of the Boston countryside in 1775.[12]

An argument of historical relevance, based on the simple fact of the locations to which the surviving maps refer, could be extended to a larger proportion of those maps made by the British headquarters' staff during the Revolution. Throughout the war, the British may have continued to make more maps than the Americans; but these often related to territory effectively held by the British for fairly long periods and therefore seldom depicted subsequently contested ground. A good illustration of this is the voluminous manuscript cartography of the New York area, accumulated by 1783: it serves to emphasize that, although Clinton's mapmakers were indeed often busy, their activity was mainly behind the lines of outer fortifications.[13] If in 1781 Washington and Rochambeau had decided to attack New York rather than march to Yorktown, then the terrain data encapsulated in these maps could have been vital. As it was, the decisive actions to end the war were in remote areas—in the southern colonies—and far from where British military surveyors had been intensively active. Viewed in this light, the cartographic resources of the two armies were probably more nearly equal than they appear when we skim a catalogue. It is clearly dangerous to erect historical argument on the basis of simple censuses of maps.

The Supply of Printed Topographical Maps and Charts

Generally at least, printed maps and charts of individual colonies and regions of North America (and of estuarine and coastal waters) were indispensable tools to naval and military commanders throughout the Revolution. It is true that they were far from perfect for many of the demands made on them; nevertheless, they could hardly have done without them. A necessary stage in following the implications of this use, indeed a temporal and spatial variable in its own right, lies in detailing the availability of those maps in North America—again, not just that maps had been published but that a supply was adequate for those who sought them. A systematic examination of this topic is beyond the scope of this study. It would involve a detailed reconstruction of ways in which printed maps reached North America (such as through the map trade) and of evidence that copies were lodged (such as through contemporary lists of colonial libraries and other map collections) where they could be used for military purposes.[14] Some of these sources will be used, but work has not proceeded far enough for us to comment on the quantity of maps available in North America during the Revolution. All that can be diagnosed is a few trends and some of their underlying causes.

An important influence on the availability of maps in 1775 had been the British policy or, more correctly, a lack of defined policy concerning the publication of materials from official surveys, such as those conducted for the Board of Trade and the Admiralty. Basically, few barriers were put in the way of crown servants who wished to publish surveys acquired during their official duties. Indeed, the practice may have been positively encouraged on occasion. In the absence of official map-making agencies in Britain (the Ordnance Survey and the Hydrographic Office were not founded until the decade after the Revolution ended), this was a way of employing private capital with useful by-products for the government. Some of the published maps of John Montresor provide a case study of how individual officers were generally free to make their own arrangements with the London map trade, and they also show the wider process by which primary surveys were transmitted to London for engraving.

For Montresor, as for other officers serving in North America, the opportunity to compile more general maps out of a mass of field observations and rough drafts (or *brouillons,* as he termed them[15]), was provided by the relatively peaceful conditions following the end of the French and Indian War. Maps and plans had been accumulating for years at regional and local headquarters of the engineers in North America.[16] In 1765–1766, Montresor turned his attention to cartographic synthesis. On 29 January 1765, he entered in his journal that he was "employed in assisting Capt Henry Gordon Chief Engineer in making a plan of part of North America shewing the upper Lakes and Posts thereon together with the several passes, Portages, Ranges of Mountains, sources of Rivers, for the Marquis of Granby, Master General of the Ordnance."[17] By 17 March "the new completed plan of great part of N. America done by the Engineers at New-York" had been dispatched to England.[18] By that December, a "General Draught" of the province of New York was available for consultation by General Gage, the commander-in-chief.[19] Shortly afterward, when Gage's cartographic awareness was sharpened by the events of the Stamp Act riots, he asked Montresor "to Sketch him a Plan of this Place [New York] on a large Scale with its environs and adjacent country together with its harbour, but particularly to shew the ground to the North and North East of the Town &c."[20] This assignment, involving a new instrumental survey, occupied the engineer inter-mittently throughout January 1766, until it was completed on 8 February (see plate 22).[21] Even these plans, drawn for what was recognized as an immediate and possibly recurrent military emergency, were not restricted in circulation to their manuscript form.

Montresor was next employed on a "reduced Plan" of New York and its environs, again for Gage.[22] In June he noted that he was still "shading and putting together the several communications in this Province in order to compile a Draught of it."[23] Montresor was probably aiming at publication throughout this spell of active map compilation. When he was given permission to go to England in October 1766, he took with him manuscript copies of several completed maps, presumably with Gage's knowledge and assent.[24] In the following spring, we find him taking the final steps towards publication of some of these maps. Perhaps after taking advice and com-paring quotations for the cost of engraving, he selected the workshop of the late John Rocque. His journal for 8 April noted that he had given "la Rocque, Engraver, my plan of Canada reduced to be engraved from Isle de Bernaby & Bic quite to Montreal."[25] On 1 May, an entry reported that he was "constantly attending at the 2 Engravers to assist them in the Executions of the severnl Draughts I have given them to Engrave for me viz.t one of Nova Scotia, one of the Province of New York, one of Canada from the first Island to Montreal and one of the City of New York and Environs with the Bosen Harbour and Channel from the Hook."[26] One of these "draughts," that of Canada, does not seem to have been published.[27] The journal also leaves other questions unanswered about Montresor's precise involve-ment with the production of these maps. It is abundantly clear, however, that manu-script surveys made for military and other official use in North America before 1775 were published without impediment and passed into general usage. Apparently there was no question of Montresor having to seek formal permission from the Board of Ordnance: a nod from his commander-in-chief was probably all that was required to release maps from the New York drawing room. There were, moreover, similar North American surveys published in this way, either before 1775 or in the early years of the Revolution. Thomas Jefferys and William Faden, with their pub-lishing houses and their semiofficial position (Jefferys was Geographer to the King), were particularly successful in exploiting this aspect of the American map trade.[28] Blaskowitz, De Brahm, Holland, and Sauthier were among the better-known cartog-raphers who contributed to a more general availability of military survey materials through these two London publishing houses.

It is the consequence of this lack of control—crown surveys were available to both armies after 1775—that is relevant to the present argument. In the matter of maps, as in many other fields, the military reality of the Revolution can scarcely have been anticipated. Had it been foreseen, it would have been in line with contemporary military thought for the North American commander-in-chief to have insisted that topographical maps and plans were restricted or classified material—as indeed they became in the course of the Revolution.[29] Frederick the Great (who as we have seen

was something of a model for eighteenth-century military commanders) was sufficiently concerned about the chance of detailed maps falling into enemy hands to
discourage Field Marshall Samuel von Schmettau from taking a trigonometrical
survey of Prussia.[30] Similar restrictive policies characterized Austrian military mapping of the same period.[31] In the North American colonies, the peaceful uses of
maps were uppermost in the minds of administrators until it was too late to prevent
their becoming tools in the hands of friend and foe alike.

Land Maps for the British. In the early years of the war, the supply of maps may
have been tipped in favor of the British. Officers posted to North America were able
to equip themselves, if they had the foresight, from the London map sellers, who
had published most of the colonial and military maps that were available for use in
1775.[32] These same map sellers were predictably quick to react to the opportunity
the Revolution gave them to sell more North American maps, and several trends can
be identified.

First, after 1775, they started to publish a few of the considerable numbers of
American manuscript maps already in London. These included the collections of the
Board of Trade,[33] the Board of Ordnance,[34] the War Office,[35] and the Admiralty;[36]
private collections, such as those of George III and other noblemen;[37] and, in one
or two cases, as with Faden, the accumulated raw materials of a map-engraving
business.[38] Some of these drafts, where they were of relevant areas, could be tidied
up for engraving. Others obviously represent the topical publication of manuscripts
that had been in Britain for some years, such as William Brasier's "A Survey of
Lake Champlain including Lake George, Crown Point and St John," surveyed by
him in 1762 but published by Sayer and Bennett in 1776, or John Montresor's "A
Map of the Province of New York," finally published by Dury in 1775.

Second, to meet the same demand, there was a spate of reissuing maps of parts of
North America from existing copperplates. This trend can be monitored from the
Comparative Cartography of Stevens and Tree. Among the maps given a new lease
on life by the intensified focus on North American affairs were Fry and Jefferson's
Virginia (republished in 1775), plans of the city of New York by John Montresor
and by Bernard Ratzer (reissued in 1775 and 1776 respectively), and Lewis Evans's
General Map of the Middle British Colonies in America (by Sayer and Bennett in
1775).[39] This last-named map appeared despite Thomas Pownall's complaint that it
had been plagiarized and "was in a most audacious Manner published by the late
Thomas Jefferys, under a false Pretence of Improvements."[40] In some cases, such
maps were republished in an atlas format—consisting of diverse maps brought
together in one binding, sometimes to customers' requirements, with variant title
pages. *The American Atlas,* issued under Jefferys's name (but with the commercial
risk taken by Sayer and Bennett), and Faden's *North American Atlas* were the
compilations most important for the supply of printed maps during the Revolution.[41]
They provided a selection of the most detailed maps on areas of potential military
activity. As further materials became available to the London engravers, they came
to embody new sheets in later "editions."[42]

A third trend, that of engraving completely new maps from fresh manuscript
sources, also affected the supply. The flow of raw materials from North America
did not dry up entirely for British mapmakers during the Revolution. Apart from
battle plans, which served a different type of user, operationally useful manuscript

drafts were still arriving in London. Examples were the "Plan of the City and Environs of Philadelphia," published by Faden in 1777, his "sketch of the Northern Frontiers of Georgia by Archibald Campbell," and some of the drafts of manuscript maps brought back to England by Sauthier.[43]

With the facilities to engrave multiple copies of useful maps, the British had an edge on the Americans. The relatively underdeveloped state of the American map engraving business (especially as disrupted by the Revolution) meant that it was not technically equipped to attempt the preparation of complicated regional maps, even when manuscript drafts were available. After the Revolution, the promoters of major map projects still tended to look to Europe for their engravers.[44] Taken together, these facts suggest that throughout the Revolution the British headquarters probably had an adequate supply of maps published in London, though relatively few printed maps have survived in the Clinton papers.[45] There is no reason to think otherwise, and printed maps also continued to be imported into American towns under British control—notably New York, where they were occasionally advertised for sale in the local newspapers.[46]

DesBarres's Atlantic Neptune. What was true of the land maps available to the British also applied to the marine charts required for naval and mercantile vessels plying vital supply routes and engaged in the amphibious operations that often were a critical element in army tactics. The older charts, such as those in *The English Pilot: The Fourth Book* (first issued in 1689, but three reissues were published during the Revolution[47]), continued to be available, but the hydrography of the period tends to be dominated by the publication of one work—*The Atlantic Neptune* by Joseph F. W. DesBarres. It has already been noted that the *Neptune* was conceived and surveyed in the decade or so preceding the Revolution. Thanks to detailed studies by John C. Webster and G. D. N. Evans,[48] the details of the administrative background to DesBarres's cartography are clearly delineated; but we have only a sketchy picture of the techniques by which the charts were compiled and engraved. DesBarres, under instructions from the Admiralty and with his headquarters at Halifax, spent the decade after 1764 surveying the coastline of Nova Scotia and charting its inshore waters. His methods, similar to those of his contemporary Murdoch Mackenzie the Elder in surveys of western Britain,[49] involved a combination of coastal triangulation, topographical mapping and sketching along the shore, and soundings—both inshore (by small boat) and in deeper waters (by schooner).

Some time before the Revolution, and probably soon after he began to send his manuscript charts back to England in the late 1760s, DesBarres started to develop a scheme to publish his Nova Scotia charts. By 1773 the idea was sufficiently formulated for him to have mentioned it to Samuel Holland.[50] In 1774 he returned to England. By May of that year, he was lobbying among the influential lords of the Admiralty to obtain financial support for the engraving and publication.[51] The first chart, as a specimen of the project, also appeared in 1774.[52] The complicated process of obtaining patronage must be seen against a background of the absence of an official hydrographic office—although such an establishment had been suggested by Lord Howe in 1766 and was to be recommended again during the Revolution.[53] By March 1775, however, the House of Commons had approved an estimate prepared by DesBarres for "the Expence of Engraving Charts of the Coast of *North*

America, between the Bay of *Chaleurs,* in the Gulph of *St Lawrence,* and the River *St. Croix,* in the Bay of *Fundy"* at a cost of £3,711 15s., based on a rate of thirty-five guineas for each copper plate.[54] From a house in Soho, in a quarter among artists and other craftsmen of Huguenot extraction,[55] DesBarres began to engage more engravers to produce the charts of the stretch of coast specified in the grant.

This venture's progress was altered by the Revolution. If the outbreak of hostilities brought a rapid halt to surveys along the coast of New England, it clearly gave impetus to the more rapid publication of the available charts. The main result, though the detailed steps still have to be unraveled from the DesBarres papers,[56] was that the Admiralty encouraged the expansion of the work beyond its Nova Scotian beginnings. In 1774 and 1775 DesBarres claimed to have spent £458 and £483, respectively, "for Contingencies to prepare and publish the Atlantic Neptune," and in the following two years this increased to £960 and £853.[57] As the work expanded in geographical scope, so did its sources to incorporate coastal surveys made by Samuel Holland and his assistants on the general survey, as well as DesBarres's own charts. Although it became a source of friction between the two men, DesBarres had obtained official approval for his step by petitioning the lords of trade for the use of manuscript maps in their possession.[58]

With these and other materials, including some maps obtained from the Board of Ordnance,[59] the *Neptune* grew from one book into five. In the contemporary division of the work as set out by DesBarres, the first book consisted of "impressions of all the charts plates of my surveys of the coast and harbours of Nova Scotia; with a small book of table of latitudes, longitudes, variations of the magnetic North, tides etc." The second book contained "charts of the coast and harbours of New England composed, by command of Government, by various surveys, but principally from those taken by Major Holland under the directions of my Lords of Trade and Plantations." The third book included charts of the Gulf of Saint Lawrence and the islands of Cape Breton and Saint John. The fourth book, based on "several surveys," extended the coverage to the coast of North America south of New York, and the fifth book contained "various views of the North American coast."[60]

In its fullest form, *The Atlantic Neptune* consisted of 115 maps or charts and 146 views engraved on 290 copper plates and printed on almost three hundred sheets of paper (see plates 23 and 24).[61] No single copy of the work included impressions of all items, but in comparison with earlier works, it was quickly recognized by contemporaries as a hydrographic masterpiece. When Lord Howe was shown some of the first charts in 1775, "They appeared so well executed" that he "hardly distinguished them at first, from the Drawings he had been allowed the pleasure of seeing at Mr. Des Barres Lodgings last year."[62] And just after the end of the Revolution, the *Neptune* was described in a French journal as "one of the most remarkable products of human industry that has ever been given to the world through the arts of printing and engraving," the "most splendid collection of charts, plans and views ever published."[63]

How available were the charts for operations during the Revolution? As soon as any impressions of charts were pulled off the press, they were very quickly placed in the service of the Admiralty. DesBarres, while he retained ownership of the copper plates, fulfilled demands for sets of the charts: one of his accounts included a claim for £1771 "to prepare Impressions for the Public Service."[64] The flow of charts to naval and merchant captains is also confirmed in his correspondence. On 14 September 1776, for example, DesBarres noted how he had "sent by the Elephant Storeship which is about sailing for New York thirty six setts of Charts of the Coast and Harbors of Nova Scotia and New England, they are contained in four cases addressed to Major Holland who will recieve of your Lordship directions for the disposal of them." He went on to add that he had also "asked the Admiralty's Pleasure with regard to the Number of Impressions the Lords Commissioners might judge proper to take for supplying His Majesty's ships."[65] In July 1779, DesBarres submitted a more detailed account of "Charts Supplyed for His Majesty's service," specifying both the items and their recipients.[66] There can be no doubt of the availability and general use of the published charts during the Revolution.

It remains to be established how often particular charts were available at the right time and for the right places in order to be useful as events unfolded during the Revolution. The publication record of the *Neptune*, as summarized in figure 3:2, indicates that they were not always available. There were delays in the com-

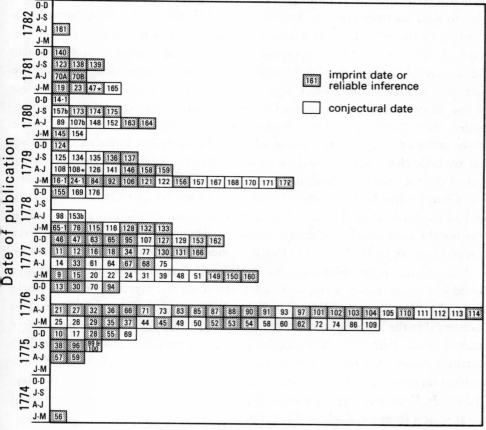

Figure 3:2 First appearance of *Atlantic Neptune* charts and views. After a diagram by Robert W. Karrow, Jr. Numbers refer to the sequence in the Stevens catalogue.

pletion of the charts for Book 2 (some of which were issued in incomplete proof states), a problem DesBarres attributed to Holland's manuscript drafts being "very deficient as yet in the Soundings and nautical Observations."[67] As a result of such delays, the publication of the whole work was not completed until after 1780— beyond the date when it could have been used in some of the critical engagements of the war. Moreover, before the publication of particular charts, manuscript copies were not always available for use in North America. A glimpse of this problem is provided in a letter from Holland to Haldimand, written in July 1775 at a critical early stage in the Revolution, when he noted with some exasperation: "I have wrote frequently to Mr DesBarres to send me a correct copy of his Nova Scotia Survey & agreeably to the Promise he made when he took Copies of my Surveys to make his Projection complete. I wish he was advised to send me without more Delay, those Plans, as he knows I must be in absolute want of them, & that it would be doing Government an essential Service."[68]

Nor did the geography of publication always coincide with the march of events. Although the value of those DesBarres charts on the vital North American supply routes (such as those of Sable Island, "the graveyard of the Atlantic") cannot be underestimated, many of the charts of the Saint Lawrence, Nova Scotia, and even parts of New England, became progressively more remote from active flashpoints of conflict. The corollary, that DesBarres was unable to provide superior charts of several important areas of activity south of New York, is borne out in several actions. One of the most striking results of a lack of elementary hydrographic information was the abortive British attack on Charleston in 1776. It had been Clinton's plan to send his troops over to Sullivan's Island by means of a ford, "confidently reported by the pilots to be in a manner joined by a ford passable on foot at low water."[69] This proved to be impossible, despite Clinton's two-day reconnaissance. He discovered, to his "unspeakable mortification and disappointment," that "the passage across the channel which separates the two islands was nowhere shallower at low water than seven feet instead of eighteen inches, which was the depth reported. This of course rendered it impracticable for the troops to take that share in the attack of . . . Sullivan's Island which had been at first intended."[70] Neither the available charts nor the local pilots, who played as vital a role throughout the war as did the guides on land, had been able to prevent this debacle. So obsessed was Clinton with the whole episode that after he returned to Charleston in 1780 he had the ford carefully sounded, as if in vindication of his own actions.[71] This was not the only occasion when an absence of adequate charts south of the areas mapped in detail by DesBarres and Holland hindered British planning of operations.

Another clue to the effectiveness of DesBarres's charts during the Revolution is found in the continuing attempts at hydrographic survey, especially in areas where the work of DesBarres or Holland had already provided some basic coverage. This confirms that the *Neptune* was no hydrographic panacea; it left many gaps where more detailed charts were necessary for operational purposes. Since 1761, an Admiralty directive had required all naval officers to collect hydrographic and navigational information.[72] This practice was continued and reinforced during the Revolution. In December 1776, for example, secret instructions had been issued to all naval vessels from the *Eagle* off New York:

Many Opportunities may probably offer in the course of the Service you have been appointed to conduct, for collecting material Intelligence and making useful Discoveries; not only of the preparations of further Resistance of the King's Authority by His Majesty's disaffected Subjects, but also of the Pilotage and Navigation on the most accessible parts of the Coasts within the Limits of your Station. . . . But to facilitate the Acquisition of such useful Knowledge, as well as the Concealment of the purpose; those Methods and Opportunities should only be taken for Sounding or other Examination of the Coasts, that will testify the least apparent Intention of that Nature.[73]

Charting had almost become a matter of espionage. It was perhaps a sequel to such orders that Frederick Mackenzie, some ten months later in October 1777, noted in his diary from Rhode Island "that the flag of truce Sloop which was lately sent up to Providence is detained there and the officer and men made prisoners, in consequence of the Officer's having been detected in taking a sketch of the River, with the Soundings, &c. &c. The Rebels are in possession of the Sketch."[74] As we move from purely cartobibliographical evidence into other historical sources, it seems less likely that either the British or the Americans had a fraction of the cartographic tools they would have liked in waging war along the extensive eastern seaboard of North America.

The Supply of Printed Maps to the Americans. From the inventory of George Washington's library (to judge by the date of many of the recorded editions) it would appear that he had been able to acquire most of the major printed surveys published in London. These included atlases, such as Jefferys's *General Topography of North America;* general maps of North America, such as those by Mitchell and Popple; and sheet maps of individual colonies. The latter extended to surveys made by British officers before the Revolution, including maps by De Brahm (South Carolina and Georgia) and Montresor (the province of New York and his plan of New York City), together with the work of colonial surveyors such as Lewis Evans (Pennsylvania, New Jersey, New York, and Delaware), Fry and Jefferson (Virginia), Henry Mouzon (North and South Carolina), and William Scull (Pennsylvania). Washington had also built up a small collection of charts, including that of Newfoundland by James Cook and Michael Lane. Even DesBarres's "Map of Boston Harbour and vicinity" seems to have reached him, although the British must have been careful to restrict the circulation of charts from the *Neptune.*[75] Presumably Washington's collection was one of the most comprehensive available to the Americans; in this regard it was not representative.

If efforts to improve the supply of maps are any indication, then a realistic assessment is that the Americans were desperately short of multiple copies of maps for everyday use in campaigning, especially in the early part of the war. The papers of Thomas Jefferson record a bill in 1779 authorizing the Virginia assembly to appoint persons to "procure such books and maps as aforesaid" and referred to the "importation of books and maps in times of war" as being "hazardous."[76] Later, in a letter to Horatio Gates of 23 September 1780, Jefferson wrote: "I have given orders to have Fry and Jeffersons and Henrys Maps of Virginia sought for and purchased. As soon as they can be got I will forward them."[77] Shortly afterward, he confirmed that "we are endeavoring to get you a copy of Fry & Jefferson's; but they are now very scarce."[78] Jefferson, with one of the largest libraries and map collections in eighteenth-century North America,[79] was obviously in touch with the map market.

Virginia was not, however, the only state to be involved in a search for maps for military use. Other state houses, too, had small collection of maps. It was as a result of a suggestion by Benjamin Franklin in the 1740s that Popple's large map of North America was hung in the Pennsylvania assembly room.[80] It was still there in 1776, as confirmed by John Adams, then Massachusetts' delegate to the Continental Congress, who noted in a letter to his wife that Popple's map was "the largest I ever saw, and the most distinct. Not very accurate. It is Eight foot square. —

There is one in the Pensilvania State House."[81] Adams also reported to his wife: "The Board of War are making a Collection of all the Maps of America, and of every Part of it, which are extant, to be hung up in the War Office. As soon as the Collection is compleated, I will send you a List of it. In the mean Time take an Account of a few already collected and framed and hung up in the Room."[82] The maps, obviously designed for military planning, included those of D'Anville, Evans, Mitchell, and William Scull, and the list ended on a flourish of cartographic patriotism: "You will ask me why I trouble you with all these dry Titles, and Dedications of Maps. —I answer, that I may turn the Attention of the Family to the subject of American Geography. —Really, there ought not to be a State, a City, a Promontory, a River, an Harbour, an Inlett, or a Mountain in all America, but what should be intimately known to every Youth, who has any Pretensions to liberal Education."[83] The American zeal for geographical self-education through maps as well as through military textbooks undoubtedly helped in their planning of the war.

To supplement copies obtainable in North America, the Americans also acquired printed maps from Europe, especially through the intermediary of the Paris map trade. Although it may have been difficult for an American to purchase a map in the Strand after 1775, London map sellers nevertheless continued to export maps to Europe throughout the Revolution. Faden's business correspondence in particular with the Paris engraver and map dealer, Lattré, confirms that this French house ordered sheet maps of the North American theater of war from 1777 onward. The transactions continued even after 1781, when France was officially at war with Britain, although trade had to be diverted through the neutral port of Ostend.[84] These direct exports were, moreover, complemented by the "translations" of maps made by geographical publishers in Paris, such as Le Rouge and Beaurain. Le Rouge had already issued a French edition of John Mitchell's *Map of the British Colonies in North America* in 1756.[85] In 1778, the same publisher brought out Jefferys's *American Atlas,* embodying many of the major surveys of the period. Such versions were yet another means of ensuring that the information in the major maps could be put to use by both sides in the Revolution.

The use of these maps by the French in military planning is confirmed by the researches of Rice and Brown, who argue that numerous engraved maps of parts of North America, mainly of English origin, were available in France and "must have been assiduously studied by the officers assigned to Rochambeau's staff."[86] "These included," they note, "both prewar maps of the British colonies and more recent 'war maps,' drawn by British engineers and subsequently issued as engraved maps by William Faden and other London publishers. They related, for example, to the 1775–1776 campaign in New England, the New York and Long Island campaign of 1776, the campaigns of 1777 and 1778 in New Jersey and Pennsylvania, and to Burgoyne's expedition down the Champlain Valley."[87] It is even possible to identify some of the specific maps brought by the French expedition to North America. For example, those of Rochambeau and Crublier D'Opterre (a headquarters engineer), now preserved in the collection of Paul Mellon, included many of the standard maps of the period already referred to.[88] Nor did the traffic in maps always flow from Europe to North America. While the Americans were denied the engraving facilities of the London map trade, some of the French officers attached to the Continental Army were able to send back drafts to Paris for publication. A map, *Theatre of War in North America,* engraved after a drawing by one of these volunteers (Lafayette's aide Michel Capitaine du Chesnoy), was published in Paris in 1779.[89] As with many other aspects of Revolutionary cartography, the circulation of printed maps, as regulated by the map trade and often by the movement of individual officers, was thoroughly international.

The same principle—to establish more precisely the historical and geographical coordinates of map use—is applicable to a study of printed battle plans as disseminators of information about the war. Again, there is no shortage of fruitful hypotheses about the historical role of these maps, but little attempt has been made to test them fully. It was Lloyd Brown, quoting the first director of the William L. Clements Library, Randolph G. Adams, who noted, "Pictorial news about the war was limited almost entirely to maps."[90] This aspect of their use has been taken up by several historians as (in Peter Guthorn's phrase) "public information news maps."[91] To William P. Cumming they were also "commercial maps to keep the public informed."[92] Such statements apart, there has been little exploration of how printed battle plans either were potentially able to or effectively did fulfill such a role. In 1974, Kenneth Nebenzahl's *Bibliography of Printed Battle Plans of the American Revolution* was published.[93] This work, including as it does nearly a total population for this cartographic genre, enables some general questions to be posed. How important was the engraving of battle plans as a cartographic activity? Did the printed battle plans give a comprehensive or balanced record of events, or were they biased toward particular battles and periods? How effective were they as a news medium?

A total of 217 published plans does seem a meagre record of well over two hundred "named incidents" during seven years of campaigning over much of a continent.[94] This tally, moreover, included maps of the West Indies theater of war and of Gibraltar; it was compiled from the sum of all printed plans (located as being published in America, Britain, and other European countries) issued either separately or in books and magazines. Standing alone, this is a crude statistic. The total excludes several variant editions of some plans and gives weight neither to the number of impressions sold of single maps nor to the circulation figures of eighteenth-century magazines.[95]

A breakdown of this total population by events is needed in order to define the type of news being communicated. By far the most published events in map form were those of the Boston campaign (including Lexington and Concord, Bunker Hill, and the siege of Boston) and the Virginia campaigns culminating in the siege of Yorktown—both with a total of over thirty published items. Below this there was a sharp drop to a group of engagements with around ten maps each: the battle of Long Island (ten); Delaware River forts, including the siege of Fort Mifflin (nine); and the 1780 Charleston expedition (ten). Still lower in the rank order came another group: White Plains (six); Newport (Rhode Island), and the naval engagement off Chesapeake Capes (five each); and then, all with three recorded plans—Arnold's march, Camden, New Jersey, and Trenton, Princeton, and the second battle at Saratoga. The remaining engagements were represented by only one or two published items. Among those conspicuously absent were any plans relating to events at Cowpen's, King's Mountain, and Moores Creek Bridge—all in the southern campaigns. Nor were there any published maps of the military activities—largely by loyalist-led corps—on the Western frontier. On the other hand,

Battle Plans as Carriers of News

twenty-eight of the published plans related to events in the West Indies, and another eleven depicted engagements at Gibraltar.[96]

It would be hazardous to read too much into these figures, for the publication of a plan depended on the outcome of a complicated chain of occurrences, including the making of a suitable map on the site of an event, its successful transmission (in many cases to London), and the assumption of a commercial risk by a map publisher. Even so, a few inferences may be drawn. The first is that the really momentous events of the Revolution—its beginnings around Boston and the humiliation of Yorktown—sent both politicians and armchair soldiers scrambling for maps portraying the topography of such military and political sensations. This likely interest was presumably carefully gauged by men such as Faden and Le Rouge. Second, as the Revolution dragged on, there were also periods when events were insufficiently newsworthy to impel the engraving of special maps. At certain times in the struggle, moreover, the British public was presumably more interested in the fate of vital commerce in the West Indies or Gibraltar than in a minor event in an obscure part of eastern North America. Nor could the beginning of the cult of visiting sites of Revolutionary battlefields, started by French officers before 1783, have greatly stimulated the demand for maps.[97] Within a few years after Bunker Hill, it is possible that the market was saturated. Indeed, in a letter to Faden dated 20 July 1778, Lattré, after requesting six copies of Jefferys and Faden's *Theatre of War in North America,* added the plea, "Please do not send me any battle maps."[98]

Third, London map sellers tended to favor publication of the victories, real or apparent, of their own armies rather than those of the Americans. No doubt William Faden, as geographer to the king, felt it his duty to present an official and optimistic view of events. The description "rebels" appears on many of his plans—at least until the peace treaty was signed. Always an astute business man, Faden then restored impartiality to a plan of the battle of Brandywine by amending the copper plate from "rebels" to "Americans" for a new edition perhaps aimed at the reopened American market. (see plate 25)[99] Such subjective considerations often impinged on the cartographic record of the Revolution as on other published news, and at best, the map image of military events was a patchy reflection of reality.

The other variable in this situation, an important aspect of availability, was the date on which the plans were published, compared with the date on which the depicted battle or engagement was fought. Figure 3:3 summarizes this relationship for plans in the Nebenzahl *Bibliography* that record discrete and datable events. This presentation tends to separate the plans into two main, if oversimplified, categories.

The first category comprises those battle plans that appeared within six months of the dates of the events they record. A major hazard for publication in Britain lay in the Atlantic crossing. Although a month was sometimes regarded as normal travel time, immense variations were recorded. Given such a capricious influence, the rapidity with which some plans were published confirms that they were rushed through the engraver's hands because of their immediate topicality. The record in this respect was held by a Faden plan, *The Attack and Defeat of the American Fleet under Benedict Arnold, By the King's Fleet Commanded by Sir Guy Carleton, upon Lake Champlain.* The event took place on 11 October 1776; the plan, "From a Sketch taken by an Officer on the Spot," was published on 3 December 1776.[100] It was not the only occasion during the Revolution when good news traveled faster

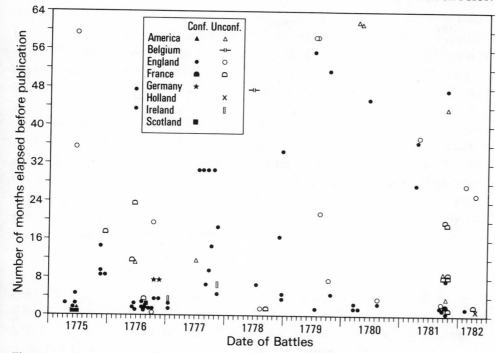

Figure 3:3 Periods between the occurrence of battles during the Revolutionary War and the publication dates of maps portraying them. Based on a diagram compiled by Robert W. Karrow, Jr.

than bad. Twenty plans were published in England within two months of the American battles they depicted, and as many again within four months (though not all were discrete events that could be shown on figure 3:3). It can perhaps be accepted that this group, including some of the earliest graphic expressions of the war, could have been a source of pictorial news. Despite the attractiveness of Lloyd Brown's concept, however, this was at most a minor contemporary use of the printed battle plan, and only about a quarter of the total were published on a time scale that would have enabled them to accompany other printed reports. Of even this small tally a number were, moreover, derived from common sources and thus represented duplicate rather than unique images when they became available in Britain. It seems inherently improbable that printed plans, which had to be laboriously engraved, should have carried the first news of a battle. They belong to a later phase of analysis, a commentary on events already generally understood. This seems to be confirmed by the publication of some plans in periodicals such as the *Gentleman's Magazine,* the *London Magazine,* and the *Remembrancer or, Impartial Repository of Public Events.*[101]

The second category consists of plans published, for whatever reason, so long after the event that their influence in the immediate aftermath of a battle—as in informing public opinion—must be ruled out. Any other news function, even allowing for the longer time lags of the eighteenth century, seems equally improbable. For this larger group, published over six months after the occurrence they represented, there were quite different roles, which help to build up a picture of eighteenth-century map use. A major usage, as the debate about events moved from periodicals to full-length books, was in the writing of contemporary history. Defeated generals, seeking to salvage tarnished reputations, were especially involved. Controversial battles were fought over again, and maps were compiled and much pored over for the light they might throw on the outcome of then recent events. With such motives, a number of plans were commissioned for the narratives and military journals of men like Burgoyne, Clinton, Graves, Simcoe, and Tarleton. Clinton, moreover, provided an interesting example of the continuing use of these published plans through annotations in his personal copy of Stedman's *History of the Origin, Progress and Termination of the American War*.[102] On *A Plan of the Operations of the Kings Army under the Command of General Sʳ William Howe, K.B.* he had noted, "This Map is very faulty: North Castle is not over the Groton, nor did the rebels retire above a mile from White Plains—Merobridge is not as placed in the Map; it is nearly in a line with Lord Cornwallis standing not above 4 miles from it" (see plate 26).[103] Beneath the bottom margin of the map Clinton had also written "Bad Map." Identifiable annotations, apart from any light they may throw on the contents of a map, are obviously primary evidence in reconstructing the extent of contemporary map use.[104]

THE OPERATIONAL SUITABILITY
OF MAPS

In 1776, British map sellers Robert Sayer and John Bennett published from their London workshop a small atlas, *The American Military Pocket Atlas; Being an approved Collection of Correct Maps, Both General and Particular, of the British Colonies; Especially those which now are, or probably may be The Theatre of War: Taken principally from the actual Surveys and judicious Observations of Engineers De Brahm and Romans; Cook, Jackson, and Collet; Maj. Holland, and other Officers, Employed in His Majesty's Fleets and Armies*.[105] The work, in the fashion of the age, was fulsomely dedicated "To Gov. Pownall, Member of Parliament, F. R. S. and F. A. S. &c." The dedication reads:

Sir, As we undertook this Work for the use of the Military Gentlemen at your recommendation, we cannot but hope that the avowed patronage, of a person so well informed in Geography, and having such a particular knowledge of the country of North America, may recommend it to the public; we therefore presumed to dedicate it to You. To You we owe our just acknowledgements for having enabled us to rectify former mistakes, to offer details hitherto unknown, and to collect a very great variety of interesting objects, within a moderate compass.[106]

The atlas contained six maps: North America as a whole, the West Indies, the northern colonies, the middle colonies, the southern colonies, and Lake Champlain. The compilers, who described themselves as "the editors," explained the purpose of their work as follows: "Surveys and Topographical Charts being fit only for a Library, such Maps as an Officer may take with him into the Field have been much wanted. The following Collection forms a PORTABLE ATLAS of NORTH AMERICA, calculated in its Bulk and Price to suit the Pockets of Officers of all Ranks."[107] For the military officer going on campaign, this was a "military Baedeker" instead of a cumbersome "Jefferys type" atlas. It was associated with no less a geographical expert on the continent than Thomas Pownall.[108] For any officers who had failed to make the necessary preparations for war by purchasing it in London, it was also on sale in New York.[109]

How should this particular atlas be assessed? Some historians of cartography have called it a publication of "particular interest."[110] It was deliberately designed for the Revolutionary War and (as Cumming noted) it was a "holster atlas" of special use to mounted officers.[111] There the argument rested. A more realistic approach, disregarding the blandishments of the publishers, is to try to reconstruct the needs of an eighteenth-century officer, detached in the North American countryside and dependent on Sayer and Bennett to plan his next movement. The result would surely be to devalue the *Atlas* as a tool of much military significance. Many of the maps were over twenty years out of date and were in any case compilations of the workshop rather than engravings from original surveys. The general map of North America carried no scale at all. The map of the West Indies was at a scale of about 150 miles to an inch. The "Middle British colonies" were protracted on a scale of about 35 miles to an inch and the "Southern Colonies," at approximately 45 miles to an inch. Despite its pretensions of being derived from "Astronomic Observations," of incorporating "Improvements . . . laid down by Persons perfectly knowing Topography," and of including "very curious nautical surveys," it is doubtful that it ever played a practical part in the actions of the war (see plate 27).

This is a cautionary tale of an extreme nature, but to a greater or lesser extent none of the printed maps of the Revolutionary period was adequate for all of the military uses to which commanders sought to put them. This was as true of the maps in Jefferys's *American Atlas* (which contained many of the most detailed and up-to-date surveys of individual colonies available between 1775 and 1783) as of Sayer and Bennett's little atlas. Some of the deficiencies in Jefferys's compilation can be summed up by the coverage of sheets in the volume (figure 3:4): these indi-

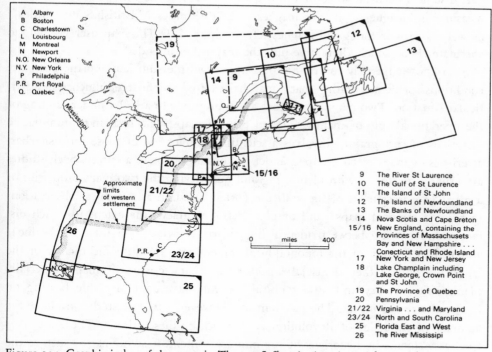

A	Albany
B	Boston
C	Charlestown
L	Louisbourg
M	Montreal
N	Newport
N.O.	New Orleans
N.Y.	New York
P	Philadelphia
P.R.	Port Royal
Q.	Quebec

9	The River St Laurence
10	The Gulf of St Laurence
11	The Island of St John
12	The Island of Newfoundland
13	The Banks of Newfoundland
14	Nova Scotia and Cape Breton
15/16	New England, containing the Provinces of Massachusets Bay and New Hampshire . . . Conecticut and Rhode Island
17	New York and New Jersey
18	Lake Champlain including Lake George, Crown Point and St John
19	The Province of Quebec
20	Pennsylvania
21/22	Virginia . . . and Maryland
23/24	North and South Carolina
25	Florida East and West
26	The River Mississipi

Figure 3:4 Graphic index of the maps in Thomas Jefferys's *American Atlas*, 1776.

cate considerable overlap and the use of incompatible projections.[112] It confirms the striking extent to which the mapping of North America in the mid-eighteenth century had been an *ad hoc* affair. This was perhaps an inevitable consequence of the great size of individual colonies and of leaving their mapping to the speculative initiatives of a few individuals. For anyone seeking to plan across colonial boundaries using different maps, the inconsistencies must have seemed of an almost irreconcilable magnitude.

A few examples will illustrate further some of the potential disadvantages of such an atlas for the military user. First, and unavoidably in such a made-up work, the maps had all been surveyed and published at different dates. Some stretched back as much as thirty years or more before the Revolution but incorporated only sporadic revisions—often on western frontiers away from areas of active campaigning. Second, to the drawback of obsolete detail in vital areas must be added the diverse points of reference to which the geographical coordinates were related. Various prime meridians were in use in eighteenth-century North America: Faden's map of New Jersey employed a Philadelphia meridian; Sauthier's map of the province of New York used New York; and later in the same year, a French map of Chesapeake Bay was plotted from the meridian of Paris.[113] Third, little reliance could be placed on the representation of north in most printed maps. Magnetic north was a changing position, and thus of practical importance when marching by compass, but the maps in Jefferys were largely uninformative on its movement. It must be assumed, from the limited observations at their disposal, that many of the mapmakers represented in the *Atlas* were attempting to show true north. Henry Mouzon's map of the Carolinas, recording magnetic north by means of two arrows on the face of the map, was exceptional in this respect.[114] Fourth, in the matter of scale, again a critical factor in military planning, hardly any two maps were alike—the very units of measure were often different. For those trying to compare or convert distances between some of the maps in the *Atlas*, the complications included measures in "leagues," "marine leagues," "English miles," "British Statute Miles," as well as various miles and leagues left unspecified.[115] The map user was left to speculate about which alternative unit the mapmaker intended.

Such knowledge may contribute to setting down the sufficient and the necessary conditions for demonstrating that a map has exerted a definable influence in a particular situation. Two main approaches are appropriate to a fuller understanding of the operational role of manuscript and printed maps. The first, more familiar to historians of cartography, involves a scientific examination of those intrinsic characteristics of maps often grouped under the heading of map accuracy. Such studies are usually concerned with identifying and quantifying the two main properties of a map: (1) assessment of the graticule (often based on astronomical observations in printed regional maps) and of planimetric accuracy (the extent to which distances and bearing between identifiable objects coincide with their true value); and (2) evaluation of the topographical content (the quantity and quality of the landscape objects they depict).[116] Both these characteristics of maps, especially planimetric accuracy and topographical content, have an undeniable bearing on their military usefulness. The fact remains, however, that few studies evaluate the accuracy of the maps of Revolutionary America by these criteria. There are, it is true, assessments by historians of the military content of some maps—such as the detailed critique of Page's *Plan of the Action at Bunkers Hill* by Allen French,[117] but this does not extend to an examination of other types of maps used in the campaigns. Nor has research harnessed to any extent the increasingly sophisticated battery of cartometric techniques that can be used to assess planimetric accuracy.[118] A notable exception is the recent attempt by Douglas Marshall and Waldo R. Tobler to assess the accuracy of distance and direction in some of the headquarters manuscript maps of Sir Henry Clinton. One such map that came under their scrutiny—they used a technique of vector analysis—was that of the roads between Philadelphia and New York, probably drawn by John Montresor during the winter of 1777–1778. They report: "The standard deviation for the towns on the map represents an average inaccuracy of 3.7 miles. Each of the positions in relation to their nearest neighbors indicates an average dislocation of 3.25 miles and a staggering distortion of 52 degrees. Thus, travel between towns would be difficult if not impossible using only this map and a compass."[119] This illustrates both the promise and the problems of such analyses of intrinsic accuracies of maps.

The potential of this approach clearly lies in establishing a range of uses to which particular maps could reasonably have been put. The problem, however, is that in any historical situation the map is only one of the variables, often a very small one. The question of specific purpose must also be posed. It is possible that when Montresor drew his sketch of the roads he had other uses in mind—perhaps to clarify a point in a conference of general officers—rather than to provide a reliable map for his commander-in-chief to use in a march across the New Jersey countryside. The characteristics of maps, far from being immutable, were infinitely varied. It is obvious that the same map could be anything from useful to totally inadequate, depending on who was using it and for what purpose. A second approach accordingly must consider the levels and types of decisions being made with maps, as well as their absolute characteristics (more helpful in defining potential than indicating actual use).

In the context of the Revolution, this second approach requires an understanding of the military hierarchy and of the complex and even chaotic command structure that reached from the secretary of state for the colonies in London down to a small unit in the field.[120] Decisions involving the use of maps were made at least at three main levels. At a political level, they were made by the British cabinet or the American Congress; at an organizational level, they were made by the British army headquarters in North America and Washington's headquarters; and at an operational level, by the army or detachment in the field. At each of these planes in the war, the same printed maps were not only likely to have played different roles but also to have contained different types of pitfalls for their users.

At the higher level, it would be difficult not to conclude that printed maps sometimes helped as much to mislead politicians as they may have assisted in informing them what was logistically possible in North America. On occasions, the Continental Congress lacked realism in their proposals, perhaps most notably in the desire for Canadian conquest in the early part of the war. As Washington realized, though he supported the venture at the time, this was a matter of maps and of imaginary conditions set down on paper: the Congress failed to appreciate all the geographical implications of such a strategy.[121] Indeed, apart from general printed maps, the only cartographic information available to the Americans at the time of Arnold's march to Quebec was the map prepared by Montresor for his journal in the 1760s.[122]

In the British direction of the war, political control was probably even more important in fashioning the major strategies. All expeditions were first approved by the king and cabinet, who were well supplied with the latest printed maps of North American available in London.[123] Presumably, they studied these maps when making their decisions. (This is not to imply a sort of cartographic determinism; maps were by no means the only evidence considered.) A recurrent strategy was to isolate New England from the middle colonies by securing military control of the Hudson; maps, especially those on a small scale, made such a plan overly attractive. Its simplicity disguised enormous logistical problems.[124] It would, of course, greatly exceed the evidence to imply that a lack of adequate maps (or an inability to use them properly) was even a major factor in the failure of the British arms in the north, culminating in Burgoyne's defeat at Saratoga. What cannot be denied is that politicians do seem to have derived some misconceptions of American space from their reading of maps. More than one contemporary, as well as modern historians, have commented that it was the environment as much as the American army that helped to defeat the British.[125] This is another way of saying that the British failed to understand the realities of North American geography and, arguably, failed to use perceptively those maps that codified the salient landscapes of the eastern seaboard.

At general headquarters there was another level of map use in which, as we have already seen, maps were frequently consulted by both the British and the Americans in reaching their decisions. Clinton, possibly the most map conscious of all British commanders, was wont to press his colleagues to pay more attention to their maps. "Take your map and I think you will see it," he wrote in the summer of 1776 when he was urging a war of expedition based on two strong points—Halifax and Chesapeake Bay.[126] Later, writing in his *Narrative,* he related how, "Upon Casting . . . [my] eye over the map of the Chesapeake," he had been constantly impressed by the defensive possibilities of a "tract of country lying between that bay and the Delaware."[127] This case, however, revealed the problem of strategic planning on the basis of unsubstantiated inferences from maps. Clinton had suggested that Cornwallis should fortify Old Point Comfort in Virginia—a spot he seems to have picked out from the map—but Cornwallis, "having caused the ground and channel to be surveyed and sounded," quickly revealed its unsuitability.[128]

Perhaps Clinton was sometimes irrationally swayed by an inspection of maps. That other officers could at least question his judgment implies that, whatever the cartometric limitations revealed by modern research, maps were also regarded with suspicion in the eighteenth century. As the commander-in-chief of the British army in North America, Thomas Gage, wrote to his principal surveyor in 1767, "There is no map of the inhabited provinces of any use, for there is none correct, even the roads are not marked."[129] There clearly were men in the Revolutionary headquarters who would have agreed with him. Washington, though an avid user of maps, could also be critical. In 1779, he noted that he had "no regular Maps of the Western Country except Evan's Hollands and such as are in print."[130] The obvious implication was that they were inadequate for military planning. In a similar vein, Jefferson wrote to Horatio Gates in 1780, enclosing a copy of Henry's map of Virginia, "It is a mere cento of blunders" and he believed it to represent only "a general idea of the courses of rivers and position of counties," suggesting that Jefferson was fully aware of its operational limitations.[131]

It is perhaps at the third level of decision-making—the local commander in the field—that we need to be most aware of the users' appraisals of maps as well as of their cartographic characteristics. After all, at this level tactics ceased to resemble armchair games, and the most exacting demands were made of maps. Significance, however, was determined by the man rather than the map. Some users were deceived by the printed image: just as politicians around polished tables miscalculated risks by trusting maps, so did unwary field commanders, who saw in blank spaces an easy passage across an inhospitable countryside. According to one historian, this happened to Horatio Gates (who, as we have seen, had obtained printed maps from Jefferson). De Kalb and other officers preferred to approach Camden, South Carolina, by way of Salisbury and Charlotte, a circuitous route but one that would have provided subsistence for the army: "Gates would have none of that. He did not know the country, but he studied the map. He saw that the most direct route to Camden was fifty miles shorter than that proposed by de Kalb. He paid no attention to the remonstrances of his officers who told him that the way led through infertile pine barrens in which deep sand alternated with swamps, and water courses given to swelling floods after a few hours' rain were everywhere."[132]

It was in the southern campaigns that both armies were least equipped with adequate maps, but other field headquarters showed greater circumspection than did Gates. Lord Francis Rawdon, second in command under Cornwallis, seems to have been a critical map user—if sometimes a frustrated one. A letter written at the approach of the "Mountain Men" indicates how baffling was the uncharted vastness of the countryside: "A numerous Army now appeared on the Frontiers drawn from Nolachucki and other Settlements beyond the mountains *whose very names had been unknown to us.*"[133] Existing maps afforded little enlightenment, as is confirmed in a more explicit letter, written to Tarleton, from Smith's plantation on 23 October 1781:

I am very much obliged to you, my dear Sir, for the pains which you have taken in looking out a position for us. All the maps of the country which I have are so very inaccurate, that I must depend totally on your judgement. . . . I am not enough acquainted with that part of the country to decide. . . . Twenty miles westward from the cross roads I should think would remove us too far from that direct communication which we wish. But I must repeat, that I speak from maps, in which I suspect the relative positions to be ill laid down.[134]

Given this kind of awareness of the inadequacy of printed maps (and a number of textbooks also stressed their limitations[135]), it is again unwise to construct arguments—either positive or negative—about their significance. Even with manuscript maps found in military archives, assuming we correctly assess the context of decision-making and their role in it, it is as easy to infer too much as too little. The cartographic historian concerned with maps in action has to face the much wider historical problem: the data that survives (especially maps in this case) were not always linked with those events for which, at first sight, they seem to offer a logical dimension of explanation.[136]

ATTITUDES TO MAPS

Given that a gap often exists between maps and events in the past, there may be a means of bridging it by the more explicit collection of data relating to the users' perception of his maps. In influencing the pace and pattern of historical change, it is a self-evident truth that attitudes toward reality are often as important as the supposed facts themselves. Thus, what users believed maps represented may be more important than the maps themselves. A willingness to use maps was determined as much by faith in their validity or by a sense of their necessity as by any belief in their absolute accuracy. It is therefore legitimate to regard prevailing attitudes toward maps as part of the Revolutionary map users' environment. It was, after all, these ideas that had hallowed the role of maps in a military education, had regulated their spread as a means of military shorthand for recording terrain features, and had influenced their uses in operational situations.

In these senses, much of this study has been concerned with eighteenth-century attitudes toward maps. It is often impossible to separate an "attitude" from other evidence for map use. If the concept of attitude is all embracing, so too are the sources that may be used to study it. The inclusion of a map in a painting or references to maps in literature can occasionally give as much insight into the place of maps in military affairs as a diary of a professional engineer.[137] A survey of attitudes provides invaluable background to the military use of maps. If linked to evidence in surviving maps, such a survey should improve our understanding of the limits to their part in particular events.

Military commanders throughout the Revolution—despite some of the poor tools they had at their disposal and their recorded criticism of them—held maps of the right sort and quality in high esteem as potentially useful, even indispensable aids to warfare. In military theory, maps were accorded an important place. The professional staff officer prided himself on his knowledge and use of maps, just as his modern counterpart might pride himself on the use of a computer for aspects of logistical management. This is consistently true of all the armies during the Revolution. Sufficient examples have been given to demonstrate this attitude in Washington and some of his general officers and in Clinton and other British commanders. It extended to both the French and the Hessians. This cartographic interest is demonstrated in a number of ways that, interestingly enough, went beyond the immediate military duties of the officers concerned.

Von Closen, one of the staff officers who accompanied Rochambeau, was already picking up hints on navigation during the voyage from Brest. He entered in his journal, "I am amusing myself by learning to calculate our position, and I will mark our course on the ocean chart given by the Admiralty to all captains of the King's ships."[138] After landing in Rhode Island, he was soon busy drawing maps and plans to illustrate his first impressions of the new World. With a comparably methodical approach to American military geography, Claude Blanchard, chief commissary to the French army, noted in the preface to his journal, "To be well acquainted with this country, we must study the maps, endeavor to know the great rivers, the position of the cities upon the banks of these rivers, from the point to which they are navigable and as far as vessels can ascend."[139] Even with campaigns in the offing, the pace of eighteenth-century war was leisurely enough for some of the French contingent to make a contribution to scientific cartography. Blanchard tells us: "M. de Cachrain took advantage of . . . [an] eclipse to make some observations upon the latitude and the longitude of the coasts of Rhode Island. He sent them to the Academy of Philadelphia; he also observes that these points are exactly marked upon the map."[140] The systematic use of maps was clearly as basic a part of the French general staff's approach to acquiring a background knowledge of America as it was integral to their detailed military planning. As another French officer summed it up after arriving at Newport, "my first care, after having performed the duties which my service required, was to study the country in which I found myself."[141]

The Hessians were no less alert to the value of maps upon their arrival in a new environment. Some of their observations of natural history and landscape add materially to our knowledge of eighteenth-century images of North America.[142] One of the first letters written home by a Hessian officer, in July 1777 from Castletown in New Hampshire, contained the suggestion, "Whoever wishes to get a clear notion of this may order from England a map: The Province of New York and New Jersey, with part of Pennsylvania and the Province of Quebec, drawn by Major Holland—1777."[143] For most educated officers of the Revolutionary period, the way to understand a country was initially through its maps. It should not be forgotten that in that era, a large part of the study of geography was a study of maps.

It will perhaps serve to sum up some of the prevailing attitudes toward maps in the Revolution, as well as one of their more important operational uses, if we consider the role they played in the acquisition and transmission of military intelligence. It was often the message rather than the medium that took precedence in the conveyance of urgent information, and military intelligence maps do not fit neatly into any of the categories enumerated in chapter 1. Indeed, some of the most inaccurate and technically inchoate maps may have been of the utmost importance. An episode was reported in the Washington papers, for example, when the American army was trying to engage the British in their march from Philadelphia; a messenger came up to Washington and drew a rough map of the British positions in the sand. This map, although ephemeral, could have been of equal importance to several of Erskine's carefully plane-tabled traverses.

Maps and plans often held what Van Doren called the secret history of the American Revolution. Even if no map drawn with the invisible ink favored by both headquarters has been recorded,[144] maps were regarded as encapsulations of major secrets. In 1776, British knowledge of the ground and fortifications at Fort Washington may have been derived in part from the treason of William Demont, adjutant to Colonel Robert Magaw of the Fifth Pennsylvania Regiment, who much later confessed that he had "sacrificed all I was worth in the world to the service of my King and Country and joined the then Lord Percy, brought in with me the plans of Fort Washington, by which plans that fortress was taken by His Majesty's troops."[145] Plans seem to have been part of the currency of deserters. It was cartographic intelligence of just this nature that John André, of the British adjutant general's department, was anxious to pick up through his secret correspondence with Benedict Arnold. In a cypher letter dated to the end of July 1779, André wrote to Arnold: "We are thankfull for the Information transmitted and hope you will continue to give it as frequently as possible. permit me to describe a little Exertion. It is the procuring an accurate plan of West Point, with the new roads, New Windsor [Washington's headquarters near Newburgh], Constitution [the fort opposite West Point] &cᵃ . . . Sketches or descriptions of Harbours to the Eastward which might be attacked and where Stores and Shipping might be destroyed."[146] Arnold later reported to André that he had "a Drawing of the works on both sides the River done by the French Engineer."[147] Judging by maps of the West Point district in Clinton's headquarters papers, some of this information was successfully passed to the British forces.[148] At the time of his capture, it was reported that André, disguised as John Anderson, had "a Parcel of Papers taken from under his Stockings, which I think of a very dangerous Tendency. . . . They contain the Number of Men at West Point and its Dependencies; the Number of Cannon &c; the different Pieces of Ground that command each Fort; & what Distance they are from the different Forts; the Situation of each Fort, and which may be set on Fire

Maps for Military Intelligence Purposes

with Bombs and Carcasses, and which are set out of Repair . . . the Situation of our Armies in General."[149] Plans of the fort and its environs doubtless were principal items of barter in the conspiracy.

The risk of espionage offered by maps, especially manuscript plans unique to one side, led to their becoming classified material during the course of the Revolution. This was often standard practice in Europe, and it is possible to trace some of the safeguards adopted by the Americans. These are illustrated in a note—with map enclosed—sent by Erskine to von Steuben in July 1779: "I beg leave to transmit you the enclosed Draught of the Adjacent Country—at the same time His Exy.[Washington] desired me to mention it as His particular request that no copies whatever be permitted to be taken of it."[150] In other cases, too, Washington urged the secure handling of maps prepared by Erskine and others.[151] His precautions were matched by British headquarters. On a pen-and-ink drawing of the ground plan and abatis of the fort of Stony Point, there is this annotation in the Clinton papers: "The exposing of this plan of the proposed work on Stony point or allowing it to be copied before it is in a thorough State of defence might possibly enable the rebels to act against it with advantage."[152] (See plate 28.)

In view of the fact that spies directed by Washington were explicitly alerted to acquire maps wherever possible, such caution was far from superfluous. In May 1780, when Washington wrote to Major General William Heath advising him of the probable arrival of the French forces on the continent, he explained that a likely objective was the "destruction of Hallifax, of the Naval arsenals and Garrison there" and ordered to be sent to Halifax: "One or Two persons of good understanding and in whose firmness and fidelity we may safely rely, to obtain the most exact accounts. . . . If they could be Draftsmen they would be so much the better, as a good plan of the Fortifications would be of essential service and is what Our Friends are very desirous of obtaining."[153] One response to this order came in August 1780. James Bowdoin informed Washington that he had "obtained, from a person who came from Halifax about a month ago, a sketch of the fortifications there, which I inclose."[154] This plan turned out to be a careful manuscript copy of Le Rouge's printed map of 1778.[155] Based on a British source, this map was presumably already available to the French. Still, Washington appreciated that a good map could be worth several thousand words. His "Instructions for Spies," issued for the briefing of agents operating near New York, required information on the "precise situation of the enemy," the location of their headquarters, the sites of new earthworks, and ended with a request for "A Description at least of Brooklyn Fort . . . and the size of it, if a plan can be had."[156]

As a result of these and similar instructions, Guthorn has been able to identify a small group of interrelated American "spy maps." All these related to New York and Long Island, including some of the targets specified by Washington:

The quite sophisticated network used pseudonyms, code numbers, well developed "cover" and was directed by a "spy master," Benjamin Tallmadge. . . . Although many of the maps were enclosed in regular correspondence, it is difficult to determine the actual authorship. The more active spies and possible mapmakers were Abraham Bancker ("Amicus Republicae"), Louis Johnson Costigan ("Z"), Abraham Woodhull ("Samuel Culper" or "722" or "C"), Robert Townsend ("Samuel Culper Jr." or "723"), Austin Roe ("724"), John Hendricks ("John Hks" or "Mrs. Elizabeth Vanderhovon"), John and Joshua Mercereau, and John Vanderhoven ("D" or "L.D.").[157]

The British, less successfully in the later years of the war, attempted to maintain a similar system. Lloyd Brown concluded:

The intelligence office of the British Army was directly under the supervision of the commander-in-chief. Scores of written reports, accompanied by crudely drawn maps and plans, found their way to general headquarters. . . . These maps show details of rebel troop movements as well as the position and size of gun emplacements in and around West Point. Maps containing secret information were almost never signed and dated, and are therefore difficult to identify.[158]

Until his capture, André directed these activities from the adjutant general's department.[159] Among the loyalists through whom he worked, Beverley Robinson, colonel of the Loyal American Regiment and later director of the guides and pioneers, was a key figure in a web of British intelligence connections throughout the Revolution.[160] Although only one map signed by him has actually been identified, it illustrates the sort of information that both the British and the Americans went to such lengths to acquire. It extended along the "Valley of the Hudson River from Fishkill River to Teller's point" and, although its detail (showing a number of roads and buildings in the West Point area) was sparse, it was amplified by "A discription of the Rebell Works in the Highlands as laid down in ye map."[161]

There can be no doubt that such maps and their accompanying reports, written or oral, were highly prized. Even where necessity had obviously been the mother of cartographic improvisation, it was the content of maps rather than their appearance that mattered to the user. All that can be garnered from fragmentary Revolutionary sources about attitudes towards maps suggests, *prima facie,* that they were at least one means by which decisions of military importance were made. Men were, after all, prepared to risk their lives (and lost them) in acquiring suitable maps. Nathanael Greene, in a February 1781 letter written from his camp on the Dan River to Washington, and surely echoing one of the better-known maxims of the century, observed that "good intelligence is the soul of an army, and ought to govern all its movements."[162] No doubt, he would have agreed that maps were an integral part of such intelligence.

However we generalize about topics such as availability, suitability, or attitudes, another problem in considering map use is that a study of decisions must involve the reconstruction of exceptional acts as well as commonly shared experiences. Thus, even when aspects of the map users' environment have been partially re-created, many unresolved questions remain about the role of certain maps in particular events. Although their place in theory can hardly be denied, the direct evidence is often impossible to find. This final section offers some tentative comment on the dilemma —more in the sense of questions raised than answered, for some questions will always remain unanswered. Factors both in the nature of the problem and in the evidence for its study are relevant to an understanding of the contribution that maps made in individual military decisions during the Revolution.

DOCUMENTED DECISIONS WITH MAPS

In ascertaining the extent to which a map influenced a particular event (even allowing for the preconceptions and knowledge of a map user), there is the problem of establishing what other types of information were just then available to the person making a decision. John K. Wright framed the matter well: "Maps are indispensable tools in human affairs. That you cannot navigate a ship without charts, however,

Maps Relative to Other Sources of Information

does not mean that you can navigate it by charts alone. Rudder and helmsman are also necessary."[163] This may serve as a reminder that specialists other than map-makers were consulted before many geographical decisions were reached. For the military events of the Revolution, this is a point on which there is some evidence. It is clear that maps were seldom, if ever, the sole basis for a commander's decision. Even under optimum conditions for military planning, the map was only one medium by which military topographical information was collected, codified, and used in reaching decisions. Contemporary printed and manuscript maps for other purposes were often accompanied by written descriptions. Text-book practice always stressed the value of a report written about the area in addition to the military map or sketch. This sort of record was demanded of both fortification and reconnaissance reports. Vallancey insisted on the importance of written military itineraries (in the manner of the French practice in the Revolution) and went as far as to imply that maps alone could be of only limited value to a general in his maneuvers.[164] Many vital pieces of geographical information were never expressed in map form. For example, tables of distances between towns (in the manner of embryonic road-books) were incorporated in the numerous printed almanacs of the Revolutionary period. In planning the attack on New York in 1776, the Howes had to derive a timetable for tides from *New York Gazette and Weekly Mercury;* from a variety of local knowledge, they made suitable allowances for the intricacies of the channel (only imperfectly charted) between the Manhattan and Brooklyn shores.[165]

Of even greater importance were guides with an adequate knowledge of the countryside. So important were they to both sides in the Revolution that it may be said their mental maps were often as valuable as the graphic maps used by the military commanders. Use of guides was advocated by contemporary European writers, with warnings to avoid treacherous ones. In North America, in often underdeveloped and unmapped countryside, they were usually indispensable. Military historians have argued that it was the local knowledge of guides (rather than any map) which decisively determined the outcome of battles in several campaigns. This may have been the case in the attack on Long Island in 1776, where loyalist guides with a detailed knowledge of local terrain directed a successful march for the British.[166] In the same campaign, Aaron Burr, Putnam's aide, led part of the American army to safety.[167] In June 1780, although Clinton was accompanied by his professional mapmakers in the march from Philadelphia (including John Hills who presumably had been instructed to prepare the best maps possible of the intended route), he still had to call on Simcoe to furnish guides to assist in route finding.[168] Even the French, the most meticulous of cartographic planners, sometimes went astray. Baron Cromot du Bourg, an aide to Rochambeau, noted after crossing the Susquehanna that "the Legion mistook the road, there being no sign posts."[169] Later he was astonished by the American practice of changing the names of taverns and ferries with their owners, so that "For this reason it is sometimes difficult to find the road."[170] (French engineers were trained to pay special attention to the verification of local names for their maps and itineraries.)[171]

Although such examples suggest that local (unmapped) knowledge rather than maps in a formal sense was frequently critical in the course of events, this is not a firmly grounded conclusion. The point is that we are back to a situation in which it is often impossible to measure the relative contribution of the several sources of information. This does not mean that guides were usually all important, nor that maps were relatively unimportant in many situations, but that we should put defined limits to our inferences about map use and influence in the Revolution. Maps were only one tool of many in the kitbag of topographical knowledge—any one of which may have provided a fact in a vital second of decision.

Another implication of exploring the relationship between the surviving sources and the events they so imperfectly mirror is perhaps the most obvious. Just as historians of cartography have intensively studied individual mapmakers, so it would be equally beneficial to document more fully the cartographic component in single events. In some respects, it is a more difficult assignment. The humblest cartographer may have left a birth or marriage certificate in addition to the graphic record of his trade, but few decision makers have actually told posterity the reason for their actions.[172] As a result, well-documented examples fall far short of their original number. There may have been an inverse relationship between the extent to which maps were in regular use and the frequency with which the instances of use were recorded. Certainly, in many situations they must have been taken for granted. If it was only the unusual incident or moment of extreme exasperation that gave rise to comment on maps, this in turn could bias our view of their significance. In the writings of Washington, his reference to maps in some periods only once or twice every two or three months probably greatly underrepresented an almost daily use of maps in military planning. Even from the surviving sample, it is clear that maps were consulted in reaching many decisions.

Manuscript maps present some particular technical problems for a study of single events. At first sight, their comparative study might appear to present few difficulties, because the manuscript maps relating to the Revolution are concentrated in fewer collections than printed maps. On the other hand, as many researchers have noted, the multiplication of duplicate or similar copies from a common source presents a major complication in any interpretation of their contemporary uses. The Revolution was one of the last major wars planned by headquarters lacking any mechanical processes for map reproduction, such as lithography.[173] As a result, one of the principal tasks of the headquarters cartographer was to make copies of maps on demand, for operational use and to accompany reports. In other cases, surveys were subsequently copied, and the historian is faced with a whole family of maps, similar in content, origin, and often appearance, but having served a variety of contemporary uses.

At present there is no agreed methodology, comparable with cartobibliography, to tackle the collation of these multiple copies as a preliminary to assessing their historical roles. An object of such a collation (as with printed maps) would be to establish the differences in topographical content and explanatory matter between interrelated copies and to arrange them in a sequence chronological with the events for which they were created. Figure 3:5 is an empirical attempt, from a knowledge of the survival and distribution of British and French surveys of the Revolution, to generalize about some of the possible stages and stemma, rather like a genealogical table, in the development of such a related group of manuscript maps.[174] The parentage of the family is rooted in a primary survey, and this developed from a field notebook, through a stage of a rough draft or *brouillon,* to a number of finished copies. In some cases a master copy of a survey was evidently kept at headquarters, though additional data might be added or subtracted at any stage in the creation of

Maps and the Events They Record

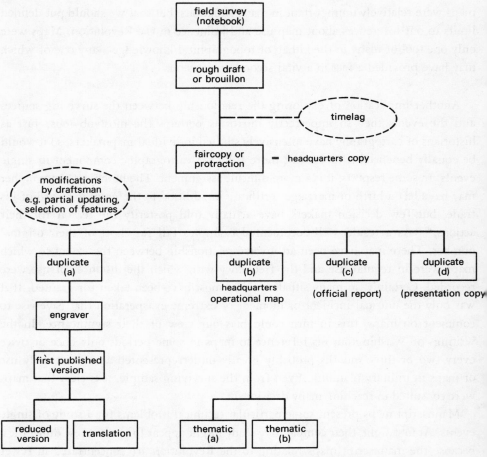

Figure 3:5 Stemma demonstrating the cartographic stages of military maps from field survey to various published versions.

new copies. In providing maps to meet changing needs, draftsmen were conveniently flexible in their treatment of topographical content. For one operation only selected information (on roads or settlements) may have been traced off, as is demonstrated by the existence of various such maps, without apparent evidence of fresh survey, among headquarters' map collections of the Revolution.[175] Despite differences between surviving copies and the fact that they were scattered both during the Revolution and in their subsequent descent through various collections, these cohorts of manuscript maps have a unity of source and sometimes interdependent use. It is necessary to reconstruct this to appreciate the full historical contributions of particular basic surveys. Such "family reconstructions," to borrow the demographer's phase, can only enlarge our appreciation of the uses of maps. Once it has been demonstrated that many manuscript surveys (like most printed maps) were put to a whole range of uses over a period of time, then the somewhat artificial distinction between manuscript and printed maps will tend to disappear from the documented study of the place of maps in events. Far from being unique, the single manuscript map was frequently a link in the larger chain along which topographical information was transmitted through time and space.

The last word in this study lies with three contemporaries who observed the events of the Revolution from different vantage points; to all of them, maps were of great importance. The first documented example of a map user of the Revolutionary era was Frederick the Great. With a map in front of him in his Potsdam Palace, he followed the course of events in the American war, delighting in the defeat of the Hessians (whom he disliked) and approving of Washington's campaign.[176] As a soldier, he regarded a map as any other weapon, for he believed: "Knowledge of the country is to a general what a rifle is to an infantryman and what the rules of arithmetic are to a geometrician. If he does not know the country he will . . . make gross mistakes. . . . Therefore study the country where you are going to act . . . the most detailed and exact maps . . . that can be found are taken and examined and re-examined frequently."[177] The emphatic last sentence expresses his deep conviction about the value of maps.

A man more often troubled than delighted by his maps was Sir Henry Clinton. Some time after the disaster at Yorktown, when he was still trying to erase blemishes from his military record, we discover him retracing events. In a recriminatory mood, he as much as accuses Cornwallis of inadequate cartographic preparation for the siege. The nub of Clinton's case was that no systematic plan of the ground was made before the siege works began, although Cornwallis had implied its existence in dispatches to New York. According to Clinton, Alexander Sutherland, Cornwallis's engineer at Yorktown, had "very honestly confessed that *he had never surveyed the ground they stood siege on, and consequently had no plan.*"[178] For Clinton, such an oversight was unthinkable. He felt it was Cornwallis's "indispensable duty to have lost no time in transmitting to me a plan of the ground with his own opinion upon it."[179] Indeed, Clinton implied that he had to obtain a full picture of the geography of events at Yorktown with the help of French plans.[180] He came back to his example of Cornwallis's professional neglect, like a dog worrying a bone, on an unfinished pen-and-ink sketch of the British works at Yorktown and Gloucester (it extended only about half a mile inland and lacked any descriptive text), where he annotated, "The only plan of York I could obtain from Southerland L.C. Chief Engineer, and the person he said that had made an Exact survey and Examination of it."[181] To Clinton at least, the lack of an adequate topographical plan of the ground contributed to the British defeat at Yorktown. This claim was made, admittedly, by an officer whose concern with facts contained in maps was almost an obsession (indeed Clinton fought more battles on paper than on the ground), and it may lead us to question its wider validity. The situation does, however, neatly demonstrate the potential historical importance of a map.[182]

A final example is provided by Joseph F. W. DesBarres, who was trying to secure greater remuneration from the Admiralty for his previous work as a chart maker. As proof of the value of his charts in the Revolution, he included in his "Statement" several first-hand testimonies by naval commanders telling how *The Atlantic Neptune* had assisted them. In one such incident:

The Phoenix, ordered to Boston under the command of Sir Hyde Parker, had had an almost continued storm for three weeks, in which it was impossible to take an observation: finding himself in soundings, all the Journals of the ship were examined, and from thence it was concluded they were off Cape Cod; but Sir Hyde Parker, comparing the quality of the bottom with the description of the soundings marked in the Atlantic Neptune, conjectured, what was truly the case, that he was off Isle Sable, and in the course of being soon a-ground; therefore, he altered his course, contrary to the remonstrances of his officers, and, while these were in constant dread of being a-shore, he arrived under an easy sail in two days off Cape Cod.[183]

There is no doubt that a critical decision in this case rested primarily on the correct use of a chart. It may encourage us, as it did DesBarres, to make wider claims: "Such instances are innumerable. In the course of the publication it was common for Officers and Commanders of vessels arriving from America, to come to Des Barres's house to thank him for having been saved from shipwreck, by his Charts."[184] Such documented case studies, when properly substantiated, are the vital raw material of the history of map use. From them, with due circumspection and with the help of appropriate theory, we can then draw wider conclusions. The surface has hardly been scratched in detailing the use of maps in eighteenth-century North America.

The Revolution—apart from its many other historical fascinations—provides a relatively well documented springboard for pursuing such studies. The fact that men of action—Des Barres's sea captains—were eager to visit with their cartographer after the voyage home shows to what extent the cartographer and his work were esteemed. We cannot help appreciating the significance of maps during this period.

4 | The Mapping of the American Revolutionary War in the Nineteenth Century

The distinguished scholar Hans Kohn, while comparing European and American nationalism at the Massachusetts Institute of Technology in the 1950s, contrasted Swiss and American attitudes toward resident aliens. My recollection is that he said the Swiss were suspicious of any alien who wished to become a citizen; Americans, on the other hand, were suspicious of aliens who did not. To the Swiss, he went on, being Swiss means being several generations a native of the soil, with bloodlines reaching back into the dim and unrecorded past, sharing one or more common languages, and having a cultural identity that could not be conferred by legislative act. To the Americans, however, being American means voluntarily choosing to share certain loosely defined common values variously described as freedom, democracy, free enterprise, or Americanism. Underscoring his point, Professor Kohn doubted that there would ever be a Swiss counterpart of the then Un-American Activities Committee.

The reasons for this emphasis on values rather than on origins lie in American history and the unique developments of the Revolutionary generation. The United States of America were a new nation and, as in a new marriage, they had very little common history. Out of thirteen former colonies strung out along some fourteen hundred miles of seacoast, and out of a population comprising some four million souls of British, European, African, and Amerind origin (a more diverse people in one nation than the world had ever seen), that remarkable first generation created a nation almost overnight. By inventing the constitutional convention at the state level and then at the national, the Founding Fathers developed a way to legitimize a revolutionary government, one that succeeded in transferring power, not only from one political party to another, but also from one generation to another. In short, they solved the constitutional problem of sovereignty, at least until the Civil War.

During the nineteenth century, the American nation took away from the Indians, the Spanish, the French, the Mexicans, and the English a territory more than four times its original size. The nation survived one of the bloodiest civil wars in history;

For author's acknowledgments, see page 167.

it freed its vast slave population (which had grown naturally more rapidly than any other slave population in the Americas); it absorbed immigrants from Europe numbering nearly five times its original population; and it changed from a society that was primarily rural, agricultural, and commercial into a vast industrial power.

THE AMERICAN REVOLUTION
AS MYTH

Lacking the "natural" ties that bound more ancient peoples together, Americans early turned to the history of the American Revolution and to biographies of their Founding Fathers for a substantial part of their national myth. George Washington, for example, became the American Ulysses, and during the nineteenth century dozens of biographies of that hero were published—in some of which he would not have recognized himself.

Ironically, in the earliest years of the new nation, its best histories—David Ramsay's two-volume masterpiece, *The American Revolution;* William Gordon's *The History of the Rise, Progress, and Establishment of the Independence of the United States;* and even John Marshall's four- volume *Life of George Washington*—relied heavily for fact, interpretation, organization, and a good deal of text on a British publication edited by Edmund Burke and known as the *Annual Register.*[1]

Even for the maps and charts that illustrate the war of the American Revolution, the new nation depended heavily on English and French cartographers and map publishers contemporary with the Revolution.[2] For years, the British author Charles Stedman's *History of the Rise, Progress, and Termination of the American War* (published in London in 1794) provided the most useful military text and maps of that war. Even as late as the 1840s, Benson J. Lossing, when writing his popular *Pictorial Field Book of the Revolution,* visited the battlefields with Stedman's work in hand.[3]

Soon, however, the new nation was ill content to rely on its early histories and its early historians, just as it was unwilling to rely on a non-American language and literature. As Noah Webster put it in 1789: "Our honor requires us to have a system of our own, in language as well as government. Great Britain, whose children we are, and whose language we speak, should no longer be *our* standard; for the taste of her writers is already corrupted, and her language on the decline."[4] Similarly, Ralph Waldo Emerson, writing half a century later argued that: "Perhaps the time is already come . . . when the sluggard intellect of this continent will . . . fill the postponed expectation of the world with something better than . . . mechanical skill. Our day of dependence, our long apprenticeship to the learning of other lands, draws to a close."[5]

As in language and literature, so also in history: Americans early generated a great deal of historical activity, on various levels, much of it focused on the Revolution and on the War for Independence. The Founding Fathers had known they were participating in great events, and they left to the nation a remarkable corpus of papers. Learned societies, such as the Massachusetts Historical Society, the American Philosophical Society, the New-York Historical Society, and the American Antiquarian Society, began to gather, preserve, and publish the nation's historical record. Even the Congress created its own library. Soon, gentlemen antiquaries were filling volumes of "proceedings" with accounts of every battle, skirmish, and encounter; new historical journals were created and carried stories of the Revolution; and general magazines, such as *Harper's Monthly,* printed extended accounts of that war.

Probably the most popular historian of the nineteenth century, and the most effective myth creator in the larger sense of the word, was George Bancroft. His monumental ten-volume *History of the United States, 1834–1874*) devoted six volumes to the Revolutionary period, 1763–1782, including two volumes on the war. In this history—based on a wide use of manuscript and other source materials, European as well as American—Bancroft depicted the Revolution, according to Page Smith, as "the golden age, the time of giants, the opening act of the extraordinary drama of American democracy."[6] "History, for Bancroft, was the working of Divine Wisdom, and God's eternal principles were discoverable through its study. . . . Seen in this light, the Revolution appeared as part of God's plan: it was intended for the edification of man and the improvement of society; it ushered in a new and brighter age of human progress."[7]

Despite Bancroft's sweeping panoramic vision—with its foundation in the Puritan view that Americans were God's chosen people—he, like other historians, wrote intensively on purely military aspects of the Revolution, criticizing this commander and that and delighting in the controversy his words engendered. Indeed, as Don Higginbotham has said, military history in the nineteenth century was, "on the whole, narrowly conceived to mean the field of combat. Captain John Parker mustering his company on Lexington Common, Washington crossing the ice-filled Delaware, Greene struggling through fog at Germantown . . . young Alexander Hamilton seizing a redoubt at Yorktown—all this, and little more, was military history."[8]

Given the nationalistic need for a historic myth, this intense interest in the battlefield, and the remarkable series of nobly conceived and executed contemporary maps already available, one would not be surprised to find in American histories an extensive and imaginative use of cartography as an adjunct to the history of the War for Independence as written in the nineteenth century. Similarly, in Europe, given the emergence during the American Revolution of both a citizen army, or armies, and very successful partisan or guerilla warfare, one would expect that the Revolutionary War—and the maps of the war—would have been extensively written about and studied in nineteenth-century Europe.

Unfortunately, in neither Europe nor America was that the case. Peter Paret, in his "Colonial Experience and European Military Reform at the end of the Eighteenth Century," finds that the colonial wars, in America and India, provided little but emotional examples, not hard case studies for tactical reform. "The decisive innovation in infantry fighting," he said, ". . . consisted in the acceptance of open order tactics by the line infantry. Close order methods—the line, the attack column, fire by volley—were now combined as a matter of course with skirmish groups and individual, aimed fire."[9] But the examples were not found in America: "many of the great and minor figures in the military reform movements of the time showed little special interest in colonial wars—Scharnhorst and Clausewitz are two examples."[10] Consequently, there was apparently no great demand in Europe for either the military annals or the maps of the American Revolution showing our ragtag and bobtail military tactics.

As for American histories, there were many. But with few exceptions, if maps were used at all extensively (Bancroft, for example, printed none in his war volumes, nor did he cite any), they were ill used and they added little to an understanding of the text they accompanied. In the history of cartography, they

Hard Times for Historical Cartography

represent a retreat from, rather than an advance over, the maps of the eighteenth century.

To be sure, there were many maps produced or reproduced during the period. With the help of David Sanders Clark's "Index to the Maps of the American Revolution," I looked at some seven hundred maps in ninety-four books and fifteen periodicals. They began appearing in the first decade of the century and they reached a numerical peak just before the Civil War, when the Revolution became at once a part of the controversy between the North and South and, as myth, a possible cement for the distintegrating nation. They peaked again, predictably, in the 1870s, the centennial of the Revolution, and their production stayed at a fairly high level to the end of the century.[11]

As one might expect, the methods of reproduction evolved parallel to the printing history of the century. The largest percentage down to 1850 were copper or steel engravings, with lithography and wood engravings frequently used for large foldout maps and small maps in books, respectively. By the end of the century, line cuts predominated, although lithography and wax engraving were still in use.

The average size of these maps was 24.5 square inches, or not quite 5-by-5 inches. For the most part, it appears, map size was technically a function of how large a map the page size would allow, for maps were mostly reproduced in books and periodicals. Intellectually, it is just barely too harsh to say that map size seems to have been a function of keeping the maps small enough to be virtually unintelligible.

The use of symbols (which in eighteenth-century maps often involved the use of different colors) also deteriorated. Examination of eighteenth-century maps reveals a score or more conventional symbols, such as a man-of-war, a ferry boat, a watch boat, cavalry, troop encampments, troop movements, redoubts, cannon, and the like. There was very little development in these symbols in the nineteenth century. Troops, ships, fortifications, and troop movements were simplified and standardized, but the loss of color greatly reduced what a given map could tell. Troop encampments and troop movements are usually indistinguishable, and many of the ornamental features of the earlier maps were lost. In short, no notable advances were made in the difficult art of depicting movement in space over time.

The publishing company Matthews-Northrup was an exception. In 1891 there appeared John Fiske's two-volume, *The American Revolution,* which contained eleven maps designed and printed in color by means of wax engraving by the publishers. Matthews-Northrup continued to produce maps of unrivaled quality in the twentieth century, culminating in Elroy McKendree Avery's *History of the United States and Its People* (7 vols., 1904–1910). Indeed, Barbara Petchenik has called this latter work "a landmark in American map-making" and "the only real contribution to the 20th-century mapping of the War of the American Revolution."[12]

Finally, concerning the technical features, one has to deal with map compilation. Again, with some notable exceptions, there were few advances in the period. Most of the maps printed in the nineteenth century were old maps. To the extent they were redrawn, redrawing was to simplify detail for reproduction in a smaller size rather than for accuracy. Apparently little effort was made to compare maps with battle terrains, with the manuscript or printed accounts of the participants, or with each other. As a single example of what could have been done, the Historical Society of Pennsylvania in 1846 commissioned a survey of the terrain of the Battle of Brandywine. The map was designed by one Joseph Townsend and has since been used at least three times, most recently in an adaptation by Douglas Southall Freeman in his *Life of Washington*. It embraces more territory than the famous Faden map, it shows roads along which troops moved, and it is, or was at least intended to be, geographically more accurate.[13]

In short, the historical cartography of the Revolutionary War during the nineteenth century lacked a systematic foundation in both theory and technique, and this was especially true for the mapping of the Revolution. Revolutionary battles in general were not seen as case studies in military tactics and strategy; still less were they viewed in light of the wider problem of the relationship between geography and human behavior. The Revolution was an episode to be celebrated, not analyzed. It is not surprising, therefore, that maps of the war were limited to reproductions within books, serving as illustrations rather than integral parts of the text.

But if historical cartography was in a rudimentary state, cartography was not. One has only to look at John Melish's *Atlas of the War of 1812* (published in 1813) to know that good maps could be, and were being, produced in America. This work includes five handsomely-engraved 16-by-21-inch maps: three are by the distinguished cartographer Henry Schenk Tanner, one is an eighteenth-century map, and one is based on a British engineer's sketch of the fighting on the Detroit River.[14] The fact is that cartographic energy was being devoted more to contemporary maps than to historical maps. America was expanding into uncharted lands: following the Louisiana Purchase, the Lewis and Clark expedition, and the emerging conquest of the West, American cartographic enterprise was more challenged by mapping a new nation than by an old war.

An account of the nineteenth-century mapping of the American Revolution could stop right here, were it not for three men. They, however, make a major difference in the story, not only because they each made a significant contribution to the cartography of the Revolution, but also because each is interesting in himself.

THREE CONTRIBUTORS TO REVOLUTIONARY CARTOGRAPHY

Benson J. Lossing

The first of these men is Benson J. Lossing, 1813–1891, publisher, editor, wood-engraver, and author. His most important writings are a series of volumes called *Field-Books*—of the Revolution, of the War of 1812, and of the Civil War. The first, *A Field-Book of the Revolution*, was published in thirty parts by Harper's during 1851–1852, then as a book in two volumes, which he twice revised.[15]

Lossing's first *Field-Book* is a narrative account of his eight-thousand-mile, five-month journey to the scenes of the Revolutionary battles, then rapidly changing. He was really more interested in depicting scenes and views and buildings than drawing maps, alas. Of the nearly twelve hundred illustrations, only seventy-six are maps and, truth be told, even the maps are often more illustrative than militarily informative. They are miniscule, the largest being about 3-by-5 inches, and they provide very little information for the general reader.

What contribution, then, did Lossing make? First, he made an effort to compare standing maps with the actual terrain. As he told a correspondent years later, he visited the battlefields with Charles Stedman's maps in hand, carrying as well a camera lucida and a drawing board to record his impressions on the spot.[16] He also interviewed aged survivors of the war. His research was necessarily unsystematic, but Lossing did gain access to many private manuscript holdings.[17] Moreover, even though the rise of the historical profession was another half-century in the future,

Lossing was in touch with the leading scholars of the time. "Mr. Irving, Mr. Sparks, Mr. Force, Mr. Frothingham and many others," he wrote, "genuinely expressed their desire to contribute all in their power to my work. . . ."[18]

Lossing, we must remember, was not an objective historian-cartographer. His *Field-Book* and his maps were designed to play a symbolic role, to build American nationality by appealing to its glorious Revolutionary past. Perhaps Lossing believed that the sectional conflicts of the 1850s could be quieted through a timely invocation of the Revolution. As an admirer wrote, the *Field-Book* was "peculiarly opportune in these foppish and degenerate days when we appear to be losing sight of our revolutionary landmarks in the fogs of partyism."[19] And when civil war came, Lossing began a new Field Book—"a Great National work"—which might help provide a new foundation on which to rebuild American unity.[20] His "unflinching national sentiments," in Lossing's own words, ran throughout his work.[21] Only at the end of the nineteenth century, with the advent of "scientific history," environmental determinism, and a greater appreciation for the interplay between geography and history, would historical cartography become more objective and scholarly.

Henry B. Carrington

Lossing provides a direct link to the second figure worth remembering, Henry Beebe Carrington, 1824–1912, for whom Lossing's on-site inspections and publishing success were an inspiration. The two men frequently corresponded in the 1870s, the older man, Lossing, being unstinting in his support, suggestions, and praise. Carrington's claim on our attention rests chiefly, of course, on his *Battles of the American Revolution, 1775–1781,* which went through at least five editions and from which was published, as a separate work, his *Battle Maps and Charts of the American Revolution* (New York, 1881).

There were several impulses that led to Carrington's interest in the military history of the Revolution. His great-grandfather had served in the colonial army, and some of his military gear was still around when Carrington was a child. Carrington tells of his youthful anger at a hired man who sharpened up the old soldier's sword "for the purpose of cutting corn stalks. . . ." "My mother," he wrote, reproved "my wicked" outburst that "I wish it had cut his head off."[22] On the annual training days in Wallingford, Connecticut, Carrington recounted:

Just after sunrise, there passed by the old home two soldiers of the Wallingford Light Infantry. This Company retained the uniform . . . worn during the Revolutionary War as a part of Lafayette's Special Light Infantry Division, with which he marched . . . to command the campaign against Cornwallis. . . . The hats of these soldiers were surmounted with a tall white feather, nearly eighteen inches in length, and tipped with red. The swallow-tail coat was also a fiery red, while the trousers were white. On the Training Days, several carriages, or large wagons, brought to the view of the people large and small the presence of surviving Revolutionary Veterans, and two or three of them used to visit the Tavern and rehearse stories of their war experience.[23]

Carrington's childhood interests in the Revolution and the military were reinforced by the career of his grandfather, James C. Carrington, who had been a partner of Eli Whitney in the manufacture of arms at Whitneyville, Connecticut, from 1800 to 1825, and was subsequently superintendent for the United States of the manufacture of arms there and inspector of works at the arsenals at Springfield and Harper's Ferry.[24]

In fact, young Carrington's interest in the military would have led him to West Point had lung trouble not prevented it. Instead he decided for Yale, where his maternal grandfather and great-grandfather had studied. Upon graduating in classics, he taught at the Irving Institute in Tarrytown, New York, for two years. There he came to know Washington Irving, who had just returned from being United States Minister to Spain. "His acquaintance," wrote Carrington, "laid the foundation for my years of subsequent labor in preparing *The Battles of the American Revolution*."[25] Irving himself followed the same course by publishing his four-volume biography of Washington between 1857 and 1859.[26]

One final influence on Carrington must be mentioned. That was John Brown, the radical abolitionist. Before attending Yale in the early 1840s, Carrington heard John Brown preach and became an immediate convert to the cause of abolitionism. After college and after teaching at the Irving Institute, Carrington moved to Ohio to practice law and there played an important role as an antislavery man in organizing the Republican Party. In 1857, he jumped at the chance to enter the military, and he reorganized the Ohio militia, becoming adjutant general. At the outbreak of the Civil War, he rushed nine regiments across the Kentucky border, saving that state for the Union, and earned a federal commission as colonel. His vigorous Republicanism and abolitionism led him to try several Copperheads or Sons of Liberty (Democrats who opposed the war) by military tribunal, but the convictions were later reversed by the United States Supreme Court. After the war, Carrington participated in various military campaigns in the West against the Indians: he built Fort Phil Kearney in Nebraska, he took part in the Red Cloud War, and he defended the Union Pacific against Indian marauders. He was severely wounded in one of those engagements and in 1869 was detailed to teach military history at Wabash College in Indiana.[27]

Reflecting later on his Indian fighting, in a speech delivered in England, he revealed the same kind of manifest-destiny nationalism that led him to participate so zealously in the Civil War. These same sentiments are everywhere evident in his book on the Revolution:

The Anglo-Saxon, in his westward march, still meets the red man. It is the old story of an issue of races in the expansion of the stronger. The inferior must perish. Bloody issues have been evoked, and earnest efforts have been made to harmonize the conflicting elements; but the waste goes on. On the one hand, all passions are stimulated to annihilate the savage as a beast, because he tears and tortures in the throes of his death struggle; and, on the other hand, we yearn for his rescue from that oblivion which buried his earlier ancestors, because we feel that his destinies, like his possessions, are in our hands.[28]

Carrington's real work on *The Battles of the American Revolution* began when he started teaching at Wabash College. As he wrote George Bancroft: "During my labors at this college for nearly five years, I have given a course of lectures upon the battlefields of the Revolution: using maps compiled from all known sources, excluding so far as possible civil history and presenting Washington, Greene, etc. as military men through the actual field operations of the War. . . . Neither at West Point nor elsewhere," he added, "has a similar enterprise been attempted."[29]

During the last year of Carrington's work before publication, there was a flurry of activity. He sent outlines, some maps, and some text to Bancroft and Lossing, both of whom encouraged him to go on, as he did Generals Sherman and Sheridan.

Bancroft urged him to use the New-York Historical Society, the Lenox Collection, and the Library of Congress. Lossing encouraged him, saying that his work "cannot fail to be exceedingly interesting to all scholars, and especially to students of American History, whether in military circles or not, and I hope you will carry out your plan, successfully. A Knowledge of the topography of the battlefield, is a very great help in rightly understanding a report of the battle. . . ."[30]

Sherman was particularly interested in the military value of Carrington's work: "I have no doubt in your studies to illustrate your lectures on the Military Science you must collect much valuable material that would warrant presentation in the form of a Book. I know of nothing of the kind about the Revolutionary War—should you desire you may use my name for I am sure such a book as you describe would be most valuable to military men and to professors engaged like yourself in the effort to save our profession from sinking clear out of mind."[31]

The climax to Carrington's research was a trip to England and Europe in 1875, recorded in his scrapbook. There he visited the British Museum, the Bodleian, the Royal Geographical Society, and the Bibliothèque Nationale. At the British Museum he checked out Stedman's *History,* Clinton's *Narrative of the Campaign of 1781* (Philadelphia, 1865), and Faden's plan of Newport, Rhode Island, 1777. To his hometown newspaper he wrote on 28 July 1875, "My time has fastened itself to regular hours, between the War Office, British Museum, and Hall of Records. Generous courtesy meets my work, and from ten to twelve, and one to five, I am at maps and books, old watercolor sketches of Charlestown in flames, pen and ink plans of battles, and even pencil plans. . . ."[32]

On his return from Europe, Carrington completed the maps and the text and, with the help of Lossing, finally found a publisher, A. S. Barnes and Company, who printed it in parts during 1876. By November of that year, General Sherman had read the third part and wrote to tell him that he would "call the attention of the officers to it, that they may Encourage you in the long effort to systematize and arrange American military history so that it may be studied."[33]

In December came a letter from George Bancroft filled with praise, but revealing a little pique that Lossing might have caught him out in an error: "I have just received your splendid volume, which I see at once is the fruit of much toil and careful research, & the advantage of military experience. One matter caught my eye: pray do not think it ungracious if I enclose to you a little memorandum on a point, where you think me in the wrong: but where I hope you will find reason to reverse your opinion."[34] Unfortunately, the little memorandum is lost.

Using the same maps, Carrington then prepared a slim volume, *Battle Maps and Charts of the Revolution,* published in 1881. It is an ugly book, with the one page of text for each map, printed in alternating lines of red and black ink. But, as did his earlier volume—which was priced at five dollars, a high price for those days—it sold well. Carrington helped; for example, he urged it on Secretary of War Robert Todd Lincoln in 1882. Wrote Lincoln in reply: "With reference to your suggestion that said work would be of value, as a text book, for the Military Academy, I beg to state that 36 copies for the use of the military schools at West Point, Willetts Point, Fort Monroe, and Fort Leavenworth were purchased by the department in July last."[35]

Since this essay is supposed to be about maps, not chaps, it is not enough that Henry Beebe Carrington was a colorful character who happens to deserve a biography of at least article length. Instead, we now have to address the question, just what did he contribute to the history of historical mapmaking, in particular of the Revolution? Several observations, it seems to me, can be made.

First, the *Battles of the American Revolution* grew out of a felt need for maps with which to teach the history of the war. The contemporary maps were already scarce, widely scattered, and probably unavailable at Wabash College where Carrington was teaching. He moved to supply that need, perhaps only coincidentally, in time for the centennial in 1876. Thus the maps were presented as deliberately patriotic history, not news.

Second, the maps are newly-compiled, not reproductions, and they are based on several sources. These include some on-site visits, research in old maps, and research in the written records of the combatants. Carrington visited at least six map repositories in the United States, and his bibliography cites three hundred sources, European as well as American. (Unfortunately, there is no record for any single map of whether Carrington visited the site, of what other maps he used, or of what written materials he consulted. The bibliography for the *Battles* is a general one.)

Third, while the book includes text as well as maps, the maps are of primary importance and the book was designed with them in mind. It is a historical atlas. As we have seen, the maps were later published separately in a small atlas, and they are quite able to stand on their own.

Fourth, as a military man experienced in topography and mapping, Carrington kept his maps uncluttered and readable, even understandable. Bancroft commented on the value of Carrington's military experience, and Lossing said that Carrington's "topographical maps will be the next best, in giving clearness to history, to an actual visit in person."[36]

Finally, a new method of map reproduction, wax-engraving, had been developed, allowing maps of considerable clarity, compared with other maps of the period. This method was invented in the United States by Sidney Edwards Morse in the 1830s. By the 1870s, a number of large map publishing companies had begun to use the process.[37] It was wax-engraving, including the use of set type for the lettering, that Carrington's publishers used. (The total costs for illustrations, composition, and plates, by the way, was $2,569.)

Despite the real advances made by Henry Beebe Carrington, the culmination of nineteenth-century and the beginning of twentieth-century cartography of the American Revolution came with Justin Winsor, Librarian of Harvard College. This formidable scholar, who became the century's leading student of the history of cartography, was born in Boston in 1831.[38] He attended Boston Latin School and there acquired a distaste for organized instruction that, at Harvard, led him to near revolt and near suspension. Winsor spent two years in France and Germany instead of finishing his college courses, and got his degree only several years later. His attitude was not mere youthful rebelliousness against all authority, however, for on his return from Europe, he lived happily with his parents—even after he was married—until his forty-ninth year. It was rather that he thought classwork got in the way of an education that was proceeding very well on its own. He was probably right, for in his freshman year he had published his first book, *A History of the Town of Duxbury*: he was then eighteen years old.[39]

Winsor turned his back on American history for some twenty years, devoting

Justin Winsor

himself to literary criticism, poetry, commentary, and fiction. For fourteen of those years he worked on a monumental study of the life and times of David Garrick, the eighteenth-century actor and playwright. When he completed it, in 1864, it comprised ten folio manuscript volumes. Never published, it sits with forty other volumes of Winsor manuscripts at the Massachusetts Historical Society.

Winsor returned to writing history after becoming head of the Boston Public Library in 1868, and he continued in that field as Librarian of Harvard College, where he succeeded John Langdon Sibley in 1887. It was while ransacking and then bringing to order the collections of the Boston Public Library and the Harvard College Library that Winsor first drew together his knowledge of the sources of the American Revolution, including the maps. As a freshman at Harvard, his diary relates, he had prepared a lecture on the Northern Campaign in the Revolution, for which he painted some "diagram like maps."[40] But it was in his *Readers Handbook of the American Revolution 1761–1783* (Boston, 1879), that he made not only his first substantial effort, but *the* first substantial effort, to bring the maps of the Revolutionary War under bibliographical control. In that volume of 328 pages there are 34 sections on maps (some only a sentence or two, others a page or more) describing printed maps, maps in books, and manuscript maps, along with their locations.

That book was a necessary background for his next work, *The Memorial History of Boston,* a vast compendium in four volumes, still very useful, and one of the first cooperative histories in America, published in 1880–1881. As general editor of *The Memorial History,* he said, he "secured seventy writers, endeavored to unify their contributions, and aimed to complete publication in two years. It was completely finished in twenty-three months."[41] There were giants in the land in those days!

In these volumes, Winsor provided the editorial apparatus—essays on sources, and the like—foreshadowing his later cooperative work, *The Narrative and Critical History of America.* The *Memorial History* apparatus includes two extensive lists of maps of Boston and its environs, in one of which appears the Battle of Bunker Hill. There Winsor listed and critically compared several maps, each of which had gone through various transformations as they were used again, and again, and again. I quote at length to illustrate the painstaking cartobibliographical detail he affords the student:

Lieutenant Page [whom Winsor identifies in a footnote] made an excellent plan, based on a survey by Montresor, of the British Engineers, showing the laying-out of Charlestown. The successive positions of the British line are indicated on a smaller superimposed sheet. This was issued in London in 1776, called *A Plan of the Action at Bunker's Hill on the 17th June, 1775, between His Majesty's Troops under the Command of Major-General Howe, and the Rebel Forces.* The same plate; with some changes, was dated April 12, 1793, and used in Stedman's *American War.* It was re-engraved, reduced, by D. Martin, substituting American for Rebel and Breeds for Bunker's in the title, with a few other changes in names, and issued by C. Smith in 1797, in *The American War from 1775 to 1783.* See Hunnewell's *Bibliography of Charlestown and Bunker Hill,* 1880, p. 18, where a heliotype is given. It was again re-engraved, much reduced (5¼ x 9 inches), for Dearborn's *Boston Notions,* 1848, p. 156; and soon after, full size, following the original of 1776 in Frothingham's *Siege of Boston. . . .*

Henry de Berniere, of the Tenth Royal Infantry, made a map similar in scale to Page's, but not so accurate in the ground plan. It was called *Sketch of the Action on the Heights of Charlestown,* and having been first mentioned in the *Gleaner,*—a newspaper published at Wilkesbarre, Pa., by Charles Miner,—as found recently in an old drawer; it was engraved, in facsimile, in the *Analectic Magazine,* February, 1818; where it is stated to have been found in the captured baggage of a British officer, and to have been copied by J. A. Chapman from an original sketch taken by Henry de Berniere, of the fourteenth regiment of infantry, now in the hands of J. Cist, Esq. General Dearborn commented on this plan in the *Portfolio,* March 1818 (reprinted in *Historical Magazine,* June, 1868), with the same plan altered in red (19½ x 12¼ inches), which alterations were criticised by Governor Brooks in June, 1818. See *N.E. Hist. and Geneal. Reg.,* July, 1858. G. G. Smith worked on this rectified plan in producing his *Sketch of the Battle of Bunker Hill, by a British Officer* (12 x 19 inches) issued in Boston at the time of the completion of the monument in 1843.

Colonel Samuel Swett made a plan (18½ x 12½ inches), based on De Berniere's which was published in his *History of the Battle of Bunker Hill,* and has been reproduced, full size, in Ellis's *Oration* in 1841; and reduced variously in Lossing's *Field Book of the Revolution,* in Ellis's *History,* and *Centennial History;* and in other places.[42]

Alas, there were only a few maps reproduced in this section of *The Memorial History,* mostly by heliotype, the best method of facsimile reproduction then available. I suspect that Winsor's disappointment over their poor legibility led him to changes in his monumental *Narrative and Critical History of America,* published in Boston, 1884–1889. It is the sixth of these eight cooperatively written volumes that concerns us.

This volume comprises eight chapters, two written by Winsor. At the end of most chapters are "Critical Essays" and "Notes" by Winsor, sometimes running nearly as long as the text. Scattered throughout the volume, frequently in these sections but also in the text, are ninety-four maps (more than twice as many as in Carrington), fifty-eight of them reproductions.

While Winsor's maps vary in size, method of reproduction, and quality, they have three important elements in common. First, each map's source is given, usually with a genealogy of the map's various transformations through book after book in the nineteenth century, as illustrated above; second, for each map Winsor indicated whether it was an exact reproduction or a sketch based on the original; and third, he indicated the method of reproduction. Even a casual study of this volume reveals much about Winsor as a cartobibliographer, as a cartographer, and as a frustrated scholar trying to fit maps of varying sizes to a set page size. Let us deal with the frustrations first.

Winsor had devoted a great amount of time to cartography and maps, as we have already seen. In the Massachusetts Historical Society are five large folio scrapbooks with facsimiles of maps (and some originals) that Winsor gathered not only for *The Narrative and Critical History* but also for his later works on Columbus, on the Mississippi Basin, and on the Far West. He was ready to do a nearly definitive work. But book publishers were not up to the job. On Bunker Hill, for example, we know he was an authority, as is shown in his *Handbook* and in his *Memorial History of Boston.* But in the chapter concerning Bunker Hill and Boston in *The Narrative and Critical History,* not one of the seven maps or the one view is as informative as he would have liked.

First appears a drawing, based on a tracing (provided him by Lossing) of the original manuscript sketch made from Beacon Hill of Charlestown following the battle. He had used a later engraving of this for *The Memorial History,* but here he wanted to get closer to the original. It was reproduced as large as his page permitted. While it does convey the sense of immediacy, the details are difficult to distinguish, and the manuscript handwriting is illegible to middle-aged eyes.

There follow: first, a sketch of Charlestown peninsula from the plan by Montresor, which is almost useless; second, a cut of the Charlestown Heights Battle plan from the *Analectic Magazine,* that, as reduced, has a legend so small Winsor had to have it set in the text on the following page; third, a full page reproduction from Stedman's *History,* showing Boston and Bunker Hill, which is much clearer than the preceding map; fourth, a reduced reproduction from the Atlas accompanying Marshall's *Life of Washington,* far inferior to the original; fifth, a map of Boston and vicinity taken from a photograph of a map in *Almon's Remembrancer;* sixth, a sketch based on a manuscript in the Library of Congress entitled "A Draught of the Town of Boston and Charlestown . . . 1775," which, while attractive, is merely an illustration here because it really cannot be read without magnification; and finally, a quite legible detail from Page's *Plan of the Town of Boston* (London, 1777) showing the British lines on the Boston Neck, but again with the legend requiring resetting in the text.[43]

These frustrations, I believe, led Winsor to become his own cartographer. They led him to try to produce pen and ink drawings, with lettering and numbering of his own, that, when reduced photographically and subsequently reproduced (by linecut, a process developed in the 1880s), would be intelligible, or at least legible to the reader. How he did this can be inferred from an examination of his scrapbook volumes in the Massachusetts Historical Society. In that work are an extended note by Winsor and two maps of the Brandywine campaign. The original map, which was Washington's, Winsor found "much crumpled and torn" in the Pennsylvania Historical Society. He had a facsimile tracing made of it, and then reduced the facsimile photographically to see how clearly the legend and detail would show. That reproduction is in his scrapbook. He then retraced it, simplifying the detail considerably. He then placed printed numbers on the map corresponding to the location of Washington's notes on the original, and these notes were then printed separately in the text.[44] In all, Winsor produced thirty-six maps by this method.

One other example of Winsor's cartobibliographical work in *The Narrative and Critical History* should be mentioned, for it shows how careful he was. The map is of the Battle of Guilford, 15 March 1781. A comparison with the original— that is, with Faden's map printed in 1787—reveals a reduction in size and, of course, the use of only black and white. Also lost are Faden's trees and underbrush. But otherwise the maps are identical, at least to the untrained eye. Wrote Winsor:

Sketched from Faden's map (March 1, 1787), which is the same as the map in Tarleton (p. 108), with the same date, and Stedman, ii. 342, with slight changes, dated Jan. 20, 1794. It is followed in the maps in *Mag. of Amer. Hist.* (1881), p. 44; in R. E. Lee's *Lee's Memoir,* etc., p. 276; and Caruthers' *Incidents* (Philadelphia, 1808), p. 108; in Lossing's *Field-Book,* ii. 608. There are among the Faden maps (nos. 52, 53) in the Library of Congress two MSS. drafts of the battle,—one showing the changes of the position of the forces. Johnson (*Greene,* ii. 5) gives five different stages of the fight, and G. W. Greene (iii. 176) copies them. His lines vary from the description of Cornwallis. Cf. Carrington's *Battles* p. 565; Hamilton's *Grenadier Guards* (ii. 245); *Harper's Monthly,* XV, 162, etc. Ed.[45]

Winsor, then, emerges as the most significant nineteenth-century cartographer and cartobibliographer of the American Revolution. He reproduced more maps, and, with the exception of Carrington, his own maps are more legible than those of most scholars restricted to book-page size. He experimented with different ways of reproducing maps, settling finally on photographically reduced tracings and eliminating what he considered unnecessary clutter to make the main lines legible, then using the linecut method of reproduction. Winsor compared different maps and different accounts in arriving at his final delineations, much as modern scholars edit a manuscript that has various versions to establish the text. He provided (unlike Carrington) documentation for each map, and he prepared a systematic cartobibliography for each battle.

If the work of Justin Winsor marks the culmination of nineteenth-century historical cartography, it also represents a significant departure from the mapmaking of Lossing and Carrington. The last decades of the nineteenth century were formative ones for the historical profession. The days of the patrician amateur were clearly numbered: an ambitious group of university-trained men were endeavoring to bring order and professional standards to their discipline. Viewing the works of earlier historians as romantic and subjective, these new scholars wanted to place history on a "scientific" basis. Winsor was among this group.[46]

THE COMING OF SCIENTIFIC HISTORY

The scientific basis of such scholarship derived in part from Darwinism, which had a tremendous impact on all aspects of American thought. In history, the impact took the form of environmental determinism. Rather than seeing American history as the unfolding of providential design or as the development of Teutonic institutions, the so-called scientific historians believed that environment was primary in shaping human thought and behavior. Frederick Jackson Turner, of course, was the preeminent spokesman for this point of view. Winsor too was influenced by this outlook, and he concluded that mapmaking must be a necessary part of historical analysis. His systematic appreciation for cartography thus contrasted significantly with the more antiquarian—and nationalistic—concerns of Lossing and Carrington. Winsor expressed his views about the importance of environment in this way: "I would not say that there are no other compelling influences, but no other is so steady."[47]

There remains to be made a brief foray into the twentieth century in anticipation of Barbara Petchenik's essay. I wanted to find out whether twentieth-century historians of the Revolution relied on nineteenth-century cartographers and cartobibliographers. With the help of Professor Don Higginbotham of the University of North Carolina, I chose eight military histories published between 1909 and 1972.[48] Of the eight works, all but one, Howard Peckham's *War for Independence,* have maps. In the others, the number of maps varies from a low of eight to a high of sixty-three—in Francis Vinton Greene, *The Revolutionary War and the Military Policy of the United States.*

The two works published earliest, Steel's *American Campaigns* and Greene's *Revolutionary War,* are the only ones that follow, in a limited way, the cartobibliographical principles developed by Winsor. They cite works by Carrington, Henry Johnston, and Fiske, all from the nineteenth century, as sources for their maps. The remaining six moderns do cite nineteenth-century works in footnotes and bibliographies.

Here the most enduring works appear to be studies of individual battles, such as those by Charles Coffin, Henry Johnston, and Richard Frothingham.[49] Willard M. Wallace's *Appeal to Arms* and Christopher Ward's *War of the American Revolution* were the heaviest users of such materials.

The two most recent works, by John Richard Alden and Don Higginbotham, probably point to the future, for they depend even less than their predecessors on nineteenth-century histories. This is indicative of the growing body of twentieth-century secondary literature on the Revolution: the increased attention being given to archival sources, the shift away from stories of battles to other aspects of military-social history, and the greater availability of contemporary maps today than at the beginning of this century. Thus nineteenth-century cartography appears to be falling into disuse. For the most part, it is of only antiquarian interest.

In my opinion, however, Justin Winsor, at least, will be consulted as long as no better critical cartobibliography exists. And, indeed, his volume 6 was recently republished, in 1972, as *The American Revolution* (New York: Lands End Press). Even so, the cartobibliographical material thus reprinted needs redoing: after nearly a hundred years, it cannot stand as definitive. *Sic transit gloria mundi.*

5 | The Mapping of the American Revolutionary War in the Twentieth Century

As time passes after the occurrence of some striking or remarkable event, it is inevitable that interest shifts from the details of the event to its broader significance—from the journalistic "who, what, where, when" to the more complex and subtle causes, effects, and meaning. By 1900 the War for American Independence had been officially over for 117 years. Considerable lay and scholarly interest persisted, but there took place around 1900 a marked change in the nature of this interest.

Most writers of the eighteenth and nineteenth centuries treated the Revolution in a way that glorified military events—the "drums and trumpets" school of history. By 1903, however, historians such as Sydney Fisher were reacting strongly to that approach. In the preface to his volume, *The True History of the American Revolution,* Fisher wrote:

I understand, of course, that the methods used by our historians have been intended to be productive of good results, to build up nationality, and to check sectionalism and rebellion. Students and the literary class do not altogether like successful rebellions; and the word revolution is merely another name for a successful rebellion. Rebellions are a trifle awkward when you have settled down. . . . The Revolution was a much more ugly and unpleasant affair than most of us imagine. I know many people who talk a great deal about their ancestors, but who I am quite sure would not now take the side their ancestors chose. Nor was it a great, spontaneous, unanimous uprising, all righteousness, perfection, and infallibility, a marvel of success at every step, and incapable of failure, as many of us very naturally believe from what we read.[1]

This point of view became so pervasive among historians that by 1925 Allen French felt called upon to react strongly to *it* in the opening sentences of his book, *The Day of Concord and Lexington:* "Modern history burrows so deeply into causes that it scarcely has room for events. In place of the old descriptions of battles, of the prominence once given to kings, statesmen and civilian or military heroes, history now occupies itself with economic and social conditions and sometimes seems to regard happenings as mere accidents, to be allowed as little space as possible."[2]

French's observation holds true not only for the history of the American Revolution but for the writing of American history in general during the twentieth century. The study of military history has remained at a low level throughout much of the present century. A 1972 bibliography of doctoral dissertations in military affairs lists only seventy dissertations in eighteenth-century American military history, and only a few of those are concerned directly with the American Revolution.[3] In considering the discipline of American history as a whole, John Higham refers to the peripheral place that military history has occupied: "As yet, however, scholars in the universities have studied little more than the politics of military groups and the details of particular military campaigns. The general history of war as an institution remains only a dimly perceived ideal. Academically speaking, military history is still a sideline."[4]

CHANGES IN MAPPING THE WAR OF THE AMERICAN REVOLUTION: 1900–1975

This essay has begun with a brief description of the writing of American history because the mapping of the Revolution in this century is intimately related to it. Virtually all maps associated with the topic of the Revolution have been made by or for historians whose chief concern was writing about historical events, not mapping them. It follows that if military history has been peripheral to the mainstream of American historical thought and writing, and if maps have been peripheral to military history, then such maps are likely to be something less than first-rate in conception and appearance.

Quantitative Variation in Mapping

There are three distinct peaks in the quantities of maps of the American Revolution produced during this century, and these peaks are somewhat related (but not identical) to qualitatively distinct periods of historical text production. The matter of quantity is illustrated in figure 5:1, a graph of the number of publications cited per year from 1780 through 1967, in David Sanders Clark's "Index to Maps of the American Revolution in Books and Periodicals."[5] It is probable that his citations are

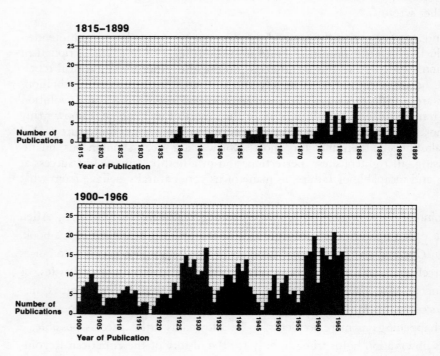

Figure 5:1

more complete for recent years, because it is more likely that such materials have been acquired by the Library of Congress, where he did his work. Nevertheless, his survey seems representative of trends in the quantity of publication on this subject, and it is used here as such.

As the graph shows, there has been a continuous, if somewhat irregular, upward trend in the amount of material published with maps. But there are distinct peaks and valleys in such publication, and they are of interest. The first peak occurs from about 1875 to 1883 and reflects the usual increase in publication that the anniversary of an event generates, here the centennial of the Revolutionary War period. There is another peak around the turn of the century, from about 1895 to 1905. This is the period of the multivolume, general American history, both popular and scholarly, more or less focused on the Revolution. Thereafter, there is a decline in the number of publications until the spurt of 1925 that lasts until about 1932; this too is an anniversary, 150 years after the Revolution. Then there is a general decline until the early part of the 1950s when there occurs a sudden increase without benefit of anniversary. Clark's work terminates in 1967, but an enormous amount of publication has taken place since then, motivated in part by the forthcoming bicentennial celebrations. I believe that shortly after the first year or two of these celebrations there will be a precipitous decline in the number of publications about the Revolutionary period and that this will last for twenty years or so, due to a natural exhaustion of undiscovered sources, novel viewpoints, and marketing opportunities.

There are three distinct subperiods of writing about the Revolution in this century, but they correlate only approximately with the trends in quantity of publication.

First, there is the period of the multivolume general history, lasting from about 1895 to about 1920. There follows a period lasting until the late 1940s during which a great many detailed studies of specific aspects of the Revolution were published. Diplomatic, political, and economic studies, as well as military studies and biographies of military figures appeared. These were certainly significant in themselves, but more important, they provided new, high quality, primary material from which could be fashioned the more synthetic general histories of the Revolution published between 1948 and the present. In other words, there is a sequence within the twentieth century from general histories based on eighteenth- and nineteenth-century sources, to meticulous primary studies of specific events, to another round of general histories based on these foregoing twentieth-century studies—synthesis to analysis to synthesis.

Although one commonly speaks of "mapping a war," war is a human activity that cannot be mapped directly. The word *war* is a verbal abstraction that summarizes and encodes a reality consisting of complex sequences of events created by the observed actions of tangibles (people) acting from intangibles (intentions and goals). When maps are made to clarify or communicate spatial aspects of the complexity of war, the mapper must select the tangible for depiction. One common approach is to map the distribution of troops at critical moments, usually before, during, or after battles. Another is to map the places that are relevant to the conduct of the war, again usually battle sites. To contemporaries of the event, the

Qualitative Variation in Mapping

Mapping the Phenomenon "War"

details of battle action are important. Hence, most eighteenth-century maps of the war are large-scale battle maps. Interest, however, has shifted to more general and abstract concerns. But the maps made to accompany texts with this new point of view have not developed much beyond eighteenth-century interests. Furthermore, no one seems to have considered what the explicit cartographic implications of these new concerns should or could be. Instead of a major rethinking, only some superficial changes have been introduced: fewer maps have been produced and of these the place-name variety is the most common; the number of names on maps has declined; the graphics have become more generalized; and random and often ridiculous selections of material have been made in order to effect some simplification.

The remainder of this essay will offer first, a selective chronological analysis of the three major periods in twentieth-century mapping, based on an extensive survey of published maps; second, a review of the three major technological developments that have affected such mapping; third, a description of the three major kinds of military map content that occur during the period; and finally, a description of the novel approach to the mapping of the Revolution recently taken in the *Atlas of Early American History*.[6]

The Twentieth Century: A Descriptive Chronology of American Revolutionary War Maps

1900–1920: The Period of the Multivolume Histories

G. O. Trevelyan's important four-volume history, *The American Revolution,* published in London between 1899 and 1903, contained a few fold-out maps like the one shown in figure 5:2, made by W. and A. K. Johnston of Edinburgh and London.[7] This is the only map included here that approximates the look of an eighteenth-century map, a quality that derives from its being engraved in metal, either copper or steel. Such intaglio maps are not common in this country after 1900.

Wax-engraving was the dominant technique for producing printed maps in books during the first third of this century, and such maps tended to be the work of a few specialist firms.[8] Figure 5:3 is a portion of a wax-engraved map that appears in the third volume (1912) of Edward Channing's *A History of the United States,* a six-volume work published between 1907 and 1925.[9] The map was prepared by the Williams Engraving Company of New York, and it is unusual in that the source map is indicated. It is a poor copy of the source, however, indicating that although the Williams Company may have had the technical facility to produce such maps, the ability was not matched by a concern for accurate data. The map in figure 5:3 is almost as illegible in its original form as it is in this reproduction.

While Trevelyan's and Channing's works were scholarly, other multivolume histories published about this time were directed to wider audiences. They were more popular in content and included many illustrations. James Wilford Garner and Henry Cabot Lodge are the authors of the four-volume *History of the United States,* published in Philadelphia in 1906.[10] The few maps appearing in these volumes are poorly done. Figure 5:4 shows an unidentified copper- or steel-engraved map that was photographed and overlaid with a dot screen. Again, the original is not much more legible than this reproduction.

Another popular history is John Clark Ridpath's *New Complete History of the United States of America,* published in twelve volumes between 1905 and 1907. A wide range of techniques was used (but not very well) to produce the maps in

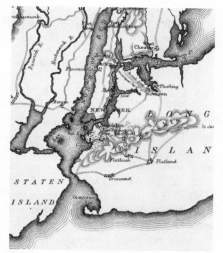

Figure 5:2

Figure 5:4

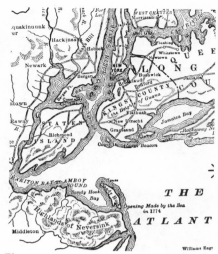

Figure 5:3

Figure 5:5

this work. Figure 5:5 shows one of two maps from the same page, a photograph of a sophisticated copper- or steel-engraved map (probably of the eighteenth century.)[11] The other (not shown) is a crude sketch map. The use of photography to make printing plates had become common by this time, allowing even amateurish drawing to be reproduced directly.

The only real contribution to twentieth-century mapping of the American Revolution is Elroy McKendree Avery's seven-volume *History of the United States and Its People,* published between 1904 and 1910. This was intended to be a sixteen-volume set, but the seventh volume was the final one—perhaps because the cost of the set's lavish production could not be met by its sales.[12] The seven extant volumes are extraordinary in graphic conception for the time and are a landmark in American mapmaking. Because these books were produced for popular consumption, few scholars are aware of the

provenance of these maps, although many have seen them reproduced in Francis Vinton Greene's *Revolutionary War and the Military Policy of the United States* (1911). It appears that Greene learned of the maps through his friend and West Point classmate, Charles William Burrows, president of the Burrows Brothers Publishing Company of Cleveland and publisher of Avery's book. Greene says of the Avery maps in the preface to *his* volume:

> They are the only maps of the Revolution that are accurate. They have been prepared in the only way in which accurate maps can be made—viz., by using careful topographic surveys (in this case those of the United States Geological Survey) as the basis, and placing on these the positions of the troops as stated in the official reports of the commanding generals, reconciling the discrepancies between different reports as well as possible. Most of them were drawn by Lieutenant Joseph

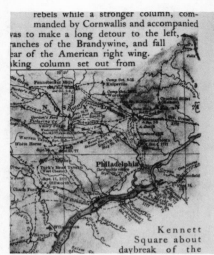

rebels while a stronger column, commanded by Cornwallis and accompanied ...was to make a long detour to the left, ...ranches of the Brandywine, and fall ...ear of the American right wing. ...king column set out from

Kennett
Square about
daybreak of the

Figure 5:6

A MAP
of the
TOWN and HARBOUR
of
BOSTON
Drawn by a Captain in
His MAJESTY's Navy

Figure 5:7

Baer, United States Army, while on duty in the Department of Drawing at West Point in 1904. . . . Prepared in this way all the maps have been engraved [i.e., wax-engraved] and printed at the Matthews–Northrup Works in a manner that leaves nothing to be desired.[13]

In volume six, which deals with the Revolution, there are sixteen reproductions of eighteenth-century maps and sixty-nine newly compiled and drawn maps. Lt. Joseph A. Baer of West Point is given sole credit for forty-six of the maps, and a number of other compilers are listed for the remainder.[14] Only two maps do not carry identification of authority or compiler, a remarkable occurrence in a century in which omission of this information is the rule rather than the exception.

Technically, all of the maps are printed in five inks: black, a dull yellow-green, a turquoise blue, a bright royal blue, and red. Register is generally poor, probably unacceptable by today's standards. The base for nearly all the maps is a shaded relief terrain drawing, printed in a half-toned version of the yellow-green ink. There is unusually good and consistent generalization, although each map is unique in scale. The maps nearly always contain a graticule and scale, though it is peculiar that in such a coherent series of maps, more than twenty different forms of scale statement and graphic scale should occur in volume six. A number of the maps extend across pages of text, with very imaginative layouts incorporating maps, drawings, photographs, and text. In figure 5:6 the arrangement of the map in relation to the text on the page amply demonstrates that the maps were conceived as an integral part of the book design.[15] This is, of course, a desirable way to handle maps, but one only rarely encountered.

The Matthews-Northrup Works, where it is presumed the designing and wax-engraving was so competently carried out from drawings, was an important mapping firm in this period, having a major geographic reference library and staff of skilled map compilers. The booklet, *The Making of Fine Maps,* describes some of the work of the firm, mentioning with justifiable pride the *Century Atlas,* a complete set of maps for the *Encyclopedia Brittanica,* and the maps for Avery's *History.*[16] The map department of Matthews-Northrup was acquired by the J. W. Clement Company of Buffalo in 1926,

and was finally discontinued in 1963.[17]

Since their original publication, Avery's maps have been copied and republished in adapted forms several times, with no credit given. It is unlikely that they will ever be surpassed, and they must surely qualify as the finest maps of the American Revolution to be made during the twentieth century.

1920–1948: An Inactive Period

As noted earlier, military history was not a popular subject between 1915 and 1948. Studies of the Revolution done in this period tended to treat various aspects of the war—political, diplomatic, economic—not directly related to military affairs. Consequently, only a few maps of the Revolution were produced. These were, with few exceptions, of deplorable quality, resulting primarily from the use of photographic reduction that rendered the originals illegible. During this period, Allen French produced several landmark studies on the early events of the war. The map shown in figure 5:7 is from his book, *The First Year of the Revolution* (1934), and is an example of the degradation of the image brought about by photography.[18] In general, French was little concerned about maps in any of his publications. Hoffman Nickerson published a landmark study of the Saratoga events in 1928, and he included a fine essay on the geography and mapping of the region. However, the map he drew (fig. 5:8) is practically meaningless, the only dominant shape being that of "mountain country" (the area with lines).[19] H. L. Landers produced an important study of Yorktown (1931), and his book has some unusually competent fold-out maps drawn by Donald Windham, although the complexity of linework on the maps frequently leads to illegibility (fig. 5:9).[20] Troyer Anderson's 1936 book about the peculiar behavior of the Howe brothers during the early years of the war is an important work, but the hand-drawn maps in it (fig. 5:10) are mere illustrations, rather feeble in appearance and content.[21]

It is important to point out that Anderson's book, like many others to be written in subsequent decades, was based on eighteenth-century sources that had just become available through acquisitions made by William L. Clements for his library in Ann Arbor, Michigan. Clements acquired the Clinton and Greene papers in 1925, the Gage papers in 1930, and

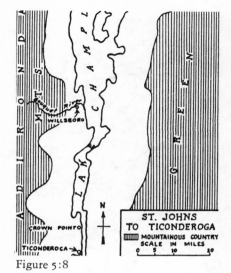

Figure 5:8

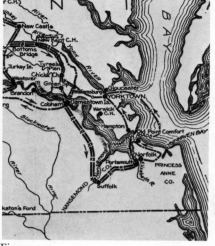

Figure 5:9

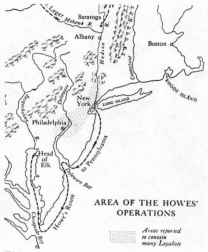

AREA OF THE HOWES' OPERATIONS

Figure 5:10

Figure 5:11

Figure 5:12

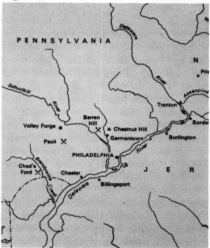

Figure 5:13

the Shelburne and Germain papers as well.[22] Although these materials have been extremely valuable as sources for scholarly writing, they seem to have had no direct impact on cartography.

1948–1975: The Synthetic Military Histories

The most recent era of synthetic military studies of the American Revolution opens in 1948 with John Miller's *Triumph of Freedom.* This book contains a number of battle maps drawn by Van H. English. As is usual in recent decades, no sources are given and the maps appear to have been treated as illustrations rather than as data (fig. 5:11).[23]

John Alden is an important scholar of the Revolution but, like many modern scholars, he has not been very interested in or concerned with mapping in his many books. Alden's first general work on the War, *The American Revolution,* published in 1954 by Harpers, contains

some banal and unauthoritative map-illustrations (fig. 5:12), apparently done by a staff artist, including neither sources nor credits.[24] The style of the maps is similar to much of the graphic illustration done in the 1950s—utterly lacking in either charm or precision.

Marshall Smelser's 1972 book, *The Winning of Independence,* includes a few neat, austere, place-name maps with, as usual, no reference to source or maker (fig. 5:13).[25]

Atlases and Reference Work Mapping

Another category of map publication—one that does not fall specifically into any single time period—is that of atlases and reference works focusing on American military history. These include the maps of the Revolution on a two-page spread in Charles O. Paullin and John K. Wright's *Atlas of the Historical Geography of the United States* (1932). Thick red and blue lines, small scales, and trun-

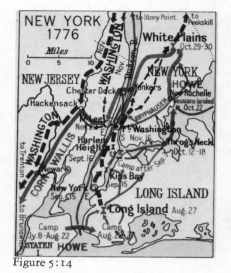

Figure 5:14

Figure 5:15

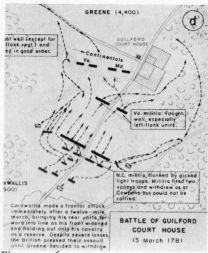

Figure 5:16

Figure 5:17

In 1959 Praeger published the first volume of *The West Point Atlas of American Wars,* covering 1689–1900, under the editorship of Vincent Esposito, with Edward Krasnorski as cartographer. In addition to a running narrative in the volume, the *West Point Atlas* includes textual notes printed on the maps, providing some help in clarifying the content—providing one already has a good understanding of the event depicted. But in general, the maps (fig. 5:16) are not of high quality, some of them having been taken directly or even traced from Henry B. Carrington's nineteenth-century atlas.[28] Lines of march in red and blue are difficult to follow, and the user must be familiar with standard military terminology and symbols.

Mark Mayo Boatner's invaluable reference work, the *Encyclopedia of the American Revolution* (1966), includes many maps that are, unfortunately, of generally lower quality than the text. Boatner himself provided full-scale sketches that were then drawn in more finished form by several draftsmen. The maps are minimal in design, both intricate and sketchy at the same time (fig. 5:17).[29] They are, however, more comprehensible than might otherwise be the case because they accompany detailed textual accounts of the action they depict.

This, then, is a descriptive survey of the twentieth-century mapping of the Revolutionary War, focusing on the wide range of content and design that has appeared. There are, however, several other ways of looking at these maps. One is to focus on the production and reproduction techniques employed to make maps during the last seventy-five years.

cated areas produce maps that are difficult or impossible to use (fig. 5:14).[26]

In 1934 James Truslow Adams and R. V. Coleman directed the production of maps for Scribner's *Atlas of American History.* These maps (fig. 5:15) were compiled by various historians, each an expert on his topic, and then converted to consistent hand-drawn artwork by a staff at Scribner's that included LeRoy Appleton, Chief Cartographer, and Arthur S. Bryant, his assistant.[27] The maps are attractively hand-lettered and meticulously drafted, but they are erratic in coverage (for example, a full page is given to Moore's Creek Bridge) and so deficient in base data that it is difficult or impossible to relate them to locations on modern maps.

Figure 5:18

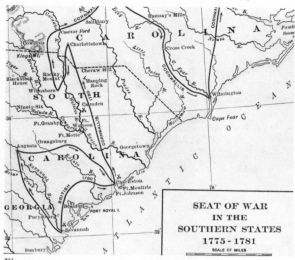

Figure 5:19

Cartographic Technology in Twentieth-Century Military Mapping

There is a general sequence of map production technology occurring within this century, beginning with the very end of the copper- and steel-engraving era, continuing through wax-engraving and letterpress printing, and culminating in the photoengraving, photolithography, scribing, and stickup lettering techniques of the present day. The development and use of photography has set the maps of this century sharply apart in appearance from maps of earlier centuries. Photography has been useful and has had good effects on cartographic production, but it has also made possible illegible reproductions of early maps and the inclusion of drawings of such poor quality that they barely qualify as maps.

Copper- and Steel-Engraving and Wax-Engraving

A late intaglio map from Trevelyan's 1903 work has already been shown in figure 5:2. The hand lettering, the tremulous coastline, and the high contrast noticeable here can be said to characterize most nineteenth-century intaglio maps.

Wax-engraved maps occur frequently from the turn of the century through the 1930s. The map in figure 5:18, from Fisher's *True History of the American Revolution,* is by the firm of W. J. Bormay.[30] Several other Bormay wax-engraved maps appear in various incarnations nearly to the present day. The map in figure 5:19 first appeared in Claude Van Tyne's *American Revolution* (1905), one of the twenty-eight volumes of Harper's *American Nation* series (1904–

1918). It reappeared in Harper's *Atlas of American History* in 1920 and was still appearing in a 1956 printing of Samuel Eliot Morison and Henry Steele Commager's *Growth of the American Republic.*[31] This is a good example of the pervasive presence of wax-engraved maps in American cartography, a point made in other contexts by David Woodward.[32]

Figure 5:20 is taken from Nathaniel Wright Stephenson and Waldo Hilary Dunn's two-volume biography of George Washington, published in 1940.[33] It is a product of the J. W. Clement Company, purchaser of the Matthews-Northrup Works, and it has the typical look of a late wax-engraved map—tidy, but rather clumsy and stilted.

Photography and Photolithography

The development of photography in the nineteenth century gave rise to widespread practical application of its advantages in the twentieth century. The results of its use in cartography are mixed: they range from abuse of the technique and production of exceedingly poor maps to excellent photographic reproductions of rare maps that otherwise would be almost inaccessible.

There is no need to do more than pass quickly over the following all-too-common examples of the abuse of photography in map reproduction. The maps from 1930s and 1940s publications by Thomas G. Frothingham (fig. 5:21) and Louis Gottschalk (fig. 5:22) are illegible because of vast reduction from the originals. At the opposite end of the spectrum, however, are two recent publications that reproduce eighteenth-century maps at or near the same scale as the originals—the

Figure 5:20

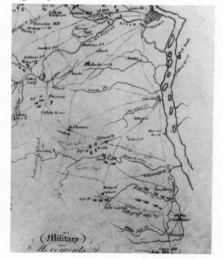

Figure 5:21

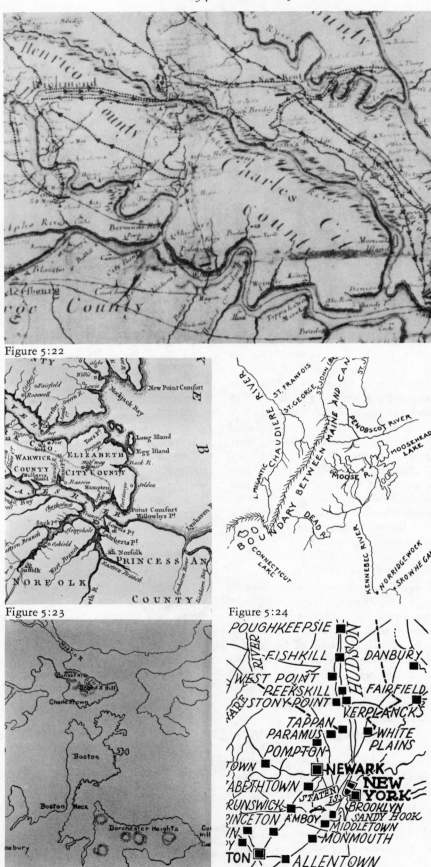

Figure 5:22

Figure 5:23

Figure 5:24

Figure 5:25

Figure 5:26

Naval History Division's *Atlas* of reproductions (fig. 5:23) and Kenneth Nebenzahl's *Atlas of the American Revolution*.[34]

Photography also makes it possible to reproduce amateur drawings such as those in figure 5:24 taken from Ridpath's 1905 *History* and in figure 5:25 from a 1948 book by Alden.[35] Of course, photography can make possible the reproduction of high quality artwork, such as that seen earlier in the 1943 Adams-Coleman *Atlas* (fig. 5:15).

Douglas Southall Freeman's four-volume biography of George Washington (1948–1957) includes textual commentary demonstrating the author's clear understanding of the geography of the period and of the reliability of various cartographic sources in such matters. But virtually none of this expertise is communicated to readers of his book through its maps, for Freeman's presentation has been effectively sabotaged by the deplorable map design of the artist, John Draper. Town names obliterate most of the coastline (fig. 5:26), while town symbols occupy space equal to almost ten square miles, when they could have been effective at one-tenth that size.[36]

Christopher Ward's fine two-volume history, *The War of the Revolution,* was published in 1952 under the editorship of John Alden, who continued the work after Ward's death in 1943. It contains many competently drawn battle maps (fig. 5:27), but nowhere in the volumes does Alden identify the mapmaker.[37] Fortunately, there is a small note in the book saying that certain of the maps were taken from Ward's 1941 work on the Delaware Continentals, where they are identified as the work of Leon DeValinger, Sr., an archivist.[38] One can assume from the similarity in style that all the rest of the maps are also DeValinger's work.

The Current Technology

At present, maps are frequently scribed on plastic film and type is set and applied in wax-backed stickup form. An early use of such type is shown on the map (fig. 5:28) by an unidentified artist in Willard M. Wallace's 1951 book.[39] The map in figure 5:29 is from *The American Heritage Atlas of United States History* (1966), done under Duncan M. Fitchet's cartographic direction, and shows a modern map made with scribing and stickup techniques.[40] For the limited purposes of book illustration, where the maps are always considered subordinate to the text

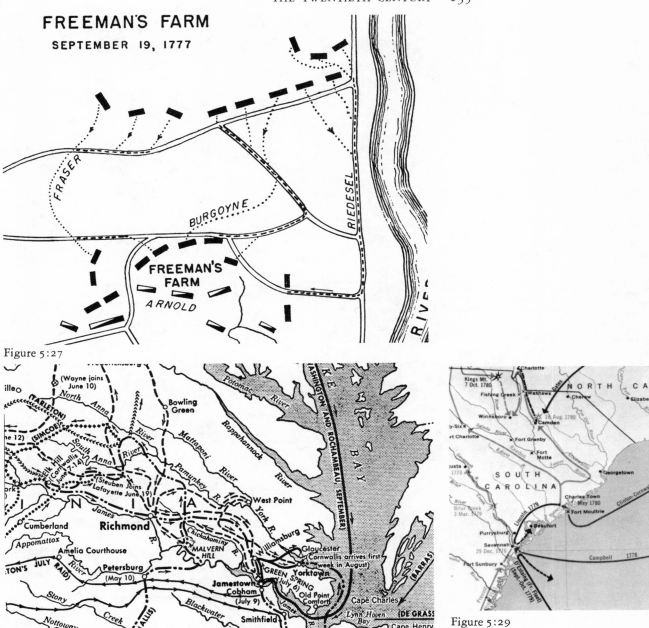

FREEMAN'S FARM
SEPTEMBER 19, 1777

Figure 5:27

Figure 5:28

Figure 5:29

(and usually to the other illustrations as well), this technology tends to be too expensive, and hand-drawn maps are consequently still common in many books.

A Typology for Twentieth-Century Military Maps

Turning from the technology of mapmaking to the content of twentieth-century Revolutionary War maps, one finds no clear linear development paralleling that of technology. The same kinds of maps recur throughout the century, the only possible trend being a decrease in the absolute number of all maps and considerably less frequent use of traditional battle maps. As will be apparent, however, battle maps have always been less common than place-name reference maps.

Place-Name Maps, Small Scale

Most of the maps made to accompany military histories are small-scale place-

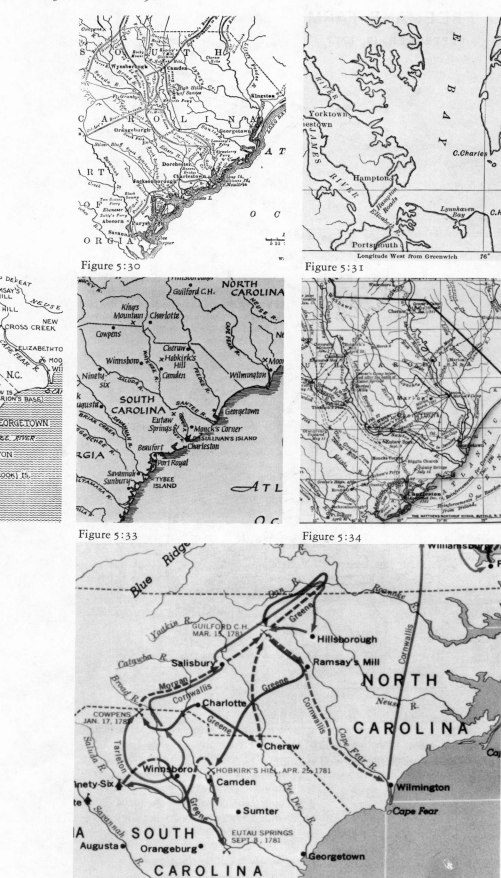

Figure 5:30

Figure 5:31

Figure 5:32

Figure 5:33

Figure 5:34

Figure 5:35

name maps. They show one or more states and simply include a variety of place-names associated with the locations of significant military actions or strategic concern. Such maps are shown in figure 5:30, from Channing (1922), and in figure 5:31, an uninformative illustration from Gardner Allen's *Naval History of the American Revolution* (1913), where the use of a full page for a miniscule amount of information is hard to understand.[41] Boatner uses rather densely covered place-name reference maps for front and back endpapers (fig. 5:32).[42] Alden, in his 1969 work, *A History of the American Revolution,* includes some place-name information on artistic maps (fig. 5:33) by Rafael Palacios—but these maps are more attractive than they are reliable.[43]

Place-Name and Line Maps, Small to Medium Scale

A second kind of map encountered frequently in military works is the "places-connected-with-lines" type, where the lines imply troop movements, either for a limited length of time or over the course of an entire campaign or war. These maps tend to be drawn at small or medium scales, covering areas ranging from several states to a portion of one state. They are generally chaotic in appearance, sometimes virtually impossible to understand, even when they cover limited time periods and appear in a good source like Avery (fig. 5:34).[44] Such maps become absolutely meaningless when they summarize campaigns that took place over the course of several years, as in figure 5:35, which appears in the 1971 Webster's *Guide to American History.*[45] The maker of this map (and others in the volume) is not identified, but stylistic evidence suggests that it was produced by the C. S. Hammond Company.

Battle Maps, Large Scale

The third and last kind of map that recurs in military histories is the more or less traditional battle map, depicting either the arrangement of troops at one point in time, or attempting to show troop movements over some limited amount of time (such as during a battle) with dashed lines, arrows, and so on, generally at large scales. These are the maps that everyone expects to see and that hardly anyone understands. Even the eminent British military historian, J. W. Fortescue, in the 1899 preface to his thirteen-volume history of the British army, reports that he found battle maps unclear and misleading.

He includes them in his book, however, because others thought that he should have them (fig. 5:36).[46] In his words:

Maps and plans have been a matter of extreme difficulty, owing to the inaccuracy of the old surveys and the disappearance of such fugitive features as marsh and forest. I have followed such contemporary plans wherever I could in fixing the dispositions of troops, but in many cases I should have preferred to have presented the reader with a map of the ground only, and left him to fill in the troops for himself from the description in the text. Blocks of red and blue are pleasing indeed to the eye, but it is always a question whether their facility for misleading does not exceed their utility for guidance. Actual visits to many of the battlefields . . . did not encourage me in my belief in the system, although in deference to the vast majority of my advisors I have pursued it.[47]

Fortescue is unique in his perceptiveness and honesty about this situation. Most authors appear to include whatever map comes to hand, as long as it has a title that seems to relate to the battle under discussion. The *West Point Atlas* is an example of this problem, at least for the lay user, although its maps may be clear enough to the military specialist. Maps such as those encountered in Samuel Smith's excellent 1960s studies are impossible to decipher without text and are rather muddled in graphic form (fig. 5:37).[48] Boatner at-

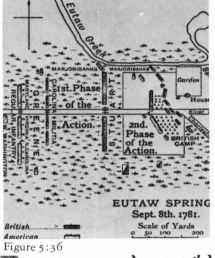

Figure 5:36

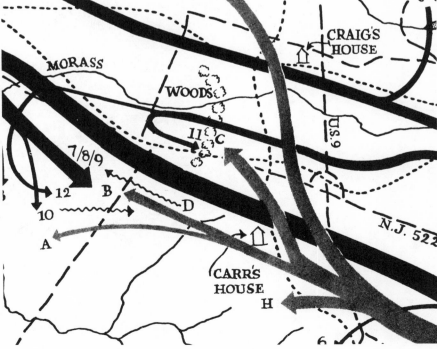

Figure 5:37

Figure 5:38a

Figure 5:38b

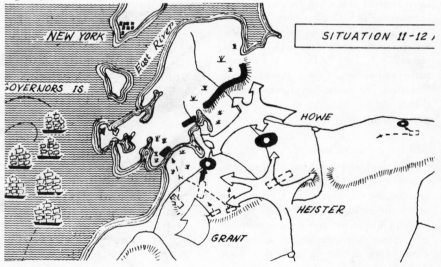

Figure 5:38c

Figure 5:39

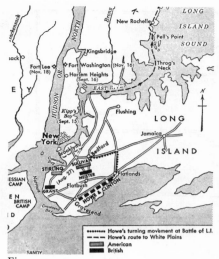

Figure 5:40

Figure 5:41

tempts to avoid complex arrays of lines and arrows in mapping troop shifts by substituting a series of maps about one event, each covering a different time period during the course of a battle (fig. 5:38).[49] Still, these remain indecipherable without the accompanying textual account.

Achronological Aspects of Twentieth-Century Mapping of the American Revolution

From a chronological survey of twentieth-century mapping of the War, we now turn to two characteristics of these maps that transcend chronology: (1) that authors and mapmakers evidence little regard for maps as data, as sources of documented and documentable information; and (2) that they also evidence little regard for the meaning of maps, or for the communication of that meaning to readers and viewers. Both of these characteristics have their origins in one fact: mapping has been secondary or peripheral to the development of text. With a few exceptions, there have been no professional cartographers involved in the making of the maps thus far discussed.

Low Regard for Maps as Data

One example of the common disregard for the quality of map data in historical works is the case of Long Island. In examining maps of the Long Island area in many books, I observed significant differences in the treatment of coastline and place locations. The most conspicuous variation occurred in the location of the town of Flushing, which was directly on a bay on some maps and far inland on others. After a systematic examination of the matter, using tracings of many coastlines and measurement of angles among a number of Long Island point locations —and such indirect measures were necessary because none of the maps identified sources—it was quite apparent that there are at least three classes of Long Island maps in books about the Revolution: the first derives from Sauthier's map of the late eighteenth century, the second is based on Carrington's map of the late nineteenth century, and the third uses Avery or the current United States Geological Survey coastline, which is, by the way, significantly different from that of the eighteenth century in some areas such as Coney Island.[50] Looking at figures 5:39 and 5:40, the former from Alden (1969) and the latter from Wallace (1951), it is hard to believe that they are both maps of the same area, especially where the northern coastline and the location of Flushing are concerned.[51] I believe that the Alden–Palacios drawing is based on Avery, or drawn from another source that was taken from Avery, though no source is given. The Wallace map has no credit; a reasonable assumption is that it was drawn by an artist for Harper and Brothers. The Wallace map derives from the Sauthier map, or possibly from the Channing map based on it, and contains considerable error.[52]

Consider this same coastline on a recent map of the Long Island area in Don Higginbotham's 1971 book, *The War of American Independence* (fig. 5:41): the same erroneous depiction. There is no credit or source, but I believe that this map is traced from Wallace, which makes it, at a minimum, a third or fourth deriva-

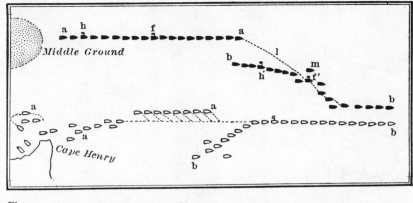

Figure 5:42a

Figure 5:42b

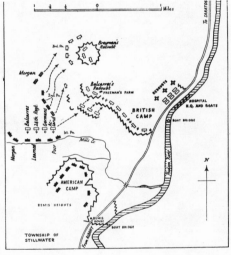

Figure 5:43a

Figure 5:43b

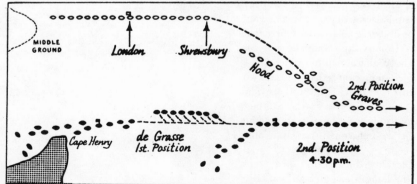

Figure 5:44a

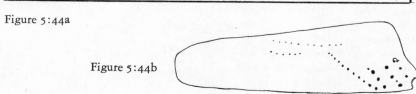

Figure 5:44b

tive from an original erroneous source.[53] I suspect that similar analytical techniques would show much the same failing in a variety of other situations. Although authors surely would not include uncredited paragraphs from tertiary sources in their texts, they do not hesitate to condone such practice when it come to maps.

Inadequate Regard for Meaning and Communication in Mapping

The second matter—inattention to meaning and communication—is far more serious and far more complex. Maps are not as self-explanatory as persons familiar with them would perhaps like to think. This can be dramatized with figures 5:42, 5:43, and 5:44, which appear to show pairs of battle maps—or could easily be so interpreted because their graphic characteristics are similar. Furthermore, as none includes an explanatory legend, they are equally meaningless. But the fact is that absolutely no one yet knows the meaning of any of the *b* images in the pairs, while the *a* images are naval and land battle maps of the traditional type.[54] The real battle maps are strikingly similar in appearance to the other images, which are actually markings made on bone and stone objects during the Upper Paleolithic Period in Europe.[55] Through familiarity, one forgets how abstract are the marks on a map, and thereby also forgets to consider how little meaning they may have for observers less familiar with the conveyance of meaning in cartography.

When a decision is made to include a map in a written text, it is imperative that several basic questions be asked: Why is this map being included? What will viewers know after they have looked at the map that they did not know before? What data can be most easily comprehended in map form, in contrast to verbal or pictorial form? In the more than two hundred publications that I examined while preparing this essay, I found little indication that such questions were ever asked. If they had been, such flagrant examples of poor mapmaking could not be displayed here.

Among the publications I reviewed, there were practically no examples to indicate that authors or publishers cared whether they were clarifying information by mapping it. One small bright spot is Henry Belcher's *First American Civil War* (1911). In his preface, Belcher takes responsibility for the maps in his book, although they were actually drawn by

Stanford's Geographical Establishment, London. Figure 5:45 illustrates Belcher's attempt to help the reader (through the addition of a scale of dates alongside the route of movement) to understand the progress through space and time of Burgoyne's army in the northern campaign.[56]

A Case Study: The Battle of Long Island

Perhaps the best way to illustrate the difficulty of extracting meaning from conventional maps of the Revolution is to describe an event and ask readers to determine for themselves how well they could reconstruct that same event from a number of representative maps of it. The Battle of Long Island is a good example, for it is a relatively simple event and has often been mapped.

This battle took place early in the war. The stage was set with the Americans fearing that the British troops at Halifax would soon attempt to take control of New York and the waterways that position commands. The Americans dug in across from New York at Brooklyn Heights. The British arrived, landed near Gravesend on Long Island, and fought the Americans briskly at two locations simultaneously. But while the British thus had engaged the Americans, they had diverted attention from their more significant movement: the bulk of the British forces moved around an unguarded American flank and were in a position to take the American fortifications from behind. They fail to move decisively, however, despite the knowledge that they can destroy the entire American army at this point. As a result, the Americans are able to slip away by boat to Manhattan Island a few nights later, ending the Battle of Long Island.

The most comprehensible visual presentation of this battle that I have ever seen appeared in a 1973 issue of the *American Way,* a publication given away to passengers who fly on American Airlines and one that normally has few pretensions to scholarly content. The colorful map-diagram (fig. 5:46) was drawn by an artist, Don Troiani, and accompanied an article by Richard Ketchum.[57]

Various presentations of the same situation appear on other maps. Freeman's map (fig. 5:47) is virtually incomprehensible, although it is accompanied by fine notes on sources.[58] It is difficult to see Avery's (fig. 5:48) and Belcher's (fig. 5:49) maps as dealing with the same situation.[59] Figure 5:50 shows the treatment in Ward's book: visually clear, but not helpful in extracting significant action.[60] Hundreds

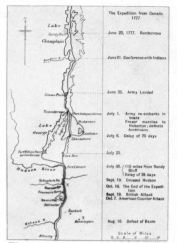

Figure 5:45

Figure 5:46

Figure 5:47

Figure 5:48

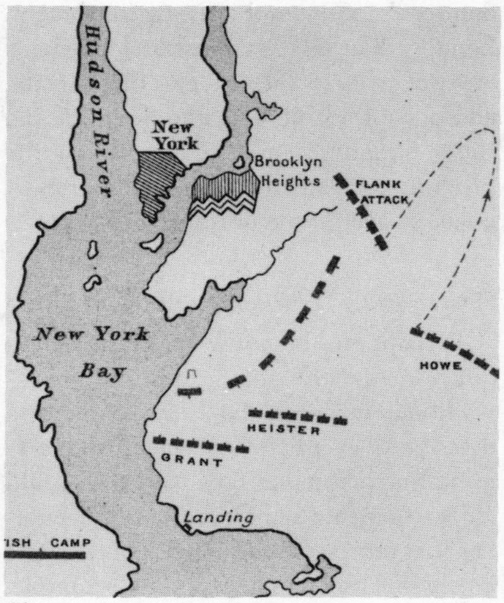

Figure 5:49

Figure 5:50

of other examples could be cited. Symbology and scale may vary, but all are similar in their failure to communicate. It is true that the clearer of them are helpful if and only if one already has a good understanding of what happened—the "known if known" situation—but they are no help to someone coming to them in ignorance.

New Maps of the American Revolution and the Atlas of Early American History Project

This was a serious matter as I considered what might be done about mapping the Revolutionary War for the *Atlas of Early American History* during 1970–1975. I had to evaluate the matter of military mapping at great length, for there were no apparent directions in which to proceed. The directions not to take were obvious, and it occurred to me that perhaps the problem lay not in the means of arriving at a goal for such mapping but rather in the nature of the goal itself.

I had one distinct advantage as I approached the matter initially: I knew virtually nothing about the Revolution. I personified the map user with little or no background in a subject, who comes to a reference work to acquire specific knowledge. I read a great many textual accounts of the war and was made aware repeatedly of the unsatisfactory nature of most of the maps I encountered; they simply did not give me the spatial information and organization that I needed.

Characteristics of "War" and the Revolution: their Bearing on Military Mapping

As I read various historical studies, I became aware of certain analytical similarities; scholars tended consistently to agree on what constituted the most important events of the war and to de-emphasize or omit others. They grouped certain events in their texts and treated others individually. From the cartographer-geographer's point of view, the texts themselves had a consistent and glaring weakness in that they lacked overall spatial organization and structure in their accounts of the War. Armies appeared here and disappeared there, with the spatial coherence and continuity of real life either assumed or ignored. Words like *meanwhile* and *at the same time* are impossible notions to deal with adequately in sequential text. I found myself wanting and needing maps as I read, but not maps of battles and places. Instead, I was constructing in my mind the maps I needed in order for events to take on spatial and temporal coherence.

It is important to note, however, that several characteristics make the War of American Independence difficult to understand as a spatial phenomenon. First, it was not an isolated conflict between colonizer and colony; it was part of a world-wide struggle among European powers for territory and trade. Britain's failure to focus its powerful naval resources on the American conflict, because of its preoccupation with events elsewhere, was among the major reasons that the American colonials were able to assert their independence successfully.

Second, there was no clear front along which fighting took place, with one side or the other gaining territory as the line was pushed back. The British took point after point in battle but found it impossible to control any extent of territory beyond these points. The British impact was that of a foot pressing down on foam rubber—a deep impression is made when the foot is there, but disappears the instant the foot is raised. As a result, there were no clear gains and losses of territory that can be conveniently mapped.

Third, military conflict during the period 1775–1781 usually occurred simultaneously at a number of places in the eastern United States. It is difficult to keep this complexity in mind when reading text that can only describe such events serially.

Finally, because of the nature of the conflict, much of the fighting was done by men other than those in formal army units. Thus it is difficult—even meaningless—to map the movements of *the* army. The American army consisted of a core of regular soldiers (the Continental Army), but the total American force grew and diminished daily, with changes in events. When intense fighting moved into a particular area, the threatened inhabitants would turn out in great numbers to attack the British. The next day, the British having been routed, the men of these local militia forces would return to their farms and shops, and Washington's army would shrink by 50 or 75 percent.

Given these and other factors, the complexity of understanding this war in its spatial structure and of presenting this structure in a series of maps becomes apparent. The need for something more than battle maps is obvious. But if not battle maps, what then? If not the samples of time and space that battle maps usually represent, what scales, extents, and units of spatial and temporal analysis would be helpful?

An Analytical Approach: Space, Time, and Military Events

The average user's difficulty in comprehending battle maps becomes easier to understand if one thinks of such maps as single snapshots that are supposed to represent complex events. Consider how difficult it would be to use a single snapshot to explain the nature of the simple physical process of running to a person who did not understand it. A single static sample of a dynamic process tells little about the essential nature of the process. But a number of snapshots taken together, ultimately a series of still frames, moving quickly enough to be perceived by the eye as real motion, becomes an adequate substitute for the process itself. A sufficient number of static images will approximate dynamism.

The first step, then, in proceeding beyond battle maps is to consider content, that is, the complex of elements that is varying over space. Battle maps usually show how particular units of troops were distributed over a relatively small space for a small unit of time. Regardless of how small this unit of time might be, however, it encompasses too many discrete, dynamic events to be portrayed clearly on any one map. Therefore, most such maps degenerate into a welter of tangled lines and symbols, rarely comprehensible.

A battle map shows the distribution of troops over some small part of the earth's surface, but *war* is a conception that involves more than just the location of troops. It is a complex abstraction that involves notions of action, movement, and intentionality as well as quantities and distribution of men. The important question at any level more general than that of

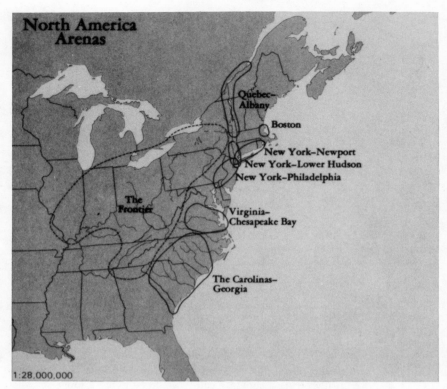

Figure 5:51

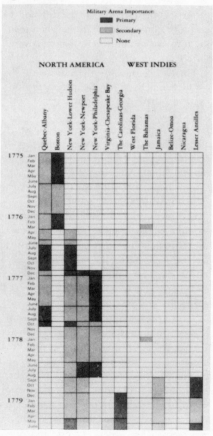

Figure 5:52

the battle buff is not "How were the troops distributed throughout the course of a battle?" but rather "How were the battles distributed over the course of the war?" With this insight, potential subjects for mapping begin to occur. Nevertheless, analyzing a war in such a way that its distribution over a surface can be mapped remains something of a problem. One must identify those aspects of it that are concrete and, preferably, quantifiable.

In producing most battle maps, the armies remain constant as the phenomenon mapped while the space on which the phenomenon occurs is varied from map to map, depending on where battles are fought. This means that a series of battle maps for any one war will always show the same two armies (the phenomenon being mapped), but distributed by small units, such as regiments, in different physical settings or spaces at different times (now on meadows near Princeton, later on swamps near Charleston). The choice of time for any one map is usually dictated by the time of crucial battle.

But it would seem equally reasonable to reverse this procedure, keeping the space constant and varying the phenomena appearing or occurring on that space. For the Revolution, this approach meant that I could choose to map the eastern United States as a constant, unchanging, relatively small-scale base, and then show how the distribution of war actions varied over this surface at different times. Ideally, it would be desirable, using this approach, to subdivide the entire subject space or area into a fine grid of small areal units, perhaps one-mile squares. Then, if it were possible to acquire perfect knowledge of every aspect of the war, each unit of the grid could be easily labeled or colored according to some system that would tell precisely the conditions of war activity at each moment of time.

But the information available in documents is not adequate for such complete mapping. On an intuitive basis, therefore, I established constant spatial units, similar to those of the theoretical grid in nature, by subdividing the eastern United States in a more pragmatic way, using the notion of *arenas* (figure 5:51).[61] The war was fought, over its seven-year course, in a number of different areas or arenas. As it happens, there are seven clearly distinguishable, almost spatially discrete arenas of war action in the area being considered here. I drew lines around these arenas, based on empirical-intuitive considerations, and modified them as I became more familiar with the details of events. These arenas closely parallel the units that historians customarily deal with in their texts (that is, discussions of events in "the Carolinas," or "New Jersey," or "Newport," and so on). Just as they have had to partition a continuous, complex war into discrete portions in order to be able to write about it conveniently in linear text, so the cartographer must devise some more or less discrete unit spaces on which to plot variation in the phenomenon being observed.

Temporal continuity is not a characteristic of conventional military maps: there are never enough of them to begin coverage of a new period where the previous one ends. Even textual chronologies often have significant and puzzling gaps. Accounting for each hour, even each day of the war would, of course, be an impossible task. But on a more general level, it seemed possible that larger time units could be used and that, when taken in total, they would be continuous for the entire period of the war. Therefore I partitioned time into one-month units, as I had used arena units to partition space. The number of months accounted for by any one map must be determined by the duration of relatively static conditions. Whenever the situation changes, whether in one arena or in more, a new map must be made which is "true" until the next significant change occurs. Thus every month of the war will be accounted for over the total map series, but the period of time mapped can, and will, vary from one map to another.

Finally, there was one other notion that the map had to reflect: the matter of emphasis on or importance of events and conditions. That is, there must be a concrete or observable substitute for the too-abstract notion of *war*. It seemed reasonable that a basic series of military maps about the War of American Independence should parallel in its selection and emphasis the scales of emphasis that the community of historians had developed in literary works about the war. After considerable study, I concluded that one could, on a simple ordinal scale, classify virtually all events and conditions of the war period by relative importance or intensity of focus (the three ordinal categories being: "no importance," "some importance," and "great importance").

Thus the three necessary ingredients of a new cartographic presentation come together: a consistent spatial base, subdivided into fixed arenas; temporal continu-

ity, based on the one-month unit; and the notion of varying "intensity" or "importance" with which war events can be characterized. Once I evolved the matrix, part of which is shown in figure 5:52,[62] I was confident that a new cartographic synthesis of the war was possible. The matrix includes units of space on one axis, units of time on the other, and levels of importance of war events (indicated by white, gray, or black tones) in each intersection space. White indicates activity of little or no importance; gray, activity of secondary importance; and black, activity of primary importance and high intensity. From this matrix it became apparent that a series of twenty-four maps, any one map showing variation among arenas but relatively homogeneous conditions within all arenas for the period mapped, would show the Revolutionary War in a spatially and temporally coherent fashion.

Visually, the cartographic techniques devised have their origins in analogy with characteristics of the staged drama (figure 5:53).[63] The base maps (at 1:15,000,000) are stages on which important dramatic action takes place; spotlights are played on the surface at different levels of intensity to convey the importance of the arena-characters for periods of time that vary in length from map to map, depending upon how rapidly the conditions yielding the particular intensity coding changed. The time period to which the conditions on each map are applicable is indicated by a time scale that appears at the top of each map.

Helpful as such maps may be in enabling one to develop a comprehensive and coherent image of spatial structure, they are, however, incapable of communicating the action, motivation, and mood of the war-drama. The burden of communicating action and intention is normally borne by verbal narrative. Consequently, the *Atlas* maps are accompanied by considerable narrative text, in the belief that concise verbal summaries of strategies and operations will make the static maps far more meaningful than they could be in isolation.

Finally, the scale of the maps is too small for readers wanting to investigate details of locations. Therefore, a section of detailed, larger scale place-name maps, one for each arena, has been included with the basic series in the *Atlas*.

Figure 5:53

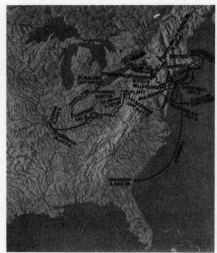

Figure 5:54a

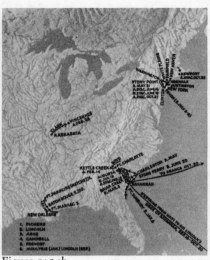

Figure 5:54b

Historical Precedents for Atlas of
Early American History *Approach*

In retrospect, it now becomes apparent
that there have been certain precedents
for the approach finally taken in the *Atlas
of Early American History.* There is Fortescue's verbal description of the way he
thought military maps should be made (in
contrast to the way he actually did make
them), showing the ground only and let-
ting the reader fill in the troop movements
on the basis of verbal description.[64] The
two maps shown in figure 5:54 are taken
from a series in the 1944 *Historical Atlas
of the United States* by Clifford L. and
Elizabeth H. Lord.[65] Poorly designed and
produced though these maps are, they do
take a similar approach to mapping the
distribution of battles, instead of the distribution of troops within battles.

W. M. James, in his 1926 book about
the British navy, has a similar summary
presentation for each year (figure 5:55).
And William Wood and Ralph Henry
Gabriel's *Winning of Freedom* (1927)
contains an interesting series of maps, one
map for each year of the war, which does
get at the problem of mapping the distribution of a war. These maps (figure 5:56)
were made by Gregor Noetzel of the
American Geographical Society.

Conclusion

The Revolutionary War has not been
mapped in exemplary fashion during the
twentieth century. There are, however,
exceptions to this conclusion, the most
notable being the Matthews-Northrup
Works–Baer maps in Avery's *History.*

Mapping the war has been peripheral
to the production of scholarly texts on the

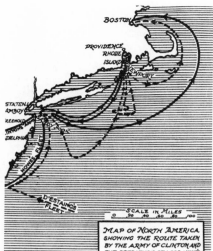

Figure 5:55a

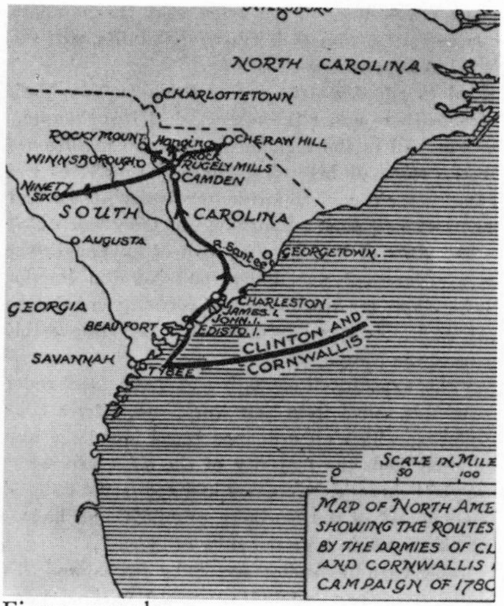

Figure 5:55b

subject. Some large-scale battle reconstruction mapping of the nineteenth century was followed in the twentieth by the production of derivative and inept map-illustrations. These maps were prepared for texts far more synthetic and remote in their approach to the details of battles than are any of the maps. Battle maps have tended to be tiny samples of space and time, inadequate for developing an understanding of the spatial and temporal coherence of events in the mind of the user. They appear to have been produced, and they continue to be produced, more from a mindless acceptance of outdated conventions than from a thoughtful, deliberative approach. A major reconsideration of this matter took place at the Atlas of Early American History project during the early 1970s, and an analytical approach to the problem of military mapping showed that there is considerable cartographic potential in mapping (at relatively small scales) intensity or importance of military events as they vary over space and time.

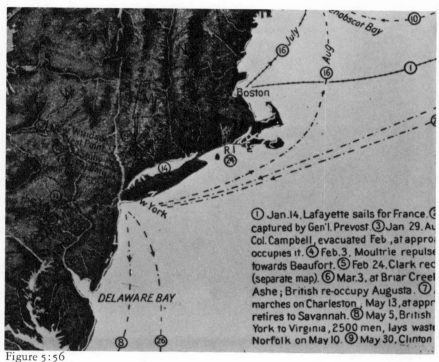

Figure 5:56

Notes

Chapter 1

My interest in military cartography has developed over a decade, during which I have been concerned with the origins and development of the Ordnance Survey of Great Britain. For a first chance to transplant these studies into North American soil, I am grateful to the trustees of the John Carter Brown Library; their award of a postdoctoral fellowship in 1966 allowed me to make a study of the American maps of William Faden, London mapseller and leading cartographic publicist of the events of the Revolution. My work was also supported by the American Philosophical Society and, subsequently, has been sustained generously by the Universities of Liverpool and Exeter. For the present opportunity, I tender sincere thanks to Mr. and Mrs. Kenneth Nebenzahl for the impetus which these lectures have provided for the exchange and publication of ideas on a relatively neglected topic, and to the Newberry Library's Hermon Dunlap Smith Center for the History of Cartography for the scholarly and congenial atmosphere it provides for the pursuit of such studies under its director, David Woodward. By nature, military maps are truly international, and my debt to scholars in several national map collections is considerable. In Britain particular thanks are due to Helen Wallis and Yolande O'Donoghue of the British Library; to Peter Clark of the Mapping and Charting Establishment, Royal Engineers; and to Peter Penfold of the Public Record Office. In the United States, I extend thanks to Walter W. Ristow, Richard W. Stephenson, and John Wolter of the Geography and Map Division, Library of Congress; to Herman Friis and Patrick D. McLaughlin in the National Archives; to Robert W. Karrow, Jr., of the Newberry Library; to William B. Willcox, the editor of the Franklin papers at Yale; and to the many other librarians and map curators who have willingly provided information by letter. Peter Guthorn of Neptune City, New Jersey; Louis De Vorsey, Professor of Geography, University of Georgia; and, in particular, Douglas W. Marshall of the William L. Clements Library, University of Michigan, have also freely shared some of their unpublished researches with me. On editorial questions I have leaned heavily on the experience of David Woodward and Jane Carley in Chicago, and of Molly Dexter and William L. D. Ravenhill, Professor of Geography, both of the University of Exeter. To Rodney Fry of the Department of Geography, University of Exeter, who designed and drew the text figures so skillfully, I also wish to express my thanks. Finally, I would like especially to note the kind help and encouragement of my fellow authors, Barbara Bartz Petchenik and Lawrence W. Towner; sharing this experience with them has been rewarding in every way.

1. Lynn Montross, *Rag, Tag, and Bobtail: The Story of the Continental Army, 1775–1783* (New York: Harper & Brothers, 1952), pp. 5–6.

2. Randolph G. Adams, "The Cartography of the British Attack on Fort Moultrie in 1776," in *Essays Offered to Herbert Putnam . . . ,* ed. William Warner Bishop and Andrew Keogh (New Haven: Yale University Press, 1929), p. 36.

3. William P. Cumming, *British Maps of Colonial America,* the Kenneth Nebenzahl, Jr., Lectures in the History of Cartography at the Newberry Library, ed. David Woodward (Chicago and London: University of Chicago Press, 1974), p. 57.

4. Peter J. Guthorn, *British Maps of the American Revolution* (Monmouth Beach, N.J.: Philip Freneau Press, 1972), p. 6.

5. For a general discussion, see David Harvey, *Explanation in Geography* (London: Edward Arnold, 1969), pp. 326–32; for further exploration of some of the cartographic implications, see Joel L. Morrison, "Recommendations for Classification of Extant Maps of the Great Lakes," mimeographed (report to David Woodward, director, Hermon Dunlap Smith Center for the History of Cartography, the Newberry Library, Chicago, 1975).

6. David L. Clarke, *Analytical Archaeology* (London: Methuen, 1968), pp. 187–99.

7. Peter J. Guthorn, *American Maps and Map Makers of the Revolution* (Monmouth Beach, N.J.: Philip Freneau Press, 1966).

8. Guthorn, *British Maps.*

9. Howard C. Rice, Jr., and Anne S. K. Brown, eds. and trans., *The American Campaigns of Rochambeau's Army, 1780, 1781, 1782, 1783,* vol. 2, *The Itineraries, Maps, and Views* (Princeton and Providence: Princeton University Press and Brown University Press, 1972), passim (hereafter cited as *American Campaigns*).

10. Peter J. Guthorn, "The Library of Congress 'Hessian Map': Its Authorship and Importance" (paper delivered at the American Congress on Surveying and Mapping, Washington, D.C., March 1975).

11. Douglas W. Marshall, "The British Engineers in America: 1775–1783," *Journal of the Society for Army Historical Research* 51 (1973): 155–63.

12. Rice and Brown, *American Campaigns* 2: 111–19.

13. Herman R. Friis, "A Brief Review of the Development and Status of Geographical and Cartographical Activities of the United States Government: 1776–1818," *Imago Mundi* 19 (1965): 68–80, and "The United States Congressional Serials and Related Records: A Significant Source for a Study of a History of Official Mapping by the Federal Government, 1774–1861" (paper delivered at the Sixth International Conference on the History of Cartography, National Maritime Museum, Greenwich, September 1975); Albert H. Heusser, *George Washington's Map Maker: A Biography of Robert Erskine,* ed. Hubert G. Schmidt (New Brunswick, N.J.: Rutgers University Press, 1966); and Walter W. Ristow, "Simeon De Witt, Pioneer American Cartographer," in *Kartengeschichte und Kartenbearbeitung . . . ,* ed. Karl-Heinz Meine [Festschrift honoring Wilhelm Bonacker] (Bad Godesberg: Kirschbaum Verlag, 1968), pp. 103–14.

14. Cumming, *British Maps,* passim; see also note 15 below.

15. David Woodward, "The Study of the History of Cartography: A Suggested Framework," *American Cartographer* 1 (1974): 102.

16. R. A. Skelton, *Maps: A Historical Survey of Their Study and Collecting,* the Kenneth Nebenzahl, Jr., Lectures in the History of Cartography at the Newberry Library, ed. David Woodward (Chicago and London: University of Chicago Press, 1972), p. 26.

17. Christopher Duffy, *Fire and Stone: The Science of Fortress Warfare, 1660–1860* (Newton Abbot, Devon: David & Charles, 1975), provides a useful introduction to the central place of cartographic skills in fortification.

18. John W. Stoye, *English Travellers Abroad, 1604–1667* (London: Jonathan Cape, 1952), pp. 66–67, 124–27.

19. Nicholas de Fer, *Les Forces de l'Europe, ou description des principales villes; avec leur fortifications* (Paris: Chez l'Auteur, 1695); British Library, Maps 3.b.18 (1.); a later variant, ca. 1710, is at Maps 2.c.51. Another example is the [Sheets of plans of fortification engraved by Bodenehr, ca. 1740], British Library, Maps 13.c.1 (222–25), the sheets of which were obviously sold separately as well as sometimes bound together, as in this volume.

20. Rice and Brown, *American Campaigns,* 2: pls. 93, 94.

21. Duffy, *Fire and Stone,* pp. 21, 40, 43, and 170–71.

22. Jay Luvaas, ed. and trans., *Frederick the Great on the Art of War* (New York: Free Press, 1966), frontispiece.

23. Thomas Williams Baldwin, ed., *The Revolutionary Journal of Col. Jeduthan Baldwin, 1775–1778* (Bangor, Me.: Printed for the De Burians, 1906); pp. 6–7, 20, 24, and 32 record Baldwin drawing fortification plans in various contexts.

24. See, for example, Whitworth Porter, *History of the Corps of Royal Engineers,* 3 vols. (Chatham, Kent: Institution of Royal Engineers, 1951–1954), 1: 150, for some published eighteenth-century instructions for drawing plans, lacking source attribution.

25. John Muller, *A Treatise Containing the Elementary Part of Fortification, Regular and Irregular, with Remarks on the Constructions . . . of Marshal de Vauban and Baron Coehorn . . . For the Use of the Royal Academy of Artillery at Woolwich,* 3d ed. (London: J. Nourse, 1774), and *A Treatise Containing the Practical Part of Fortification . . . For the Use of the Royal Academy of Artillery at Woolwich,* 3d ed. (London: Printed for W. Strahan [etc.], 1774).

26. Muller, *Elementary Part of Fortification,* p. 19.

27. Ibid., p. 148; the reference at the end of the quotation is to another of Muller's texts.

28. Elizabeth S. Kite, *Brigadier-General Louis Lebègue Duportail: Commandant of Engineers in the Continental Army, 1777–1783* (Baltimore: Johns Hopkins Press, 1933), p. 23.

29. Gideon Delaplaine Scull, ed., *The Montresor Journals,* Collections of the New-York Historical Society, Publication Fund, vol. 14 (New York: New-York Historical Society, 1881), passim.

30. Baldwin, *Revolutionary Journal,* pp. 20–21.

31. See, for example, Jacques Ozanam, *A Treatise of Fortification, Containing the Ancient and Modern Method of the Construction and Defense of Places . . . ,* trans. J. T. Desaguliers (Oxford: J. Nicholson, 1711).

32. For later developments relating to British military cartography, see Yolande Jones, "Aspects of Relief Portrayal on Nineteenth-Century British Military Maps," *Cartographic Journal* 11 (1974): 19–33.

33. Randolph G. Adams, *British Headquarters Maps and Sketches Used by Sir Henry Clinton While in Command of the British Forces Operating in North America during the War for Independence, 1775–1782: A Descriptive List of the Original Manuscripts and Printed Documents . . . in the William L. Clements Library at the University of Michigan* (Ann Arbor: William L. Clements Library, 1928), p. 38 (hereafter cited as *British Headquarters Maps*); Christian Brun, *Guide to the Manuscript Maps in the William L. Clements Library* (Ann Arbor: University of Michigan, 1959), p. 90.

34. Muller, *Practical Part of Fortification,* p. 148.

35. Muller, *Elementary Part of Fortification*, p. 14.

36. Porter, *History of the Royal Engineers* 1:150.

37. Ibid. In a North American context this is confirmed by the "surveying chains" of 100 feet and 50 feet in the 1754 Board of Ordnance list, "Stores for the Intended Expedition to North America," in *Military Affairs in North America, 1748–1765: Selected Documents from the Cumberland Papers in Windsor Castle*, ed. Stanley Pargellis (New York: Archon Books, 1969), pp. 484–85. See also Samuel Holland's list of instruments below, p. 27.

38. British Museum, *Catalogue of the Manuscript Maps, Charts, and Plans, and of the Topographical Drawings in the British Museum*, comp. John Holmes and R. H. Major, 3 vols. (London, 1844–1861).

39. Brun, *Guide to the Manuscript Maps*.

40. Ibid., pp. 15–34.

41. P.R.O. 325/1. I owe this reference to Douglas W. Marshall.

42. Ibid., fol. 6.

43. Ibid.

44. Adams, *British Headquarters Maps*.

45. For example, the Revolutionary maps of Hugh Earl Percy (1742–1817) listed in Cumming, *British Maps*, pp. 79–84.

46. Great Britain, Public Record Office, *Maps and Plans in the Public Record Office*, vol. 2, *America and West Indies*, ed. P. A. Penfold (London: Her Majesty's Stationery Office, 1974), passim.

47. Among the plans or maps enumerated by Brun, *Guide to Manuscript Maps*, the following scales occur:

Scale	Number of Gunter's Chains	Page Reference
one inch to 528 feet	8	276
one inch to 660 feet	10	380, 636
one inch to 1,056 feet	16	434
one inch to 1,320 feet (440 yards)	20	417
one inch to 1,980 feet	30	34, 329
one inch to 2,112 feet	32	177
one inch to 2,640 feet	40	319
one inch to 3,960 feet	60	175
one inch to 4,224 feet	64	274

The scales in these, as in other cases, enable us to identify the type of chain in use on particular surveys.

48. Guthorn, *American Maps*, p. 33, reproduces "A Plan of Fort Montgomery," ca. 1776, drawn at a scale of "50 paces 3 f to a pace."

49. Porter, *History of the Royal Engineers* 1: 150.

50. See below, pp. 17–21.

51. Muller, *Elementary Part of Fortification*, pp. 14–15.

52. Marshall, "British Engineers in America," pp. 162–63, gives a list of engineers on station during the Revolution. Not all, however, were capable of making maps. See also Douglas W. Marshall and Howard Henry Peckham, *Campaigns of the American Revolution: An Atlas of Manuscript Maps* (Ann Arbor: University of Michigan Press; Maplewood, N.J.: Hammond, 1976), pp. 15, 37 (hereafter cited as *Campaigns*).

53. Adams, *British Headquarters Maps*, p. 29.

54. Ibid., p. 122.

55. For example, Muller, *Elementary Part of Fortification*, pp. 218–40, is "An Explanation of the principal terms used in Fortification, digested in an alphabetical manner." John Muller, *A Treatise of Artillery . . .*, 2d ed. (London: John Millan, 1768), contains an "Artillery Dictionary," 32 pp. [separately paginated]; Thomas Simes, *The Military Guide for Young Officers* (London: J. Millan, 1772) also contains "A Military, Historical, *and* Explanatory Dictionary" that provides very full definitions of contemporary terms found on military maps of the Revolutionary period.

56. Heinrich Friedrich Rumpf, *Allgemeine Literatur der Kriegswissenschaften, . . . Littérature universelle des sciences militaires* [German and French text], 2 vols. (Berlin: G. Reimer, 1824–1825), 1: 40–56, lists encyclopedias and dictionaries (hereafter cited as *Allgemeine Literatur*).

57. Reproduced in Kenneth Nebenzahl, *Atlas of the American Revolution* (Chicago: Rand McNally & Co., 1974), p. 42.

58. François de Dainville, *Le Langage des géographes: Termes, signes, couleurs des cartes anciennes, 1500–1800* (Paris: Editions A. & J. Picard & Cie, 1964).

59. P.R.O. 325/1; see also Muller, *Practical Part of Fortification*, pp. 128–32.

60. Louis Gottschalk, ed., *The Letters of Lafayette to Washington, 1777–1799* (New York: privately printed by Helen Fahnestock Hubbard, 1944), p. 34.

61. Guthorn, *American Maps*, p. 30.

62. Kite, *Louis Lebègue Duportail*, pp. 165–66.

63. Jared Sparks, ed., *Correspondence of the American Revolution: Being Letters of Eminent Men to George Washington . . .*, 4 vols. (Boston: Little, Brown & Co., 1853), 3:310.

64. Adams, *British Headquarters Maps*, pp. 127–28.

65. Ibid., p. 128.

66. James M. Hadden, *Hadden's Journal and Orderly Books: A Journal Kept in Canada and upon Burgoyne's Campaign in 1776 and 1777, by Lieut. James M. Hadden, Roy. Art.*, explanatory chapter and notes by Horatio Rogers (Albany, N.Y.: Joel Munsell's Sons, 1884), p. 174.

67. Adams, *British Headquarters Maps*, pp. 2–5.

68. Kite, *Louis Lebègue Duportail*, p. 175.

69. Louis André de La Mamie de Clairac, *The Field Engineer of M. le Chevalier De Clairac ... With Observations and Remarks on each Chapter ...*, trans. John Muller, 2d ed. (London: John Millan, 1773), p. 2.

70. Roger Stevenson, *Military Instructions for Officers Detached in the Field: Containing, A Scheme for forming a Corps of a Partisan. Illustrated with Plans of the Manoeuvres Necessary in carrying on the Petite Guerre* (Philadelphia: R. Aitken, 1775), p. 3.

71. Coolie Verner, *Maps of the Yorktown Campaign, 1780–1781: A Preliminary Checklist of Printed and Manuscript Maps Prior to 1800*, Map Collectors' Series, no. 18 (London: Map Collectors' Circle, 1965).

72. Rice and Brown, *American Campaigns*, 2: pls. 87–89, where the overlay is reproduced.

73. Verner, *Maps of the Yorktown Campaign*, p. 38. Fage was also active as a mapmaker during the British occupation of Rhode Island, as demonstrated by Guthorn, *British Maps*, pp. 20–21.

74. J. D. C. Pirscher, *Coup d'oeil militaire, oder Kurzer Unterricht, wie man sich ein militarisch Augenmaass erwerben, ... praktisch beschrieben* (Berlin: Arnold Wever, 1775); three of the engraved plates at the end of the volume show symbols.

75. France, Dépôt Général de la Guerre, *Mémorial topographique et militaire, rédigé au Dépôt Général de la Guerre ...*, 5 vols. (Paris: L'Imprimerie de la République, 1802–1803), 5: 1–64.

76. For the use of the *bateaux* symbols see Hadden, *Journal and Orderly Books*, p. 152.

77. William Siborne, *Instructions for Civil and Military Surveyors in Topographical Plan-Drawing; ... founded upon the system of J. G. Lehmann ...* (London: G. & W. B. Whittaker, 1822), pl. 4. Lehmann had codified the various symbols being used by military draftsmen toward the end of the eighteenth century and to this extent Siborne's treatise is a guide to practices at the time of the Revolution.

78. France, Dépôt Général de la Guerre, *Mémorial* 5: pl. 7.

79. Nebenzahl, *Atlas*, pp. 166–67.

80. Rice and Brown, *American Campaigns*, 2: pl. 87.

81. Ibid., pl. 5.

82. Ibid., pp. 125–26.

83. Guthorn, *American Maps*, p. 22.

84. Frederick Mackenzie, *Diary of Frederick Mackenzie: Giving a Daily Narrative of His Military Service as an Officer of the Regiment of Royal Welch Fusiliers during the Years 1775–1781 in Massachusetts, Rhode Island, and New York*, 2 vols. (Cambridge: Harvard University Press, 1930), 2: 361, 385.

85. Bernhard A. Uhlendorf, ed. and trans., *The Siege of Charleston, ... Diaries and Letters of Hessian Officers from the von Jungkenn Papers in the William L. Clements Library* (Ann Arbor: University of Michigan Press, 1938), p. 295.

86. Another example is "A Plan of the Siege & Surrender of Charlestown ... to His Majesty's Fleet and Army ... May 12th 1780. Surveyed during and after the Siege by Charles Blaskowitz, Capt. Guides & Pioneers," in *Maps and Plans in the Public Record Office*, no. 2856.

87. Alexander A. Lawrence, *Storm over Savannah: The Story of Count d'Estaing and the Siege of the Town in 1779* (Athens: University of Georgia Press, 1951), pp. 201–202.

88. William B. Willcox, ed., *The American Rebellion: Sir Henry Clinton's Narrative of His Campaigns, 1775–1782, with an Appendix of Original Documents* (New Haven: Yale University Press, 1954), pp. 30–31. The maps described by Adams, *British Headquarters Maps*, nos. 301–305 reveal Clinton's concern with establishing the topographical reasons for the British failure in 1776.

89. Reproduced in Nebenzahl, *Atlas*, pp. 182–83.

90. Stevenson, *Military Instructions for Officers*, p. 80.

91. Ibid., p. 88.

92. John Count O'Rourke, *A Treatise on the Art of War: or, Rules for Conducting an Army in all the Various Operations of Regular Campaigns* (London: T. Spilsbury, 1778), p. 21.

93. Ibid., pp. 21–23.

94. Ibid., p. 87.

95. Stevenson, *Military Instructions for Officers*, p. 84.

96. Pirscher, *Coup d'oeil militaire*.

97. Edward Barrington de Fonblanque, *Political and Military Episodes ... Derived from the Life and Correspondence of the Right Hon. John Burgoyne, General, Statesman, Dramatist* (London: Macmillan & Co., 1876), p. 20.

98. Charles Vallancey, "An Essay on Military-Surveys accompanied with Military Itineraries" [1779], Map Library 6. Tab. 64., British Library, London, [pp. 8–9] (hereafter cited as "Essay").

99. Ibid., [p. 21].

100. Brun, *Guide to the Manuscript Maps*, no. 400; on Martin, see Guthorn, "Library of Congress 'Hessian Map,'" p. 7. As an engineer, Martin had been detailed to record the Hessian part in the Revolution in maps.

101. Rice and Brown, *American Campaigns*, 2: 136–37, pl. 43, for example, can be compared with p. 157, pl. 87.

102. Mackenzie, *Diary* 1: 1; see John Richard Alden, *General Gage in America: Being Principally a History of His Role in the American Revolution* (Baton Rouge: Louisiana State University Press, 1948), pp. 226–27, for further details of Gage's preparations—cartographic and otherwise.

103. Ibid.

104. Guthorn, *British Maps,* p. 15.

105. Ibid., p. 18.

106. Thomas Gage, *General Gage's Instructions, of 22nd February, 1775* ... (Boston: J. Gill, 1779) reprinted in *Massachusetts Historical Society Collections,* 2d ser., 4 (1816): 205–15 (to which all further page numbers refer), and in *American Archives: Fourth Series, Containing a Documentary History of the English Colonies in North America* (Washington, D.C.: M. St. Clair Clarke & Peter Force, 1837), 1: 1264–68.

107. Gage, *Instructions,* pp. 205–14.

108. Guthorn, *British Maps,* p. 18, items 1–3 now in the Library of Congress, listed under De Berniere.

109. Gage to Holland, 27 July 1767, Gage Papers, William L. Clements Library, University of Michigan, Ann Arbor. I owe this reference to Douglas W. Marshall.

110. Gage, *Instructions,* p. 205.

111. Ibid., p. 206.

112. Ibid., pp. 207–208.

113. "Calendar of the Correspondence of Major-General Nathanael Greene, Quartermaster-General U.S.A., in the Library of the American Philosophical Society," *Proceedings of the American Philosophical Society* 39 (1900): 252; John Sullivan, *Journals of the Military Expedition of Major General John Sullivan Against the Six Nations of Indians in 1779 . . . ,* ed. Frederick Cook (Auburn, N.Y.: Knapp, Peck & Thomson Printers, 1887), p. 288.

114. Guthorn, *American Maps,* p. 27, quoting the endorsement on the original map in the collection of the New-York Historical Society.

115. Adams, *British Headquarters Maps,* p. 89.

116. Ibid., p. 68.

117. Scull, *Montresor Journals,* p. 419.

118. Rice and Brown, *American Campaigns,* 2: pl. 107a.

119. This is true of many of Washington's instructions when he was commander-in-chief of the Continental Army; see John C. Fitzpatrick, ed., *The Writings of George Washington from the Original Manuscript Sources, 1745–1799,* 39 vols. (Washington, D.C.: U.S. George Washington Bicentennial Commission, 1931–1944), passim.

120. The eleven maps in the Mackenzie *Diary* are listed in Guthorn, *British Maps,* p. 34.

121. Rice and Brown, *American Campaigns,* 2: 136–38.

122. Ibid., 1: 252.

123. Ibid., and 2: 138.

124. Ibid., 2: 137–38.

125. Ibid., 1: 252.

126. Vallancey, "Essay," [p. 10].

127. Christopher Duffy, *The Army of Frederick the Great* (Newton Abbot, Devon: David & Charles, 1974), p. 146.

128. R. A. Skelton, *The Military Survey of Scotland,* Royal Scottish Geographical Society, Special Publication no. 1 (Edinburgh: Royal Scottish Geographical Society, 1967).

129. Cumming, *British Maps,* and *The Southeast in Early Maps, with an Annotated Check List of Printed and Manuscript Regional and Local Maps of Southeastern North America during the Colonial Period* (Chapel Hill: University of North Carolina Press, 1958); Louis De Vorsey, Jr., ed., *De Brahm's Report of the General Survey in the Southern District of North America* (Columbia: University of South Carolina Press, 1971) (his bibliography, pp. 301–16, lists others items); Marshall, "British Engineers in America"; Marshall and Peckham, *Campaigns;* and Nathaniel N. Shipton, "General James Murray's Map of the St. Lawrence," *Cartographer* 4 (1967): 93–101 [now *Canadian Cartographer*].

130. Shipton, "James Murray's Map," p. 93.

131. Louis De Vorsey, Jr., "La Florida Revealed: The De Brahm Surveys of British East Florida, 1765–1771," in *Pattern and Process: Research in Historical Geography,* ed. Ralph E. Ehrenberg (Washington, D.C.: Howard University Press, 1975), pp. 89–90.

132. Brun, *Guide to the Manuscript Maps,* pp. 15–31.

133. P.R.O., A.O. 3/140 6, printed in *Holland's Description of Cape Breton Island and Other Documents,* comp. D. C. Harvey, Public Archives of Nova Scotia Publication no. 2 (Halifax: Public Archives of Nova Scotia, 1935), pp. 132–33.

134. Great Britain, Admiralty, Hydrographic Department, *A Summary of Selected Manuscript Documents of Historic Importance Preserved in the Archives of the Department,* Hydrographic Department, Admiralty, Professional Paper no. 13 (London, 1950), pp. 17–23 (hereafter cited as *Summary*).

135. P.R.O., C.O. 323/24, pp. 231 ff.; Holland, *Description,* p. 46.

136. De Vorsey, *De Brahm's Report,* p. 34.

137. P.R.O., A.O. 3/140; Holland, *Description,* p. 36.

138. Holland, *Description,* p. 36.

139. Ibid., pp. 37–38.

140. Ibid., p. 36.

141. Ibid.

142. The proposals bear close comparison, for example, with the almost contemporary scheme by William Roy for a "General Military Map of England," discussed in the Introduction by J. B. Harley and Yolande O'Donoghue to *The Old Series Ordnance Survey Maps of England and Wales., Scale: One Inch to One Mile: A Reproduction of the 110 Sheets of the Survey in Early State in 10 Volumes,* vol. 1, Kent, Essex, E. Sussex, and S. Suffolk (Lympne Castle, Kent: Harry

Margary, 1975), pp. xiii–xv. For French developments, see Roger Hahn, *The Anatomy of a Scientific Institution: The Paris Academy of Sciences, 1666–1803* (Berkeley, Los Angeles, and London: University of California Press, 1971), pp. 90–91.

143. Holland, *Description*, pp. 42–43, 59.

144. Charles Hutton, George Shaw, and Richard Pearson, *The Philosophical Transactions of the Royal Society of London, from their Commencement, in 1665, to the year 1800; Abridged, with Notes and Biographic Illustrations . . .* , vol. 12, *From 1763 to 1769* (London: C. & R. Baldwin, 1809), pp. 507, 642–44.

145. Ibid., pp. 566–79.

146. For the North American background and its European links see Brooke Hindle, *The Pursuit of Science in Revolutionary America, 1735–1789* (Chapel Hill: University of North Carolina Press, 1956); also Philip Phineas Stearns, *Science in the British Colonies of America* (Urbana and Chicago: University of Illinois Press, 1970).

147. William H. Goetzmann, *Army Exploration in the American West, 1803–1863* (New Haven: Yale University Press, 1959), and *Exploration and Empire: The Explorer and the Scientist in the Winning of the American West* (New York: Random House, Vintage Books, 1972).

148. Douglas Stewart Brown, "The Iberville Canal Project: Its Relation to Anglo-French Commercial Rivalry in the Mississippi Valley, 1763–1775," *Mississippi Valley Historical Review* 32 (1946): 491–516.

149. Brun, *Guide to the Manuscript Maps,* passim; British Museum, *Catalogue of the Manuscript Maps,* 3: 508–58.

150. Scull, *Montresor Journals.*

151. Hindle, *Pursuit of Science,* pp. 174–75.

152. Marshall, "British Engineers in America," p. 157.

153. Clarence Edwin Carter, ed., *The Correspondence of General Thomas Gage with the Secretaries of State and with the War Office and the Treasury, 1763–1775,* 2 vols. (New Haven: Yale University Press, 1931), 1: 347.

154. Thomas Hutchins, *A Topographical Description of Virginia, Pennsylvania, Maryland, and North Carolina . . .* (London, 1778; reprint ed., ed. Frederick Charles Hicks, Cleveland: Burrows Brothers Co., 1904); Guthorn, *British Maps,* pp. 30–31, gives a list of Hutchins's maps, which illustrates the diversity of his assignments.

155. Geraint N. D. Evans, "North American Soldier, Hydrographer, Governor: The Public Careers of J. F. W. DesBarres, 1721–1824" (Ph.D. diss., Yale University, 1965), p. 90.

156. De Vorsey, *De Brahm's Report,* pp. 51–52.

157. British Library, Add. Ms. 21731 (Haldimand Collection), fol. 176.

158. Holland to Pownall, 20 December 1774, P.R.O., C.O. 323, vol. 29, p. 45.

159. Ibid., pp. 60–61, in "The Petition of Samuel Holland to the Lords Commissioners for Trade and Plantations" (Paper read at London, 6 February 1776).

160. Luvaas, *Frederick the Great on the Art of War,* p. 86.

161. Great Britain, Quarter-Master General's Department, *Special Instructions for Officers of the Quarter-Master General's Department* (London: Parker, Furnivall, & Parker, 1854), p. 12. This is a reprint of instructions issued to British staff officers during the Peninsula War (1807–1814); they were, in turn, based on similar eighteenth-century instructions.

162. "A Collection of Plan's &c. &c. &c. in the Province of New Jersey. By John Hills Ass:ᵗ Eng.ʳ," in *A List of Geographical Atlases in the Library of Congress, with Bibliographical Notes,* comp. under the direction of Philip Lee Phillips, vol. 1, *Atlases* (Washington: Government Printing Office, 1909), pp. 740–41; Guthorn, *British Maps,* pp. 24–27.

163. Marshall and Peckham, *Campaigns,* pp. 3, 35, 48–49, 52–53, 55, 67, 72–73, 78–79, 83, 84–85, and 123.

164. Lloyd A. Brown, *Early Maps of the Ohio Valley: A Selection of Maps, Plans, and Views Made by Indians and Colonials from 1763 to 1783* (Pittsburgh: University of Pittsburgh Press, 1959), map 32; Adams, *British Headquarters Maps,* nos. 157, 218; Scull, *Montresor Journals,* p. 379.

165. Fitzpatrick, *Writings of George Washington,* 8: 443.

166. Guthorn, *American Maps,* pp. 13–22.

167. Some military mapmakers adopted the asterisk symbol to represent a waterwheel, a device widely used in eighteenth-century cartography. Examples are found in British headquarters' maps of parts of New Jersey in *Maps and Plans in the Public Record Office,* 2: 449, MPH 569, MR 958.

168. For sources of the diagram, see notes 44–46 above.

169. Adams, *British Headquarters Maps,* passim; *Maps and Plans in the Public Record Office,* 2: passim.

170. Rice and Brown, *American Campaigns,* 2: pl. 43.

171. Ibid., pl. 46.

172. Ibid., pls. 4, 42, and 162.

173. Ibid., pl. 40.

174. See chapter 2, p. 55 below.

175. Fitzpatrick, *Writings of George Washington,* 16: 60.

176. In George Washington Papers, Ms., Manuscript Division, Library of Congress, Washington, D.C., quoted in Heusser, *George Washington's Map Maker,* pp. 163–65; Erskine's specification was much fuller than the few sentences actually quoted.

177. Heusser, *George Washington's Map Maker,* pp. 3–23.

178. Much of the evidence for these techniques is inferred from the surviving maps; see Guthorn, *American Maps,* p. 18.

179. Heusser, *George Washington's Map Maker*, p. 209; see also John P. Snyder, *The Mapping of New Jersey: The Men and the Art* (New Brunswick, N.J.: Rutgers University Press, 1973); pp. 65–74 includes an index map showing the coverage of Erskine's road surveys and "contractions."

180. Guthorn, *American Maps*, pp. 17–18.

181. Ibid., p. 21, map 100.

182. *New York Packet and the American Advertiser*, 30 August 1781, quoted in Walter W. Ristow, ed., *A Survey of the Roads of the United States . . . 1789, by Christopher Colles* (Cambridge: Harvard University Press, Belknap Press, 1961), p. 66 (hereafter cited as *Survey of the Roads*).

183. Guthorn, *American Maps*, p. 14, map 66.

184. Fitzpatrick, *Writings of George Washington*, 26: 496.

185. U.S. Continental Congress, *Journals of the Continental Congress, 1774–1789 . . .* , 34 vols. (Washington: U.S. Government Printing Office, 1904–1937), 24: 711.

186. Ristow, *Survey of the Roads*.

187. Oliver Lyman Spaulding, Jr., Hoffman Nickerson, and John Womack Wright, *Warfare: A Study of Military Methods from the Earliest Times* (London: George G. Harrap & Co., 1925), p. 535.

188. Notably Samuel Holland, Thomas Hutchins, and Bernard Ratzer.

189. John F. C. Fuller, *British Light Infantry in the Eighteenth Century* (London: Hutchinson & Co., 1925), p. 98.

190. Vallancey, "Essay," [pp. 3–4] implies, however, that itineraries were made in connection with all military topographical maps, whereas French practice specifically associates them with routes of marches.

191. Dupain de Montesson, *Les Connoissances géométriques, à l'usage des officiers employés dans les détails des marches, campements & subsistances des armées* (Paris: Chez Charles-Antoine Jombert, père, Libraire du Roi pour l'Artillerie & le Génie, 1774).

192. Dupain de Montesson, *L'Art de lever les plans de tout ce qui a rapport à la guerre & à l'architecture civile & champêtre . . .* , 2d ed., rev. (Paris: Chez Charles-Antoine Jombert, père, Libraire du Roi pour le Génie et l'Artillerie, 1775), pp. 179–86, deals with the method of itinerary compilation. The translation of the passage is from Rice and Brown, *American Campaigns*, 2: 3.

193. Rice and Brown, *American Campaigns*, 2: 23.

194. U.S. Adjutant-General's Office, *Legislative History of the General Staff of the Army of the United States (Its Organization, Duties, Pay, and Allowances), from 1775 to 1901*, comp. Raphael P. Thian (Washington: Government Printing Office, 1901), p. 139 (hereafter cited as *Legislative History*).

195. "Calendar of the Correspondence of Nathanael Greene," p. 226.

196. Ibid., letters cited on pp. 161, 180, 190, 196, 246, 277, 288, 299, and 344.

197. Fitzpatrick, *Writings of George Washington*, 20: 124, 391–92.

198. Ibid., 17: 135. The order—characteristic of many others during the Revolution—gives the impression of having been read from a map.

199. Ibid., 23: 68–69.

200. Guthorn, *American Maps*, pp. 14–15.

201. R. E. Scouller, *The Armies of Queen Anne* (Oxford: Clarendon Press, 1966), pp. 62–63; Clifford Walton, *History of the British Standing Army, A.D. 1660 to 1700* (London: Harrison & Sons, 1894), pp. 621–22.

202. Thomas Simes, *A Treatise on the Military Science, which comprehends the Grand Operations of War . . .* (London: Printed by H. Reynell, 1780), p. 1.

203. R. H. Thoumine, *Scientific Soldier: A Life of General Le Marchant, 1766–1812* (London: Oxford University Press, 1968), pp. 99–119.

204. See, for example, "Formation of a Company and a Regiment, Drawing by Pierre-Charles L'Enfant, for Regulations for the Order and Discipline of the Troops of the United States," in Rice and Brown, *American Campaigns* 1: xxiii–iv, pl. following p. 142, which was designed to illustrate the drill manual prepared by Baron von Steuben for the use of the Continental Army.

205. Fuller, *British Light Infantry*, "Bouquet's Order of March," fig. facing p. 108.

206. Lawrence Martin, ed., *The George Washington Atlas* (Washington, D.C.: U.S. George Washington Bicentennial Commission, 1932), reproduced as pl. 13 (lower).

207. Fitzpatrick, *Writings of George Washington*, 12: 4–5.

208. Ibid., 7: 359; 9: 124–25, 307; 11: 465–67; 12: 90, 196, 198, and 460–62; 13: 295; and 19: 273, 335–37, and 425.

209. Ibid., 12: 74.

210. Justin Winsor, ed., *Narrative and Critical History of America*, 8 vols. (Boston and New York, 1884–89; reprint ed., New York: AMS Press, 1967), 6: 628.

211. Hadden, *Journal and Orderly Books*, p. 152.

212. Rice and Brown, *American Campaigns*, 2: pl. 108, where the symbols used in the succeeding maps are identified.

213. Herbert George Fordham, *The Road-Books and Itineraries of Great Britain, 1570 to 1850: A Catalogue . . . and a Bibliography* (Cambridge: Cambridge University Press, 1924), and *Les Routes de France: Etude bibliographique sur les cartes-routières, et les itinéraires, et guides-routiers de France, suivie d'un catalogue des itinéraires et guides-routiers, 1552–1850* (Paris: Libraire Ancienne Honore Champion, 1929).

214. Rice and Brown, *American Campaigns*, 2: 119.

215. Brown, *Early Maps of the Ohio Valley*, p. 117, pl. 45 (lower).

216. Hills, "Collection of Plans," in *List of Geographical Atlases in the Library of Congress*, 1: nos. 5–10, 17; see note 162 above.

217. Sullivan, *Journals of the Military Expedition*, p. 288.

218. Ibid., for reproductions of these route maps, and p. 293, for a list of the maps now in the Erskine-De Witt Collection; Guthorn, *American Maps*, p. 26.

219. Guthorn, *American Maps*, pp. 26, 39, where part of the map is reproduced; also Marshall and Peckham, *Campaigns*, p. 97.

220. Sullivan, *Journals of the Military Expedition*, p. 288.

221. Ibid.

222. Cumming, *British Maps*, p. 71. For other manuscript examples by British cartographers, see Marshall and Peckham, *Campaigns*, pp. 55 (by John André), 84–85 (by Alexander Sutherland), and 116–17 (by Edward Fage).

223. Guthorn, "Library of Congress 'Hessian Map,' " p. 3; sections are reproduced in black and white in Winsor, *Narrative and Critical History*, 6: 327, 345, 409, 422, 428, 433, 442, and 556.

224. Adams, *British Headquarters Maps*, p. 44, no. 143. This can be compared with the map by André cited in note 222 above; the compilation of such maps may have been regarded as among the routine responsibilities of senior staff officers with cartographic skills.

225. Rice and Brown, *American Campaigns*, 2: pl. 162.

226. Frederick the Great, "Frederick the Great: Military Instructions for the Generals," in *Roots of Strategy: A Collection of Military Classics,* ed. Thomas Raphael Phillips (Harrisburg, Pa.: Military Service Publishing Co., 1940 [subsequently reissued]; London: John Lane, 1943), p. 178.

227. Dupain de Montesson, *L'Art de lever les plans* (1763 ed.), pp. 166–84.

228. Humphrey Bland, *A Treatise of Military Discipline; in which is laid down and Explained the Duty of the Officer and Soldier, thro' the several Branches of the Service,* 2d ed. (London: S. Buckley, 1727), p. 250. Nine further editions of Bland's *Treatise* were printed at London between 1727 and 1762.

229. There were indeed attempts to regulate the scale of such drawings: "Sketches of positions should never be made upon a smaller scale than four inches to an English mile. More general Sketches may be made upon a scale of two inches to a mile, and Tracings of Roads upon a scale of one inch to a mile" (Great Britain, Quarter-Master General's Department, *Special Instructions*, p. 14, footnote).

230. "Calendar of the Correspondence of Nathanael Greene," p. 157.

231. Fitzpatrick, *Writings of George Washington*, 17: 167–68.

232. Ibid., pp. 168–69.

233. Ibid., p. 240.

234. Luvaas, *Frederick the Great on the Art of War*, p. 113.

235. Fitzpatrick, *Writings of George Washington*, 17: 271.

236. Kite, *Louis Lebègue Duportail*, pp. 165–66.

237. Kenneth Nebenzahl, *A Bibliography of Printed Battle Plans of the American Revolution, 1775–1795* (Chicago and London: University of Chicago Press, 1975).

238. France, Dépôt Général de la Guerre, *Mémorial* 5: pl. 9, "Signes conventionnels pour l'armée de mer." For an example of the use of such symbols in Revolutionary cartography, see Marshall and Peckham, *Campaigns*, pp. 60–61.

239. National Gallery of Canada, *Thomas Davies, c. 1737–1812: An Exhibition Organized by the National Gallery of Canada, Ottawa,* ed. R. H. Hubbard (Ottawa, 1972). For an example of the work of another military artist-cartographer, see British Museum, *The American War of Independence, 1775–83: A Commemorative Exhibition Organised by the Map Library and the Department of Manuscripts of the British Library Reference Division, 4 July to 11 November 1975* (London, 1975), pp. 56–57.

240. Luvaas, *Frederick the Great on the Art of War*, pp. 41, 150.

241. Gottschalk, *Letters of Lafayette to Washington*, pp. 102–103.

242. Fitzpatrick, *Writings of George Washington*, 20: 428–34.

243. Johann David Erdmann Preuss, ed., "Plans relatifs aux oeuvres militaires de Frédéric le Grand, réimprimés sur les planches originales," in *Oeuvres de Frédéric le Grand . . . ,* 31 vols. and atlas (Berlin: Chez Rodolphe Decker, 1846–1857).

244. Hadden, *Journal and Orderly Books*, facing p. 164; also the much neater diagram in Fitzpatrick, *Writings of George Washington*, 10: facing p. 138.

245. John Burgoyne, *A State of the Expedition from Canada, as Laid before the House of Commons . . . and Verified by Evidence; with a Collection of Authentic Documents* (London: J. Almon, 1780), advertisement.

246. Adams, *British Headquarters Maps*, pp. 105–106.

247. Nebenzahl, *Bibliography;* nos. 55, 129, 145, 177, and 195, for plans derived from Hills, and no. 116 for the Sauthier plan; all these were published by William Faden. For an earlier example, see Henry Pelham to Susanna Copley, 23 July 1775, in *Letters and Papers of John Singleton Copley and Henry Pelham, 1739–1776* (Boston: Massachusetts Historical Society, 1914), p. 346.

248. As with the Barrette plan, note 246 above.

249. Nebenzahl, *Bibliography*, no. 126.

Chapter 2

1. Cumming, *British Maps.*

2. Guthorn. *American Maps,* and *British Maps.* The same author is working on comparable biographies of Hessian mapmakers.

3. Where evidence such as diaries, journals, or notebooks is available, more systematic studies could profitably be made of the "action space" and mobility of individual military surveyors. For a historical application, see R. Lawton and C. G. Pooley, "David Brindley's Liverpool: An Aspect of Urban Society in the 1880s," *Transactions of the Historic Society of Lancashire and Cheshire for the Year 1974* 125 (1975): 149–68.

4. Ira D. Gruber, *The Howe Brothers and the American Revolution* (New York: Atheneum, 1972), p. 56; William B. Willcox, *Portrait of a General: Sir Henry Clinton in the War of Independence* (New York: Alfred A. Knopf, 1964), pp. 10–44.

5. de Fonblanque, *Episodes from the Life of John Burgoyne*, pp. 1–107; George Athan Billias, "John Burgoyne: Ambitious General," in *George Washington's Opponents: British Generals and Admirals in the American Revolution*, ed. George Athan Billias (New York: William Morrow & Co., 1969), pp. 142–92.

6. Franklin Wickwire and Mary Wickwire, *Cornwallis and the War of Independence* (London: Faber & Faber, 1971), pp. 17–29; Hugh F. Rankin, "Charles Lord Cornwallis: Study in Frustration," in *George Washington's Opponents*, ed. Billias, pp. 193–232.

7. Guthorn, "Library of Congress 'Hessian Map,'" pp. 3–4.

8. Mark Mayo Boatner III, *Encyclopedia of the American Revolution* (New York: David McKay Co., 1974), s.v. "Lee, Charles," who was educated in England and Switzerland and served not only on Braddock's expedition in North America, but also in England and Portugal and as an officer attached to the Polish army; John W. Shy, "Charles Lee: The Soldier as Radical," in *George Washington's Generals*, ed. George Athan Billias (New York: William Morrow & Co., 1964), pp. 22–53.

9. Fuller, *British Light Infantry*, pp. 97–99.

10. Boatner, *Encyclopedia*, s.v. "Kalb, Johann," "Lafayette, Marquis de," and "Pulaski, Casimir."

11. John McAuley Palmer, *General Von Steuben* (New Haven: Yale University Press, 1937), pp. 37–39.

12. Fitzpatrick, *Writings of George Washington*, 20: 463.

13. Boston Athenaeum, *A Catalogue of the Washington Collection in the Boston Athenaeum*, comp. Appleton P. C. Griffin (Boston, 1897), pp. 537–42, is a list of the military books in Washington's library. It is said that when asked by the Marquis de Chastellux which professional military books he had read with the greatest pleasure, Washington replied, "The King of Prussia's Instructions to His Generals and The Tactics of M. de Guibert" (Quoted in *History of the George Washington Bicentennial Celebration*, vol. 1, *Literature Series* [Washington, D.C.: U.S. George Washington Bicentennial Commission, 1932], p. 108).

14. The acquisition of maps and plans as prizes of war is suggested by the presence of some foreign maps in a number of British collections, for which see Cumming, *British Maps*, p. 34. When Lord Jeffery Amherst conquered Montreal in 1759, he captured French maps there. Captured French plans of Louisbourg also occur in Add. Ms. 57703/3, Amherst Collection, British Library, London. Another example in a letter of John Graves Simcoe to Clinton: "I take this opportunity of enclosing to your Excellency two sketches, taken amongst the papers of the Marquis de la Fayette" (*Simcoe's Military Journal: A History of the Operations of a Partisan Corps, called the Queen's Rangers, Commanded by Lieut. Col. J. G. Simcoe . . . Now First Published with a Memoir of the Author . . .* [New York: Bartlett & Welford, 1844], p. 304).

15. P.R.O., C.O. 325/1, fol. 6.

16. John Clarence Webster, "Life of John Montrésor," *Transactions of the Royal Society of Canada*, sec. 11, ser. 111, 22 (1928): 1–31.

17. Harry Miller Lydenberg, ed., *Archibald Robertson . . . His Diaries and Sketches in America, 1762–1780* (New York: New York Public Library, 1930), pp. 9–10.

18. Marshall, "British Engineers in America," pp. 162–63.

19. De Vorsey, *De Brahm's Report*, pp. 7–9.

20. Willis Chipman, "The Life and Times of Major Samuel Holland, Surveyor General, 1764–1801," *Ontario Historical Society Papers and Records* 21 (1924): 11–90.

21. Evans, "Soldier, Hydrographer, Governor," pp. 1–6.

22. Cumming, *British Maps*, pp. 72–74.

23. See below, p. 72.

24. In this respect Debbeig's comment that "he was seven years employed upon the survey of Scotland (the greatest work of this sort ever performed by British subjects and perhaps for the fine Representations of the Country not to be equalled in the World)," if it is not impartial, is suggestive of its influence (P.R.O., C.O. 325/1, fol. 6).

25. For example, Fitzpatrick, *Writings of George Washington*, 3: 322, 325; 4: 61, 196, and 528; 5: 108, 117, 132, 154, and 318; 6: 160–61, 214, 340, and 400–401; and 7: 388.

26. Boatner, *Encyclopedia*, s.v. "Gridley, Richard."

27. Guthorn, *American Maps*, p. 30.

28. Boatner, *Encyclopedia*, s.v. "Putnam, Rufus."

29. Kite, *Louis Lebègue Duportail*, p. 2.

30. U.S. Adjutant-General's Office, *Legislative History*, pp. 487–88.

31. Duportail was an able military theoretician, and during the summer of 1776 before going to America, he had prepared a new set of rules for the French engineer corps, for which see Kite, *Louis Lebègue Duportail*, p. 1.

32. See U.S. Adjutant-General's Office, *Legislative History*, pp. 487–95, for a complete list of engineering commissions to 1783.

33. Kite, *Louis Lebègue Duportail*, p. 50.

34. Ibid., p. 52.

35. Ibid., p. 245. Niven was of Huguenot descent and came from the region around New York.

36. This, for example, includes civilians who made the occasional map for military purposes (or those that turn up in an archival context which is military) and as well as the professional officers who made the bulk of maps.

37. See Philip Lee Phillips, *Notes on the Life and Works of Bernard Romans,* Publication of the Florida State Historical Society, no. 2 (Deland: Florida State Historical Society, 1924), for details on Romans's association with De Brahm's project.

38. R. A. Skelton, "The Military Surveyor's Contribution to British Cartography in the 16th Century," *Imago Mundi* 24 (1970): 77–83.

39. William Richard Mead, "The Eighteenth-Century Military Reconnaissance of Finland: A Neglected Chapter in the History of Finnish Geography," *Acta Geographica* 20 (1968): 255–71.

40. Brian Bond, *The Victorian Army and the Staff College, 1854–1914* (London: Eyre Methuen, 1972), p. 11.

41. Henri M. A. Berthaut, *Les Ingénieurs géographes militaires, 1624–1831: Etude historique,* 2 vols. (Paris: Imprimerie du Service Geographique, 1902), 1: 6, 13, 15, and 17–116 passim.

42. Bond, *Victorian Army,* p. 11.

43. Pierre Joseph de Bourcet, *Principes de la guerre de montagnes . . . 1775* (Paris: Imprimerie Nationale, 1888).

44. Ibid., pp. 9–12. See also Spencer Wilkinson, *The Defence of Piedmont, 1742–1748: A Prelude to the Study of Napoleon* (Oxford: Clarendon Press, 1927), p. 59.

45. Berthaut, *Ingénieurs géographes,* pp. 15–116 passim.

46. Walter Görlitz, *The German General Staff: Its History and Structure, 1657–1945, with a Preface by Cyril Falls* (London: Hollis & Carter, 1953), p. 4.

47. Bond, *Victorian Army,* p. 11.

48. Duffy, *Army of Frederick the Great,* p. 146.

49. James D. Hittle, *The Military Staff: Its History and Development* (Harrisburg, Pa.: Military Service Publishing Co., 1949), p. 52.

50. Duffy, *Army of Frederick the Great,* p. 146.

51. Ibid., pp. 37–38; Hittle, *Military Staff,* pp. 52–53.

52. Luvaas, *Frederick the Great on the Art of War,* p. 86.

53. Duffy, *Army of Frederick the Great,* p. 123.

54. Hittle, *Military Staff,* p. 84.

55. The Royal Military College's senior department was founded at High Wycombe, Bucks., in 1799; its junior department was established at Great Marlowe, Bucks., in 1802, for which see Thoumine, *Scientific Soldier,* pp. 61–79. It is a nice illustration of the argument in this chapter that the first director of instruction at High Wycombe was General François Jarry who, though French by birth, had been employed in Prussia for thirteen years as governor of the Académie des Nobles.

56. Oliver F. G. Hogg, *The Royal Arsenal: Its Background, Origin, and Subsequent History,* 2 vols. (London: Oxford University Press, 1963), 1: 305, for the artillery warrant of 1716; Porter, *History of the Royal Engineers,* 1: 139–44.

57. Great Britain, Royal Military Academy, *Records of the Royal Military Academy (1741–1840),* comp. William D. Jones (Woolwich: Royal Artillery Institution, 1851), p. 1 (hereafter cited as *Records*); Hogg, *Royal Arsenal,* p. 345.

58. *Dictionary of National Biography,* s.v. "Muller, John."

59. Muller, *Practical Part of Fortification,* p. xviii.

60. Muller, *Elementary Part of Fortification,* p. 13.

61. Great Britain, Royal Military Academy, *Records,* p. 31.

62. Ibid., p. 18.

63. Ibid., p. 1.

64. Ibid., pp. 13–15, reproduces the 1764 "Rules and Orders."

65. Great Britain, Royal Military Academy, *Rules and Orders for the Royal Military Academy at Woolwich 1776* (printed tract, P.R.O., W.O. 30/120), pp. 16–17 (hereafter cited as *Rules and Orders*).

66. Ibid., p. 18.

67. Skelton, *Military Survey of Scotland,* p. 4; Adolph Paul Oppé, *The Drawings of Paul and Thomas Sandby in the Collection of His Majesty the King, at Windsor Castle* (Oxford and London: Phaidon Press, 1947), p. 7.

68. "List and Dates . . . Appointments of Officers, Professors, and Masters . . . ," in Great Britain, Royal Military Academy, *Records,* at front of volume [unpaginated].

69. Great Britain, Royal Military Academy, *Rules and Orders,* p. 20.

70. Ibid., p. 19.

71. Eva G. R. Taylor, *The Mathematical Practitioners of Hanoverian England, 1714–1840* (Cambridge: Cambridge University Press, 1966), pp. 226, 235.

72. Vallancey, "Essay" [p. 8].

73. Great Britain, Royal Military Academy, *Rules and Orders,* pp. 11–12.

74. Great Britain, Royal Military Academy, *Records,* p. 8.

75. Ibid., p. 25.

76. P.R.O., W.O. 47/75, p. 268.

77. Hogg, *Royal Arsenal,* p. 371.

78. Great Britain, Royal Military Academy, *Records,* passim.

79. Hogg, *Royal Arsenal,* p. 371.

80. Charles M. Clode, *The Military Forces of the Crown: Their Administration and Government,* 2 vols. (London: John Murray, 1869), 1: 456–70.

81. *Dictionary of National Biography,* s.v. "Gomme, Sir Bernard de."

82. Adrian H. W. Robinson, *Marine Cartography in Britain: A History of the Sea Chart to 1855* (Leicester: Leicester University Press, 1962), p. 88.

83. Ibid., pp. 87–96.

84. *Gentleman's Magazine and Historical Chronicle,* 1746, p. 383.

85. Henry Popple, *A Map of the British Empire in America with the French and Spanish Settlements adjacent thereto, by Henry Popple* [Facsimile ed.] (Lympne Castle, Kent: Harry Margary, 1972), includes introductory notes by William P. Cumming and Helen Wallis.

86. Oppé, *Drawings of Paul and Thomas Sandby,* pp. 4–7.

87. P.R.O., W.O. 55/2281.

88. Marshall and Peckham, *Campaigns,* p. 15. Of the twenty-one members of the Corps of Engineers arriving for duty in North America in 1776, six had been commissioned after service in the Drawing Room of the Tower of London.

89. See, for example, the draftsmen recorded as appointed or employed in P.R.O., W.O. 54/199, 54/207, 54/208, and 54/214.

90. The most convenient source of information about the staff of the Drawing Room is the annual volumes of the *Court and City Kalendar; or, Gentleman's Register, for England, Scotland, Ireland, and America...* (London, 1745–) from which the figures in the text are derived. I owe this source to Douglas W. Marshall.

91. In P.R.O., MPH 14 and MPH 15, for example, the names, ages, and lengths of service of Drawing Room personnel are tabulated.

92. India, Survey of India Department, *Historical Records of the Survey of India,* comp. Reginald Henry Phillimore, vol. 1, *Eighteenth Century* (Dehra Dun, U.P., 1945), pp. 316–17, notes that Reuben Burrow, who had been appointed as a mathematics instructor at the Drawing Room, took his charges and several Woolwich cadets to survey part of the Essex and Sussex coast in 1777. P.R.O., W.O. 34/206 notes similar surveys along the Thames in September 1780.

93. P.R.O., MPH 14, MPH 15.

94. See p. 53 above.

95. P.R.O., W.O. 34/206 in the "Report of the Drawing Room" for March 1782.

96. Great Britain, Royal Military Academy, *Records,* p. 39.

97. P.R.O., W.O. 47/109, 1 June 1787.

98. Boatner, *Encyclopedia,* s.v. "Knox, Henry"; Francis S. Drake, *Life and Correspondence of Henry Knox, Major-General in the American Revolutionary Army* (Boston: Samuel G. Drake, 1873), p. 15; and North Callahan, "Henry Knox: American Artillerist," in *George Washington's Generals,* ed. Billias, pp. 239–59.

99. Edward S. Holden, "Origins of the United States Military Academy, 1777–1802," in *The Centennial of the United States Military Academy at West Point, New York, 1802–1902,* vol. 1, *Addresses and Histories* (Washington: Government Printing Office, 1904), pp. 201–202.

100. Ibid., p. 202.

101. Ibid., p. 203.

102. Boatner, *Encyclopedia,* s.v. "Nicola, Lewis."

103. Holden, "Origins of the U.S. Military Academy," p. 203

104. Reproduced in ibid., facing p. 204; also in Winsor, *Narrative and Critical History,* 6: 459.

105. Fitzpatrick, *Writings of George Washington,* 12: 40; U.S. Adjutant-General's Office, *Legislative History,* p. 489.

106. Kite, *Louis Lebègue Duportail,* pp. 269–70; Palmer, *General Von Steuben,* p. 321; and for their original context and other suggestions, see Holden, "Origins of the U.S. Military Academy," pp. 205–209.

107. See the works listed in Maurice J. D. Cockle, *A Bibliography of Military Books up to 1642* (London: Holland Press, 1900), pp. ix–xi; for many other leads, see Besterman, *A World Bibliography of Bibliographies,* 4th ed., s.v. "Military Arts and Sciences."

108. For example, Thomas M. Spaulding and Louis C. Karpinski, *Early Military Books in the University of Michigan Libraries* (Ann Arbor: University of Michigan Press, 1941), pp. 34–38 provides a start for military books published in North America during the Revolution; see also note 131 below.

109. Rumpf, *Allgemeine Literatur;* Cockle, *Bibliography of Military Books,* p. xii, concludes that Rumpf is generally unreliable. For lack of a better source, Rumpf's listing is adequate for the preliminary and purely illustrative analysis in this chapter.

110. Rumpf, *Allgemeine Literatur,* p. 154 ff.

111. It was not printed until 1888; see Spenser Wilkinson, *The French Army before Napoleon: Lectures Delivered before the University of Oxford in Michaelmas Term, 1914* (Oxford: Clarendon Press, 1915), p. 34.

112. Frederick the Great, "Military Instructions for the Generals," in *Roots of Strategy,* ed. Thomas Raphael Phillips, pp. 166–67; it was revised in 1748 under the title *Principes generaux de la guerre.* In 1753 an edition of fifty copies was printed and sent to officers whom Frederick considered model soldiers. The books were delivered with an order enjoining each recipient (by oath) not to take it into the field and to insure that in the event of his death the volume would be returned to the king. When the Austrians captured General Czettertiz in 1760, he was carrying a copy of this secret treatise. It was published in German in 1761, translated back into French and published in France that same year, and then translated into English in 1762 and published as *Military Instructions by the King of Prussia.*

113. Rice and Brown, *American Campaigns,* 2: 114.

114. Dupain de Montesson, *La Science des ombres, par rapport au dessein...* (Paris: Chez Charles-Antoine Jombert, Libraire du Roi pour l'Artillerie & le Génie, 1750); another edition was published in 1786.

115. Rice and Brown, *American Campaigns* 2: 111–20, is an excellent background essay on the French cartography of the Revolution.

116. Rumpf, *Allgemeine Literatur,* title no. 4045.

117. Pirscher, *Coup d'oeil militaire.*

118. Rumpf, *Allgemeine Literatur,* title no. 4064.

119. Cockle, *Bibliography of Military Books,* passim.

120. See J. B. Harley and Gwyn Walters, "William Roy's Maps, Mathematical Instruments, and Library: The Christie's Sale of 1790," *Imago Mundi* 29 (1977): at press, for a discussion of books on military sciences—many of Continental origin—owned by a leading British military engineer at the time of the Revolution. Such sale catalogues, especially those containing a record of both maps and books, deserve fuller exploitation by historians of cartography.

121. Vallancey, "Essay," [p. 25].

122. J. H. Andrews, "Charles Vallancey and the Map of Ireland," *Geographical Journal* 132 (1966): 48–61.

123. F. J. G. Robinson and P. J. Wallis, *Book Subscription Lists: A Revised Guide* (Newcastle upon Tyne: Harold Hill & Son, 1975), passim.

124. I owe this statistic to Douglas W. Marshall.

125. Marshall, "British Engineers in America," facing p. 158, is also a reproduction of the portrait.

126. Simes, *Treatise on the Military Science,* subscription list; for one general officer's familiarity with these works in an American context, see Charles Knowles Bolton, ed., *Letters of Hugh Earl Percy from Boston and New York, 1774–1776* (Boston: Charles E. Goodspeed, 1902), pp. 58–59.

127. Taylor, *Mathematical Practitioners,* passim; see also Nicholas Hans, *New Trends in Education in the Eighteenth Century* (London: Routledge & Kegan Paul, 1951); and for Scotland, Duncan K. Wilson, *The History of Mathematical Teaching in Scotland to the End of the Eighteenth Century* (London: University of London Press, 1935).

128. As one of the subscribers to Simes's *Treatise,* he styles himself as of the "Royal Military Academy, Little Chelsea."

129. For a helpful discussion of this subject from the standpoint of historical literature—but with many implications for the history of geography and the role of textbooks as carriers of cartographical information—see H. Trevor Colbourn, *The Lamp of Experience: Whig History and the Intellectual Origins of the American Revolution* (Chapel Hill: University of North Carolina Press, 1965), pp. 4–20, and pp. 199–232 (appendix 11) for a list of catalogues.

130. See note 102 above.

131. For these titles, see Evans, *American Bibliography;* Spaulding and Karpinski, *Early Military Books,* pp. 32–37; and John Henry Stanley, "Preliminary Investigation of Military Manuals of American Imprint prior to 1800" (Master's thesis, Brown University, 1964), pp. 79–97, for a fuller listing (1775–1783) that indicates the majority of titles were concerned with general matters of drill and discipline rather than advanced tactics.

132. Stevenson, *Military Instructions for Officers,* pp. 1–7.

133. Ibid., p. 85.

134. Ibid., p. 86.

135. Fitzpatrick, *Writings of George Washington,* 6: 243; 16: 60, 195.

136. Stevenson, *Military Instructions for Officers,* dedication.

137. Montross, *Rag, Tag, and Bobtail,* pp. 271–72.

138. Drake, *Life and Correspondence of Henry Knox,* p. 15.

139. Ibid., p. 20; also [Worthington Chauncey Ford], "Henry Knox and the London Book-Store in Boston, 1771–1774," *Proceedings of the Massachusetts Historical Society* 61 (1928): 225–304, for catalogues and dealers' lists that provide an indication of the military books available to Knox.

140. Theodore Thayer, *Nathanael Greene: Strategist of the American Revolution* (New York: Twayne Publishers, 1960), pp. 23–24.

141. Thomas G. Frothingham, *Washington: Commander in Chief* (Boston and New York: Houghton Mifflin Co., Riverside Press, 1930), p. 24; also reproduced in Martin, *George Washington Atlas,* pl. 13 (lower). In 1756 Washington had counseled on military matters: "Let us read . . . Blands and other Treatises which will give us the wished for information" (Fitzpatrick, *Writings of George Washington,* 1: 271); for Blands' text, see chapter 1 note 228. For a summary of the context of Washington's military development, see Oliver L. Spaulding, "The Military Studies of George Washington," *American Historical Review* 69 (1924): 675–80.

142. Fitzpatrick, *Writings of George Washington,* 9: 92–93.

143. Boston Athenaeum, *Catalogue of the Washington Collection,* pp. 537–42; also Fitzpatrick, *Writings of George Washington,* 4: 81, offers evidence that at the beginning of the war Washington's advice was sought in the choice of books that offered the best preparation for prospective officers.

144. Fitzpatrick, *Writings of George Washington,* 10: 238. Such book knowledge could commend an officer to Washington: he endorsed Timothy Pickering for the post of adjutant general on the grounds that Pickering's "Military Genius" had been "cultivated by an industrious attention to the Study of War" (Ibid., 7: 114).

145. See, for example, U.S. Adjutant-General's Office, *Legislative History,* p. 189, where provision for the geographers is made under the quartermaster's department.

146. See chapter 1 note 13.

147. Fitzpatrick, *Writings of George Washington,* 6: 243.

148. Ibid., 7: 65.

149. Ibid.
150. Ibid., 8: 372.
151. Ibid., p. 443.
152. Ibid., p. 372 note 94, quoting *Journals of the Continental Congress;* U.S. Adjutant-General's Office, *Legislative History,* p. 488.
153. Fitzpatrick, *Writings of George Washington,* 8: 495–96.
154. Ibid., 9: 52–53.
155. For the delay in full implementation see Goetzmann, *Army Exploration in the American West,* pp. 6–7; Henry P. Beers, "A History of the United States Topographical Engineers, 1813–1863," *Military Engineer* 34 (1942): 287–91.
156. See note 151 above.
157. Kenneth Roberts, comp., *March to Quebec: Journals of the Members of Arnold's Expedition* (New York: Doubleday & Co., 1940), pp. 651–714; Pierce had joined Arnold's detachment as an engineer and surveyor.
158. Not all the names of the assistant surveyors in the geographer's department can be identified; see Ristow, *Survey of the Roads,* p. 63.
159. U.S. Adjutant-General's Office, *Legislative History,* p. 493.
160. Ibid., p. 495, quoting *Journals of the Continental Congress* for 12 November 1782.
161. Fitzpatrick, *Writings of George Washington,* 16: 60.
162. Ibid., 15: 255–56.
163. Guthorn, *American Maps,* p. 26.
164. "Calendar of the Correspondence of Nathanael Greene," p. 212.
165. Sullivan, *Journals of the Military Expedition.*
166. Fitzpatrick, *Writings of George Washington,* 19: 154–55.
167. Ibid., 15: 19; for some of the detailed cartographic preparations for this expedition, 14: 150–51, 159–60, 292, 314–18, and 322.
168. Ibid., 15: 212.
169. Ibid., pp. 297–98.
170. Walter W. Ristow, "Maps of the American Revolution: A Preliminary Survey," *Quarterly Journal of the Library of Congress* 28 (1971): 196–215.
171. Marshall and Peckham, *Campaigns,* pp. iv–v.
172. Guthorn, "Library of Congress 'Hessian Map.'"
173. Mackenzie, *Diary,* 2: 662, 669, demonstrates that in 1781, for example, there were detachments of the guides and pioneers with Cornwallis in the south and with Clinton in New York.
174. See Simcoe, *Military Journal,* passim, for evidence that the skilled mapmaker of the corps seems to have been George Spencer; Guthorn, *British Maps,* pp. 43–44, gives a list of items attributable to Spencer.
175. Marshall and Peckham, *Campaigns,* p. 37; also chapter 1, pp. 22–23 above.
176. India, Survey of India Department, *Historical Records,* pp. 90–97.
177. Boatner, *Encyclopedia,* s.v. "Montresor, John," for a brief sketch.
178. P.R.O. 30/55, Carleton Papers.
179. See pp. 56–58 above; also chapter 1 notes 201, 202.
180. Skelton, *Military Survey of Scotland,* p. 2.
181. British Library, K. Top., VI, 103.
182. In 1746 he drew a map of the "March of the Royal Army in Scotland with an exact Plan of their different Encampm:ᵗˢ" (P.R.O., W.O. 55/2281).
183. Brown, *Early Maps of the Ohio Valley,* pp. 117–18.
184. Herbert George Fordham, "'Paterson's Roads': Daniel Paterson, His Maps and Itineraries, 1738–1825," *Transactions of the Bibliographical Society,* n.s. 5 (1925): 332–56.
185. Willcox, *American Rebellion,* pp. 404–405.
186. Guthorn, *British Maps,* p. 27; for a comment on Holland's value to the British army at this date, see Edward H. Tatum, Jr., ed., *The American Journal of Ambrose Serle, Secretary to Lord Howe, 1776–1778* (San Marino, Calif.: Huntingdon Library, 1940), pp. 145–46.
187. Guthorn, *British Maps,* pp. 27–29.
188. He is not, for example, listed in P.R.O., W.O. 65/164, p. 76; nor in W.O. 65/165, p. 20; and not in W.O. 65/166, p. 45.
189. P.R.O., W.O. 65/165, p. 20.
190. Guthorn, *British Maps,* p. 12.
191. Marshall and Peckham, *Campaigns,* p. 132.
192. Scull, *Montresor Journals,* pp. 538–39; also p. 517 where, in a return of the Corps of Engineers for June 1777, he is identified as a draftsman attached to the commander in chief.
193. I. H. Adams, "George Taylor, A Surveyor o' Pairts," *Imago Mundi* 27 (1975): 55–63; R. H. Fairclough, "'Sketches of the Roads in Scotland, 1785': The Manuscript Roadbook of George Taylor," *Imago Mundi* 27 (1975): 65–72.
194. See note 173 above.
195. P.R.O. 30/55, vol. 87, p. 9,712, Carleton Papers.
196. Guthorn, *British Maps,* p. 12, map 11.
197. Ibid., p. 14, maps 14, 15.
198. Ibid., p. 12, map 9.
199. Marshall and Peckham, *Campaigns,* pp. 34–35.
200. Scull, *Montresor Journals,* p. 144.
201. See Carl Van Doren, *Secret History of the American Revolution* (New York: Viking Press, 1941), passim, for information on the role of the adjutant general's department in intelligence work; see also p. 75 below.

202. Marshall and Peckham, *Campaigns,* pp. 128–29.

203. Adams, *British Headquarters Maps.*

204. Cumming, *British Maps,* p. 72–74.

205. Guthorn, *British Maps,* p. 47.

206. Ibid., pp. 24–27; Marshall and Peckham, *Campaigns,* p. 133.

207. Marshall and Peckham, *Campaigns,* p. 134; Adams, *British Headquarters Maps,* pp. 18–19.

208. Rice and Brown, *American Campaigns,* 2: 117–18.

209. The most obvious faults are the lack of biographical information on particular map-makers, the tendency for some officers to change regiments during the course of their career, and the large number of anonymous manuscript maps during this period; for the anonymous maps see Guthorn, *British Maps,* pp. 49–60.

210. Boatner, *Encyclopedia,* s.v. "Robinson, Beverley"; Van Doren, *Secret History,* passim; Brun, *Guide to the Manuscript Maps,* p. 108, map 453, is, however, the only map actually drawn by him to have been so identified.

Chapter 3

1. J. A. Williamson, *The Voyages of John and Sebastian Cabot,* Historical Association [Great Britain] Pamphlet, no. 106 (London: Historical Association, 1937), p. 7; also quoted by R. A. Skelton, *Looking at an Early Map* (Lawrence: University of Kansas Libraries, 1965), p. 4.

2. The Conference on the History of Cartography, London, September 1967, had as its main theme "Early Maps as Historical Evidence."

3. Arthur H. Robinson, "The Potential Contribution of Cartography in Liberal Education," *Cartographer* 2 (1965): 1–8 [now *Canadian Cartographer*].

4. C. Board, "Maps as Models," in *Models in Geography,* ed. Richard J. Chorely and Peter Haggett (London: Methuen & Co., 1967), pp. 671–725; Arthur H. Robinson and Barbara Bartz Petchenik, "The Map as a Communication System," *Cartographic Journal* 12 (1975): 7–15.

5. Cornelis Koeman, "The Principle of Communication in Cartography," in *International Yearbook of Cartography,* vol. 11 (London: George Philip, 1971), pp. 169–75.

6. Summarized in Robinson and Petchenik, "Map as a Communication System," pp. 8–11.

7. Ibid., pp. 10–11.

8. Phillip C. Muehrcke and Juliana O. Muehrcke, "Maps in Literature," *Geographical Review* 64 (1974): 320.

9. John L. Allen, "Exploration and the Creation of Geographical Images of the Great Plains: Comments on the Role of Subjectivity," in *Images of the Plains: The Role of Human Nature in Settlement,* ed. Brian W. Blouet and Merlin P. Lawson (Lincoln: University of Nebraska Press, 1975), pp. 3–11.

10. George Kitson Clark, *The Critical Historian* (London: Heinemann Educational Books, 1967), p. 58.

11. Ristow, "Maps of the American Revolution," p. 209.

12. In addition, in June 1775 Gage admitted: "In our present state all warlike preparations are wanting. No survey of the adjacent country [exists] . . . ." (Gage to Lord North, 12 June 1775 in *The Correspondence of King George the Third, from 1760 to December 1783,* ed. John Fortescue, 6 vols. [London: Macmillan & Co., 1927–1928], 3: 215–16).

13. Adams, *British Headquarters Maps,* pp. 34–67.

14. For a general discussion of the place of such an approach in studies of map users in the past, see J. B. Harley, "The Map User in Eighteenth-Century North America: Some Preliminary Observations," in *The Settlement of Canada: Origins and Transfer,* ed. Brian S. Osborne, Proceedings of the 1975 British-Canadian Symposium on Historical Geography (Kingston, Ont.: Department of Geography, Queen's University, 1976), pp. 47–69.

15. Scull, *Montresor Journals,* pp. 232, 345, 347, 350, 359, 387, and passim for other examples.

16. Montresor's map collection (apparently scattered) is a good example of this process. When it was sold in 1800, it was described as consisting of: "Three Port Folios, containing near 2,000 Drawings of different Fortifications and Plans of Forts"; his North American holdings included items relating to "Quebec, Bellisle, Montreal, Louisbourgh, Fort George, . . . St. Augustine, New York, Pensacola, St. Mark, Niagara, . . . Halifax, Cumberland, Detroit, . . . with Plans of the Rivers Mississippi, Iberville, St. Lawrence, Mobile, Cheesapeak, Delaware, . . . Lake Ontario, and others too numerous to mention; Draughts of Roads of the different Routs in America . . . Plans of Block Houses, Barracks, &c. of the above mentioned places . . . and most of them taken on the Spot by him" (R. H. Evans, *Catalogue of an Useful, Curious, and Valuable Collection of Books For the Year 1880* . . . [British Library, 130.k.1.(2)], p. 5, item 123). See also British Library, Add. Ms. 21886, which contains a list of over one hundred and eighty maps and plans collected at the headquarters of Frederick Haldimand, governor and commander-in-chief in Canada; likewise there is reference made in context of the garrison at Halifax to: "All the books belonging to this office with the Plans, Sections, Estimates, & locked up in the Stationery Chest, the Desk and Large Press in the Drawing Room Buildings" (P.R.O., W.O. 55/1820, pt. 11, p. 2); and Pargellis, *Military Affairs in North America,* p. 462, refers to a collection of maps belonging to William Eyre.

17. Scull, *Montresor Journals,* p. 322.

18. Ibid., p. 323.

19. Ibid., p. 341.

20. Ibid., p. 342.

21. Ibid., p. 349.

22. Ibid., pp. 351–52.

23. Ibid., p. 375.

24. Ibid., p. 392, where Montresor notes that the published plan of New York was to be dedicated ("addressed") to Gage.

25. Ibid.

26. Ibid.

27. The published maps are listed in Guthorn, *British Maps*, pp. 61–66; see also Henry Stevens and Roland Tree, *Comparative Cartography*, Map Collectors' Circle, no. 39 (London: Map Collectors' Circle, 1967), passim.

28. J. B. Harley, "The Bankruptcy of Thomas Jefferys: An Episode in the Economic History of Eighteenth Century Map-Making," *Imago Mundi* 20 (1966): 27–48, contains a description of Jefferys's role in publishing maps of North America.

29. See p. 93 below.

30. Duffy, *Army of Frederick the Great*, p. 146.

31. Josef Breu, "Official Mapping under the Hapsburg Monarchy since Maria Theresa" (paper delivered at the Sixth Technical Conference of the International Cartographic Association, Ottawa, August 1972).

32. Lester J. Cappon, "Geographers and Map-Makers, British and American, from about 1750 to 1789," *Proceedings of the American Antiquarian Society* 81 (1971): 263–64.

33. "List of Maps, Plans, &c: Belonging to the Right Honble: the Lords Commissioners for Trade and Plantations. under the care of Francis Aegidius Assiotti, Draughtsman. 1780," Ms., P.R.O FE 515 (IND 8315), London.

34. P.R.O., W.O. 55/2281.

35. The War Office maps of the period are identified in *Maps and Plans in the Public Record Office*, 2: passim.

36. Great Britain, Admiralty, Hydrographic Department, *Survey*, pp. 3–23. During the Seven Years' War the Admiralty began to take an increased interest in charting; from 1761, all officers, whether serving in home or foreign waters, were required to submit full information on all subjects of value to navigation or hydrography, as noted by Howard T. Fry, *Alexander Dalrymple (1737–1808) and the Expansion of British Trade* (London: Frank Cass & Co., 1970), p. 248.

37. British Museum, *Catalogue of the Manuscript Maps*, vol. 3; Cumming, *British Maps*, pp. 75–84, gives lists of the American maps of Francis Bernard and Earl Percy.

38. "Catalogue of Drawings & Engraved Maps, Charts and Plans; the Property of Mr. Thomas Jefferys; Geographer to the King 1775," Ms., Royal Geographical Society, London.

39. Stevens and Tree, *Comparative Cartography*, pp. 323–4, 330, and 360–61.

40. Lois Mulkearn, ed., *A Topographical Description of the United States of America . . . by Thomas Pownall . . .* (Pittsburgh: University of Pittsburgh Press, 1949 [based on the first published ed., London, 1776]), p. 10.

41. Walter W. Ristow, Introduction to *Thomas Jefferys, The American Atlas, London 1776* [Facsimile ed.] (Amsterdam: Theatrum Orbis Terrarum, 1974).

42. Library of Congress, *List of Geographical Atlases*, 1: 591–96; 3: 471–73.

43. Stevens and Tree, *Comparative Cartography*, pp. 320, 334–35, and 351–52. The map of Philadelphia, which incorporated new material recently acquired by Faden, was a larger version of a 1752 map, for which see Nicholas B. Wainwright, "Scull and Heap's Map of Philadelphia," *Pennsylvania Magazine of History and Biography* 81 (1957): 69–75.

44. See, for example, Coolie Verner, "Mr. Jefferson Makes a Map," *Imago Mundi* 14 (1959): 96–108.

45. Adams, *British Headquarters Maps*.

46. Rita S. Gottesman, comp., *The Arts and Crafts in New York, 1777–1799*, Collections of the New-York Historical Society, no. 81 (New York: New-York Historical Society, 1954), pp. 50–54.

47. Coolie Verner, Introduction to *The English Pilot, The Fourth Book, London, 1689* [Facsimile ed.] (Amsterdam: Theatrum Orbis Terrarum, 1967), pp. xv–xviii; for general background to the charting of North America, see Lawrence C. Wroth, *Some American Contributions to the Art of Navigation, 1519 to 1802* (Providence, R.I.: Associates of the John Carter Brown Library, 1947).

48. John Clarence Webster, *The Life of Joseph Frederick Wallet Des Barres* (Shediac, N.B.: n.p., 1933); Evans, "North American Soldier, Hydrographer, Governor," and its revision, G. N. D. Evans, *Uncommon Obdurate: The Several Public Careers of J. F. W. Des Barres* (Salem, Mass.: Peabody Museum, 1969).

49. Geraint N. D. Evans, "Hydrography: A Note on Eighteenth-Century Methods," *Mariner's Mirror* 52 (1966): 247–50; Louis De Vorsey, Jr., "Hydrography: A Note on the Equipage of Eighteenth-Century Survey Vessels," *Mariner's Mirror* 58 (1972): 173–77; and Robinson, *Marine Cartography in Britain*, pp. 60–70.

50. Holland, *Description of Cape Breton Island*, pp. 131–32.

51. DesBarres to Philip Stephens [Secretary of the Admiralty, 1763–1795], 28 May 1774, ser. 5 [Transcripts of documents in the Public Record Office, London, relating to his surveys and their publication], pp. 111–12, DesBarres Papers, Public Archives of Canada, Ottawa.

52. Henry Stevens, ed., "Catalogue of the Henry Newton Stevens Collection of the Atlantic Neptune together with a Concise Bibliographical Description of every Chart, View, and Leaf of Text Contained Therein, as also of Certain Other States Observed Elsewhere, by the Late Henry Newton Stevens, M.A., F.R.G.S. Corrected, Revised, and Augmented by Henry Stevens," typescript (London: Henry Stevens, Son & Stiles [1934]), p. 116 [contains additions to June 1937].

53. Fry, *Alexander Dalrymple*, pp. 248–49.

54. Great Britain, *House of Commons Journal* 35 (29 November 1774 to 15 October 1776):

177; Joseph Frederick Wallet DesBarres, *A Statement Submitted by Lieutenant Colonel Des-Barres, for Consideration: Respecting his Services, from the Year 1775, to the present Time . . .*, n.p., n.d. [London, 1795?], p. 5.

55. DesBarres appears in the ratebooks for Soho in Charlotte Street, 1774–1776, and Denmark Street, 1777–1779. I owe this information to W. R. Maidment, Director of Libraries and Arts, London Borough of Camden.

56. Material relating to *The Atlantic Neptune* can be found in ser. 3 and 5, DesBarres Papers.

57. DesBarres, *Statement*, p. 5.

58. The "Memorial" of DesBarres to the lords commissioners of trade and plantations, dated 16 May 1776, to grant him access to "Surveys and Geographical Observations" in order to render his work "as compleat as possible" (ser. 3, p. 93, DesBarres Papers).

59. DesBarres to Admiral Richard Howe, 14 September 1776, ser. 5, p. 147, DesBarres Papers.

60. Evans, "North American Soldier, Hydrographer, Governor," p. 89, quoting ser. 3, p. 97, DesBarres Papers; a similar breakdown occurs in pp. 277–79.

61. Calculation made by Robert W. Karrow from Stevens, "Catalogue of the Henry Newton Stevens Collection."

62. Admiral Richard Howe to DesBarres, 3 March 1775, ser. 5, p. 118, DesBarres Papers.

63. *L'Esprit des Journaux* (Paris, 1784), 3: 459–74; quoted by Evans, "North American Soldier, Hydrographer, Governor," p. 87, following the translation of Isaac N. P. Stokes, *The Iconography of Manhattan Island, 1498–1909*, 6 vols. (New York: Robert H. Dodd, 1915–1928), 1: 349.

64. DesBarres, *Statement*, p. 91.

65. DesBarres to Admiral Richard Howe, 14 September 1776, ser. 5, p. 145, DesBarres Papers.

66. DesBarres to the Admiralty, 20 and 24 July 1779 [includes accounts of charts supplied], ser. 5, pp. 183–90, DesBarres Papers.

67. DesBarres to Richard Cumberland, ca. 20 December 1778, ser. 3, p. 97, DesBarres Papers; see also Evans, "North American Soldier, Hydrographer, Governor," pp. 90–91.

68. Holland to Haldimand, 4 July 1775, Add. Ms. 21731, fols. 220–21, British Library, London.

69. Willcox, *American Rebellion*, p. 30.

70. Ibid., p. 31.

71. Ibid., p. 35.

72. See note 36 above.

73. P.R.O., ADM 1/487, 174.

74. Mackenzie, *Diary*, 1: 191; for another comment on the inadequacy of charts in this coastal region, see Tatum, *American Journal of Ambrose Serle*, p. 280.

75. Boston Athenaeum, *Catalogue of the Washington Collection*, pp. 561–65.

76. Julian P. Boyd et al., eds., *The Papers of Thomas Jefferson* (Princeton: Princeton University Press, 1950–), 2: 544.

77. Ibid., 3: 658.

78. Ibid., 4: 41.

79. Library of Congress, *Catalogue of the Library of Thomas Jefferson*, comp. E. Millicent Sowerby, 5 vols. (Washington, 1952–1959), 4: 85–357 contains the section "Geography" and includes many maps.

80. Leonard W. Labaree, et al., eds., *The Papers of Benjamin Franklin* (New Haven: Yale University Press, 1959–), 3: 77.

81. Lyman H. Butterfield, ed., *Adams Family Correspondence*, 4 vols. (Cambridge: Harvard University Press, Belknap Press, 1963), 2: 92. I owe this reference to Douglas W. Marshall.

82. Ibid., p. 90.

83. Ibid., p. 91.

84. George Kish [Georges Kiss], "The Correspondence of Continental Mapmakers of the 1770s and 80s with a London Firm," *Imago Mundi* 4 (1947): 75–77.

85. Richard W. Stephenson, comp., "Table for Identifying Variant Editions and Impressions of John Mitchell's Map of the British and French Dominions in North America," in *A la Carte: Selected Papers on Maps and Atlases*, comp. Walter W. Ristow (Washington: Library of Congress, 1972), pp. 110–13.

86. Rice and Brown, *American Campaigns*, 2: 115.

87. Ibid.

88. Ibid., p. 116.

89. Ibid., p. 115.

90. Lloyd A. Brown, Introduction to *British Maps of the Revolution: A Guide to an Exhibit in the William L. Clements Library*, Bulletin 24 of the William L. Clements Library, University of Michigan (Ann Arbor: n.p., 1936), p. 1.

91. Guthorn, *American Maps*, p. 4.

92. Cumming, *British Maps*, p. 57.

93. Nebenzahl, *Bibliography*.

94. Carrington, *Battles of the American Revolution, 1775–1781 . . .*, and *Battle Maps and Charts of the American Revolution . . .* (New York and Chicago, [1881]; reprint ed., New York: New York Times & Arno Press, 1967), provides a yardstick with which to assess the coverage of the published cartography.

95. Christopher M. Klein, "Maps in Eighteenth-Century British Magazines," typescript (Hermon Dunlap Smith Center for the History of Cartography, The Newberry Library, Chicago), quotes Edward Cave's 1746 claim that the *Gentleman's Magazine* had a circulation of 15,000, a figure which, however, may be exaggerated.

96. I owe this data and figure 3:2 to Robert W. Karrow, Jr.

97. Rice and Brown, *American Campaigns*, 1: 50, shows that the river forts below Philadelphia were described in the journals of Clermont-Crevecoeur, Von Closen, and Cromot Dubourg, and were also visited by Rochambeau and by Chastellux; 11: map 57 gives the position of these forts in relation to the French itinerary.

98. Kish, "Correspondence of Continental Mapmakers," p. 75.

99. Item 78, Faden Collection, Geography and Map Division, Library of Congress, Washington, D.C. Manuscript additions have been made in red to the battle plan, first published in 1778; a revised edition was issued on 13 April 1784. Apart from other changes, the word *rebels* has been deleted in four cases and *Americans* substituted. A list of the entire collection, unique in the insight it provides into the contents of a leading British mapmaker's workshop during the Revolutionary period, can be found in [Edward Everett Hale, comp.], *Catalogue of a Curious and Valuable Collection of Original Maps and Plans of Military Positions Held in the Old French and Revolutionary Wars . . .* (Boston: n.p., 1862).

100. Nebenzahl, *Bibliography*, pp. 32–33 (plan 47).

101. Ibid., passim; Klein, "Maps in Eighteenth-Century British Magazines," passim.

102. Charles Stedman, *The History of the Origin, Progress, and Termination of the American War*, 2 vols. (London: J. Murray, 1794); copy in the John Carter Brown Library.

103. Nebenzahl, *Bibliography*, pp. 66–67 (plan 101), was originally published by Faden on 25 February 1777; a variant is incorporated in Stedman's *History*.

104. For other examples of military map endorsements by Clinton, see Adams, *British Headquarters Maps*, nos. 132–33, 166, 208, 212, 232, 235, 259, 272, 300, 303, 305, 318, and 349; see also Martin, *George Washington Atlas*, pls. 14–17, for examples of maps annotated by Washington during the Revolution.

105. British Library, Map Library, Maps 30.b.1.

106. Ibid., p.v.

107. Ibid., p. vii.

108. At least through the dedication just quoted.

109. *Rivington Gazette*, 4 October 1777; printed in Gottesman, *The Arts and Crafts in New York*, pp. 50–51. At least one map was reengraved and offered for sale to "all the officers of the Continental Army" (Alfred Coxe Prime, comp., *The Arts and Crafts in Philadelphia, Maryland, and South Carolina, 1721–1785 . . .* [Philadelphia: Walpole Society, 1929], p. 24).

110. Ristow, "Maps of the American Revolution," p. 205.

111. Cumming, *British Maps*, p. 98.

112. This is a neglected subject in the history of American regional cartography in the eighteenth century. The convergence of meridians on a number of maps in *The American Atlas* indicates that regular projections were in use, but these have not been specified by the cartographers nor have they been identified by modern scholars. For some of the projections available to eighteenth-century cartographers, see Johann Heinrich Lambert, *Notes and Comments on the Composition of Terrestial and Celestial Maps (1772)*, trans. Waldo R. Tobler, University of Michigan, Department of Geography, Geographical Publication no. 8 (Ann Arbor: Department of Geography, University of Michigan, 1972).

113. Louis De Vorsey, Jr., "A Background to Surveying and Mapping at the Time of the American Revolution: An Essay on the State of the Art," in U.S. Department of the Navy, Naval History Division, *The American Revolution, 1775–1783: An Atlas of Eighteenth-Century Maps and Charts, Theatres of Operations*, comp. W. Bart Greenwood (Washington, 1972), p. 11.

114. Ibid., pp. 14–16; for the lack of information encountered by De Witt in this respect, see p. 109 above.

115. See Conrad E. Heidenreich, "Measures of Distance Employed on Seventeenth and Early Eighteenth Century Maps of Canada," *Canadian Cartographer* 12 (1975): 121–37, for a fuller discussion of the problem.

116. Paul Laxton, "The Geodetic and Topographical Evaluation of English County Maps, 1740–1840," *Cartographic Journal* 13 (1976): 37–54.

117. Allen French, *The First Year of the American Revolution* (Boston and New York, 1934; reprint ed., New York: Octagon Books, 1968), pp. 241–42, 741–42, and 747–49. Page's artistically pleasing plan is often regarded as the most accurate representation of the engagement; but the cruder map of de Berniere is more reliable for some details.

118. Morrison, "Recommendations for Classification of Extant Maps of the Great Lakes," passim; for an application in eighteenth-century regional cartography, see William Ravenhill and Andrew Gilg, "The Accuracy of Early Maps? Towards a Computer Aided Method," *Cartographic Journal* 11 (1974): 48–52.

119. In Marshall and Peckham, *Campaigns*, p. 130; for another approach to distortions in an early map of the Revolutionary period (the Mitchell map), see Lester J. Cappon et al., eds., *Atlas of Early American History: The Revolutionary Era, 1760–1790* (Princeton: Princeton University Press, 1976), pp. 58 (map), 125–26.

120. The British decision-making process was quite complex; the power of the secretary for America was hedged about by the "quite separate, independent, and uncoordinated activities of the Ordnance, Treasury, and Navy Boards, the Paymaster's Office, and the Board of Trade" (Alan Valentine, *Lord George Germain* [Oxford: Clarendon Press, 1962], pp. 112, 101–94).

121. See Fitzpatrick, *Writings of George Washington*, 4: 419; 6: 243, 339; 7: 115; 13: 205; 17: 257; 19: 81; and 21: 171, 366, for occasions when Washington, in instructions or suggestions to his generals, emphasized that he was speaking only from printed maps and not from any first-hand knowledge of the particular area.

122. Roberts, *March to Quebec*, p. 5; Marshall and Peckham, *Campaigns*, p. 12; and see also the comments of Christopher L. Ward, *The War of the Revolution*, ed. John Richard Alden, 2 vols. (New York: Macmillan Co., 1952), 1: 163–64.

123. Eric Robson, "The Expedition to the Southern Colonies, 1775–1776," *English Historical Review* 66 (1951): 535–60, cites some of the evidence.

124. R. Arthur Bowler, *Logistics and the Failure of the British Army in America, 1775–1783* (Princeton: Princeton University Press, 1975), curiously lacks reference to maps, which were constantly used in logistical planning; an older but still valuable discussion of the same issues is Edward C. Curtis, *The Organization of the British Army in the American Revolution* (New Haven: Yale University Press, 1926).

125. Valentine, *Lord George Germain*, pp. 120–21; Eric Robson, *The American Revolution in Its Political and Military Aspects, 1763–1783* (Hamden, Conn.: Archon Books, 1965), pp. 93–97, quotes a range of contemporary opinion on the difficulty of military operations in the American countryside and in particular on the inability of strategic and tactical planners to acquire sufficient knowledge of the terrain.

126. Willcox, *Portrait of a General*, p. 63, quoting a memorandum by Clinton.

127. Willcox, *American Rebellion*, p. 274.

128. Ibid., p. 323.

129. Gage to Holland, 27 July 1767, Gage Papers; quoted by Marshall and Peckham, *Campaigns*, p. iv.

130. Fitzpatrick, *Writings of George Washington*, 16: 302.

131. Boyd, *Papers of Thomas Jefferson*, 4: 41.

132. M. F. Treacy, *Prelude to Yorktown: The Southern Campaign of Nathanael Greene, 1780–1781* (Chapel Hill: University of North Carolina Press, 1963), p. 25.

133. Quoted in ibid., p. 48.

134. Banastre Tarleton, *A History of the Campaigns of 1780 and 1781, in the Southern Provinces of North America* (London: T. Cadell, 1787), p. 197.

135. To give one example, Stevenson envisaged the officer beginning with a printed map but then using observation and inquiry "to correct the errors . . . which the map may have led [him] to make" (*Military Instructions for Officers*, pp. 85–87).

136. Alan R. H. Baker, "The Limits of Inference in Historical Geography," in *Settlement of Canada: Origins and Transfer*, ed. Osborne, pp. 169–82 [see note 14 above].

137. Clark Kinnaird, *George Washington: The Pictorial Biography* (New York: Hastings House, 1967), p. 130, reproduces one portrait of Lafayette showing a plan of a star-shaped fort spread out in front of him; J. B. Harley, "George Washington, Map Maker," *Geographical Magazine*, 48 (1976): 588–94, shows that Washington, appropriately enough, was also painted with maps and plans in front of him.

138. Evelyn M. Acomb, ed. and trans., *The Revolutionary Journal of Baron Ludwig Von Closen, 1780–1783* (Chapel Hill: University of North Carolina Press, 1958), p. 13.

139. Thomas Balch, ed., *The Journal of Claude Blanchard, Commissary of the French Auxiliary Army . . . During the American Revolution, 1780–1783*, trans. William Duane (Albany, N.Y.: J. Munsell, 1876), p. xvi.

140. Ibid., p. 74.

141. "Diary of a French Officer, 1781 (Presumed to be that of Baron Cromot du Bourg, Aide to Rochambeau.) From an unpublished Manuscript in the possession of C. Fiske Harris, of Providence, R.I.," [Translated for] *Magazine of American History*, March 1880, p. 210. Such an attitude permeated the writings of many French officers serving during the Revolution; for a checklist of their journals and memoirs, see Rice and Brown, *American Campaigns*, 1: 283–345.

142. Ernst Kipping, *The Hessian View of America, 1776–1783* (Monmouth Beach, N.J.: Philip Freneau Press, 1971), pp. 13–21.

143. Ray W. Pettengill, trans., *Letters from America, 1776–1779: Being Letters of Brunswick, Hessian, and Waldeck Officers with the British Armies during the Revolution* (Port Washington, N.Y.: Kennikat Press, 1924), pp. 76–77.

144. For examples of this practice, see Fitzpatrick, *Writings of George Washington*, 14: 468, 479; 15: 274, 483; 17: 44, 58, and 492; 18: 237, 350, and 355; and 20: 255.

145. The incident is quoted by Troyer Steele Anderson, *The Command of the Howe Brothers during the American Revolution* (New York: Oxford University Press, 1936), p. 194; see also Sparks, *Correspondence of the American Revolution*, 3: 165, for another example of the acquisition of a fort's plan (Detroit) by espionage.

146. André to Arnold, July 1779, printed in Van Doren, *Secret History*, p. 453.

147. Ibid., p. 462.

148. Adams, *British Headquarters Maps*, pp. 53–54.

149. Van Doren, *Secret History*, p. 486; see Henry Cabot Lodge, ed., *The Complete Works of Alexander Hamilton*, 9 vols. (New York: Putnam, 1885–1886), 9: 210, for confirmation that André's papers did include a plan of West Point.

150. Heusser, *George Washington's Map Maker*, p. 195.

151. Fitzpatrick, *Writings of George Washington*, 8: 372, where he urged the utmost circumspection ("Secrecy and Caution") in the execution of a survey, and 14: 93–94, 160, 182–83, and 341–42.

152. Adams, *British Headquarters Maps*, p. 50; see also *Letters and Papers of John Singleton Copley and Henry Pelham*, pp. 350–51, for Gage's deliberations over the publication of a plan of Charlestown in 1775.

153. Fitzpatrick, *Writings of George Washington*, 18: 361; 19: 9.

154. Sparks, *Correspondence of the American Revolution*, 3: 61–62.

155. Guthorn, *American Maps*, p. 9.

156. Fitzpatrick, *Writings of George Washington*, 20: 26.

157. Guthorn, *American Maps*, pp. 38–40; see also Morton Pennypacker, *General Washington's Spies on Long Island and in New York* (Brooklyn, N.Y.: Long Island Historical Society, 1939), passim.

158. Brown, "Maps in the Manuscript Collections," p. 285. The group known as the Associated Loyalists, with headquarters at Lloyd's Neck on Long Island, maintained a regular intelligence network: "The Associated Loyalists had no trouble in obtaining intelligence; their members and friends were scattered over every part of Connecticut and New York. Through them Sir Henry Clinton was kept informed on the moves of Washington's army, its size and probable effectiveness. Reports came in on the location and size of storehouses and ammunition dumps, with the number of the guard set to watch them. Raiding parties were furnished with advance information, frequently on maps, regarding the best anchorages along the Connecticut shore, and the depth of the water in each. Low shores where cattle could be driven down to the boats were specially marked . . ." (Lloyd A. Brown, *Loyalist Operations at New Haven: Including Capt. Patrick Ferguson's Letter with Map, dated May 27, 1779, and Capt. Nathan Hubbel's Report and Map of His Raid on New Haven, April 19, 1781* [Meriden, Conn.: Printed by the Timothy Press for the William L. Clements Library, 1938], [lacking pagination, 2d–3d text p.]).

159. André's high degree of map conciousness is suggested by the many cases of map use implied by his journal, *Major André's Journal: Operations of the British Army under Lieutenant Generals Sir William Howe and Sir Henry Clinton, June 1777 to November 1778 . . .* (Tarrytown, N.Y.: William Abbatt, 1930), passim; Guthorn, *British Maps*, pp. 9–10, lists over fifty maps actually drawn by André.

160. Robinson's role as a clearinghouse for military intelligence (mainly relating to the location of American detachments) is made clear by the reports—in many cases consisting of information passed on by other correspondents—forwarded to British headquarters between 1777 and 1781; see, for example, his reports of 15 and 22 August 1777; 10 July 1778; 9 March, 13 April, 20 July, 13 September, and 9, 11, 13, 15, and 29 November 1779; and 5 March, 5 June, and 4 July 1781 in CCP.

161. Brun, *Guide to the Manuscript Maps*, p. 108 (map 453); see also a written description [1780?] in CCP.

162. Sparks, *Correspondence of the American Revolution*, 3: 234.

163. John Kirkland Wright, *Human Nature in Geography: Fourteen Papers, 1925–1965* (Cambridge: Harvard University Press, 1966), p. 52.

164. Vallancey, "Essay," [p. 3].

165. Anderson, *Command of the Howe Brothers*, p. 173.

166. Wilbur C. Abbott, *New York in the American Revolution* (New York: Charles Scribner's Sons, 1929), pp. 211.

167. Ibid., p. 198.

168. Simcoe, it appears, had systematized such information: "Lieutenant Colonel Simcoe had a book, in which was inserted the names of every soldier in his corps, the counties in which they were born, and where they had ever lived, so that he seldom was at a loss for guides in his own corps" (Simcoe, *Military Journal*, p. 66).

169. "Diary of a French Officer," p. 441.

170. Ibid., p. 443.

171. A 1777 French army memorandum addressed to the topographical engineers had stipulated: "Officers are requested to pay scrupulous attention to the correct spelling of proper names; they should note instances where names have been changed or disfigured on existing maps and record differences between official nomenclature and local usage" (Rice and Brown, *American Campaigns*, 2: 4).

172. I owe this formulation of the problem to John Andrews of Trinity College, Dublin.

173. P. K. Clark and Yolande Jones, "British Military Mapmaking in the Peninsular War" (paper delivered at the Seventh International Conference on Cartography, ICA, Madrid, Spain, April–May 1974), p. 10.

174. I am indebted to Donald Hodson for our discussions on the problem of evolving a methodology for the "bibliographical" description of manuscript maps; his *Maps of Portsmouth before 1801: A Catalogue* (Portsmouth: Portsmouth Record Series, forthcoming) lays down some new principles for the enumeration and description of military plans relating to this town.

175. Adams, *British Headquarters Maps*, passim.

176. Howard Henry Peckham, *The War for Independence: A Military History* (Chicago: University of Chicago Press, 1958), p. 57.

177. Frederick the Great, "Military Instructions for the Generals," p. 182.

178. Willcox, *American Rebellion*, p. 348.

179. Ibid., p. 347.

180. Ibid., p. 337.

181. Adams, *British Headquarters Maps*, p. 86 (map 272).

182. For another example of how a map may have played a key role in a single military episode, see Allen French, *General Gage's Informers: New Material upon Lexington and Concord . . .* (Ann Arbor, 1932; reprint ed., New York: Greenwood Press, 1968), pp. 31–33, 76–87; see also Douglas Southall Freeman, *George Washington: A Biography*, 7 vols. (New York: Charles Scribner's Sons; London: Eyre & Spottiswoode, 1948–1957), 4: 223, 228, where it is argued that a misunderstanding of distances as represented in Sauthier's *Plan of the Operations of the King's Army under the Command of General Sir William Howe . . . from the 12th of October to the 28th November, 1776* could have contributed to British misconceptions of American positions in the area around White Plains.

183. DesBarres, *Statement*, p. 3.

184. Ibid.

Chapter 4

This essay is a foray into unknown and dangerous territory for a hurried and harried pinch hitter. Without the help of many people, I would have had even less to say than is said, and there would be more errors of fact and interpretation than there are. My first helper was my daughter Elizabeth (see note 11). Charles Steffen, doctoral candidate at Northwestern University, did a lot of research and drafting for me, including a visit to the Huntington Library where he searched the Lossing Papers. David Woodward introduced me to cartographic printing and reproduction; Kenneth Nebenzahl lent me the proofs of two of his works (see note 2); Robert Karrow's excellent exhibit, set up for the lectures, was most instructive; and Don Higginbotham of the University of North Carolina, Chapel Hill, counseled me by telephone in my occasional desperation. None of the above can be blamed for this study's deficiencies, alas.

1. R. Kent Newmyer, "Charles Stedman's *History of the American War*," *American Historical Review* 63 (1958): 924–25.
2. Two works by Kenneth Nebenzahl are fundamental to assessing contemporary mapping of the war. They are: *Atlas of the American Revolution* (Chicago: Rand McNally & Co., 1974) and *A Bibliography of Contemporary Printed Battle Plans of the American Revolution: 1775–1795* (Chicago and London: University of Chicago Press, 1975).
3. Benson J. Lossing to Henry B. Carrington, 13 April 1875, Box 6, Henry B. Carrington Papers, Yale University Library.
4. Noah Webster, *Dissertations on the English Language . . .* (Boston: I. Thomas and Co., 1789), p. 20.
5. Ralph Waldo Emerson, *An Oration, Delivered before the Phi Beta Kappa Society, at Cambridge, August 31, 1837* [Usually entitled "The American Scholar"] (Boston: James Munroe & Co., 1837), p. 1.
6. Page Smith, "David Ramsay and the Causes of the American Revolution," *William and Mary Quarterly,* 3d ser., 17 (1960): 60.
7. Ibid., pp. 60–61.
8. Don Higginbotham, "American Historians and the Military History of the American Revolution," *American Historical Review* 70 (1965): 20, 24.
9. *Bulletin of the Institute of Historical Research* 37 (1964): 51.
10. Ibid., p. 59.
11. David Sanders Clark, "Index to Maps of the American Revolution in Books and Periodicals Illustrating the Revolutionary War and Other Events of the Period 1763–1789," mimeographed (Washington, D.C.: n.p., 1969). Elizabeth G. Towner spent a tedious month using Clark's "Index," identifying works I should examine, writing the call slips, locating the maps, measuring them, putting them in chronological order of publication, and the like. This work could not have been written without her intelligent help.
12. John Fiske, *The American Revolution,* 2 vols. (Cambridge, Mass.: Riverside Press, 1896). See below, Barbara B. Petchenik, "The Mapping of the American Revolutionary War in the Twentieth Century."
13. Joseph Townsend, "Plan of the Battle of Brandywine, September 11th 1777" in "Some Account of the British Army . . . and of the Battle of Brandywine . . . ," *Bulletin of the Historical Society of Pennsylvania* 1 (September 1846): opp. p. 8. See also an adapted version of the same map in Douglas Southall Freeman, *George Washington: A Biography,* 7 vols. (New York, Charles Scribner's Sons, 1948–1957), 4 (1951): 473. John Long of the staff of the Newberry Library's Hermon Dunlap Smith Center for the History of Cartography brought this map to my attention.
14. John Melish, *A Military and Topographical Atlas of the United States . . .* (Philadelphia: printed by G. Palmer, 1813).
15. Benson J. Lossing, *The Pictorial Field-Book of the Revolution . . . ,* 2 vols. (New York: Harper & Brothers, 1851–1852); *The Pictorial Field-Book of the War of 1812 . . . ,* (New York: Harper & Brothers, 1868); *The Pictorial Field-Book of the Civil War in the United States of America,* 3 vols. (New York: T. Belknap, 1868–1869; first published as *The Pictorial History . . .* Philadelphia: G. W. Childs, 1866–1868).
16. Alexander Davidson, Jr., "How Benson J. Lossing Wrote His 'Field Books' of the Revolution, the War of 1812, and the Civil War," *Papers of the Bibliographical Society of America* 32 (1938): 63.
17. Lossing to Helen Lossing, 5 October 1858, Lossing Papers, Henry E. Huntington Library and Art Gallery.
18. Lossing to J. J. Smith, 23 December 1850, Lossing Papers.
19. Josiah D. Channing to Lossing, 11 April 1853, Lossing Papers.
20. Amos Dean to George W. Childs, 12 April 1862, Lossing Papers.
21. Lossing to Helen Lossing, 22 April 1861, Lossing Papers.
22. Henry B. Carrington, "E. Yale, 1841–1845: A Glance at College Life by Carrington" (Typescript), Box 10, 5, Carrington Papers.
23. Ibid.
24. *Dictionary of American Biography,* s.v. "Carrington, Henry Beebee."
25. Carrington, "E. Yale," Carrington Papers, pp. 6–7.
26. Washington Irving, *Life of George Washington,* 5 vols. (New York: G. P. Putnam & Co., 1855–1859).
27. See note 24 above.
28. Unidentified British newspaper account, "Indians of North America," Box 12, Scrapbook, 38, Carrington Papers.
29. Carrington to George Bancroft, 26 March 1875, Massachusetts Historical Society.
30. Lossing to Carrington, 13 April 1875, Box 6, Carrington Papers; and letters from Bancroft, Sherman, and Sheridan, ibid.
31. Sherman to Carrington, 29 March 1875, Box 6, Carrington Papers.

32. Box 12, Scrapbook, Carrington Papers.

33. Sherman to Carrington, 17 November 1876, Box 6, Carrington Papers.

34. Bancroft to Carrington, 7 December 1876, Massachusetts Historical Society.

35. Robert Todd Lincoln to Carrington, 11 November 1882, Box 6, Carrington Papers.

36. Lossing to Carrington, 13 April 1875, Box 6, Carrington Papers.

37. David Woodward, *The All-American Map* (Chicago and London: University of Chicago Press, 1977), p. 30.

38. For bibliographical information on Winsor, see Horace E. Scudder, "Memoir of Justin Winsor, L.L.D.," *Proceedings of the Massachusetts Historical Society,* 2d ser., 12 (1899): 457–82; and Joseph Alfred Borome, "The Life and Letters of Justin Winsor" (Ph.D. diss., Columbia University, 1950).

39. Justin Winsor, *History of the Town of Duxbury, Massachusetts . . .* (Boston: Crosby & Nichols, 1849).

40. Scudder, "Memoir," p. 464.

41. Quoted in ibid., p. 477.

42. Justin Winsor, ed., *The Memorial History of Boston . . . 1630–1800,* 4 vols. (Boston: J. R. Osgood & Co., 1880–1881), 3: i–ii.

43. Justin Winsor, ed., *Narrative and Critical History of America,* 8 vols. (Boston and New York: Houghton Mifflin & Co., 1884–1889), 6: 197–211.

44. "American Maps, Vol. III 1750–1885," Justin Winsor Papers, Massachusetts Historical Society.

45. Winsor, *Narrative and Critical History,* 6: 540.

46. John Higham, with Leonard Krieger and Felix Gilbert, *History: The Development of Historical Studies in the United States* (Englewood Cliffs, N.J.: Prentice-Hall, 1965), pp. 6–25, 92–103.

47. Quoted in Ray Allen Billington. *Frederick Jackson Turner: Historian, Scholar, Teacher* (New York: Oxford University Press, 1973), p. 113. See Billington's discussion of the intellectual background of the frontier thesis in chap. 5, pp. 108–31.

48. Matthew Forney Steele, *American Campaigns,* 2 vols. (Washington, D.C.: B. S. Adams, 1909); Francis Vinton Greene, *The Revolutionary War and the Military Policy of the United States* (London: John Murray, 1911); Willard M. Wallace, *Appeal to Arms: A Military History of the American Revolution* (New York: Harper & Brothers, 1951); Christopher Ward, *The War of the Revolution,* ed. John Richard Alden, 2 vols. (New York: Macmillan Co., 1952); John Richard Alden, *The American Revolution, 1775–1783* (New York: Harper & Brothers, 1954); Howard Henry Peckham, *The War of American Independence: A Military History* (Chicago: University of Chicago Press, 1958); Don Higginbotham, *The War of American Independence: Military Attitudes, Policies, and Practice, 1763–1789* (New York: Macmillan Co., 1971); and Marshall Smelser, *The Winning of Independence* (Chicago: Quadrangle Books, 1972).

49. Charles Carleton Coffin, *The Boys of '76: A History of the Battles of the Revolution* (New York: Harper & Brothers, 1876); Richard Frothingham, *History of the Siege of Boston . . .* (Boston: C .C. Little & J. Brown, 1849), *Battle of Bunker Hill* (Boston: Little, Brown & Co., 1889); and Henry Phelps Johnston, *The Campaign of 1776 around New York and Brooklyn . . . ,* Memoirs of the Long Island Historical Society, vol. 3 (Brooklyn, N.Y.: Long Island Historical Society, 1878), *The Yorktown Campaign and the Surrender of Cornwallis, 1781* (New York: Harper & Brothers, 1881), *The Battle of Harlem Heights, September 16, 1776, with a Review of the Events of the Campaign* (New York: Published for Columbia University Press by Macmillan Co.; London: Macmillan & Co., 1897).

Chapter 5

1. Sydney George Fisher, *The True History of the American Revolution,* 2d ed. (Philadelphia and London: J. B. Lippincott Co., 1903), pp. 8–9.

2. Allen French, *The Day of Concord and Lexington, The Nineteenth of April, 1775* (Boston: Little, Brown & Co., 1925), p. 1.

3. Allen R. Millett and B. Franklin Cooling III, *Doctoral Dissertations in Military Affairs: A Bibliography,* Kansas State University Bibliographical Series, no. 10 (Manhattan: Kansas State University, 1972).

4. John Higham, with Leonard Krieger and Felix Gilbert. *History: The Development of Historical Studies in the United States* (Englewood Cliffs, N.J.: Prentice-Hall, 1965), p. 49.

5. David Sanders Clark, "Index to Maps of the American Revolution in Books and Periodicals Illustrating the Revolutionary War and Other Events of the Period 1763–1789," mimeographed (Washington, D.C.: n.p., 1969).

6. The Atlas of Early American History Project was begun in late 1970 at the Newberry Library in Chicago, with Lester J. Cappon, editor in chief and Barbara Bartz Petchenik, cartographic editor; it was jointly sponsored by the Newberry Library and the Institute of Early American History and Culture, Williamsburg, Virginia. The volume ultimately produced by the project is the *Atlas of Early American History: The Revolutionary Era, 1760–1790* (Princeton: Princeton University Press, 1976).

7. George Otto Trevelyan, *The American Revolution,* 2d ed., 4 vols. (London: Longmans, Green & Co., 1899–1903), 2: pt. 2, unnumbered foldout.

8. David Woodward, "Cerotyping and the Rise of Modern American Commercial Cartography" (Ph.D. diss., University of Wisconsin, 1970).

9. Edward Channing, *A History of the United States,* 6 vols. (New York: Macmillan Co., 1907–1925), 3: 231.

10. James Wilford Garner and Henry Cabot Lodge, *The History of the United States,* 4 vols. (Philadelphia: John D. Morris & Co., 1906), 2: 499.

11. John Clark Ridpath, *The New Complete History of the United States of America,* 12 vols. (Washington, D.C.: Ridpath History Co.; Cincinnati, O.: Jones Brothers Publishing Co., 1905–1907), 5: opp. p. 2424.

12. Elroy McKendree Avery, *A History of the United States and Its People,* 7 vols. (Cleveland: Burrows Brothers Co., 1904–1910), 6: 76. According to an article in the *North American* (Philadelphia), 28 June 1906, Mr. Burrows had already spent "a fair fortune—nearly $200,000" by that date. Anyone seeing the Avery *History,* particularly anyone interested in cartography, must wonder how these volumes were assembled, how such fine maps (and other graphic materials) were produced in what was clearly a complicated, cooperative publishing venture.

To begin with, it is not likely that very many people will ever have access to this set of books, especially not scholars. The set was directed toward a lay audience, and the text is at quite a simple level. Consequently most academic libraries would not have purchased the books in the first place.

Second, the paper on which the books were printed is deteriorating seriously and at an accelerating rate. If some copies are not deacidified soon, there may not be any copies of this cartographic monument around in 100 years.

Third, the publisher is no longer in business, and none of the principals involved in the production of the maps seem to be alive in 1977. Some research into these matters was done during the course of preparation of this essay, and the findings were not encouraging. There do not appear to be any readily accessible archives that would enable us to understand who deserves what kind of credit for the Avery maps.

Elroy McKendree Avery was born in 1844 and died in 1935, long after the last volume of his *History* appeared. He is described in *Who Was Who in America* (vol. 1, 1897–1942) as "author," although he had a long and active career in a number of other fields. He wrote a great variety of books, ranging from *Physical Technics* (1879) to *First Principles of Natural Philosophy* (1884) to *Words Correctly Spoken* (1887). Avery lived in Cleveland for some time, so the connection with the Burrows Brothers Publishing Company was a logical one. He retired to New Port Richey, Florida, and founded a library there. The New Port Richey Library, however, has no Avery papers, though it does have bound manuscripts for the unpublished volumes of his *History,* and some late correspondence is bound in with these. Substantial quantities of material were hauled to the dump in the early 1960s when the library moved to a new location. The current librarian there speculates that some Avery papers may have been destroyed at the time of the move (phone conversation of September 1974). There are no Avery archives at several locations where they might be expected: the Cleveland Public Library, Western Reserve Historical Society, and the Ohio State Historical Society.

Contemporary newspaper articles about the production of the *History* offer considerable indication that the real responsibility for the unusual production aspects of the volumes lies with Charles William Burrows (1849–1932) rather than with Avery. It was Burrows, apparently, who initiated the concept of the book and hired Avery to write it. The Burrows Brothers Company was justifiably proud of the money and time (more than twenty years) that were spent on this work, but their archives also defy location. There is a newspaper account of how Charles Francis Adams at first refused a free copy of the set, "buried under the accumulations of generations of bookcollecting" as he was. Later, however, the publishers received Adams's order for the complete set at the regular price. The explanation for this change of heart is an interesting one in the context of this study: "The reason, he explains, is that he found better maps and charts than he had seen elsewhere" (*Cleveland Leader,* 8 April 1910, ["Boston Tribute to Cleveland Books"]).

13. Francis Vinton Greene, *The Revolutionary War and the Military Policy of the United States* (London: John Murray, 1911), p. ix.

14. There is very little information available about Lt. Joseph A. Baer, who was born in 1878 and died in 1958. The West Point Library has no archives relating to his work. I was unable to track down his married daughter. Presumably he was involved in the Avery project because of Burrows's West Point background.

15. Avery, *History of the U.S. and Its People,* 6: 76.

16. J. W. Clement Co., *The Making of Fine Maps* (Buffalo, N.Y., 1927).

17. Crawford C. Anderson to David Woodward, 24 September 1968 (Hermon Dunlap Smith Center for the History of Cartography, The Newberry Library, Chicago). Mr. Anderson, a former employee, is given credit for the map shown in figure 5: 20.

18. Allen French, *The First Year of the Revolution* (Boston and New York, 1934; reprint ed., New York: Octagon Books, 1968), p. 10.

19. Hoffman Nickerson, *The Turning Point of the Revolution; or, Burgoyne in America* (Boston and New York: Houghton Mifflin Co., 1928), p. 121.

20. Howard L. Landers, *The Virginia Campaign and the Blockade and Siege of Yorktown, 1781* (Washington: U.S. Government Printing Office, 1931), unnumbered foldout.

21. Troyer Steele Anderson, *The Command of the Howe Brothers during the American Revolution* (London and New York: Oxford University Press, 1936), p. 14.

22. William L. Clements Library, University of Michigan, *History of the William L. Clements Library, 1923–1973: Its Development and Its Collection* (Ann Arbor, 1973).

23. John C. Miller, *Triumph of Freedom, 1775–1783* (Boston: Little, Brown & Co., Atlantic Monthly Press Book, 1948), p. 49.

24. John Richard Alden, *The American Revolution, 1775—1783* (New York: Harper & Brothers, 1954), p. 98.

25. Marshall Smelser, *The Winning of Independence* (Chicago: Quadrangle Books, 1972), p. 175.

26. Charles O. Paullin and John K. Wright, *Atlas of the Historical Geography of the United States* (Washington and New York: the Carnegie Institution & the American Geographical Society, 1932), pl. 160.

27. James Truslow Adams and R. V. Coleman, *Atlas of American History* (New York: Charles Scribner's Sons, 1943), p. 71.

28. Vincent J. Esposito, ed., *The West Point Atlas of American Wars*, vol. 1, *1689–1900* (New York: Frederick A. Praeger, 1959), map 8d; Henry B. Carrington, *Battle Maps and Charts of the American Revolution . . .* , (New York and Chicago [1881]; reprint ed., New York: New York Times & Arno Press, 1967), p. 214.

29. Mark Mayo Boatner III, *Encyclopedia of the American Revolution* (New York: David McKay Co., 1966), p. 648.

30. Fisher, *True History of the American Revolution*, opp. p. 420.

31. Claude Halstead Van Tyne, *The American Revolution, 1776–1783*, vol. 9, The American Nation: A History, ed. Albert Bushnell Hart (New York and London: Harper & Brothers, 1905); Harper & Brothers, *Harper's Atlas of American History* (New York and London, 1920); and Samuel Eliot Morison and Henry Steele Commager, *The Growth of the American Republic,* 4th ed., 2 vols. (New York: Oxford University Press, 1950).

32. See note 8 above.

33. Nathaniel Wright Stephenson and Waldo Hilary Dunn, *George Washington*, 2 vols. (New York: Oxford University Press, 1940), 1: opp. p. 360.

34. Thomas G. Frothingham, *Washington: Commander in Chief* (Boston and New York: Houghton Mifflin Co., 1930), opp. p. 214; Louis Gottschalk, *Lafayette and the Close of the American Revolution* (Chicago: University of Chicago Press, 1942), opp. p. 238; U.S. Department of the Navy, Naval History Division, *The American Revolution, 1775–1783: An Atlas of Eighteenth-Century Maps and Charts* (Washington, 1972), map 12 (fig. 5: 23) is a portion of the reproduction of Fry and Jefferson's *Map of Virginia* (1775); and Kenneth Nebenzahl, *Atlas of the American Revolution* (Chicago: Rand McNally & Co., 1974).

35. Ridpath, *New Complete History of the U.S.,* 5: opp. p. 2476; John Richard Alden, *General Gage in America: Being Principally A History of His Role in the American Revolution* (Baton Rouge: Louisiana State University Press, 1948), opp. p. 254.

36. Douglas Southall Freeman, *George Washington: A Biography,* 7 vols. (New York: Charles Scribner's Sons, 1948–1957), 4: endpapers.

37. Christopher L. Ward, *The War of the Revolution*, ed. John Richard Alden, 2 vols. (New York: Macmillan Co., 1952), 2: 509.

38. Christopher L. Ward, *The Delaware Continentals, 1776–1783* (Wilmington: Historical Society of Delaware, 1941).

39. Willard M. Wallace, *Appeal to Arms: A Military History of the American Revolution* (New York: Harper & Brothers, 1951), p. 249.

40. American Heritage Publishing Co., *The American Heritage Pictorial Atlas of United States History* (New York, 1966), p. 102.

41. Channing, *History of the U.S.,* 3: 316; Gardner W. Allen, *A Naval History of the American Revolution,* 2 vols. (Boston and New York: Houghton Mifflin Co., 1913), 2: opp. p. 396.

42. Boatner, *Encyclopedia,* back endpapers.

43. John Richard Alden, *A History of the American Revolution* (New York: Alfred A. Knopf, 1969), p. 399.

44. Avery, *History of the U.S. and Its People,* 6: 284.

45. Charles Van Doren and Robert McHenry, eds., *Webster's Guide to American History* (Springfield, Mass.: G. & C. Merriam Co., 1971), p. 657.

46. John William Fortescue, *A History of the British Army,* 13 vols. in 14 (London: Macmillan & Co.; New York: Macmillan Co., 1899–1930 [Set includes *Maps and Plans Illustrating Fortescue's History of the British Army . . . ,* 6 vols. (London: Macmillan & Co., 1906–1930)]), 3: pl. 4.

47. Ibid., 1: ix.

48. Samuel Stelle Smith, *The Battle of Monmouth* (Monmouth Beach, N.J.: Philip Freneau Press, 1964), p. 17.

49. Boatner, *Encyclopedia,* pp. 650, 652–53.

50. Claude Joseph Sauthier, *A Chorographical Map of the Province of New York* (London, 1779), the relevant portion of which is reproduced in *The American Rebellion: Sir Henry Clinton's Narrative of His Campaigns, 1775–1782,* ed. William B. Willcox (New Haven: Yale University Press, 1954), opp. p. 40; Carrington, *Maps and Charts,* p. 214; Avery, *History of the U.S. and Its People,* 6: 11; and U.S. Geological Survey, "Newark" and "New York" Sheets, 1:250,000 map series (Washington: U.S.G.S., 1964, 1960).

51. Alden, *History of the American Revolution,* p. 264.

52. Wallace, *Appeal to Arms,* p. 109. See also note 9 above.

53. Don Higginbotham, *The War of American Independence: Military Attitudes, Policies, and Practice, 1763–1789* (New York: Macmillan Co., 1971), p. 157.

54. The left-hand images are taken from the following sources, respectively: Alfred T. Mahan, *The Major Operations of the Navies in the War of American Independence* (Boston: Little, Brown & Co., 1913), opp. p. 218; John F. C. Fuller, *The Decisive Battles of the Western World and Their Influence upon History,* vol. 2, *From the Defeat of the Spanish Armada to the Battle of Waterloo* (London: Eyre & Spottiswoode, 1955), p. 305, 329.

55. The right-hand images are taken from Alexander Marshack, "Cognitive Aspects of Upper Paleolithic Engraving," *Current Anthropology* 13 (1972): 447, 449, and 454.

56. Henry Belcher, *The First American Civil War*, 2 vols. (London: Macmillan & Co., 1911), 2: opp. p. 227.

57. Richard M. Ketchum, "The Unwinnable War," *American Way*, October 1973, pp. 36–37.

58. Freeman, *George Washington*, 4: 160–61.

59. Avery, *History of the U.S. and Its People*, 6: 11; Belcher, *First American Civil War*, 2: opp. p. 155.

60. Ward, *War of the Revolution*, 1: 217.

61. Lester J. Cappon et al., eds., *Atlas of Early American History*, p. 43, compilation by Barbara B. Petchenik.

62. A complete version of this matrix for North America and the West Indies appears in *Atlas of Early American History*.

63. The entire series of 24 maps for North America is printed (in six colors) in ibid., pp. 44–49.

64. See note 46.

65. Clifford L. Lord and Elizabeth H. Lord, *Historical Atlas of the United States* (New York: Henry Holt & Co., 1944), p. 38.

66. William Milburne James, *The British Navy in Adversity: A Study of the War of American Independence* (London, New York [etc.]: Longmans, Green & Co., 1926), pp. 96, 226; William Charles Henry Wood and Ralph Henry Gabriel, *The Winning of Freedom*, vol. 6, The Pageant of America, Independence ed. (New Haven: Yale University Press, 1927), pp. 220–21.

Selected Bibliography

Abbott, Wilbur C. *New York in the American Revolution.* New York: Charles Scribner's Sons, 1929.

Acomb, Evelyn M., ed. and trans. *The Revolutionary Journal of Baron Ludwig Von Closen, 1780–1783.* Chapel Hill: University of North Carolina Press for the Institute of Early American History and Culture at Williamsburg, Virginia, 1958.

Adams, I. H. "George Taylor, A Surveyor o' Pairts." *Imago Mundi* 27 (1975): 55–63.

Adams, James Truslow and Coleman, R. V. *Atlas of American History.* New York: Charles Scribner's Sons, 1943.

Adams, Randolph G. *British Headquarters Maps and Sketches Used by Sir Henry Clinton while in Command of the British Forces Operating in North America during the War for Independence, 1775–1782: A Descriptive List of the Original Manuscripts and Printed Documents Preserved in the William L. Clements Library at the University of of Michigan.* Ann Arbor: William L. Clements Library, 1928.

———. "The Cartography of the British Attack on Fort Moultrie in 1776." In *Essays Offered to Herbert Putnam. . . .* Edited by William Warner Bishop and Andrew Keogh. New Haven: Yale University Press, 1929.

Alden, John Richard. *General Gage in America: Being Principally a History of His Role in the American Revolution.* Baton Rouge: Louisiana State University Press, 1948.

———. *The American Revolution, 1775–1783.* New York: Harper & Brothers, 1954.

———. *A History of the American Revolution.* New York: Alfred A. Knopf, 1969.

Allen, Gardner W. *A Naval History of the American Revolution.* 2 vols. Boston and New York: Houghton Mifflin Co., 1913.

Allen, John L. "Exploration and the Creation of Geographical Images of the Great Plains: Comments on the Role of Subjectivity." In *Images of the Plains: The Role of Human Nature in Settlement,* edited by Brian W. Blouet and Merlin P. Lawson. Lincoln: University of Nebraska Press, 1975.

American Heritage Publishing Co. *The American Heritage Pictorial Atlas of United States History.* New York, 1966.

Anderson, Troyer Steele. *The Command of the Howe Brothers during the American Revolution.* London and New York: Oxford University Press, 1936.

Andrews, J. H. "Charles Vallancey and the Map of Ireland." *Geographical Journal* 132 (1966): 48–61.

Avery, Elroy McKendree. *A History of the United States and Its People.* 7 vols. Cleveland: Burrows Brothers Co., 1904–1910.

Baker, Alan R. H. "The Limits of Inference in Historical Geography." In *Settlement of Canada: Origins and Transfer,* edited by Brian S. Osborne. Proceedings of the 1975 British-Canadian Symposium on Historical Geography. Kingston, Ont.: Department of Geography, Queen's University.

Balch, Thomas, ed. *The Journal of Claude Blanchard, Commissary of the French Auxiliary Army . . . during the American Revolution, 1780–1783.* Translated by William Duane. Albany, N.Y.: J. Munsell, 1876.

Baldwin, Thomas Williams, ed. *The Revolutionary Journal of Col. Jeduthan Baldwin, 1775–1778*. Bangor, Me.: Printed for the De Burians, 1906.

Belcher, Henry. *The First American Civil War*. 2 vols. London: Macmillan & Co., 1911.

Berthaut, Henri M. A. *Les Ingénieurs géographes militaires, 1624–1831: Etude historique*. 2 vols. Paris: Imprimerie du Service Géographique, 1902.

Billias, George Athan, ed. *George Washington's Generals*. New York: William Morrow & Co., 1964.

————. *George Washington's Opponents: British Generals and Admirals in the American Revolution*. New York: William Morrow & Co., 1969.

Bland Humphrey. *A Treatise of Military Discipline; in which is laid down and Explained the Duty of the Officer and Soldier, thro' the several Branches of the Service*. 2d ed. London: S. Buckley, 1727.

Board, C. "Maps as Models." In *Models in Geography*, edited by Richard J. Chorley and Peter Haggett. London: Methuen & Co., 1967.

Boatner, Mark Mayo III. *Encyclopedia of the American Revolution*. New York: David McKay Co., 1966, 1974.

Bolton, Charles Knowles, ed. *Letters of Hugh Earl Percy from Boston and New York, 1774–1776*. Boston: Charles E. Goodspeed Co., 1902.

Boston Athenaeum. *A Catalogue of the Washington Collection in the Boston Athenaeum*. Compiled by Appleton P. C. Griffin. Boston, 1897.

Bourcet, Pierre Joseph de. *Principes de la guerre de montagnes . . . 1775*. Paris: Imprimerie Nationale, 1888.

Bowler, R. Arthur. *Logistics and the Failure of the British Army in America, 1775–1783*. Princeton: Princeton University Press, 1975.

British Museum. *The American War of Independence, 1775–83: A Commemorative Exhibition Organised by the Map Library and the Department of Manuscripts of the British Library Reference Division, 4 July to 11 November 1975*. London, 1975.

Brown, Douglas Stewart. "The Iberville Canal Project: Its Relation to Anglo-French Commercial Rivalry in the Mississippi Valley, 1763–1775." *Mississippi Valley Historical Review* 32 (1946): 491–516.

Brown, Lloyd A. Introduction to *British Maps of the Revolution: A Guide to an Exhibit in the William L. Clements Library*. Bulletin 24 of the William L. Clements Library, University of Michigan. Ann Arbor: n.p., 1936.

————. "Maps in the Manuscript Collections." In *Guide to the Manuscript Collections in the William L. Clements Library* [Appendix B]. Ann Arbor: University of Michigan Press, 1942.

————. *Early Maps of the Ohio Valley: A Selection of Maps, Plans, and Views Made by Indians and Colonials from 1763 to 1783*. Pittsburgh: University of Pittsburgh Press, 1959

Brun, Christian. *Guide to the Manuscript Maps in the William L. Clements Library*. Ann Arbor: University of Michigan, 1959.

Burgoyne, John. *A State of the Expedition from Canada, as Laid before the House of Commons . . . and Verified by Evidence; with a Collection of Authentic Documents*. London: J. Almon, 1780.

Cappon, Lester J. "Geographers and Map-Makers, British and American, from about 1750 to 1789." *Proceedings of the American Antiquarian Society* 81 (1971): 243–71.

Cappon, Lester J. et al., eds. *Atlas of Early American History: The Revolutionary Era, 1760–1790*. Princeton: Princeton University Press for the Newberry Library and the Institute of Early American History and Culture, 1976.

Carrington, Henry B. *Battles of the American Revolution, 1775–1781: Historical and Military Criticism with Topographical Illustration. . . .* New York, Chicago [etc.]: A. S. Barnes & Co., 1876.

————. *Battle Maps and Charts of the American Revolution. . . .* New York and Chicago, [1881]. Reprint. New York: New York Times & Arno Press, 1967.

Carter, Clarence Edwin, ed. *The Correspondence of General Thomas Gage with the Secretaries of State and with the War Office and the Treasury, 1763–1775*. 2 vols. New Haven: Yale University Press, 1931.

Channing, Edward. *A History of the United States*. 6 vols. Vol. 3, *The American Revolution, 1761–1789*. New York: Macmillan Co., 1912.

Chipman, Willis. "The Life and Times of Major Samuel Holland, Surveyor General, 1764–1801." *Ontario Historical Society Papers and Records* 21 (1924): 11–90.

Clairac, Louis André de La Mamie de. *The Field Engineer of M. le Chevalier De Clairac . . . With Observations and Remarks on each Chapter. . . .* Translated by John Muller. 2d ed. London: John Millan, 1773.

Clark, David Sanders. "Index to Maps of the American Revolution in Books and Periodicals Illustrating the Revolutionary War and Other Events of the Period 1763–1789." Mimeographed. Washington, D.C.: n.p., 1969.

Clarke, David L. *Analytical Archaeology.* London: Methuen & Co., 1968.

Clement, J. W., Co. *The Making of Fine Maps.* Buffalo, N.Y., 1927.

Clode, Charles M. *The Military Forces of the Crown, Their Administration and Government.* 2 vols. London: John Murray, 1869.

Cockle, Maurice J. D. *A Bibliography of Military Books up to 1642.* London: Holland Press, 1900.

Coffin, Charles Carleton. *The Boys of '76: A History of the Battles of the Revolution.* New York: Harper & Brothers, 1876.

Colbourn, H. Trevor. *The Lamp of Experience: Whig History and the Intellectual Origins of the American Revolution.* Chapel Hill: University of North Carolina Press for the Institute of Early American History and Culture at Williamsburg, Virginia, 1965.

Cumming, William P. *The Southeast in Early Maps, with an Annotated Check List of Printed and Manuscript Regional and Local Maps of Southeastern North America during the Colonial Period.* Chapel Hill: University of North Carolina Press, 1958.

———. *British Maps of Colonial America.* The Kenneth Nebenzahl, Jr., Lectures in the History of Cartography at the Newberry Library, edited by David Woodward. Chicago and London: University of Chicago Press for the Hermon Dunlap Smith Center for the History of Cartography, The Newberry Library, 1974.

Curtis, Edward C. *The Organization of the British Army in the American Revolution.* New Haven: Yale University Press, 1926.

Dainville, François de. *Le Langage des géographes: Termes, signes, couleurs des cartes anciennes, 1500–1800.* Paris: Editions A. & J. Picard & Cie, 1964.

Davidson, Alexander, Jr. "How Benson J. Lossing Wrote His 'Field Book' of the Revolution, the War of 1812, and the Civil War." *Papers of the Bibliographical Society of America* 32 (1938): 57–64.

DesBarres, Joseph Frederick Wallet. *A Statement Submitted by Lieutenant Colonel DesBarres, for Consideration: Respecting his Services, from the Year 1755, to the present Time. . . .* n.p., n.d. [London, 1795?]

De Vorsey, Louis, Jr. "A Background to Surveying and Mapping at the Time of the American Revolution: An Essay on the State of the Art." In introduction to *The American Revolution, 1775–1783: An Atlas of Eighteenth-Century Maps and Charts. . . .* Compiled by W. Bart Greenwood. Washington: Naval History Division, Department of the Navy, 1972.

———. "Hydrography: A Note on the Equipage of Eighteenth-Century Survey Vessels." *Mariner's Mirror* 58 (1972): 173–77.

———. "La Florida Revealed: The De Brahm Surveys of British East Florida, 1765–1771." In *Pattern and Process: Research in Historical Geography.* Edited by Ralph E. Ehrenberg. Washington, D.C.: Howard University Press, 1975.

De Vorsey, Louis, Jr., ed. *De Brahm's Report of the General Survey in the Southern District of North America.* Columbia: University of South Carolina Press, 1971.

Drake, Francis S. *Life and Correspondence of Henry Knox, Major-General in the American Revolutionary Army.* Boston: Samuel G. Drake, 1873.

Duffy, Christopher. *The Army of Frederick the Great.* Newton Abbot, Devon: David & Charles, 1974.

———. Fire and Stone: *The Science of Fortress Warfare: 1660–1860.* Newton Abbot, Devon: David & Charles, 1975.

Dupain de Montesson. *La Science des ombres, par rapport au dessein. . . .* Paris: Chez Charles-Antoine Jombert, Libraire du Roi pour l'Artillerie & le Génie, 1750.

———. *Les Connoissances géométriques, à l'usage des officiers employés dans les details des marches, campements & subsistances des armées.* Paris: Chez Charles-Antoine Jombert, père, Libraire du Roi pour l'Artillerie & le Génie, 1774.

———. *L'Art de lever les plans de tout ce qui a rapport à la guerre & à l'architecture civile & champêtre. . . .* 2d ed., rev. Paris: Chez Charles-Antoine Jombert, père, Libraire du Roi pour le Génie et l'Artillerie, 1775.

Esposito, Vincent J., ed. *The West Point Atlas of American Wars.* Vol. 1, *1689–1900.* New York: Frederick A. Praeger, 1969.

Evans, Geraint N. D. "Hydrography: A Note on Eighteenth-Century Methods." *Mariner's Mirror* 52 (1966): 247–50.

———. *Uncommon Obdurate: The Several Public Careers of J. F. W. DesBarres.* Salem, Mass.: Peabody Museum, 1969.

Fairclough, R. H. " 'Sketches of the Roads of Scotland, 1785': The Manuscript Roadbook of George Taylor." *Imago Mundi* 27 (1975): 65–72.

Fisher, Sydney George. *The True History of the American Revolution.* 2d ed. Philadelphia and London: J. B. Lippincott Co., 1903.

Fiske, John. *The American Revolution.* 2 vols. Cambridge, Mass.: Riverside Press, 1896.

Fonblanque, Edward Barrington de. *Political and Military Episodes . . . Derived from the Life and Correspondence of the Right Hon. John Burgoyne, General, Statesman, Dramatist.* London: Macmillan & Co., 1876.

Fordham, Herbert George. *The Road-Books and Itineraries of Great Britain, 1570 to 1850: A Catalogue . . . and a Bibliography.* Cambridge: Cambridge University Press, 1924.

———. " 'Paterson's Roads': Daniel Paterson, His Maps and Itineraries, 1738–1825." *Transactions of the Bibliographical Society,* n.s. 5 (1925): 332–56.

———. *Les Routes de France: Etude bibliographique sur les cartes-routières, et les itineraires, et guides-routiers de France, suivie d'un catalogue des itineraires et guides-routiers, 1552–1850.* Paris: Librarie Ancienne Honore Champion, 1929.

Fortescue, John William. *A History of the British Army.* 13 vols. in 14. London: Macmillan & Co.; New York: Macmillan Co., 1899–1930 [Set includes *Maps and Plans Illustrating Fortescue's History of the British Army.* . . . 6 vols. London: Macmillan & Co., 1906–1930].

France, Dépôt Général de la Guerre. *Mémorial topographique et militaire, rédigé au Dépôt Général de la Guerre.* . . . Six vols. Paris: L'Imprimerie de la République, 1803–1805.

French, Allen. *The Day of Concord and Lexington, the Nineteenth of April, 1775.* Boston: Little, Brown & Co., 1925.

———. *General Gage's Informers: New Material upon Lexington and Concord.* . . . Ann Arbor, 1932. Reprint. New York: Greenwood Press, 1968.

———. *The First Year of the American Revolution.* Boston and New York, 1934. Reprint. New York: Octagon Books, 1968.

Friis, Herman R. "A Brief Review of the Development and Status of the Geographical and Cartographical Activities of the United States Government: 1776–1818." *Imago Mundi* 19 (1965): 68–80.

Frothingham, Richard. *History of the Siege of Boston.* . . . Boston: C. C. Little & J. Brown, 1849.

———. *Battle of Bunker Hill.* Boston: Little, Brown & Co., 1889.

Frothingham, Thomas G. *Washington: Commander in Chief.* Boston and New York: Houghton Mifflin Co., Riverside Press, 1930.

Fry, Howard T. *Alexander Dalrymple (1737–1808) and the Expansion of British Trade.* London: Frank Cass & Co. for the Royal Commonwealth Society, 1970.

Fuller, John F. C. *British Light Infantry in the Eighteenth Century.* London: Hutchinson & Co., 1925.

———. *The Decisive Battles of the Western World and Their Influence upon History.* Vol. 2, *From the Defeat of the Spanish Armada to the Battle of Waterloo.* London: Eyre & Spottiswoode, 1955.

Garner, James Wilford and Lodge, Henry Cabot. *The History of the United States.* 4 vols. Vols. 1 and 2. Philadelphia: John D. Morris & Co., 1906.

Goetzmann, William H. *Army Exploration in the American West, 1803–1863.* New Haven: Yale University Press, 1959.

———. *Exploration and Empire: The Explorer and the Scientist in the Winning of the American West.* New York: Random House, Vintage Books, 1972.

Görlitz, Walter. *The German General Staff: Its History and Structure, 1657–1945, with a Preface by Cyril Falls.* Translated by Brian Battershaw. London: Hollis & Carter, 1953.

Gottesman, Rita S., comp. *The Arts and Crafts in New York, 1777–1799.* Collections of the New-York Historical Society, no. 81. New York: New-York Historical Society, 1954.

Gottschalk, Louis. *Lafayette and the Close of the American Revolution.* Chicago: University of Chicago Press, 1942.

Gottschalk, Louis, ed. *The Letters of Lafayette to Washington, 1777–1799.* New York: privately printed by Helen Fahnestock Hubbard, 1944.

Great Britain, Admiralty, Hydrographic Department. *A Summary of Selected Manuscript Documents of Historic Importance Preserved in the Archives of the Department.* Hydrographic Department, Admiralty, Professional Paper no. 13. London, 1950.

Great Britain, Quarter-Master General's Department. *Special Instructions for Officers of the Quarter-Master General's Department.* London: Parker, Furnivall, & Parker, 1854.

Great Britain, Royal Military Academy. *Records of the Royal Military Academy (1741–1840).* Compiled by William D. Jones. Woolwich: Royal Artillery Institution, 1851.

Greene, Francis Vinton. *The Revolutionary War and the Military Policy of the United States.* London: John Murray, 1911.

Guthorn, Peter J. *American Maps and Map Makers of the Revolution.* Monmouth Beach, N.J.: Philip Freneau Press, 1966.

————. *British Maps of the American Revolution.* Monmouth Beach, N.J.: Philip Freneau Press, 1972.

Hadden, James M. *Hadden's Journal and Orderly Books: A Journal Kept in Canada and upon Burgoyne's Campaign in 1776 and 1777, by Lieut. James M. Hadden, Roy. Art. . . . with an explanatory chapter and notes by Horatio Rogers.* Albany, N.Y.: Joel Munsell's Sons, 1884.

Hahn, Roger. *The Anatomy of an Institution: The Paris Academy of Sciences, 1666–1803.* Berkeley, Los Angeles, and London: University of California Press, 1971.

Hans, Nicholas. *New Trends in Education in the Eighteenth Century.* London: Routledge & Kegan Paul, 1951.

Harley, J. B. "The Bankruptcy of Thomas Jefferys: An Episode in the Economic History of Eighteenth Century Map-Making." *Imago Mundi* 20 (1966): 27–48.

————. "George Washington, Map Maker." *Geographical Magazine* 48 (1976): 588–94.

————. "The Map User in Eighteenth-Century North America: Some Preliminary Observations." In *The Settlement of Canada: Origins and Transfer,* edited by Brian S. Osborne. Proceedings of the 1975 British–Canadian Symposium on Historical Geography. Kingston, Ont.; Department of Geography, Queen's University, 1976.

Harley, J. B. and O'Donoghue, Yolande. Introduction to *The Old Series Ordnance Survey Maps of England and Wales. Scale: One Inch to One Mile: A Reproduction of the 110 Sheets of the Survey in Early State in 10 Volumes.* Vol. 1, *Kent, Essex, E. Sussex, and S. Suffolk.* Lympne Castle, Kent: Harry Margary, 1975.

Harley, J. B. and Walters, Gwyn. "William Roy's Maps, Mathematical Instruments, and Library: The Christie's Sale of 1790." *Imago Mundi* 28 (1977), in press.

Harper & Brothers. *Harper's Atlas of American History.* New York and London, 1920.

Harvey, David. *Explanation in Geography.* London: Edward Arnold; New York: St. Martin's Press, 1969.

Heidenreich, Conrad E. "Measures of Distance Employed on Seventeenth and Early Eighteenth Century Maps of Canada." *Canadian Cartographer* 12 (1975): 121–37.

Heusser, Albert H. *George Washington's Map Maker: A Biography of Robert Erskine.* Edited with an introduction by Herbert G. Schmidt. New Brunswick, N.J.: Rutgers University Press, 1966.

Higginbotham, Don. "American Historians and the Military History of the American Revolution." *American Historical Review* 70 (1965): 18–34.

————. *The War of American Independence: Military Attitudes, Policies, and Practice, 1763–1789.* New York: Macmillan Co., 1971.

Higham, John; with Krieger, Leonard; and Gilbert, Felix. *History: The Development of Historical Studies in the United States.* Englewood Cliffs, N.J.: Prentice-Hall, 1965.

Hindle, Brooke. *The Pursuit of Science in Revolutionary America, 1735–1789.* Chapel Hill: University of North Carolina Press for the Institute of Early American History and Culture, Williamsburg, Virginia, 1956.

Hittle, James D. *The Military Staff: Its History and Development.* Harrisburg, Pa.: Military Service Publishing Co., 1949.

Hogg, Oliver F. G. *The Royal Arsenal: Its Background, Origin, and Subsequent History.* 2 vols. London: Oxford University Press, 1963.

Holden, Edward S. "Origins of the United States Military Academy, 1777–1802." In *The Centennial of the United States Military Academy at West Point, New York, 1802–1902.* Vol. 1, *Addresses and History.* Washington: Government Printing Office, 1904.

Holland, Samuel. *Holland's Description of Cape Breton Island and Other Documents.* Compiled with an introduction by D. C. Harvey. Public Archives of Nova Scotia Publication no. 2. Halifax: Public Archives of Nova Scotia, 1935.

Hutchins, Thomas. *A Topographical Description of Virginia, Pennsylvania, Maryland, and North Carolina. . . .* London, 1778. Reprint, edited by Frederick Charles Hicks. Cleveland: Burrows Brothers Co., 1904.

James, William Milburne. *The British Navy in Adversity: A Study of the War of American Independence.* London, New York [etc.]: Longmans, Green & Co., 1926.

Johnston, Henry Phelps. *The Campaign of 1776 around New York and Brooklyn . . . Containing Maps, Portraits, and Original Documents.* Memoirs of the Long Island Historical Society, vol. 3. Brooklyn, N.Y.: Long Island Historical Society, 1878.

————. *The Yorktown Campaign and the Surrender of Cornwallis, 1781*. New York: Harper & Brothers, 1881.

————. *The Battle of Harlem Heights, September 16, 1776, with a Review of the Events of the Campaign*. New York: Published for Columbia University Press by Macmillan Co.; London: Macmillan & Co., 1897.

Jones, Yolande. "Aspects of Relief Portrayal on Nineteenth-Century British Military Maps." *Cartographic Journal* 11 (1974): 19–33.

Kinnaird, Clark. *George Washington: The Pictorial Biography*. New York: Hastings House, 1967.

Kipping, Ernst. *The Hessian View of America, 1776–1783*. Monmouth Beach, N.J.: Philip Freneau Press, 1971.

Kish, George. "The Correspondence of Continental Mapmakers of the 1770s and 80s with a London Firm." *Imago Mundi* 4 (1947): 75–77.

Kite, Elizabeth S. *Brigadier-General Louis Lebègue Duportail: Commandant of Engineers in the Continental Army, 1777–1783*. Baltimore: Johns Hopkins University Press for Institut Français de Washington, 1933.

Koeman, Cornelis. "The Principle of Communication in Cartography." In *International Yearbook of Cartography*, vol. 11. London: George Philip, 1971.

Lambert, Johann Heinrich. *Notes and Comments on the Composition of Terrestrial and Celestial Maps (1772)*. Translated by Waldo R. Tobler. University of Michigan, Department of Geography, Geographical Publication no. 8. Ann Arbor: Department of Geography, University of Michigan, 1972.

Landers, Howard L. *The Virginia Campaign and the Blockade and Siege of Yorktown, 1781*. Washington: U.S. Government Printing Office, 1931.

Lawrence, Alexander A. *Storm over Savannah: The Story of Count d'Estaing and the Siege of the Town in 1779*. Athens: University of Georgia Press. 1951.

Laxton, Paul. "The Geodetic and Topographical Evaluation of English County Maps, 1740–1840." *Cartographic Journal* 13 (1976) 37–54.

Library of Congress. *Catalogue of the Library of Thomas Jefferson*. Compiled by E. Millicent Sowerby. 5 vols. Washington, 1952–1959.

Lord, Clifford L. and Lord, Elizabeth H. *Historical Atlas of the United States*. New York: Henry Holt & Co., 1944.

Lossing, Benson J. *The Pictorial Field-Book of the Revolution; or, Illustration by Pen and Pencil, of the History, Biography, Scenery, Relics, and Traditions of the War for Independence*. 2 vols. New York: Harper & Brothers, 1851–52.

Luvaas, Jay, ed. and trans. *Frederick the Great on the Art of War*. New York: Free Press, 1966.

Lydenberg, Harry Miller, ed. *Archibald Robertson, Lieutenant-General Royal Engineers, His Diaries and Sketches in America, 1762–1780*. New York: New York Public Library, 1930.

Mahan, Alfred T. *The Major Operations of the Navies in the War of American Independence*. Boston: Little, Brown & Co., 1913.

Marshall, Douglas W. "The British Engineers in America: 1755–1783." *Journal of the Society for Army Historical Research* 51 (1973): 155–63.

Marshall, Douglas W. and Peckham, Howard Henry. *Campaigns of the American Revolution: An Atlas of Manuscript Maps*. Ann Arbor: University of Michigan Press; Maplewood, N.J.: Hammond, 1976.

Martin, Lawrence, ed. *The George Washington Atlas*. Washington, D.C.: U.S. George Washington Bicentennial Commission, 1932.

Mead, William Richard. "The Eighteenth-Century Military Reconnaissance of Finland: A Neglected Chapter in the History of Finnish Geography." *Acta Geographica* 20 (1968): 255–71.

Melish, John. *A Military and Topographical Atlas of the United States. . . .* Philadelphia: Printed by G. Palmer, 1813.

Miller, John C. *Triumph of Freedom, 1775–1783*. Boston: Little, Brown & Co., Atlantic Monthly Press Book, 1948.

Millett, Alan R. and Cooling, B. Franklin III. *Doctoral Dissertations in Military Affairs: A Bibliography*. Kansas State University Library Bibliographical Series, no. 10. Manhattan: Kansas State University Library, 1972.

Montross, Lynn. *Rag, Tag, and Bobtail: The Story of the Continental Army, 1775–1783*. New York: Harper & Brothers, 1952.

Morison, Samuel Eliot and Commager, Henry Steele. *The Growth of the American Republic*. 4th ed. 2 vols. New York: Oxford University Press, 1950.

Muehrcke, Phillip C. and Muehrcke, Juliana O. "Maps in Literature." *Geographical Review* 64 (1974): 317–38.

Muller, John. *A Treatise Containing the Elementary Part of Fortification, Regular and Irregular, with Remarks on the Constructions of . . . Marshal de Vauban and Baron Coehorn . . . For the Use of the Royal Academy of Artillery at Woolwich.* 3d ed. London: J. Nourse, 1774.

———. *A Treatise Containing the Practical Part of Fortification . . . For the Use of the Royal Academy of Artillery at Woolwich.* 3d ed. London: Printed for W. Strahan [etc.], 1774.

National Gallery of Canada. *Thomas Davies, c. 1737–1812: An Exhibition Organized by the National Gallery of Canada, Ottawa.* Edited with an introduction and catalogue by R. H. Hubbard. Foreword by Jean Sutherland Boggs. Essay by C. P. Stacey. Ottawa, 1972.

Nebenzahl, Kenneth. *Atlas of the American Revolution.* Chicago: Rand McNally & Co., 1974.

———. *A Bibliography of Printed Battle Plans of the American Revolution, 1775–1795.* Chicago and London: University of Chicago Press for Hermon Dunlap Smith Center for the History of Cartography at the Newberry Library, 1975.

Newmyer, R. Kent. "Charles Stedman's *History of the American War.*" *American Historical Review* 63 (1958): 924–34.

Nickerson, Hoffman. *The Turning Point of the Revolution; or, Burgoyne in America.* Boston and New York: Houghton Mifflin Co., 1928.

O'Rourke, John Count. *A Treatise on the Art of War; or, Rules for Conducting an Army in all the Various Operations of Regular Campaigns.* London: T. Spilsbury, 1778.

Ozanam, Jacques. *A Treatise of Fortification, Containing the Ancient and Modern Method of the Construction and Defense of Places. . . .* Translated by J. T. Desaguliers. Oxford: J. Nicholson, 1711.

Palmer, John McAuley. *General Von Steuben.* New Haven: Yale University Press, 1937.

Pargellis, Stanley, ed. *Military Affairs in North America, 1748–1765: Selected Documents from the Cumberland Papers in Windsor Castle.* New York: Archon Books, 1969.

Paullin, Charles O. and Wright, John K. *Atlas of the Historical Geography of the United States.* Washington and New York: Carnegie Institution and the American Geographical Society, 1932.

Peckham, Howard Henry. *The War of American Independence: A Military History.* Chicago: University of Chicago Press, 1958.

Pennypacker, Morton. *General Washington's Spies on Long Island and in New York.* Brooklyn, N.Y.: Long Island Historical Society, 1939.

Pettengill, Ray W., trans. *Letters from America, 1776–1779: Being Letters of Brunswick, Hessian, and Waldeck Officers with the British Armies during the Revolution.* Port Washington, N.Y.: Kennikat Press, 1924.

Phillips, Philip Lee. *Notes on the Life and Works of Bernard Romans.* Publication of the Florida State Historical Society, no. 2. Deland: Florida State Historical Society, 1924.

Phillips, Thomas Raphael, ed. *Roots of Strategy: A Collection of Military Classics.* Harrisburg, Pa.: Military Service Publishing Co., 1940 [subsequently reissued]; London: John Lane, 1943.

Pirscher, J. D. C. *Coup d'oeil militaire, oder Kurzer Unterricht, wie man sich ein militarisch Augenmaass erwerben, . . . praktisch beschrieben.* Berlin: Arnold Wever, 1775.

Porter, Whitworth. *History of the Corps of Royal Engineers.* 3 vols. Chatham, Kent: Institution of Royal Engineers, 1951–1954.

Preuss, Johann David Erdmann, ed. "Plans relatifs aux oeuvres militaires de Frédéric le Grand, réimprimés sur les planches originales." In *Oeuvres de Frédéric le Grand . . .* 31 vols. and atlas. Berlin: Chez Rodolphe Decker, 1846–1857.

Ravenhill, William, and Gilg, Andrew. "The Accuracy of Early Maps? Towards a Computer Aided Method." *Cartographic Journal* 11 (1974): 48–52.

Rice, Howard C., Jr., and Brown, Anne S. K., eds. and trans. *The American Campaigns of Rochambeau's Army, 1780, 1781, 1782, 1783.* Vol. 2, *The Itineraries, Maps, and Views.* Princeton and Providence: Princeton University Press and Brown University Press, 1972.

Ridpath, John Clark. *The New Complete History of the United States of America.* 12 vols. Vols. 5 and 6. Washington, D.C.: Ridpath History Co.; Cincinnati, O.: Jones Brothers Publishing Co. [1905].

Ristow, Walter W. "Simeon De Witt, Pioneer American Cartographer." In *Kartengeschichte und Kartenbearbeitung . . .* [Festschrift, honoring Wilhelm Bonacker]. Edited by Karl-Heinz Meine. Bad Godesburg: Kirschbaum Verlag, 1968.

———. "Maps of the American Revolution: A Preliminary Survey." *Quarterly Journal of the Library of Congress* 28 (1971): 196–215.

————. Introduction to *Thomas Jefferys, The American Atlas, London 1776* [Facsimile ed.]. Amsterdam: Theatrum Orbis Terrarum, 1974.

Ristow, Walter W., ed. *A Survey of the Roads of the United States of America, 1789, by Christopher Colles*. Cambridge: Harvard University Press, Belknap Press, 1961.

Roberts, Kenneth, comp. *March to Quebec: Journals of the Members of Arnold's Expedition.* New York: Doubleday & Co., 1940.

Robinson, Adrian H. W. *Marine Cartography in Britain: A History of the Sea Chart to 1855.* Leicester: Leicester University Press, 1962.

Robinson, Arthur H. "The Potential Contribution of Cartography in Liberal Education." *Cartographer* [now *Canadian Cartographer*] 2 (1965): 1–8.

Robinson, Arthur H. and Petchenik, Barbara Bartz. "The Map as a Communication System." *Cartographic Journal* 12 (1975): 7–15.

Robinson, F. J. G. and Wallis, P. J. *Book Subscription Lists: A Revised Guide.* Newcastle upon Tyne: Harold Hill & Son for the Book Subscriptions List Project, 1975.

Robson, Eric. "The Expedition to the Southern Colonies, 1775–1776." *English Historical Review* 66 (1951): 535–60.

————. *The American Revolution in Its Political and Military Aspects, 1763–1783.* Hamden, Conn.: Archon Books, 1965.

Rumpf, Heinrich Friedrich. *Allgemeine Literatur der Kriegswissenschaften, . . . Littérature universelle des sciences militaires* [German and French text]. 2 vols. Berlin: G. Reimer, 1824–1825.

Scouller, R. E. *The Armies of Queen Anne.* Oxford: Clarendon Press, 1966.

Scudder, Horace E. "Memoir of Justin Winsor, L.L.D." *Proceedings of the Massachusetts Historical Society,* 2d ser., 12 (1899): 457–82.

Scull, Gideon Delaplaine, ed. *The Montresor Journals.* Collections of the New-York Historical Society, Publication Fund, vol. 14. New York: New-York Historical Society, 1881.

Shipton, Nathaniel N. "General James Murray's Map of the St. Lawrence." *Cartographer* [now *Canadian Cartographer*] 4 (1967): 93–101.

Siborne, William. *Instructions for Civil and Military Surveyors in Topographical Plan-Drawing; . . . founded upon the system of J. G. Lehmann. . . .* London: G. & W. B. Whittaker, 1822.

Simcoe, John Graves. *Simcoe's Military Journal: A History of the Operations of a Partisan Corps, called the Queen's Rangers, Commanded by Lieut. Col. J. G. Simcoe . . . Now First Published with a Memoir of the Author. . . .* New York: Bartlett & Welford, 1844 [Based on *A Journal of the Operations of the Queen's Rangers. . . .* Exeter, Devon: n.p., 1787].

Simes, Thomas. *The Military Guide for Young Officers.* London: J. Millan, 1772.

————. *A Treatise on the Military Science, which comprehends the Grand Operations of War. . . .* London: Printed by H. Reynell, 1780.

Skelton, R. A. *Looking at an Early Map.* Lawrence: University of Kansas Libraries, 1965.

————. *The Military Survey of Scotland.* Royal Scottish Geographical Soicety, Special Publication no. 1. Edinburgh: Royal Scottish Geographical Society, 1967.

————. *Maps: A Historical Survey of Their Study and Collecting.* Edited by David Woodward. The Kenneth Nebenzahl, Jr., Lectures in the History of Cartography at the Newberry Library. Chicago and London: University of Chicago Press for the Hermon Dunlap Smith Center for the History of Cartography, The Newberry Library, 1972.

Smelser, Marshall. *The Winning of Independence.* Chicago: Quadrangle Books, 1972.

Smith, Samuel Stelle. *The Battle of Monmouth.* Monmouth Beach, N.J.: Philip Freneau Press, 1964.

Spaulding, Oliver Lyman, Jr.; Nickerson, Hoffman; and Wright, John Womack. *Warfare: A Study of Military Methods from the Earliest Times.* London: George C. Harrap & Co., 1925.

Spaulding, Thomas M. and Karpinski, Louis C. *Early Military Books in the University of Michigan Libraries.* Ann Arbor: University of Michigan Press, 1941.

Stedman, Charles. *The History of the Origin, Progress, and Termination of the American War.* 2 vols. London: J. Murray, 1794.

Steele, Matthew Forney. *American Campaigns.* U.S. War Department, Office of the Chief of Staff, Document no. 324. 2 vols. Washington, D.C.: B. S. Adams, 1909.

Stephenson, Richard W., comp. "Table for Indentifying Variant Editions and Impressions of John Mitchell's Map of the British and French Dominions in North America." In *A la Carte: Selected Papers on Maps and Atlases.* Compiled by Walter W. Ristow. Washington: Library of Congress, 1972.

Stevens, Henry and Tree, Roland. *Comparative Cartography.* Map Collectors' Series, no. 39. London: Map Collectors' Circle, 1967.

Stevenson, Roger. *Military Instructions for Officers Detached in the Field: Containing, A Scheme for forming a Corps of Partisan, Illustrated with Plans of the Manoeuvres Necessary in carrying on the Petite Guerre.* Philadelphia: R. Aitken, 1775.

Tarleton, Banastre. *A History of the Campaigns of 1780 and 1781, in the Southern Provinces of North America.* London: T. Cadell, 1787.

Taylor, Eva G. R. *The Mathematical Practitioners of Hanoverian England, 1714-1840.* Cambridge: Cambridge University Press for the Institute of Navigation, 1966.

Thayer, Theodore. *Nathanael Greene: Strategist of the American Revolution.* New York: Twayne Publishers, 1960.

Thoumine, R. H. *Scientific Soldier: A Life of General Le Marchant, 1766-1812.* London: Oxford University Press, 1968.

Treacy, M. F. *Prelude to Yorktown: The Southern Campaign of Nathanael Greene, 1780-1781.* Chapel Hill: University of North Carolina Press, 1963.

Trevelyan, George Otto. *The American Revolution.* 2d ed., 4 vols. London: Longmans, Green & Co., 1899-1903.

Uhlendorf, Bernhard A., ed. and trans. *The Siege of Charleston, . . . Diaries and Letters of Hessian Officers from the von Jungkenn Papers in the William L. Clements Library.* Ann Arbor: University of Michigan Press, 1938.

U.S. Adjutant-General's Office. *Legislative History of the General Staff of the Army of the United States (Its Organization, Duties, Pay, and Allowances), from 1775 to 1901.* Compiled and annotated . . . by Raphael P. Thian. Washington: Government Printing office, 1901.

U.S. Department of the Navy, Naval History Division. *The American Revolution, 1775-1783: An Atlas of Eighteenth-Century Maps and Charts.* Washington, 1972.

Van Doren, Carl. *Secret History of the American Revolution.* New York: Viking Press, 1941.

Van Doren, Carl and McHenry, Robert, eds. *Webster's Guide to American History.* Springfield, Mass.: G. & C. Merriam Co., 1971.

Van Tyne, Claude Halstead. *The American Revolution, 1776-1783.* Vol. 9. The American Nation: A History, edited by Albert Bushnell Hart. New York and London: Harper & Brothers, 1905.

Verner, Coolie. "Mr. Jefferson Makes a Map." *Imago Mundi* 14 (1959): 96-108.

————. *Maps of the Yorktown Campaign, 1780-1781: A Preliminary Checklist of Printed and Manuscript Maps prior to 1800.* Map Collectors' Series, no. 18. London: Map Collectors' Circle, 1965.

————. Introduction to *The English Pilot, The Fourth Book, London, 1689* [Facsimile ed.]. Amsterdam: Theatrum Orbis Terrarum, 1967.

Wallace, Willard M. *Appeal to Arms: A Military History of the American Revolution.* New York: Harper & Brothers, 1951.

Ward, Christopher L. *The Delaware Continentals, 1776-1783.* Wilmington: Historical Society of Delaware, 1941.

————. *The War of the Revolution.* Edited by John Richard Alden. 2 vols. New York: Macmillan Co., 1952.

Webster, John Clarence. "Life of John Montrésor." *Transactions of the Royal Society of Canada,* sec. 11, ser. III, 22 (1928): 1-31.

————. *The Life of Joseph Frederick Wallet Des Barres.* Shediac, N.B.: n.p., 1933.

Wickwire, Franklin and Wickwire, Mary. *Cornwallis and the War of Independence.* London: Faber & Faber, 1971.

Wilkinson, Spenser. *The French Army before Napoleon: Lectures Delivered before the University of Oxford in Michaelmas Term, 1914.* Oxford: Clarendon Press, 1915.

Willcox, William B. *Portrait of a General: Sir Henry Clinton in the War of Independence.* New York: Alfred A. Knopf, 1964.

Willcox, William B., ed. *The American Rebellion: Sir Henry Clinton's Narrative of His Campaigns, 1775-1782, with an Appendix of Original Documents.* New Haven: Yale University Press, 1954.

William L. Clements Library, University of Michigan. *History of the William L. Clements Library, 1923-1973: Its Development and Its Collection.* Ann Arbor, 1973.

Wilson, Duncan K. *The History of the Mathematical Teaching in Scotland to the End of the Eighteenth Century.* London: University of London Press, 1935.

Winsor, Justin, ed. *Narrative and Critical History of America.* 8 vols. Vol. 6, *The United States of North America.* Boston and New York: Houghton Mifflin Co., 1888. Reprint ed., New York: AMS Press, 1967.

Wood, William Charles Henry and Gabriel, Ralph Henry. *The Winning of Freedom.* Vol. 6. The Pageant of America. Independence ed. New Haven: Yale University Press, 1927.

Woodward, David. "The Study of the History of Cartography: A Suggested Framework." *American Cartographer* 1 (1974): 101-15.

———. *The All-American Map.* Chicago and London: University of Chicago Press, 1977.

Wright, John Kirtland. *Human Nature in Geography: Fourteen Papers, 1925-1965.* Cambridge: Harvard University Press, 1966.

Index

Abeel, James F., 41
Adams, John, 59, 66, 91–92
Adams, J. T., 132, 134
Adams, Randolph G., 1, 93
Alden, John, 131, 134, 137, 139
Aldington, John, 74
Allen, Gardner, 137
America, map of the state of war in, 34
American Atlas, 86, 92, 96
American Military Pocket Atlas, 96–97
American nationalism, aspects of, 111–13
American waterways: coastal charts, 26, 88;
    harbors, survey of, 10
Anderson, Troyer, 130
André, John, 40, 103, 105
Appleton, LeRoy, 132
Army, standing, 46
Arnold, Benedict, 103
Atlantic Neptune, The, 16, 26, 27, 87–91
Avery, Elroy McKendree, 114, 129, 130, 137,
    139, 141, 146

Baer, Joseph A., 130, 146
Baldwin, Jeduthan, 6, 8
Bancroft, George, 113
Barrettè, Thomas G.L., 43, 77
Bastide, John Henry, 49
Battle, order of, 43
Battlefields, 94
Battle maps, 41–44, 93–96, 128, 137–39, 140,
    143–45; market for, 94; publication lag, 95
Bauman, Sebastian, 19
Beckmann, Martin, 57
Belcher, Henry, 140–41
Berniere, Henry de, 22, 23
Berthier, Louis-Alexandre, 16, 24, 63
Berthier, Victor-Léopold, 16, 63
Bibliographies, of 18th-century military texts,
    60, 62
Blanchard, Claude, 102
Bland, Humphrey, 40
Blaskowitz, Charles, 31, 59, 73, 74, 85

Boatner, Mark Mayo, 132, 137
Boston: campaign, 93; harbor, map of, 91;
    plan of, 13
Bouquet, Henry, 39, 47
Bowdoin, James, 104
Braddock, Edward, 66
Brandywine, map of battle of, 114–15
Brasier, William, 86
Britain, survey of western, 87
Brooklyn, line of defense at, 22
Brown, Anne S. K., 17, 38, 63, 76, 92
Brown, John, 22, 23
Brown, Arthur S., 132
Burgoyne, John, 21, 37, 43, 47
Burke, Edmund, 112
Burr, Aaron, 106
Burrow, Reuben, 58
Butler, William, 39

Camden, map of battle of, 43
Campbell, Archibald, 87
Campbell, James, 28
Canada, maps of, 85, 91
Cape Breton, and Nova Scotia, survey of, 26,
    88
Carleton, Sir Guy, 72
Carolinas, maps of, 91, 98
Carrington, Henry B., 116–19, 132, 139
Cartographic archives, 58, 70
Cartographic information, spread of, 45–78
Cartographic units, military, 67–78;
    American, 67–71; British, 71–75; French,
    76; regimental, 77
Cartography: history of, 4, 13, 46, 80;
    scientific, 102, 123–24; theory of, 82. *See
    also* Mapping; Maps; Map use
Castramentation. *See* Encampment
Channing, Edward, 129, 137
Charleston, siege of, 18, 19, 90
Charlestown: fortification of, 15; siege of,
    120, 122
Chesnoy, Michel du, 93

184   INDEX

Clairac, *Field Engineer,* 64, 66
Clark, David Sanders, 114, 126–27
Clark, George Kitson, 82
Clausewitz, Karl von, 113
Clement Co (publisher), 133
Clinton, Sir Henry, 10, 18, 43, 47, 50, 71, 98, 100, 103, 104, 109
Close, Abraham, 74
Closen, Ludwig von, 47, 102
Coleman, R. V., 132, 134
Colles, Christopher, 34
Color, use of: in fortification plans, 11–12; 19th-century, 114; in siege mapping, 17; in topographic surveys, 26–27; 20th-century, 130
Commager, H. S., 133
Cook, James, 91
Cornwallis, Charles, 19, 47, 109
Corps of Guides and Pioneers, 71–72
Corps of Invalids, 59–60
Cowley, John Lodge, 56
Croghan, George, 29
Cromot du Bourg, Baron, 106
Cumming, William P., 1, 26, 40, 46, 93, 96

Dainville, François de, 13, 16
D'Aubant, Abraham, 12, 14, 59, 75
Davies, Thomas, 42
Debbeig, Hugh, 10, 13, 48
De Brahm, William Gerard, 26–30, 33, 49, 50, 85, 91; surveys of South Carolina, Georgia, and Florida, 26, 91
Decision-making, influence of maps on, 4, 79, 99–102, 105–7
De Gomme, Bernard, 57
De Kalb, Johann, baron, 101
Delaware, map of, 91
Demont, William, 103
DesBarres, Joseph F. W., 16, 26, 27, 29, 49, 87–91, 109–10
DeValinger, Leon, Sr., 134
DeWitt, Simeon, 34–37, 69
Distance tables, 106
Dixon, Jeremiah, 28
Draper, John, 134
Drawing Room, Tower of London, 57–59, 64
Dunn, W. H., 133
Dupain de Montesson, 35, 40, 62–63
Duportail, Louis Lebegue, 7, 13, 15, 41, 49, 60, 74

Education: cartographic, 52–57, 58, 103; military, 52–57, 103
Elevation, in fortification, 8
Encampment, maps of, 40–41, 72
Engineers, military, 29, 48–49, 58, 70; American school for, 60; shortage of, in American army, 49; training of, 52–57, 64
English, Van H., 131
Engraving, copper- and steel-, 133; wax-, 129–30, 133

Erskine, Robert, 24, 33–34, 35, 39, 41, 68–69, 104
Espionage and reconnaissance mapping, 91, 104
Evans, G. D. N., 87
Evans, Lewis, 86, 91, 92
Ewald, Johann, 63

Faden, William, 13, 17, 44, 85, 86, 92, 94
Fage, Edward, 16, 18, 75
Field mapping, standards for, 24
Field observations, 35–36
Fiske, John, 114
Fitchet, Duncan M., 134
Fleury, François de, 18
Fleury, Louis, 49
Fort Constitution, plans of, 13, 103
Fortescue, J. W., 137, 146
Fortification: schools of, 12, 57; science of, 6, 12
Fortification cartography, 5–15; in textbooks, 7–12
Fortification plans: British, 9, 11–12; making of, 7, 49, 70, 106; types of, 8, 9
Fort Mifflin, siege plan of, 18
Fort Washington, plans of, 103
Franklin, Benjamin, 91
Frederick the Great, 6, 25, 40–43, 48, 61–62, 85–86, 108–9
Freehand sketching, 20, 24
Freeman, Douglas Southall, 115, 134
French, Allen, 98, 130
French and Indian War, 25, 83, 84. *See also* Seven Years' War
French strip maps, 38–39
Frothingham, Thomas G., 133
Fry and Jefferson, Virginia, 86, 91

Gage, Thomas, 22, 23, 27, 28, 72, 85, 100
Garner, J. W., 129
Gates, Horatio, 100, 101
"General maps," of line of march, 39–40
Geodetic accuracy, 28, 34, 98. *See also* Latitude and longitude
Geography, North American, 100, 103
Georgia, map of, 87
Gordon, Henry (Harry), 29, 84
Gordon, William, 112
Gottschalk, Louis, 133
Gray, William, 39
Greene, Francis Vinton, 129
Greene, Nathanael, 14, 19, 36, 41, 66, 70, 105
Gridley, Richard, 49
Gunter's chain, 11
Guthorn, Peter J., 1, 40, 46, 50, 76, 93, 104

Hadden, James, 14, 38, 43
Haldimand, Frederick, 47
Halifax, fortifications at, 14; plans of, 104
Henrichs, Johann, 18
Heymell, W., 24

Higginbotham, Don, 113, 123, 139
Hills, John, 30, 31, 39, 44, 75, 77, 106
Historical cartography, 113–15; of Revolutionary War, 115–24
Historical context, of maps, 3–5
History, cartographic, 2
History of cartography. *See* Cartography, history of
Holland, Samuel, 26–30, 33, 48, 49, 73–75, 85, 87, 88
Holtzendorff, Baron de, 66
Howe, Sir William, 47, 72, 74
Hutchins, Thomas, 29, 39, 48, 69–70
Hutton, Charles, 56
Hydrographic surveys, 29–30, 87–91

Iberville Canal project, 28
"Ichnography," in fortification, 8
Imbret, Jean-Louis, 49
Innes, Alexander, 72
Intelligence, military, and maps, 103–5.
    See also Espionage
Ireland, survey of, 21

Jefferson, Thomas, 91, 100
Jefferys, Thomas, 85, 86, 91, 92, 94, 96–97

Ketchum, Richard, 141
Knox, Henry, 59, 66
Kohn, Hans, 111
Kosciuzko, Thaddeus, 49
Krasnorski, Edward, 132

Lafayette, Marquis de, 13, 42
Lake Champlain, survey of, 86
Landers, H. L., 130
Landmann, Isaac, 55
Lane, Michael, 91
Latitude and longitude, determination of, 28, 33, 56, 102
Laumoy (engineer under Duportail), 15, 49
Le Blond, Jacob Christophe, 66
Lee, Charles, 47
Lempriere, Clement, 57
L'Enfant, Pierre-Charles, 49
Lochée, Louis, 64
Lodge, Benjamin, 24, 39, 70, 76
Lodge, H. C., 129
Long Island, battle of, 141–42
Lord, Clifford L. and Elizabeth H., 146
Lossing, Benson J., 112, 115–16

MacAlpine, William, 74
Mackenzie, Frederick, 18, 22, 71, 77, 91
Mackenzie, Murdoch, the Elder, 87
Map classification, Revolutionary War, 1–5, 135–39
Map culture, European, 3, 4
Mapmakers, Revolutionary War, 51, 56–58.
    See also Engineers, military; Surveyors and draftsmen

Mapping conventions, 16–18, 26–27, 42, 114
Mapping, 18th-century, 1–44; extent of, 1; national types, 3, 31–32; technology of, 133–35; of wars, 127–28, 142–43. *See also* Historical cartography
Mapping, of Revolutionary War in 20th century, 126, 142–43
Maps, 18th-century: accuracy of, 98–99, 139; American use of European, 112; attitudes toward, 100, 101–5; availability of, 83–93; as communications systems, 80, 140; as data sources, 139; historical significance of, 79, 101; influence of, 98, 107; information content of, 82; out-of-date, 96, 97; purpose of, 99; quality of, 127; as records, 107–10; as symbol systems, 80; topographical information in, 98; traffic in, 92–93
Maps, manuscript, 107–10
Maps, military: function of, 1–5, 102; making, 5, 108; and map type, 4–6; texts on, 62
Maps, printed, 84–96; adequacy of, 99–101; methods of reproduction, 114
Map use: analytical approach to, 143–45; annotation during, 96; conditions of, 82–83; Revolutionary War, 79–110
March, order of, 37–38, 43
Marshall, Douglas, 26, 48, 98
Marshall, John, 112, 122
Martin, Reinhard Jacob, 21, 71
Mason, Charles, 28
Massiot, Gabriel, 55
Matthews-Northrup publishing company, 114, 130, 133, 146
Measure, units of, 9, 11, 31, 98
Military movement, cartography of, 19–41
Military theory, 18th-century, 5, 102
Miller, John, 131
Mitchell, John, 91, 92
Montresor, Henry, 72
Montresor, James, 48
Montresor, John, 8, 23, 24, 26, 29, 48, 64, 72, 74, 75, 84, 85, 86, 91, 99, 120, 122
Morison, S. E., 133
Mouzon, Henry, 91, 98
Muehrcke, Phillip, 82
Muller, John, 7, 8–9, 11, 12, 54–55, 64, 66
Murray, James, 9

Narraganset Bay, plan of islands in, 14
Nebenzahl, Kenneth, 93, 94, 134
New England, coastal survey of, 29–30, 88
Newport, R. I., plans for defense of, 14, 17
New York, maps of, 83, 85, 86, 91
New York–New Jersey boundary: maps of, 91; survey of, 29
Nickerson, Hoffman, 130
Nicola, Lewis, 59, 64
Nicole, Pierre, 73, 74
North America: general survey of, 27, 86; large map of, 86
North American Atlas, 86

Nova Scotia, survey of, 87. *See also* Cape Breton

O'Connor, Antoine, 18
Officers: experience of, 47; mobility of, 46–52
Opterre, Henri Crublier d', 17, 92
O'Rourke, John Count, 20
"Orthography," in fortification, 8
Overlay technique, 16, 42
Ozanam, Jacques, 62

Page, Thomas Hyde, 13, 57, 98
Palacios, Rafael, 137
Paret, Peter, 113
Paterson, Daniel, 73, 74
Pattison, James, 55
Paullin, C. O., 131
Pennsylvania, maps of, 91
Petchenik, Barbara, 82, 114, 123
Philadelphia, map of, 87
Photography and photolithography, 133–34
Pierce, John, 69
Pirscher, J. D. C., 20, 63
Pittman, Philip, 28
Popple, Henry, 57, 91
Pownall, Thomas, 86, 96
Prussia, trigonometric survey of, 86
Putman, Rufus, 49

Quebec, plan of defenses of, 14

Ramsay, David, 112
Ratzer, Bernard, 86
Rawdon, Lord Francis, 101
Reconnaissance mapping, 19–25, 27, 30, 42, 72, 106
"Register of Draughts in the Drawing Room," 58. *See also* Drawing Room
Revolutionary War: battles of, 112, 115; cartographic history of, 2; contemporary accounts of, 95; histories of, 112; military cartography of, 45; as myth, 112–13; "secret history" of, 103
Rhode Island, maps of, 32, 102; siege of, 18, 93
Rice, Howard C., Jr. 17, 38, 63, 76, 92
Ridpath, John Clark, 129, 134
Rittenhouse, David, 29
Roads, 30–31, 41
Robertson, Archibald, 48
Robinson, Arthur F., 80, 82
Robinson, Beverley, 77–78, 105
Rochambeau, Comte de, 16, 24, 38, 47, 63, 83, 92
Rocque, John, 85
Romans, Bernard, 13, 49, 50
Route maps, 35–37, 38–39, 72
Roy, William, 10, 25, 49, 56, 57, 72
Rumpf, Heinrich Friedrich, 60–62

Saint Lawrence valley, survey of, 9, 26, 29, 83

Sandby, Paul, 56, 57
Sandby, Thomas, 57
Saratoga, march to, 37, 38
Sauthier, Claude Joseph, 44, 49, 75, 85, 87, 139
Savannah, plan of siege of, 17; siege of, 18
Saxe, Maurice, 66
Sayer and Bennett (publishers), 96–97
Scale: in fortification plans, 6, 8–9, 11, 30; in topographical surveys, 26, 28, 30, 32, 34, 98; of 20th-century maps, 130
Scharnhorst, Gerhard van, 113
Scotland, survey of, 10, 25, 49, 56, 57, 72
Scull, William, 91, 92
Seven Years' War, 25. *See also* French and Indian War
Shipton, Nathaniel, 26
Siege cartography, 15–19, 42
Simes, Thomas, 37, 66
Skelton, R. A., 5, 79
Skinner, Andrew, 31, 73–75
Smelser, Marshall, 131
Smith, Page, 113
Smith, Samuel, 137
Soldiers, mercenary, 47
Spry, William, 12, 14
"Spy maps," 104
Stamp Act riots, 85
Stedman, Charles, 96, 112, 115
Stephenson, N. W., 133
Steuben, Frederick, Baron von, 48, 60
Stevenson, Roger, 15, 19–20, 64–66
Stony Point, fort at, 104
Strategy, military, 11
Straton, James, 24
Sullivan, John, 70
Surveying: difficulties in, 39; equipment, 7–8, 9, 27, 33; methods, 7–8; skills, 29, 56
Surveyors and draftsmen, 56, 58, 69–70, 74. *See also* Engineers, military; Mapmakers
Sutherland, Alexander, 109
Symbols, in military cartography, 16, 42. *See also* Mapping conventions

Tactical planning maps, 42–43
Tactics, 62; and terrain, 30–31
Tallmadge, Benjamin, 104
Taylor, George, 8, 31, 73–75
Terminology, fortification, 12–13
Terrain, 30–31, 42
Textbooks, military, 60–67
Tobler, W. R., 98
Topographical surveys, 20, 21, 25–35, 53, 70
Townsend, Joseph, 114
Trevelyan, G. O., 129, 133
Troiani, Don, 141
Turenne, Henri, vicomte de, 66

United States Military Academy, 59–60

Vallancey, Charles, 21, 23, 25, 35, 63, 71, 106

Van Blarenberghe, Louis-Nicholas, 6
Van Tyne, Claude, 133
Vauban, Sebastien de, 55, 56
Verner, Collie, 15
Villefranche, Jean de, 50
Virginia, maps of, 91, 100

Wade, Benjamin, 14
Wallace, Willard M., 134, 139
Ward, Christopher, 134
Washington, George, 11, 13, 24, 36, 37, 41,
   48, 50, 59, 60, 65, 66–67, 67–71, 83, 91,
   100, 103, 104, 107, 109, 112; biographies
   of, 112, 133, 134
Wax-engraving. *See* Engraving

Webster, John C., 87
Werner, S. W., 44
West Point, 59, 60; plans of, 103
Wheeler, Thomas, 75
Williamson, J. A., 79
Windham, Donald, 130
Winsor, Justin, 119–23
Wolfe, James, 64
Woodward, David, 133
Woolwich, Royal Military Academy at, 7,
   54–57, 59, 63–64
Wright, John K., 105, 131
Wright, Thomas, 29

Yorktown, French maps of route to, 32, 39;
   siege of, 15–16, 17, 19, 93, 109